尾田栄一郎

When I grab a bag to carry with me when I go out, I sometimes also carry a new tune with me. Happens all the time with everyone, right?! Volume 49, starting now!

-Eiichiro Oda, 2008

Eiichiro Oda began his manga career at the age of 17, when his one-shot cowboy manga **Wanted!** won second place in the coveted Tezuka manga awards. Oda went on to work as an assistant to some of the biggest manga artists in the industry, including Nobuhiro Watsuki, before winning the award for new artists. His pirate **One Piece**, which debuted in honen Jump in 1997, quickly became most popular manga in Japan.

ONE PIECE VOL. 49
THRILLER BARK PART 4

SHONEN JUMP Manga Edition

STORY AND ART BY EIICHIRO ODA

English Adaptation/Jason Thompson
Translation/Labaaman, HC Language Solutions, Inc.
Touch-up Art & Lettering/Primary Graphix
Design/Sean Lee
Supervising Editor/Yuki Murashige
Editor/Alexis Kirsch

ONE PIECE © 1997 by Eiichiro Oda. All rights reserved.
First published in Japan in 1997 by SHUEISHA Inc., Tokyo.
English translation rights arranged by SHUEISHA Inc.

The stories, characters and incidents mentioned in this publication are
entirely fictional.

Printed in the U.S.A.

Published by VIZ Media, LLC
P.O. Box 77010
San Francisco, CA 94107

10 9 8 7 6
First printing, June 2010
Sixth printing, December 2016

www.viz.com

THE WORLD'S
MOST POPULAR MANGA
www.shonenjump.com

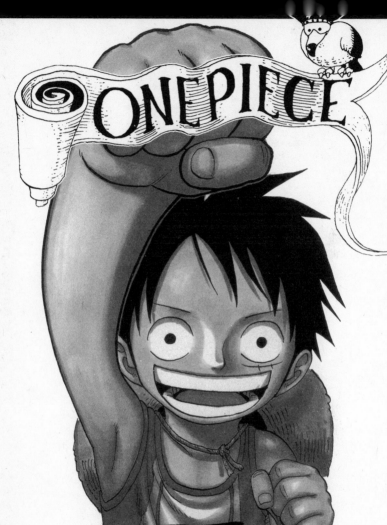

ONEPIECE

JUMP
55
PIRATES

Vol. 49
NIGHTMARE LUFFY
STORY AND ART BY
EIICHIRO ODA

A musician swordsman whose shadow was stolen. He's on a quest to take it back.

Brook

The Straw Hats

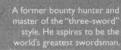

Boundlessly optimistic and able to stretch like rubber, he is determined to become King of the Pirates.

Monkey D. Luffy

A former bounty hunter and master of the "three-sword" style. He aspires to be the world's greatest swordsman.

Roronoa Zolo

A thief who specializes in robbing pirates. Nami hates pirates, but Luffy convinced her to be his navigator.

Nami

A village boy with a talent for telling tall tales. His father, Yasopp, is a member of Shanks's crew.

Usopp

The bighearted cook (and ladies' man) whose dream is to find the legendary sea, the "All Blue."

Sanji

A blue-nosed man-reindeer and the ship's doctor.

Tony Tony Chopper

A mysterious woman in search of the Ponegliff on which true history is recorded.

Nico Robin

A softhearted cyborg and talented shipwright.

Franky

The zombie who possesses Luffy's shadow

"The Beast" Oars

The zombie who possesses Zolo's shadow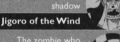

Jigoro of the Wind

The zombie who possesses Sanji's shadow

Inuppe

The zombie who possesses Brook's shadow

Samurai Ryuma

THE STORY OF ONE PIECE

Volume 49

Monkey D. Luffy started out as just a kid with a dream—to become the greatest pirate in history! Stirred by the tales of pirate "Red-Haired" Shanks, Luffy vowed to become a pirate himself. That was before the enchanted Devil Fruit gave Luffy the power to stretch like rubber, at the cost of being unable to swim—a serious handicap for an aspiring sea dog. Undeterred, Luffy set out to sea and recruited some crewmates—master swordsman Zolo; treasure-hunting thief Nami; lying sharpshooter Usopp; the high-kicking chef Sanji; Chopper, the walkin' talkin' reindeer doctor; mysterious archaeologist Robin; and cyborg shipwright Franky.

Having entered the world's greatest ocean, the Grand Line, Luffy and crew replace their old ship with the *Thousand Sunny*. Their next destination—Fish-Man Island! But before they realize it, they are caught up in a storm and end up in the Florian Triangle instead. There they meet Brook, a musically inclined skeleton. In an unexpected twist, the ghost island, Thriller Bark, beckons *Sunny* to it. This creepy island is positively crawling with zombies, and the one who controls those zombies is one of the Seven Warlords of the Sea, Gecko Moria! He grows his undead army by stealing people's shadows and inserting them into the zombies that Dr. Hogback creates. Luffy's shadow is taken and placed inside "The Beast" Oars, known for his legendary strength.

Humans with no shadow will die the moment they touch sunlight, so the Straw Hats must recover their shadows before dawn! Luffy and crew decide that the quickest way to regain their shadows is to defeat Gecko Moria! Zolo and the others have already defeated Samurai Ryuma and all but one of the Mysterious Four, and they're now up against Oars! But with such a huge difference in power, the situation seems hopeless...

Thriller Bark

The Mysterious Four

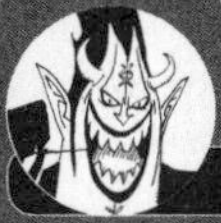

One of the Seven Warlords of the Sea

Gecko Moria

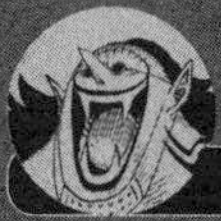

A prodigal surgeon

Doctor Hogback

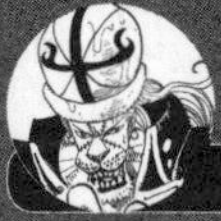

Commander of the Zombie Soldiers & Zombie Generals

Absalom of the Cemetery

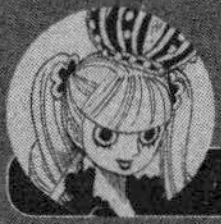

Commander of the Wild Zombies & Surprise Zombies

Ghost Princess Perona

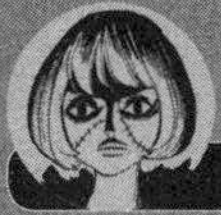

Victoria Cindry

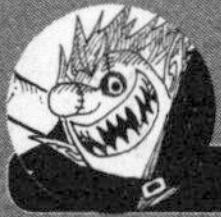

Hildon

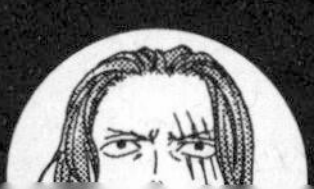

A pirate that Luffy ido

Vol. 49
Nightmare Luffy

CONTENTS

Chapter 471: My Friend		8
Chapter 472: Down		29
Chapter 473: Warlord Bartholomew Kuma Appears		49
Chapter 474: We Have to Do It!		69
Chapter 475: Pirates of the Forest		89
Chapter 476: Nightmare Luffy		109
Chapter 477: 3/8		129
Chapter 478: Luffy vs. Luffy		149
Chapter 479: Warrior of Hope		169
Chapter 480: Interception		189
Chapter 481: Shadows Asgard		209

MY FRIEND

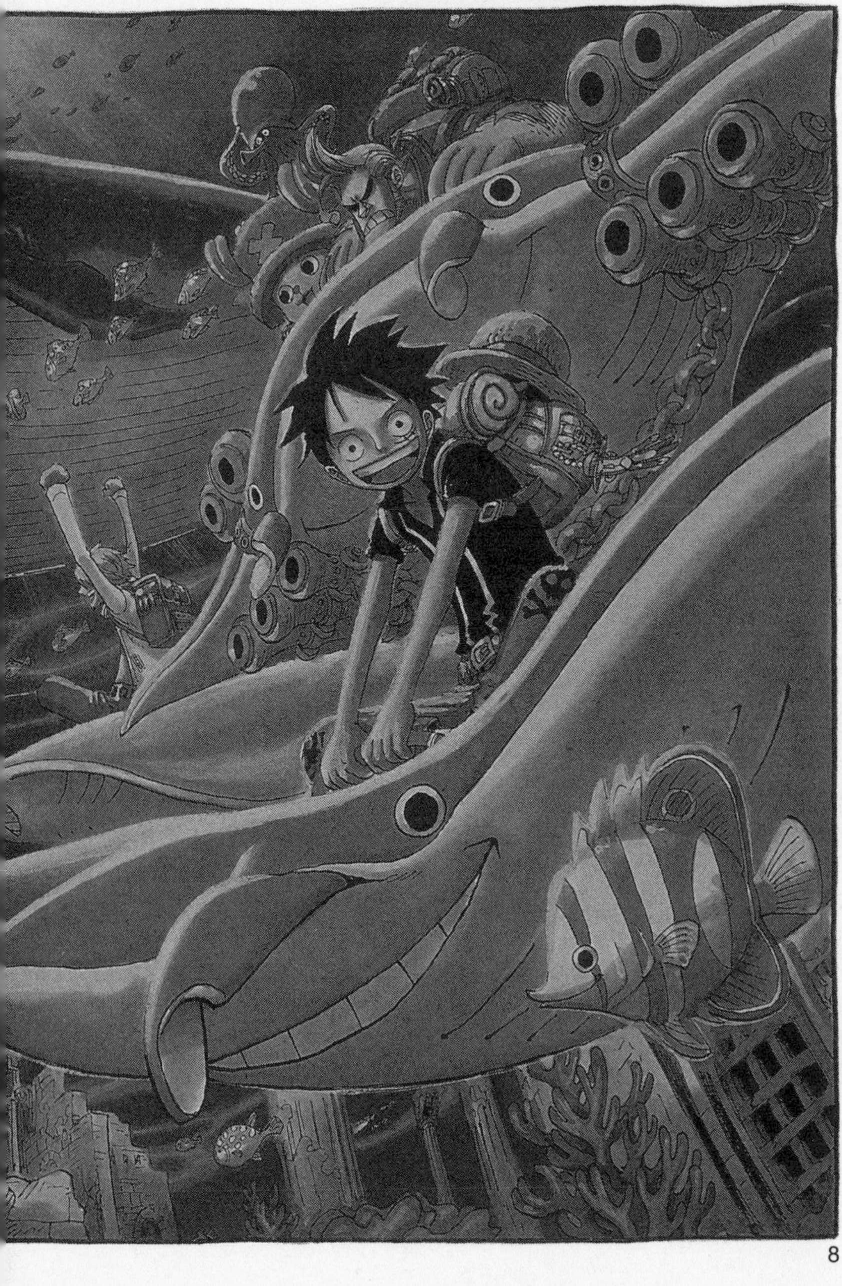

Chapter 471:

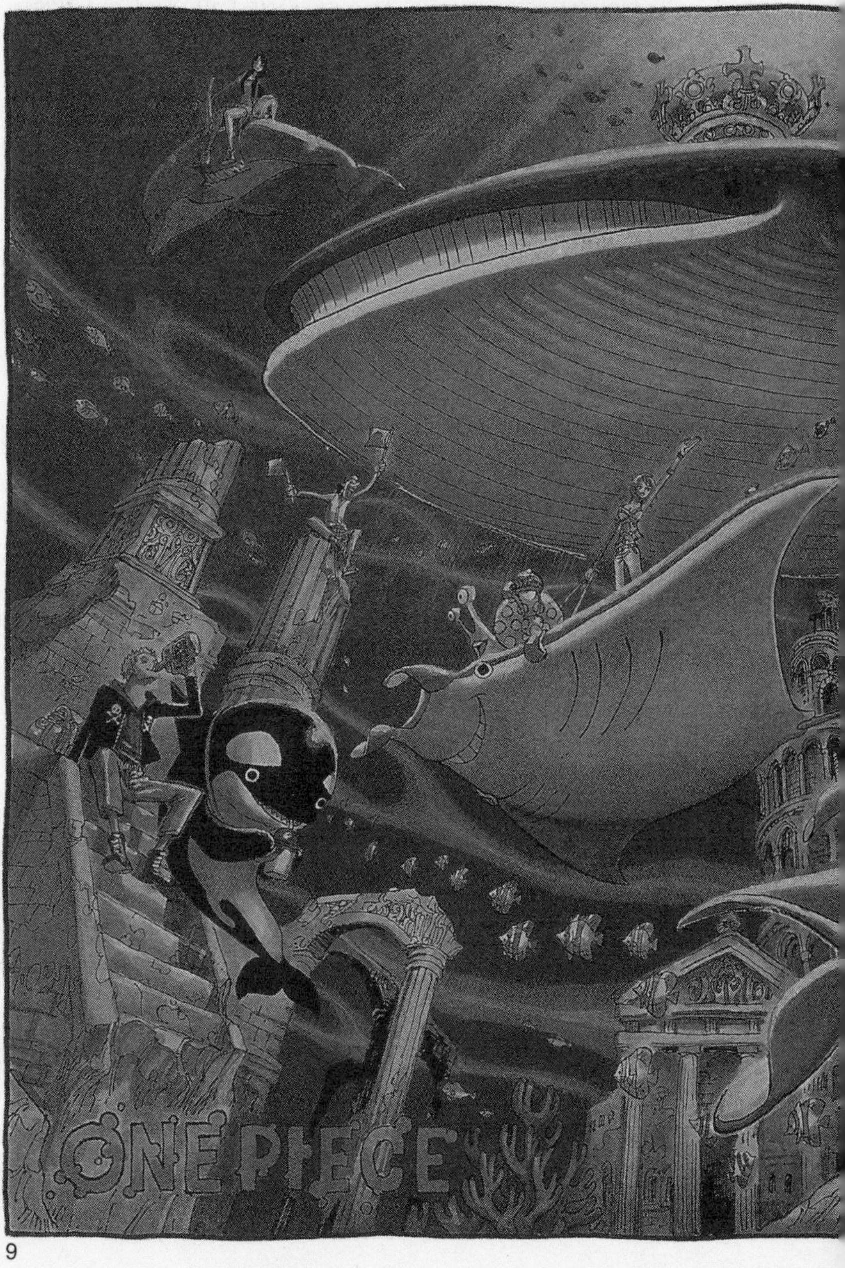
ONE PIECE

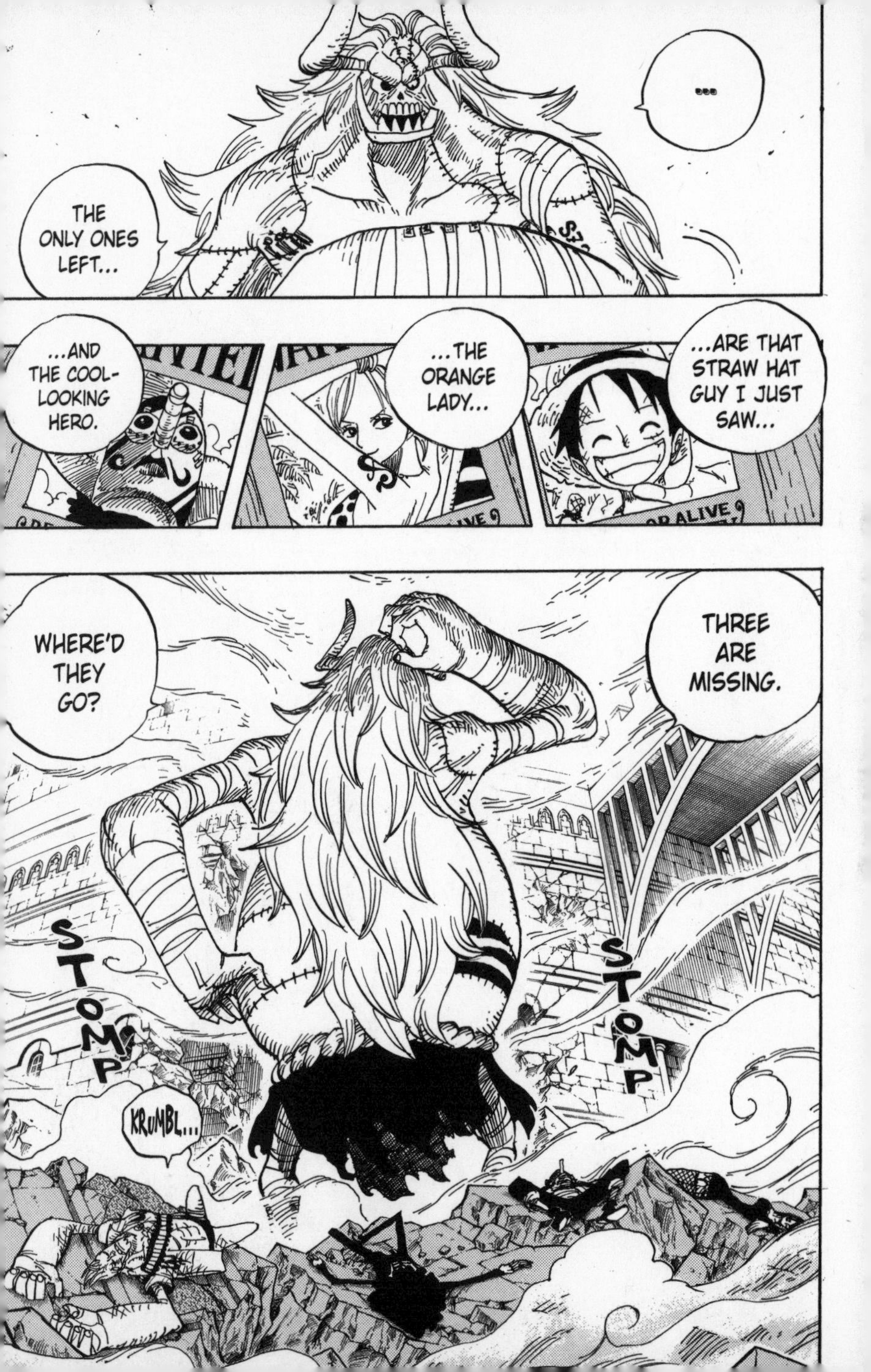
...
THE ONLY ONES LEFT...
...ARE THAT STRAW HAT GUY I JUST SAW...
...THE ORANGE LADY...
...AND THE COOL-LOOKING HERO.
THREE ARE MISSING.
WHERE'D THEY GO?
STOMP
STOMP
KRUMBL...

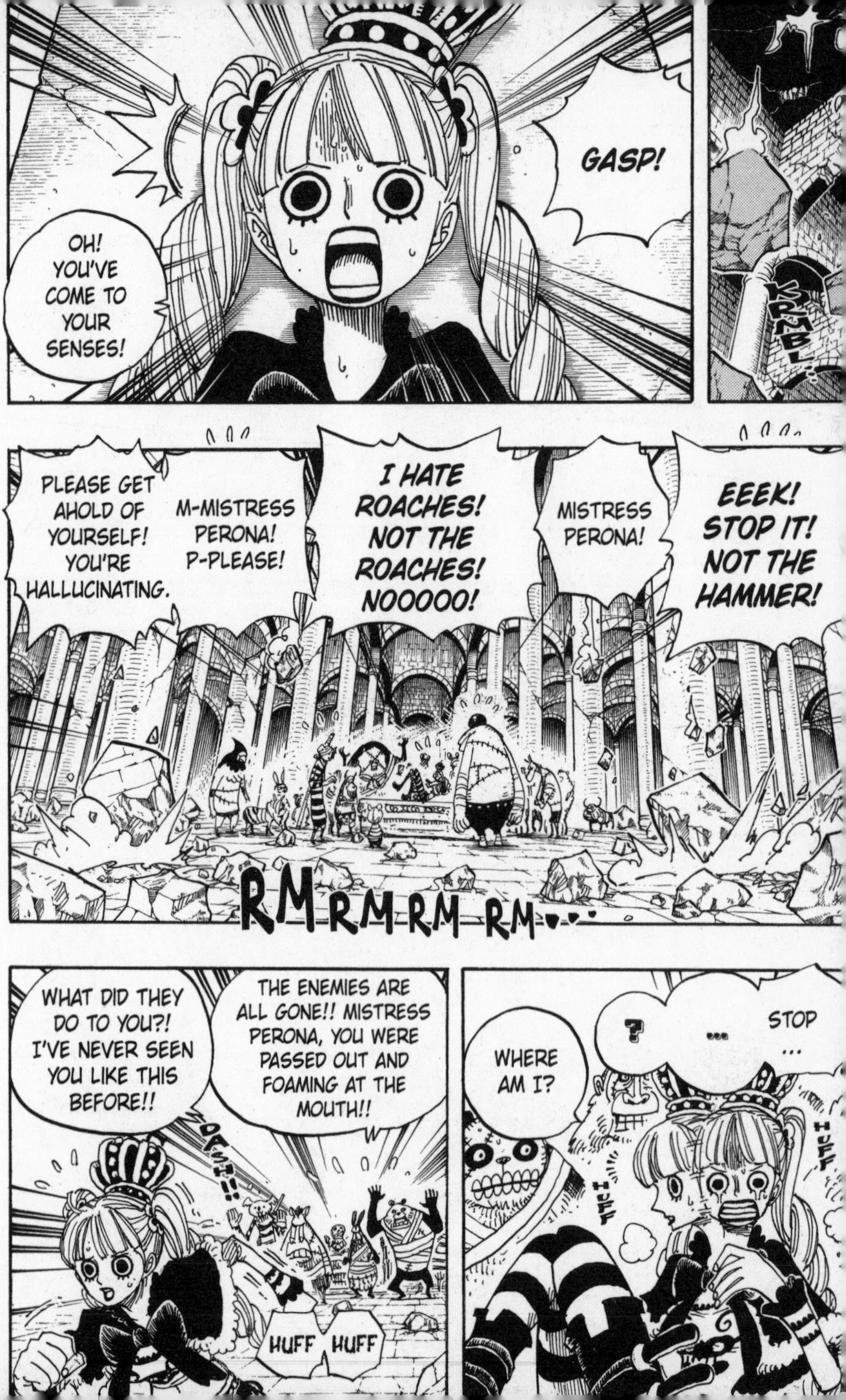
KRMBL
GASP!
OH! YOU'VE COME TO YOUR SENSES!
EEEK! STOP IT! NOT THE HAMMER!
MISTRESS PERONA!
I HATE ROACHES! NOT THE ROACHES! NOOOOO!
M-MISTRESS PERONA! P-PLEASE!
PLEASE GET AHOLD OF YOURSELF! YOU'RE HALLUCINATING.
RM RM RM RM RM...
STOP ...
? ...
WHERE AM I?
HUFF
HUFF
THE ENEMIES ARE ALL GONE!! MISTRESS PERONA, YOU WERE PASSED OUT AND FOAMING AT THE MOUTH!!
WHAT DID THEY DO TO YOU?! I'VE NEVER SEEN YOU LIKE THIS BEFORE!!
DASH!!
HUFF HUFF

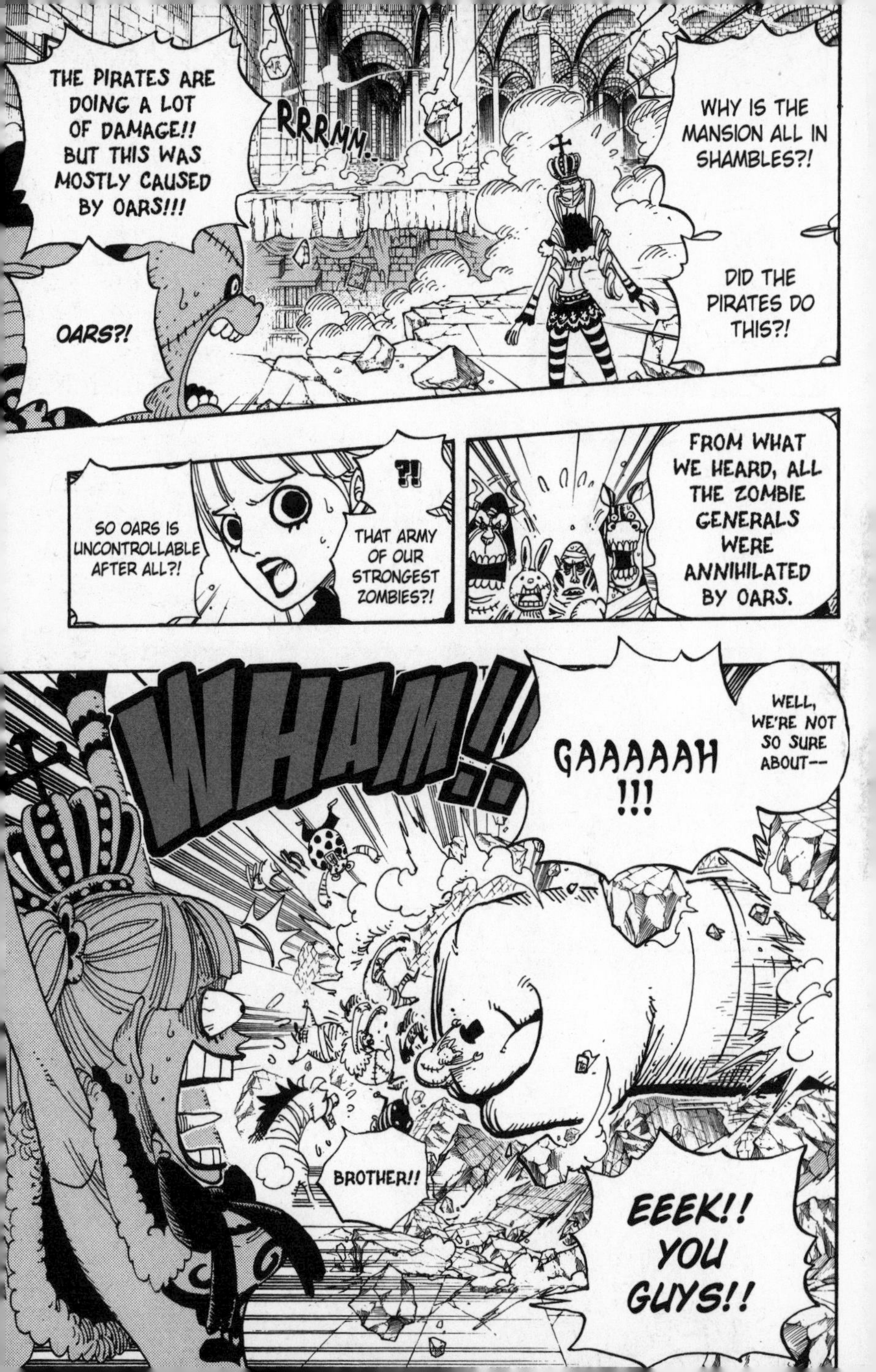
WHY IS THE MANSION ALL IN SHAMBLES?!
DID THE PIRATES DO THIS?!
RRRMM..
THE PIRATES ARE DOING A LOT OF DAMAGE!! BUT THIS WAS MOSTLY CAUSED BY OARS!!!
OARS?!
FROM WHAT WE HEARD, ALL THE ZOMBIE GENERALS WERE ANNIHILATED BY OARS.
?!
THAT ARMY OF OUR STRONGEST ZOMBIES?!
SO OARS IS UNCONTROLLABLE AFTER ALL?!
WELL, WE'RE NOT SO SURE ABOUT--
GAAAAAH !!!
WHAM!!
EEEK!! YOU GUYS!!
BROTHER!!

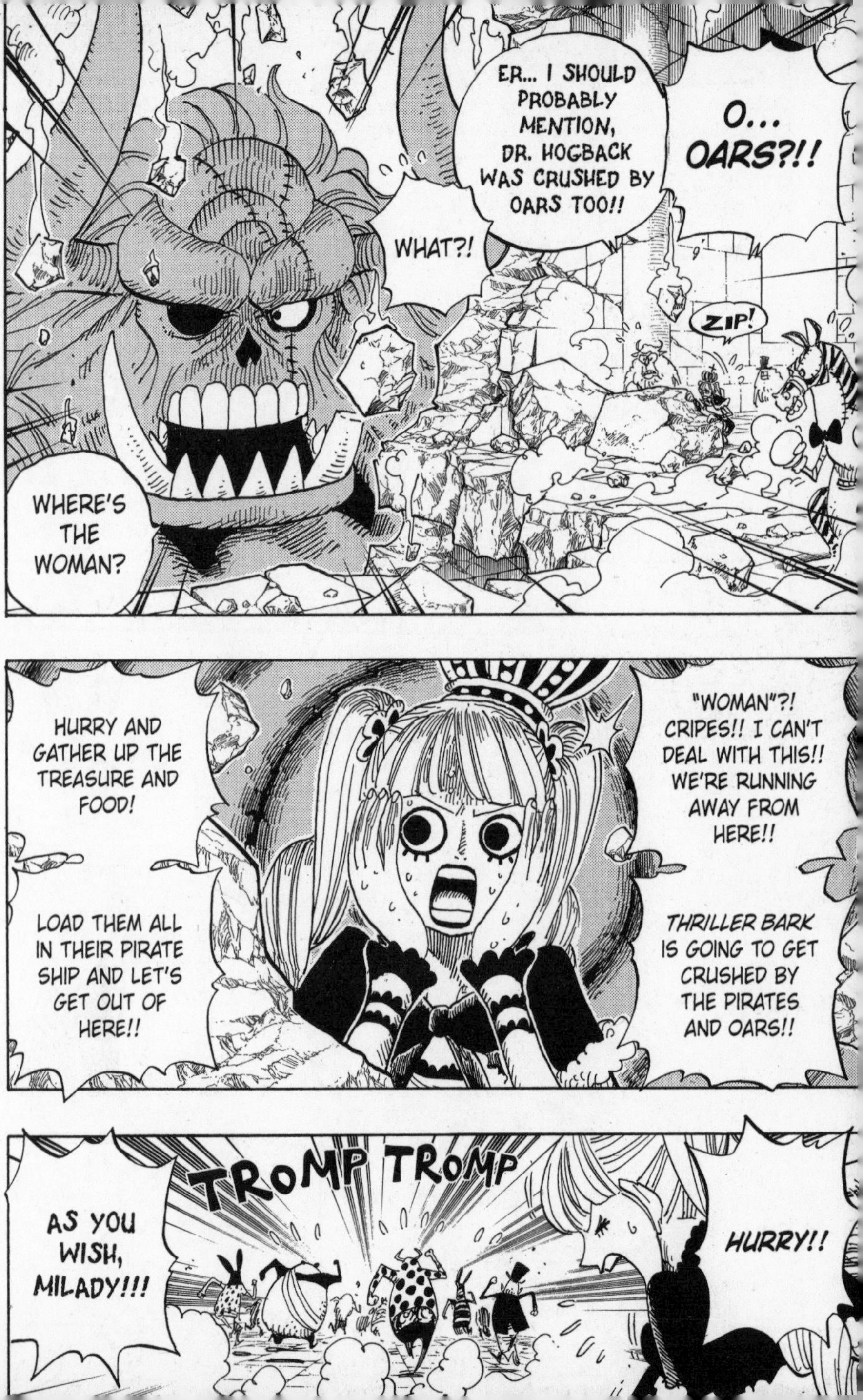
O... OARS?!!
ER... I SHOULD PROBABLY MENTION, DR. HOGBACK WAS CRUSHED BY OARS TOO!!
WHAT?!
ZIP!
WHERE'S THE WOMAN?
"WOMAN"?! CRIPES!! I CAN'T DEAL WITH THIS!! WE'RE RUNNING AWAY FROM HERE!!
THRILLER BARK IS GOING TO GET CRUSHED BY THE PIRATES AND OARS!!
HURRY AND GATHER UP THE TREASURE AND FOOD!
LOAD THEM ALL IN THEIR PIRATE SHIP AND LET'S GET OUT OF HERE!!
HURRY!!
TROMP TROMP
AS YOU WISH, MILADY!!!

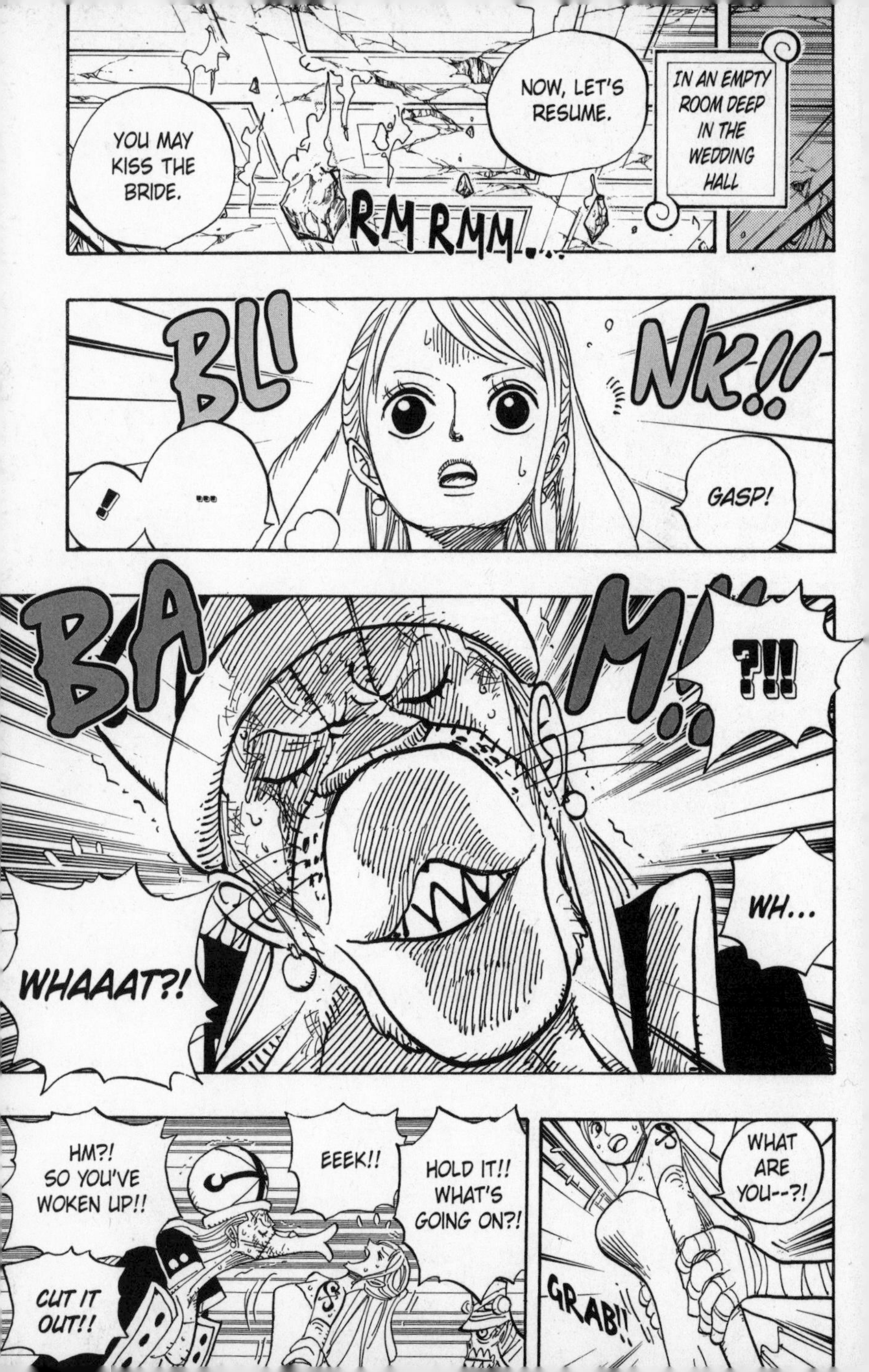
IN AN EMPTY ROOM DEEP IN THE WEDDING HALL
NOW, LET'S RESUME.
RM RMM...
YOU MAY KISS THE BRIDE.
BLINK!!
GASP!
...
!
BAM!!
?!!
WH...
WHAAAT?!
WHAT ARE YOU--?!
GRAB!!
HOLD IT!! WHAT'S GOING ON?!
EEEK!!
HM?! SO YOU'VE WOKEN UP!!
CUT IT OUT!!

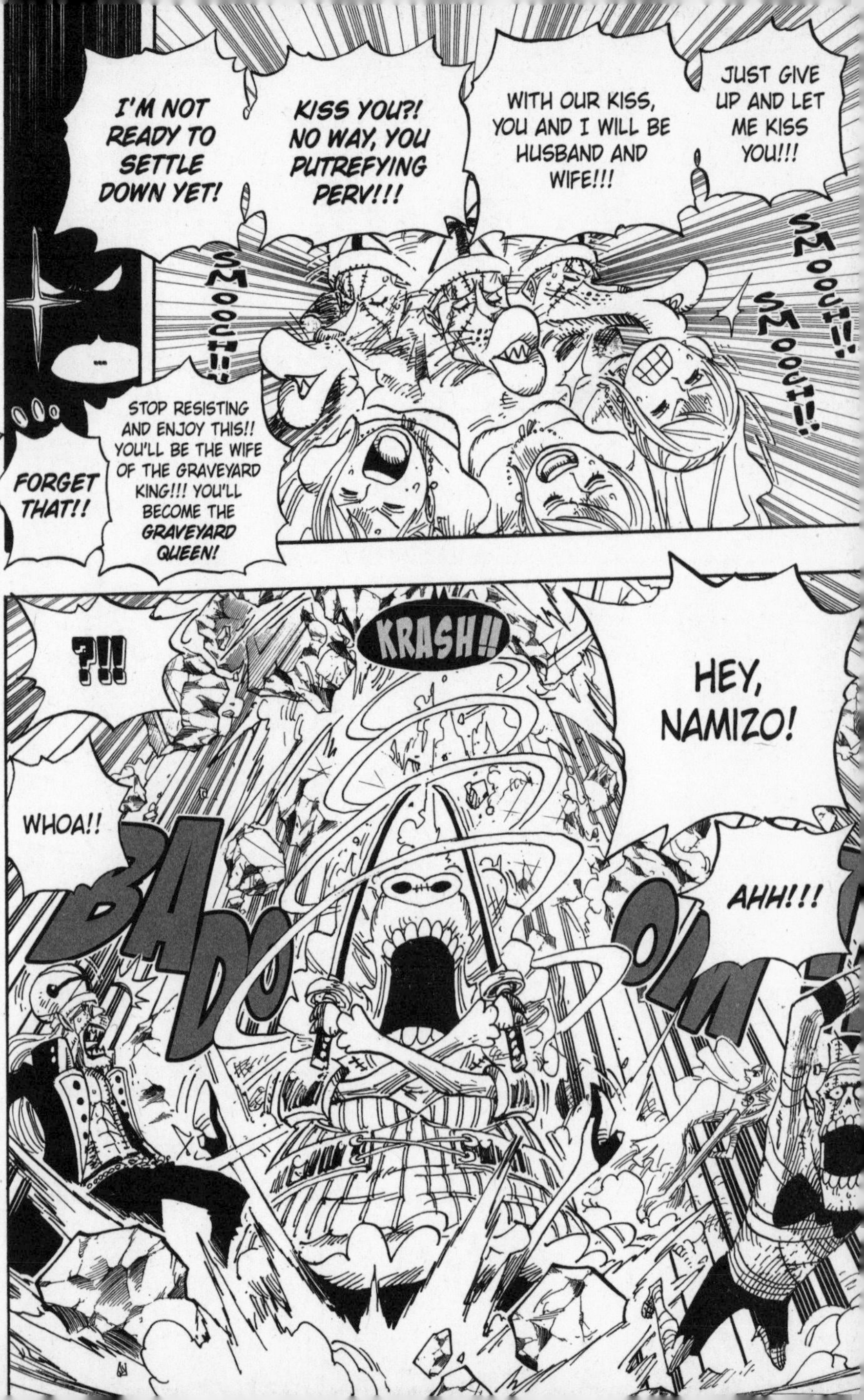
JUST GIVE UP AND LET ME KISS YOU!!!
WITH OUR KISS, YOU AND I WILL BE HUSBAND AND WIFE!!!
KISS YOU?! NO WAY, YOU PUTREFYING PERV!!!
I'M NOT READY TO SETTLE DOWN YET!
SMOOCH!!
SMOOCH!!
SMOOCH!!
STOP RESISTING AND ENJOY THIS!! YOU'LL BE THE WIFE OF THE GRAVEYARD KING!!! YOU'LL BECOME THE GRAVEYARD QUEEN!
FORGET THAT!!
KRASH!!
HEY, NAMIZO!
?!!
AHH!!!
WHOA!!
BADOOM

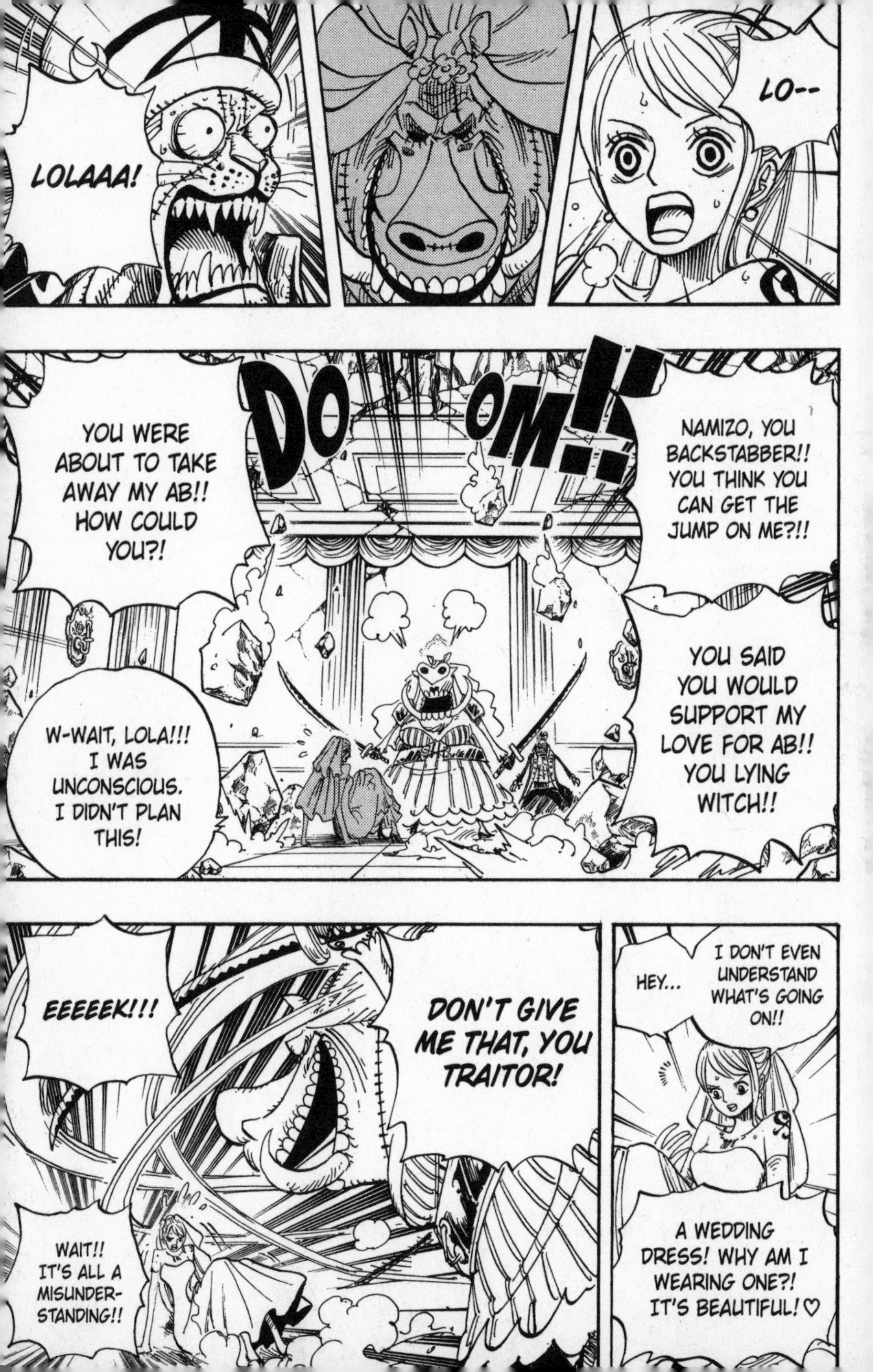
LO--
LOLAAA!
NAMIZO, YOU BACKSTABBER!! YOU THINK YOU CAN GET THE JUMP ON ME?!!
DOOM!!
YOU WERE ABOUT TO TAKE AWAY MY AB!! HOW COULD YOU?!
YOU SAID YOU WOULD SUPPORT MY LOVE FOR AB!! YOU LYING WITCH!!
W-WAIT, LOLA!!! I WAS UNCONSCIOUS. I DIDN'T PLAN THIS!
I DON'T EVEN UNDERSTAND WHAT'S GOING ON!!
HEY...
A WEDDING DRESS! WHY AM I WEARING ONE?! IT'S BEAUTIFUL! ♡
DON'T GIVE ME THAT, YOU TRAITOR!
EEEEEK!!!
WAIT!! IT'S ALL A MISUNDER-STANDING!!

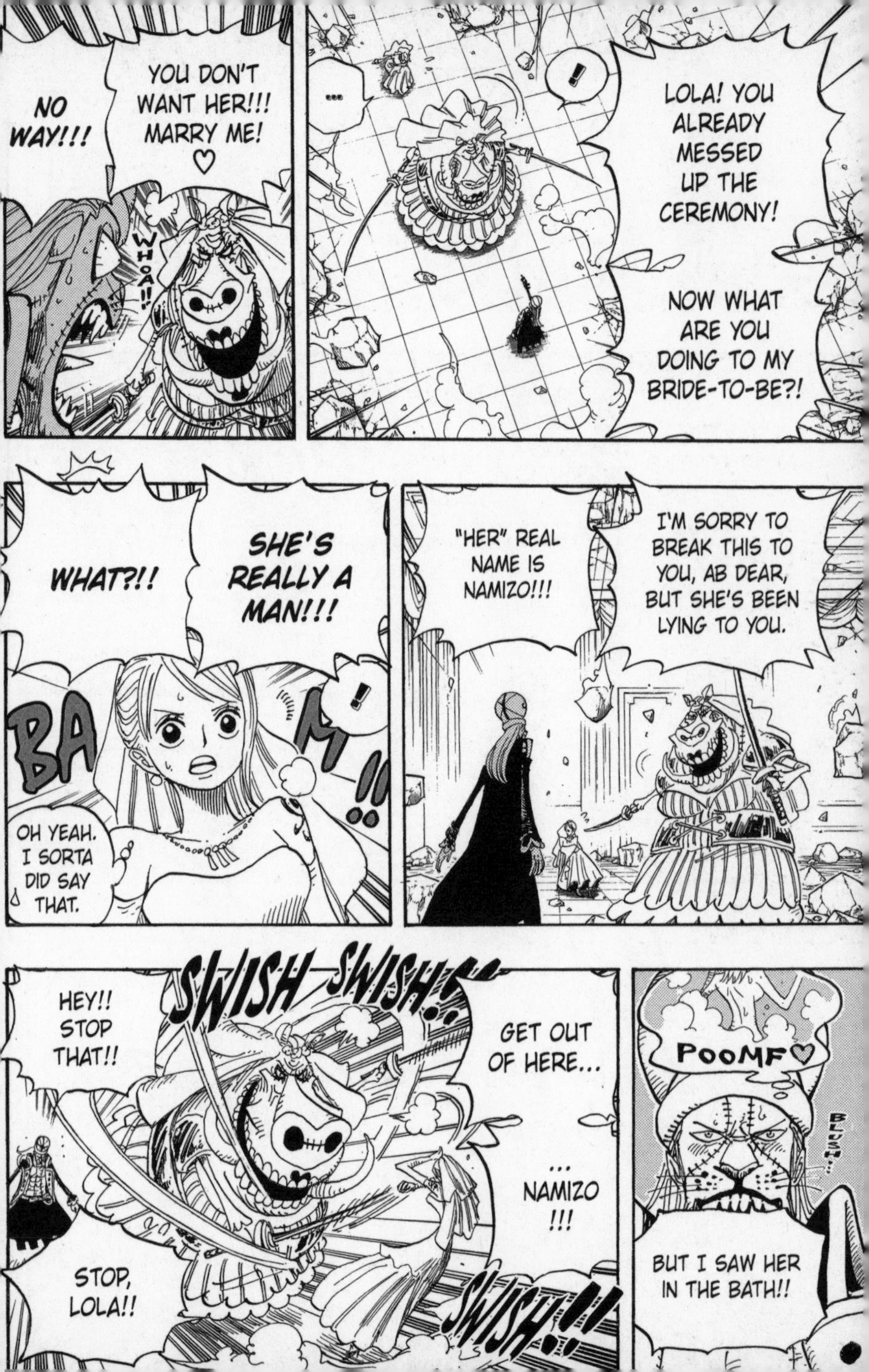
LOLA! YOU ALREADY MESSED UP THE CEREMONY!
NOW WHAT ARE YOU DOING TO MY BRIDE-TO-BE?!
!
...
YOU DON'T WANT HER!!! MARRY ME! ♡
NO WAY!!!
WHOA!!
I'M SORRY TO BREAK THIS TO YOU, AB DEAR, BUT SHE'S BEEN LYING TO YOU.
"HER" REAL NAME IS NAMIZO!!!
SHE'S REALLY A MAN!!!
WHAT?!!
!
BA M!!
OH YEAH. I SORTA DID SAY THAT.
POOMF♡
BLUSH...
BUT I SAW HER IN THE BATH!!
SWISH SWISH...
GET OUT OF HERE...
HEY!! STOP THAT!!
... NAMIZO !!!
STOP, LOLA!!
SWISH!!

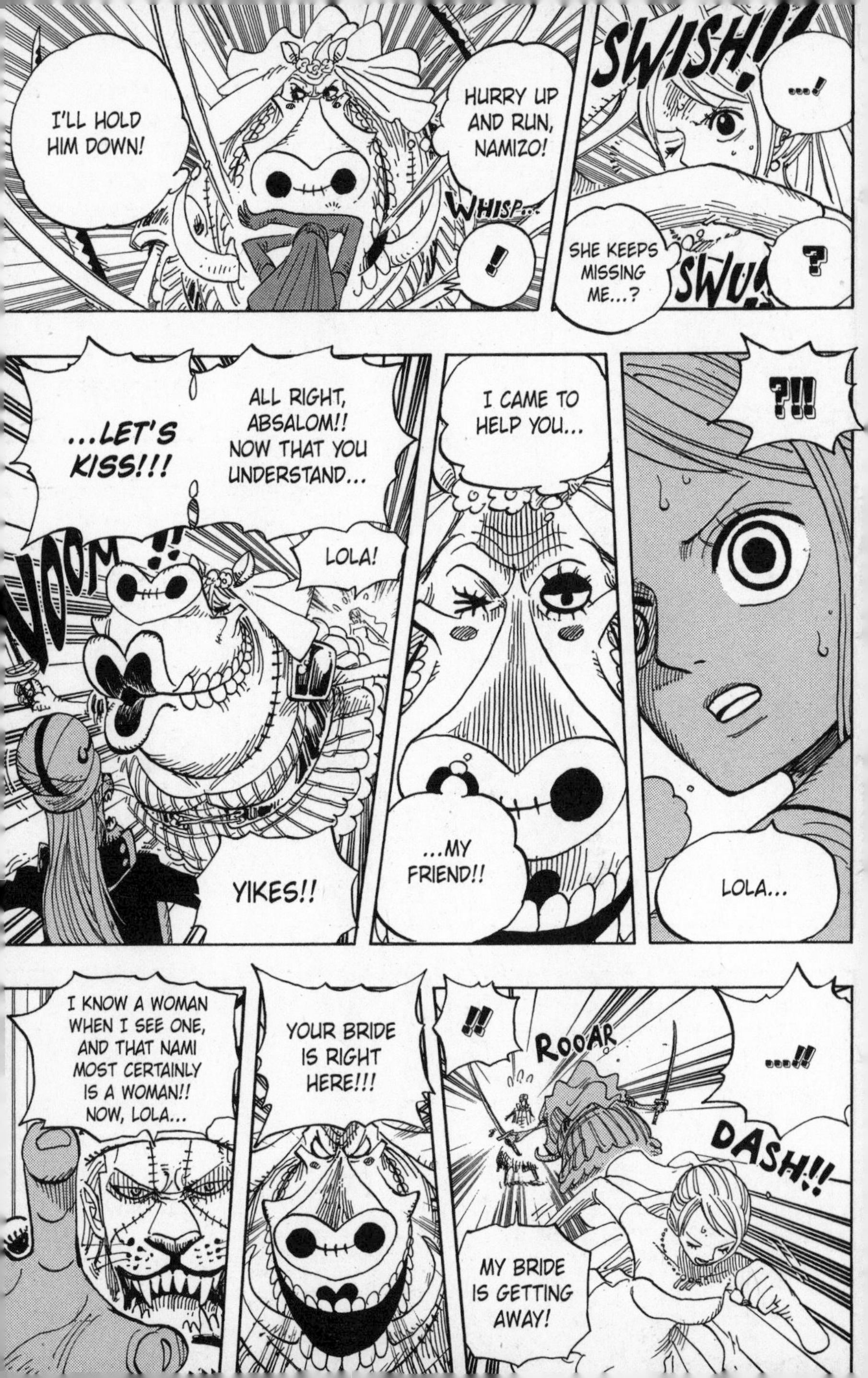
SWISH!!
...!
SHE KEEPS MISSING ME...?
?
HURRY UP AND RUN, NAMIZO!
WHISP...
!
I'LL HOLD HIM DOWN!
?!!
LOLA...
I CAME TO HELP YOU...
...MY FRIEND!!
ALL RIGHT, ABSALOM!! NOW THAT YOU UNDERSTAND...
...LET'S KISS!!!
LOLA!
YIKES!!
!!
ROOAR
...!!
DASH!!
MY BRIDE IS GETTING AWAY!
YOUR BRIDE IS RIGHT HERE!!!
I KNOW A WOMAN WHEN I SEE ONE, AND THAT NAMI MOST CERTAINLY IS A WOMAN!! NOW, LOLA...

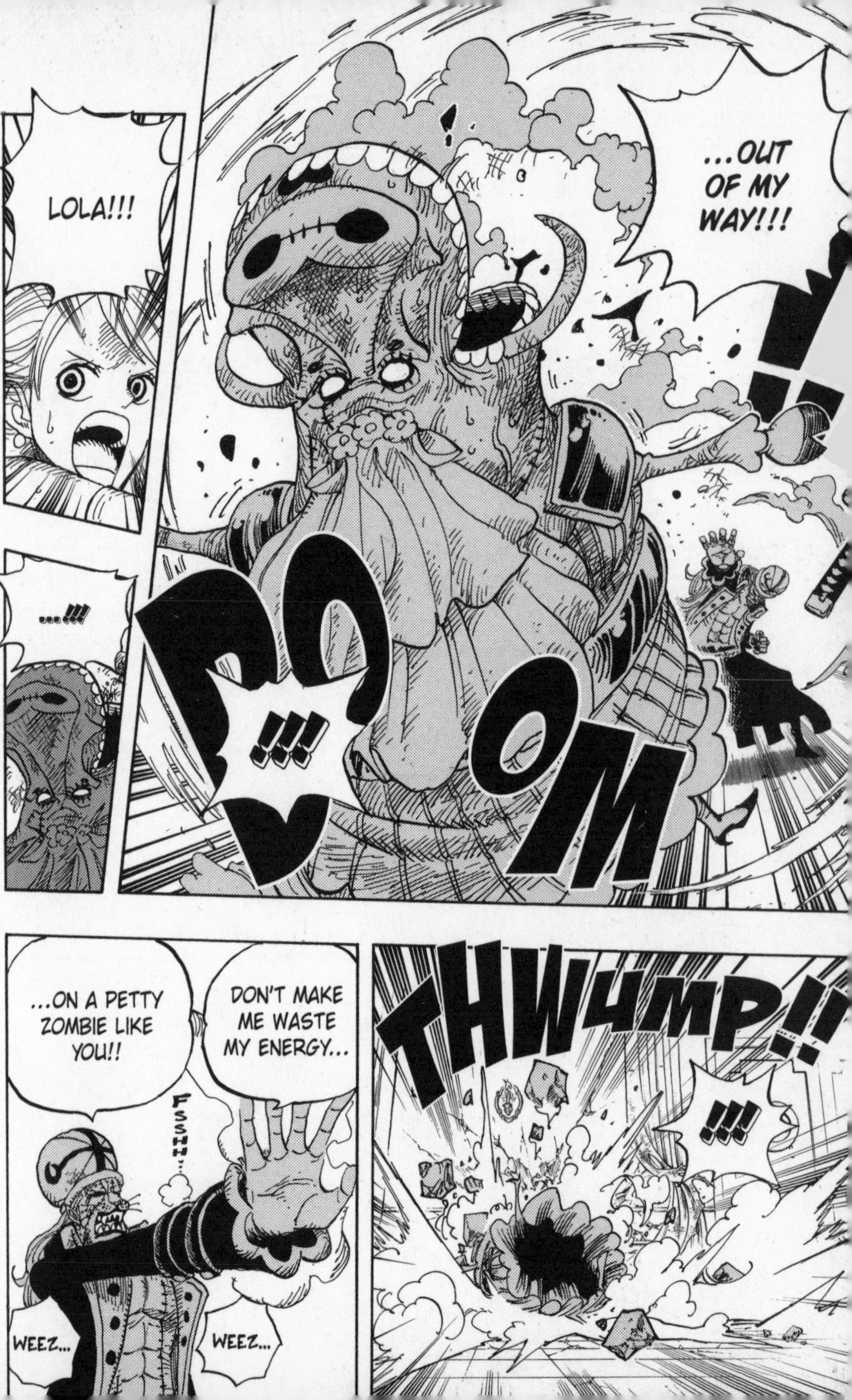
...OUT OF MY WAY!!!
DOOM!!!
LOLA!!!
...!!!
THWUMP!!
!!!
DON'T MAKE ME WASTE MY ENERGY...
...ON A PETTY ZOMBIE LIKE YOU!!
FSSHH...
WEEZ...
WEEZ...

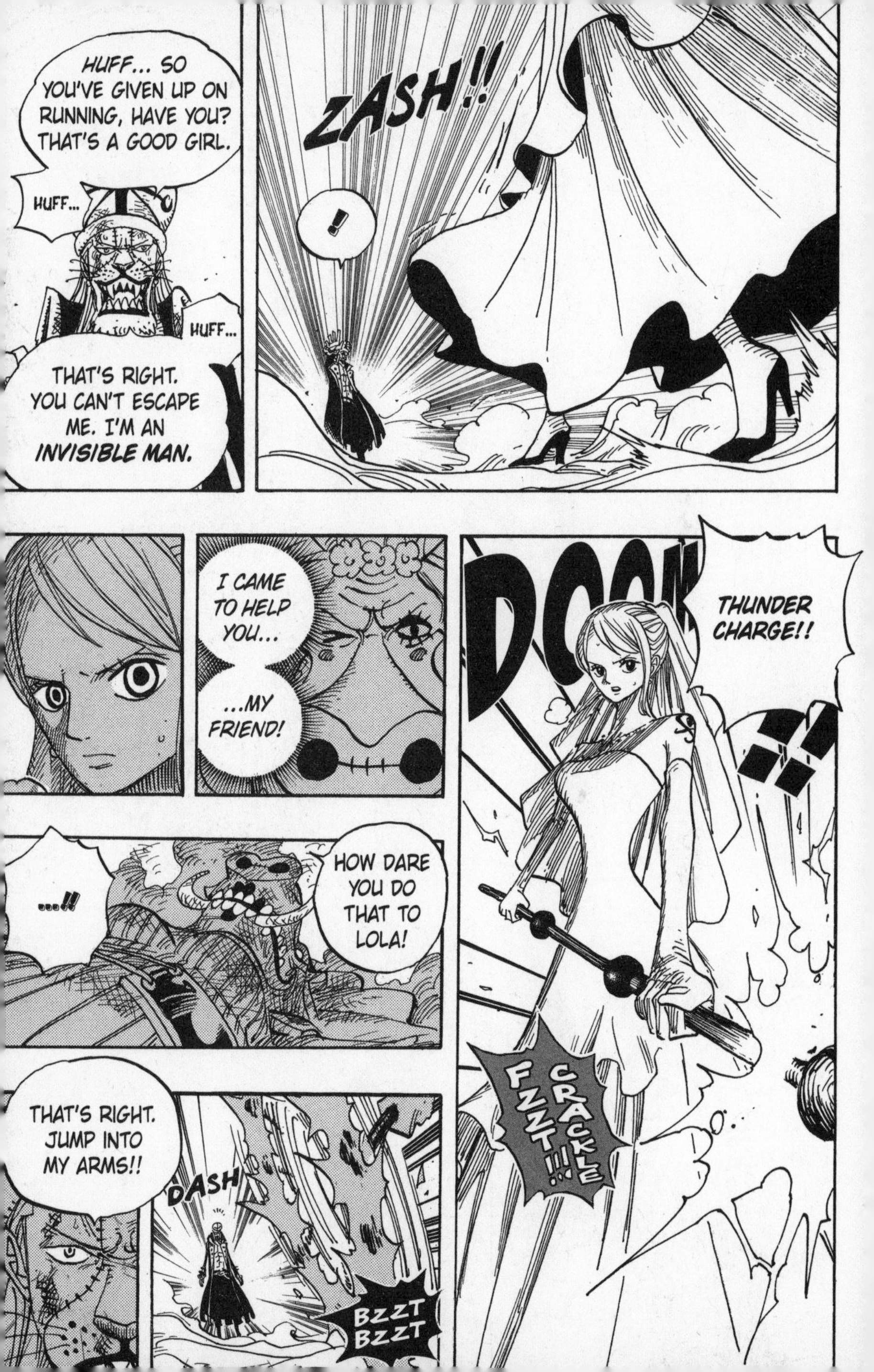
ZASH!!
!
HUFF... SO YOU'VE GIVEN UP ON RUNNING, HAVE YOU? THAT'S A GOOD GIRL.
HUFF...
HUFF...
THAT'S RIGHT. YOU CAN'T ESCAPE ME. I'M AN INVISIBLE MAN.
DOO
THUNDER CHARGE!!
FZZT CRACKLE !!!
I CAME TO HELP YOU...
...MY FRIEND!
HOW DARE YOU DO THAT TO LOLA!
...!!
DASH
BZZT BZZT
THAT'S RIGHT. JUMP INTO MY ARMS!!

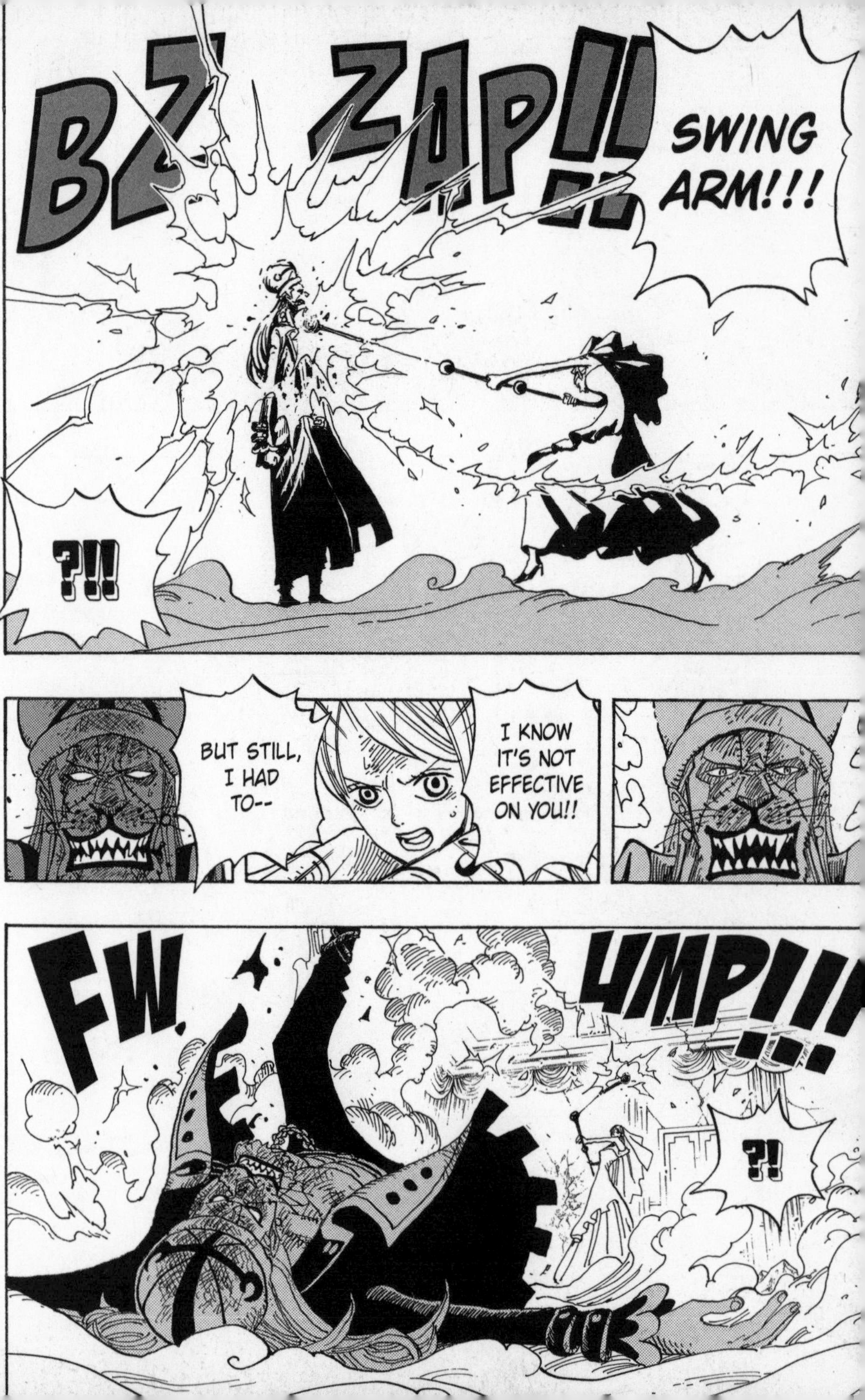
SWING ARM!!!
BZZAP!!
?!!
I KNOW IT'S NOT EFFECTIVE ON YOU!!
BUT STILL, I HAD TO--
FWUMP!!!
?!

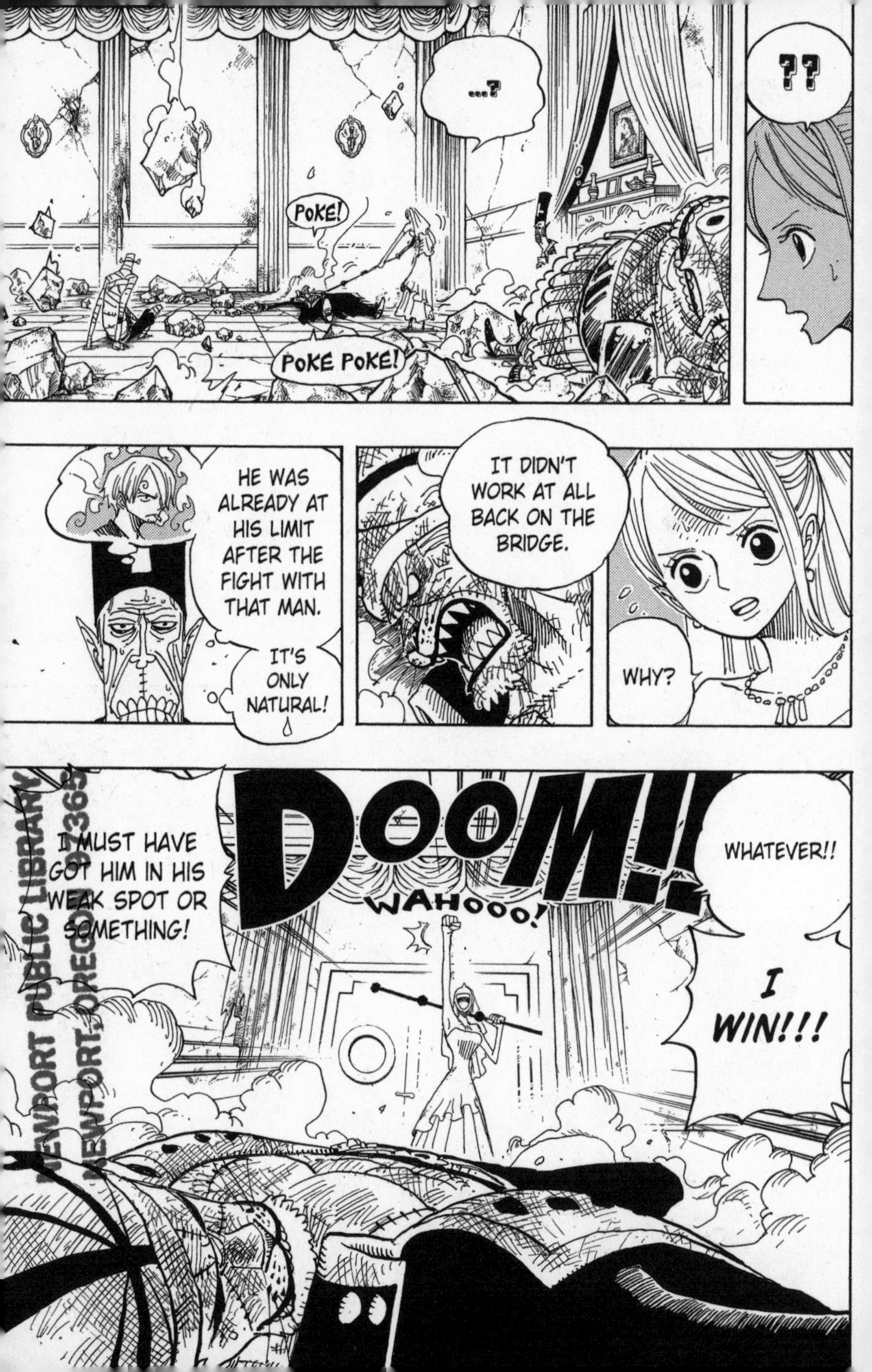
??
...?
POKE!
POKE POKE!
WHY?
IT DIDN'T WORK AT ALL BACK ON THE BRIDGE.
HE WAS ALREADY AT HIS LIMIT AFTER THE FIGHT WITH THAT MAN.
IT'S ONLY NATURAL!
WHATEVER!!
I WIN!!!
DOOM!!
WAHOOO!
I MUST HAVE GOT HIM IN HIS WEAK SPOT OR SOMETHING!

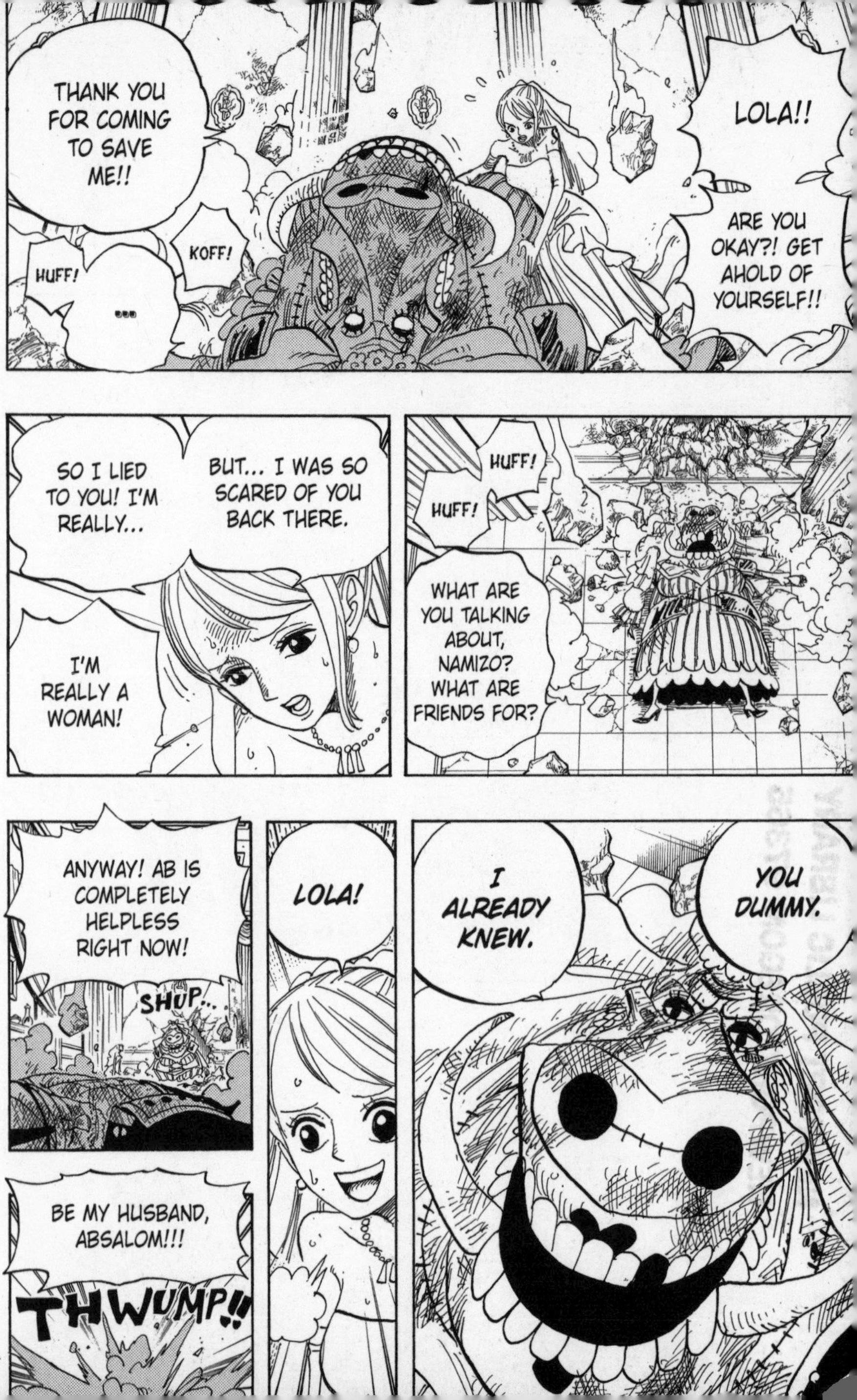
LOLA!!
ARE YOU OKAY?! GET AHOLD OF YOURSELF!!
THANK YOU FOR COMING TO SAVE ME!!
KOFF!
HUFF!
...
HUFF!
HUFF!
WHAT ARE YOU TALKING ABOUT, NAMIZO? WHAT ARE FRIENDS FOR?
BUT... I WAS SO SCARED OF YOU BACK THERE.
SO I LIED TO YOU! I'M REALLY...
I'M REALLY A WOMAN!
YOU DUMMY.
I ALREADY KNEW.
LOLA!
ANYWAY! AB IS COMPLETELY HELPLESS RIGHT NOW!
SHUP...
BE MY HUSBAND, ABSALOM!!!
THWUMP!!

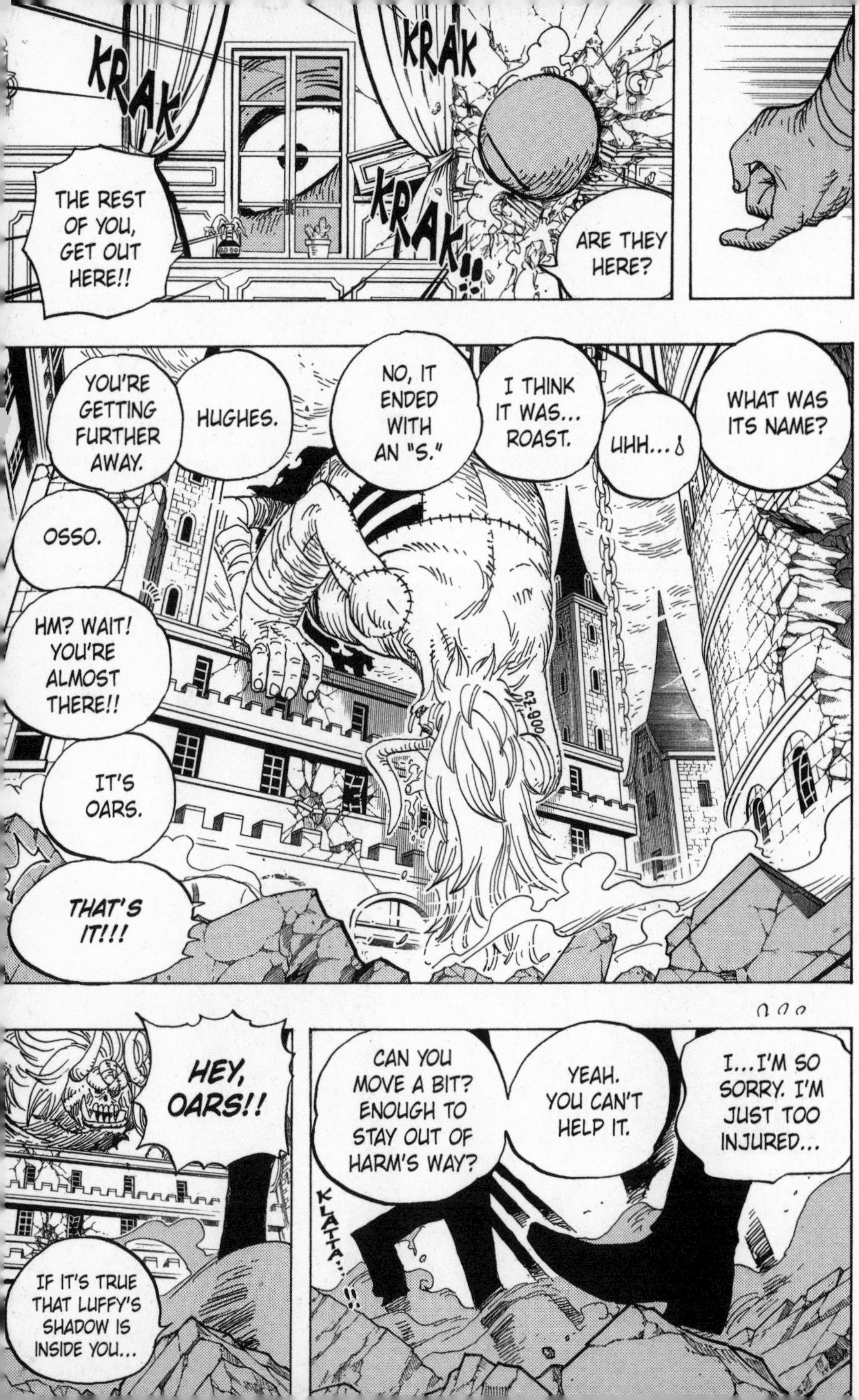
KRAK
ARE THEY HERE?
KRAK!!
KRAK
THE REST OF YOU, GET OUT HERE!!
WHAT WAS ITS NAME?
UHH...
I THINK IT WAS... ROAST.
NO, IT ENDED WITH AN "S."
HUGHES.
YOU'RE GETTING FURTHER AWAY.
OSSO.
HM? WAIT! YOU'RE ALMOST THERE!!
IT'S OARS.
THAT'S IT!!!
I...I'M SO SORRY. I'M JUST TOO INJURED...
YEAH. YOU CAN'T HELP IT.
CAN YOU MOVE A BIT? ENOUGH TO STAY OUT OF HARM'S WAY?
KLATTA..!!
HEY, OARS!!
IF IT'S TRUE THAT LUFFY'S SHADOW IS INSIDE YOU...

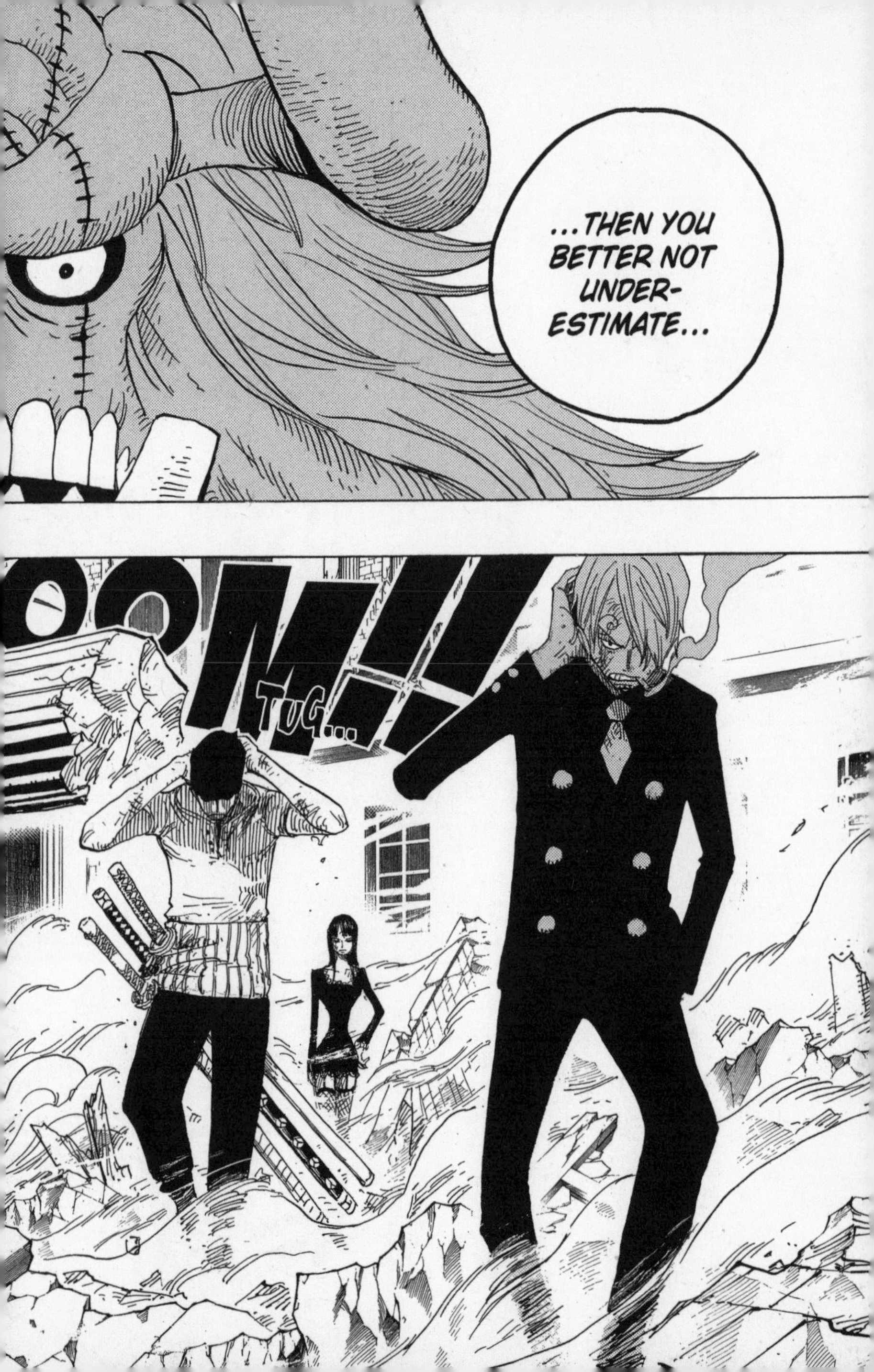
...THEN YOU BETTER NOT UNDER-ESTIMATE...
OOM!!
TUG...

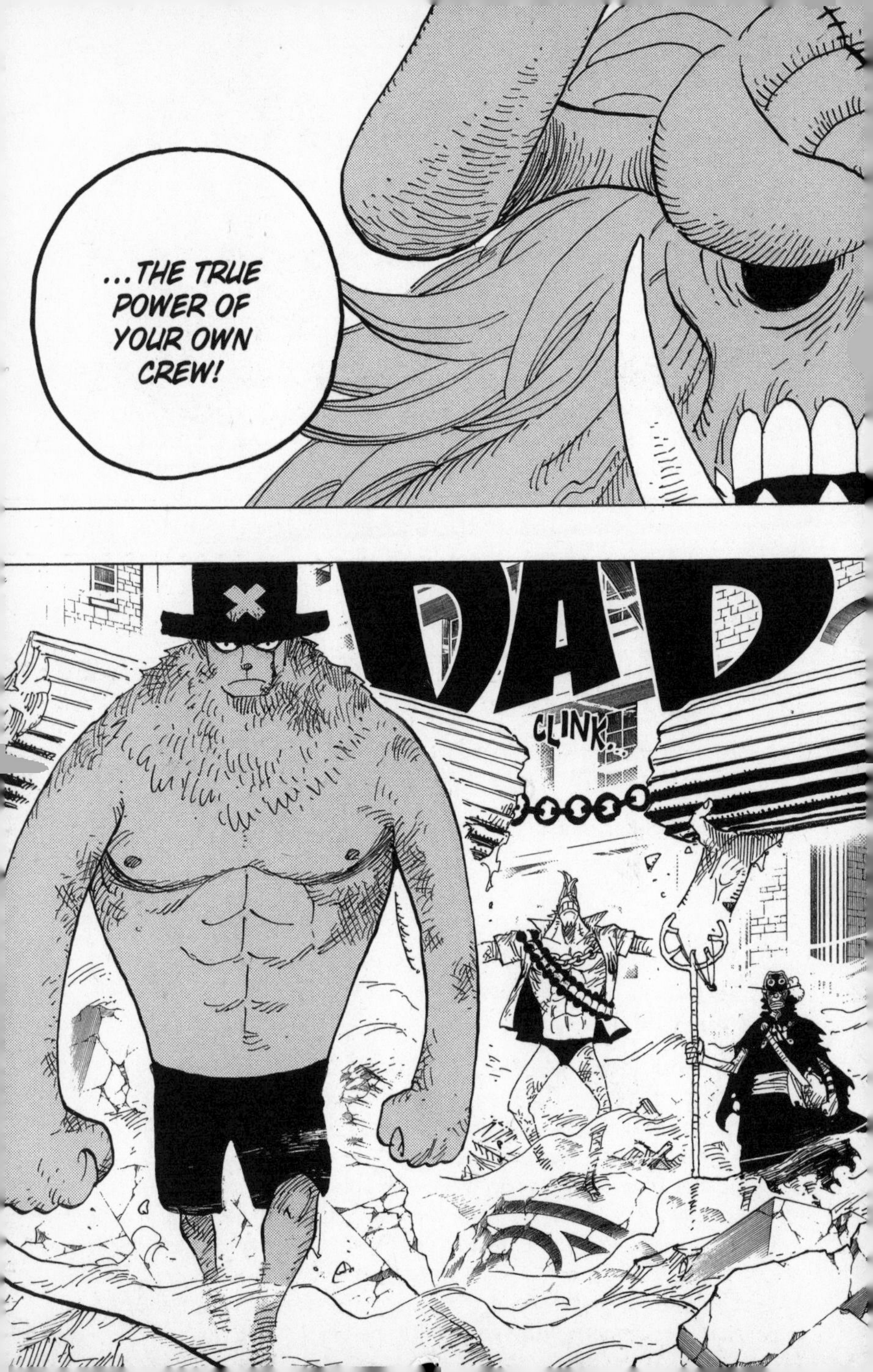
...THE TRUE POWER OF YOUR OWN CREW!
DAD
CLINK...

Question Corner SBS

Oda(A): Hello! How is everyone?! It's me, the author. I'm first. No one gets to hijack this position! And now I'd like to get things started! Ready, and... Time to starf the Question Corner! Whoops, I meant "start." Start. Aww, crap! If I were to be reborn, I would want to become a wall in the women's bath. (← Full of hope)

Reader(Q): With Usopp's razor sharp wit and my natural talent in making dumb jokes, we'd rise to the top as a comedy duo! Please! Let me team up with Usopp! --Please Think of Our Duo's Name

A: Okay! Go ahead and become comedians! Your duo's name is...AWOL.

Q: Everyone in my family is a huge fan of *One Piece,* so we always enjoy reading it. I have a question here. In volume 48, chapter 460, Robin called Nami, "Nami." Before that, she just referred to her as "Navigator." Did Robin have some kind of change of heart?! Please tell me. By the way, when my mom wakes up, she looks exactly like Brook! --Forest Bear

A: Your mom looks like Brook... That's awesome! Really funky. Oh, about Robin I'm glad to see that lots of readers picked up on this. In this volume in chapter 475, you'll see Robin say, "Are you okay, Nami?!" It seems that she now refers to Nami by name. The same goes for the rest of crew. You'll see her referring to them by their names too. After the incident at Enies Lobby, Robin is really starting to open up to the rest of the crew. Even if the stories that occur in One Piece get bigger, I want to continue to draw out these really minor, yet crucial, human relationships.

Chapter 472:
DOWN

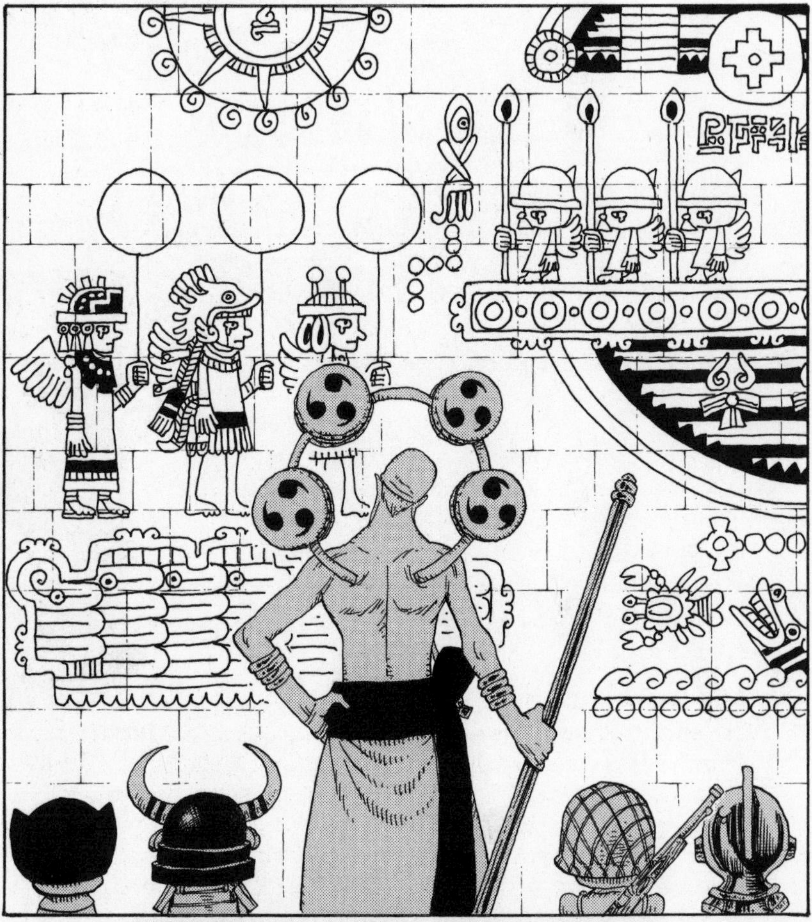

ENERU'S GREAT SPACE MISSION, VOL. 36,
"THE MOON CITY BILKA. THEY FLED TO THE
BLUE PLANET IN SEARCH OF RESOURCES"

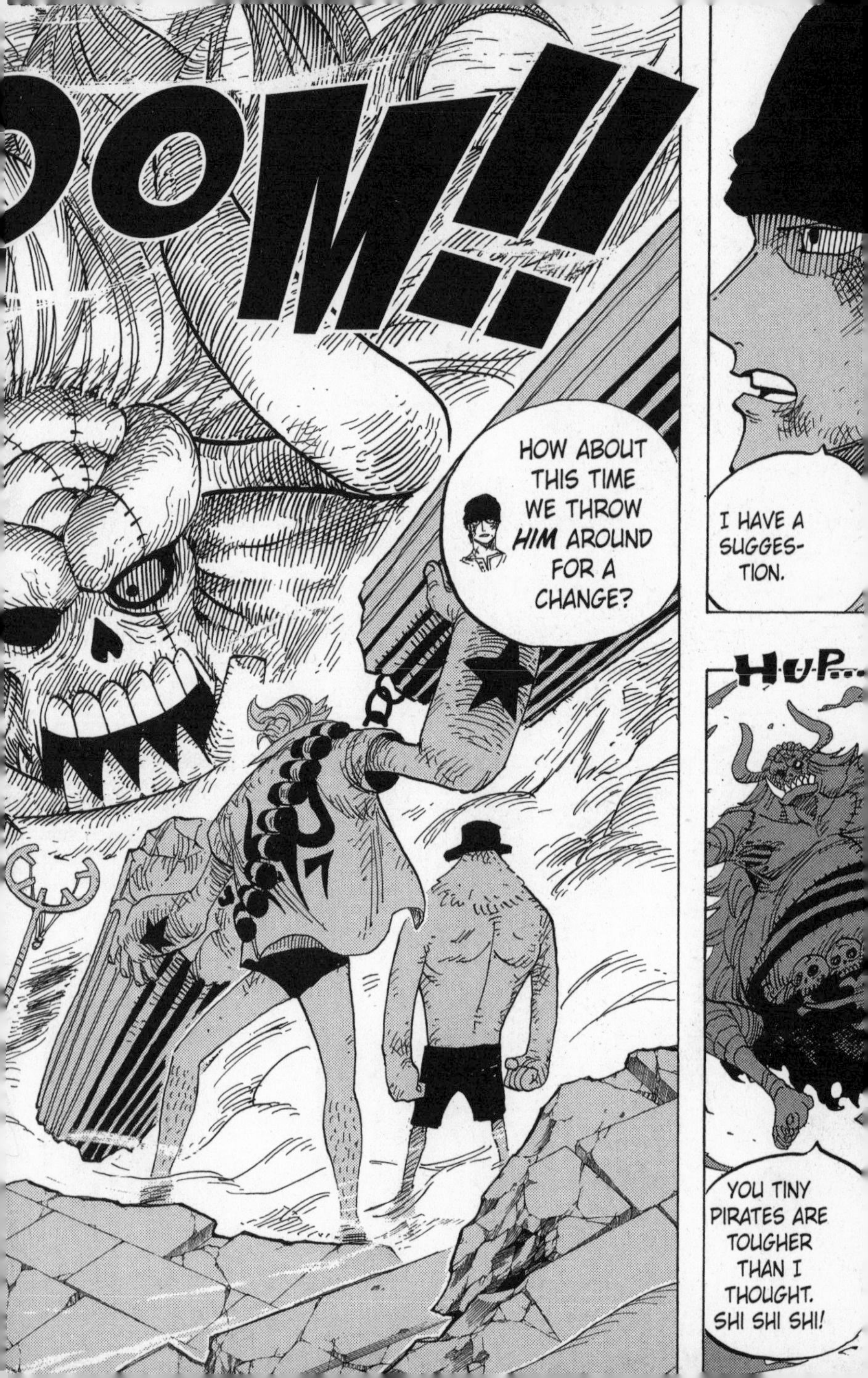
I HAVE A SUGGES-TION.
HUP...
YOU TINY PIRATES ARE TOUGHER THAN I THOUGHT. SHI SHI SHI!
HOW ABOUT THIS TIME WE THROW *HIM* AROUND FOR A CHANGE?

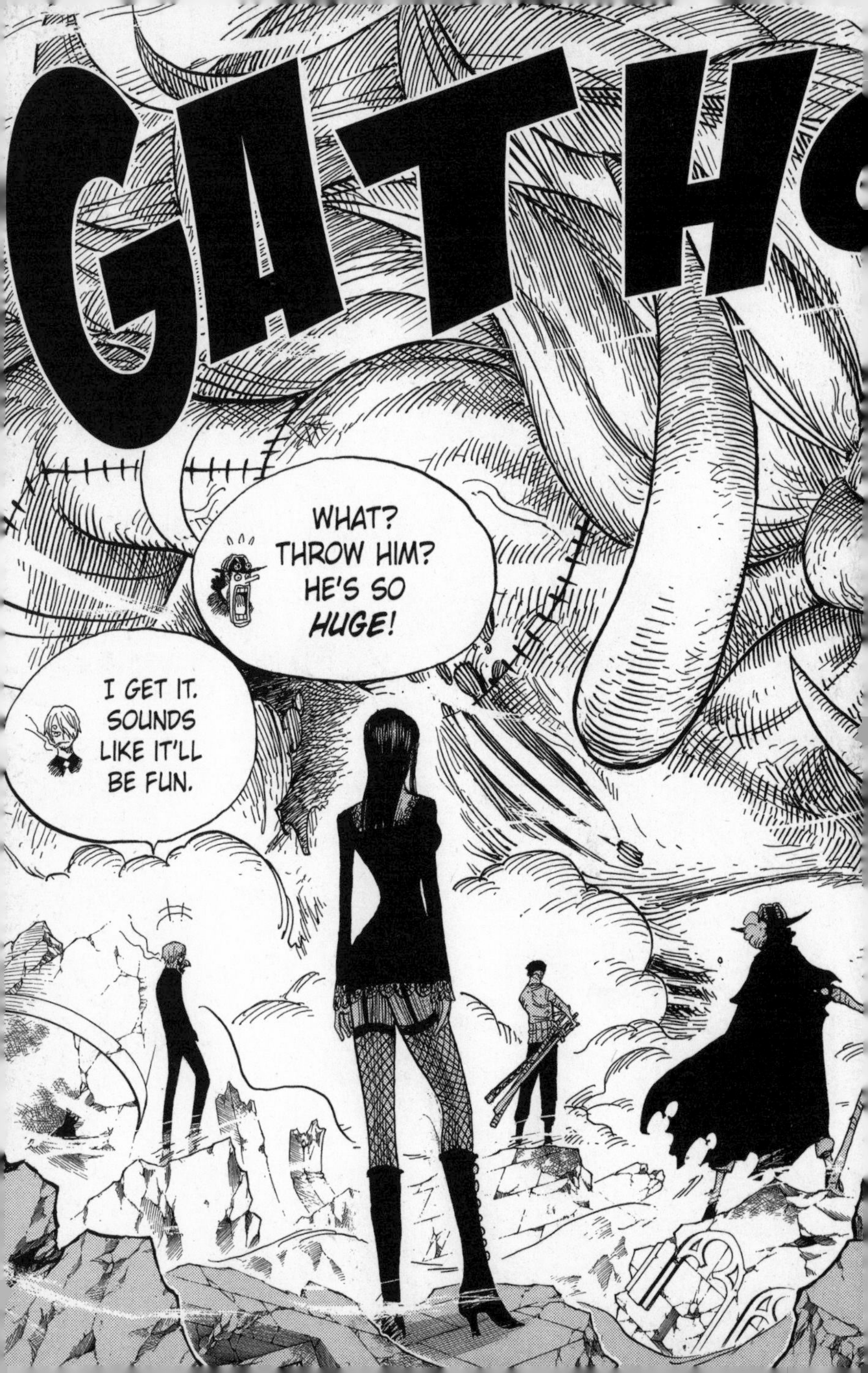
GATHO
WHAT? THROW HIM? HE'S SO *HUGE!*
I GET IT. SOUNDS LIKE IT'LL BE FUN.

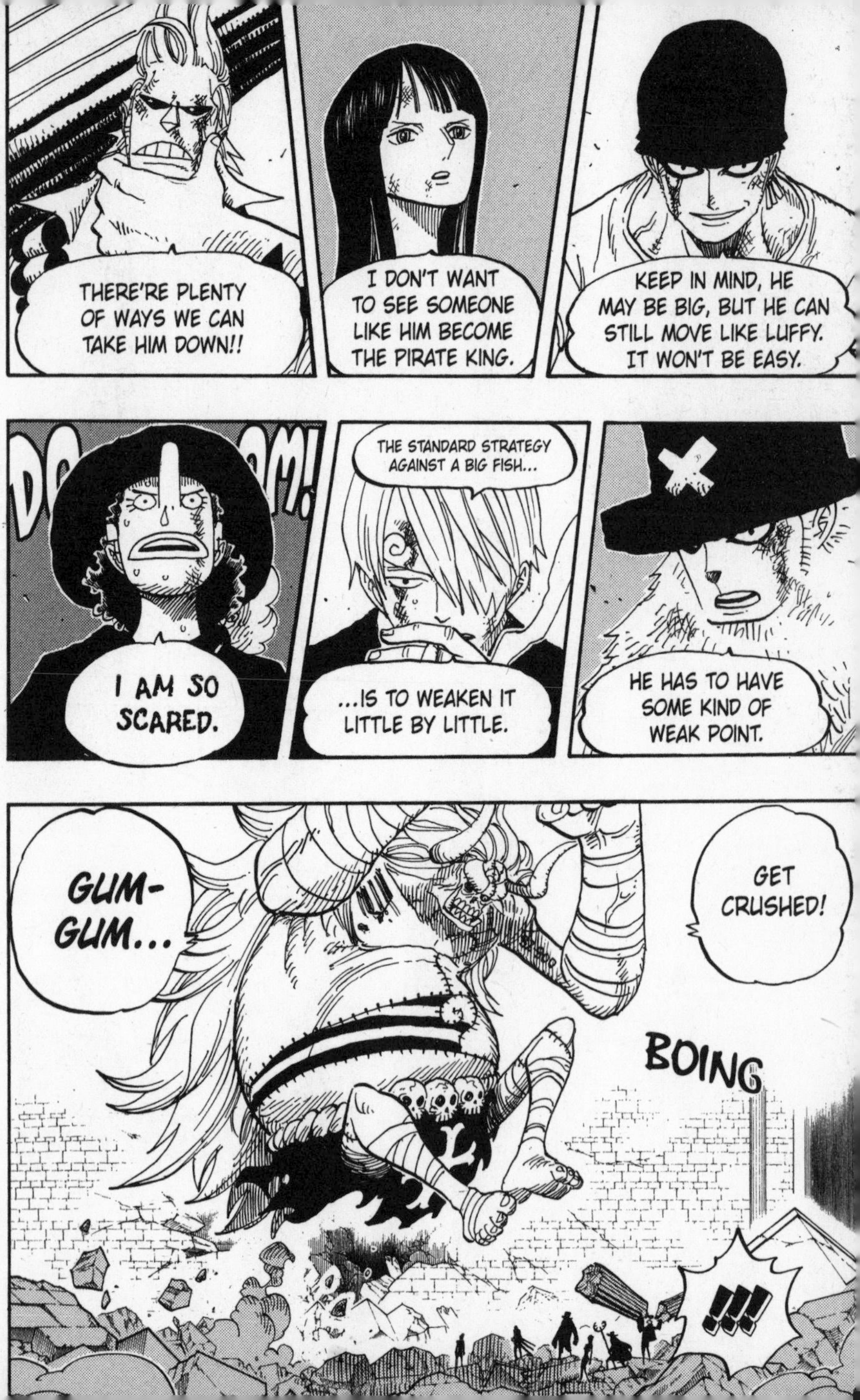
KEEP IN MIND, HE MAY BE BIG, BUT HE CAN STILL MOVE LIKE LUFFY. IT WON'T BE EASY.
I DON'T WANT TO SEE SOMEONE LIKE HIM BECOME THE PIRATE KING.
THERE'RE PLENTY OF WAYS WE CAN TAKE HIM DOWN!!
HE HAS TO HAVE SOME KIND OF WEAK POINT.
THE STANDARD STRATEGY AGAINST A BIG FISH...
...IS TO WEAKEN IT LITTLE BY LITTLE.
I AM SO SCARED.
GET CRUSHED!
GUM-GUM...
BOING
!!!

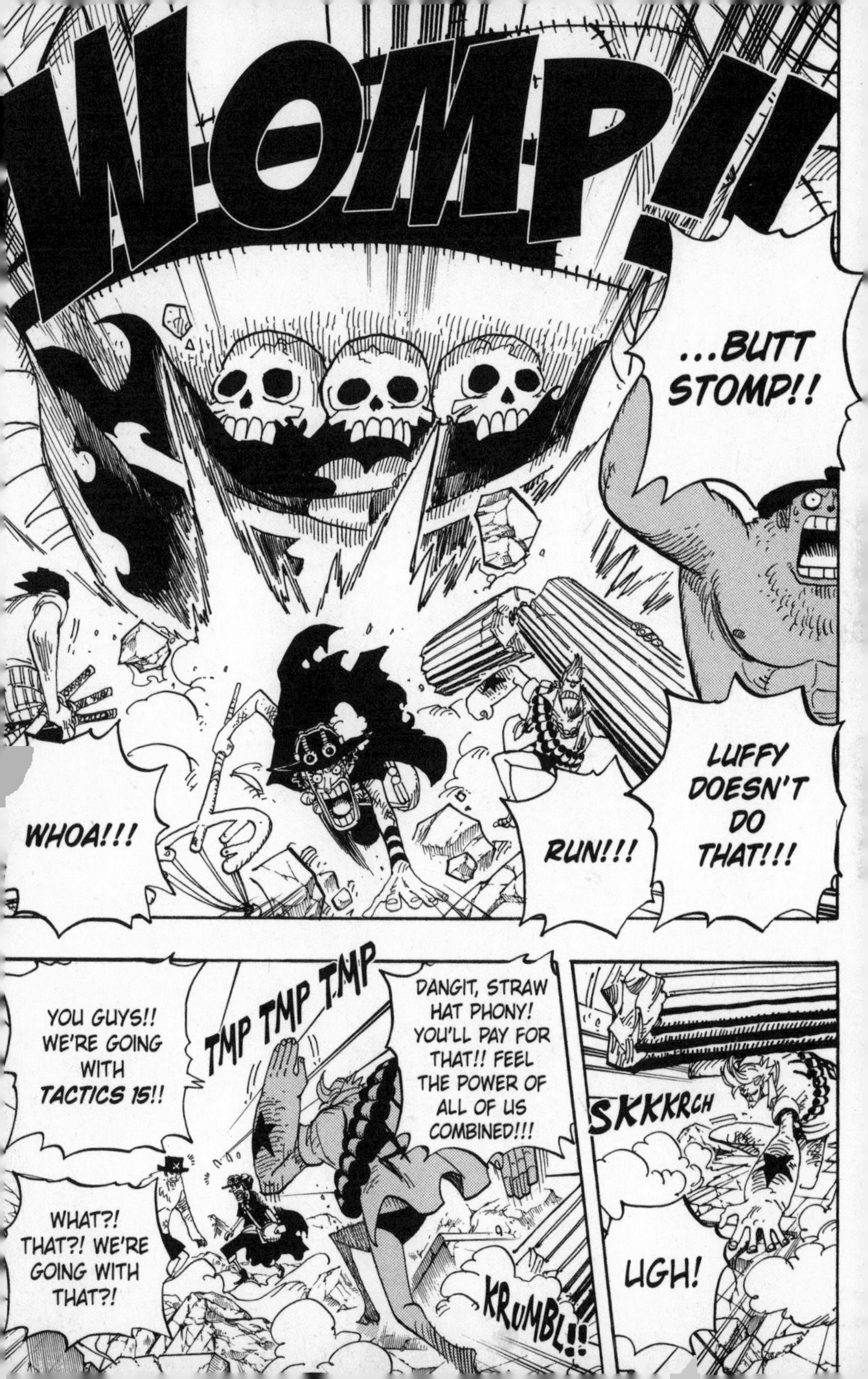
WOMP!!
...BUTT STOMP!!
LUFFY DOESN'T DO THAT!!!
RUN!!!
WHOA!!!
SKKRCH
UGH!
DANGIT, STRAW HAT PHONY! YOU'LL PAY FOR THAT!! FEEL THE POWER OF ALL OF US COMBINED!!!
TMP TMP TMP
YOU GUYS!! WE'RE GOING WITH TACTICS 15!!
KRUMBL!!
WHAT?! THAT?! WE'RE GOING WITH THAT?!

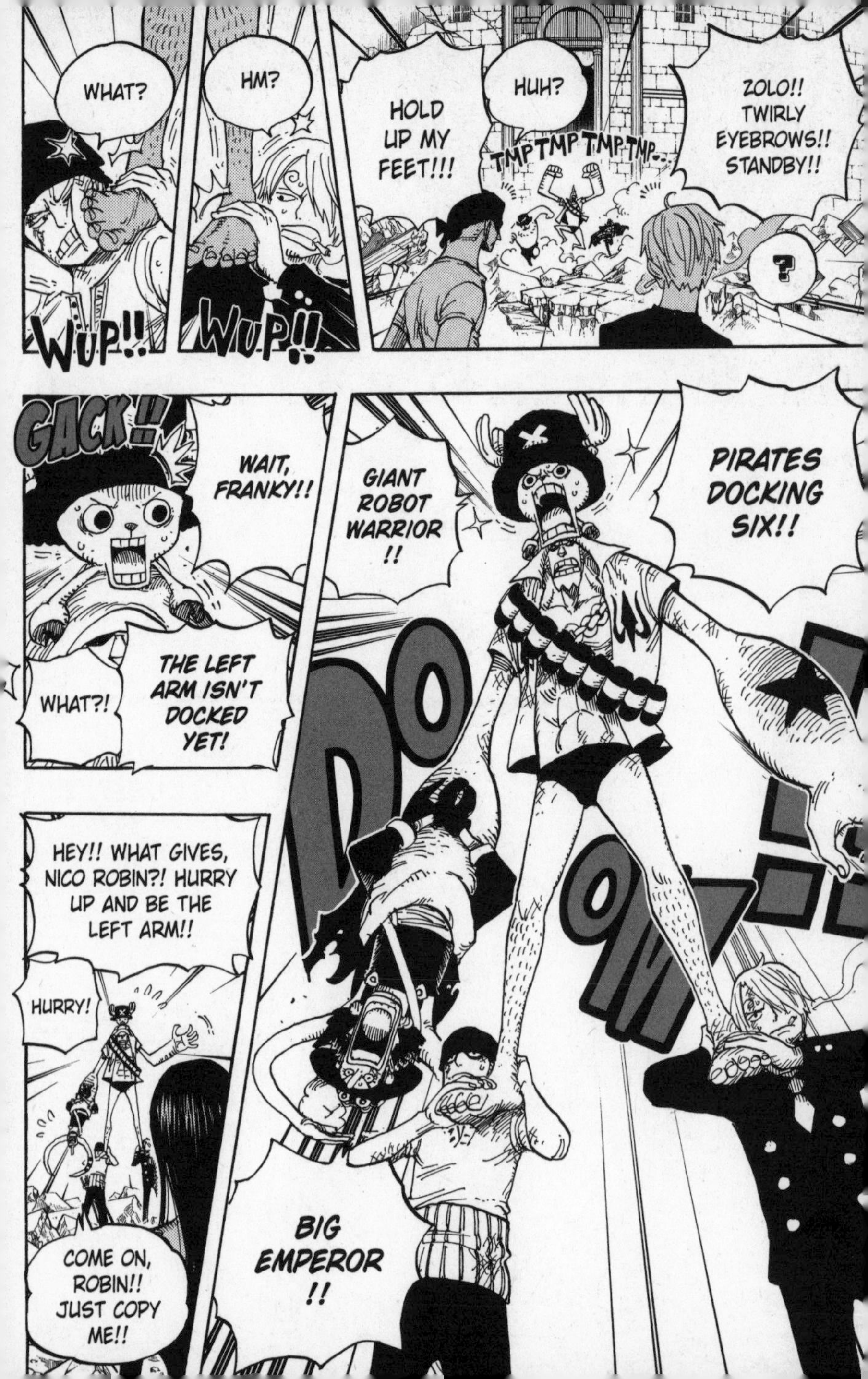
ZOLO!! TWIRLY EYEBROWS!! STANDBY!!
?
HUH?
HOLD UP MY FEET!!!
TMP TMP TMP TMP...
HM?
WUP!!
WHAT?
WUP!!
PIRATES DOCKING SIX!!
GIANT ROBOT WARRIOR!!
DOOM!!
BIG EMPEROR!!
GACK!!
WAIT, FRANKY!!
THE LEFT ARM ISN'T DOCKED YET!
WHAT?!
HEY!! WHAT GIVES, NICO ROBIN?! HURRY UP AND BE THE LEFT ARM!!
HURRY!
COME ON, ROBIN!! JUST COPY ME!!

I FIND IT EMBARRASS-ING...

...AS A HUMAN BEING.

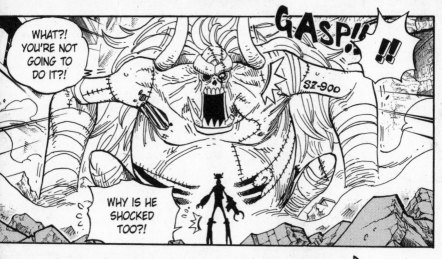

WHAT?! YOU'RE NOT GOING TO DO IT?!

GASP!! !!

SZ-900

WHY IS HE SHOCKED TOO?!

YOU GOT ME EXCITED THERE!!!

DO IT!!!

DOCK IN!!!

VOOP!

AHHHH!

VIP!!

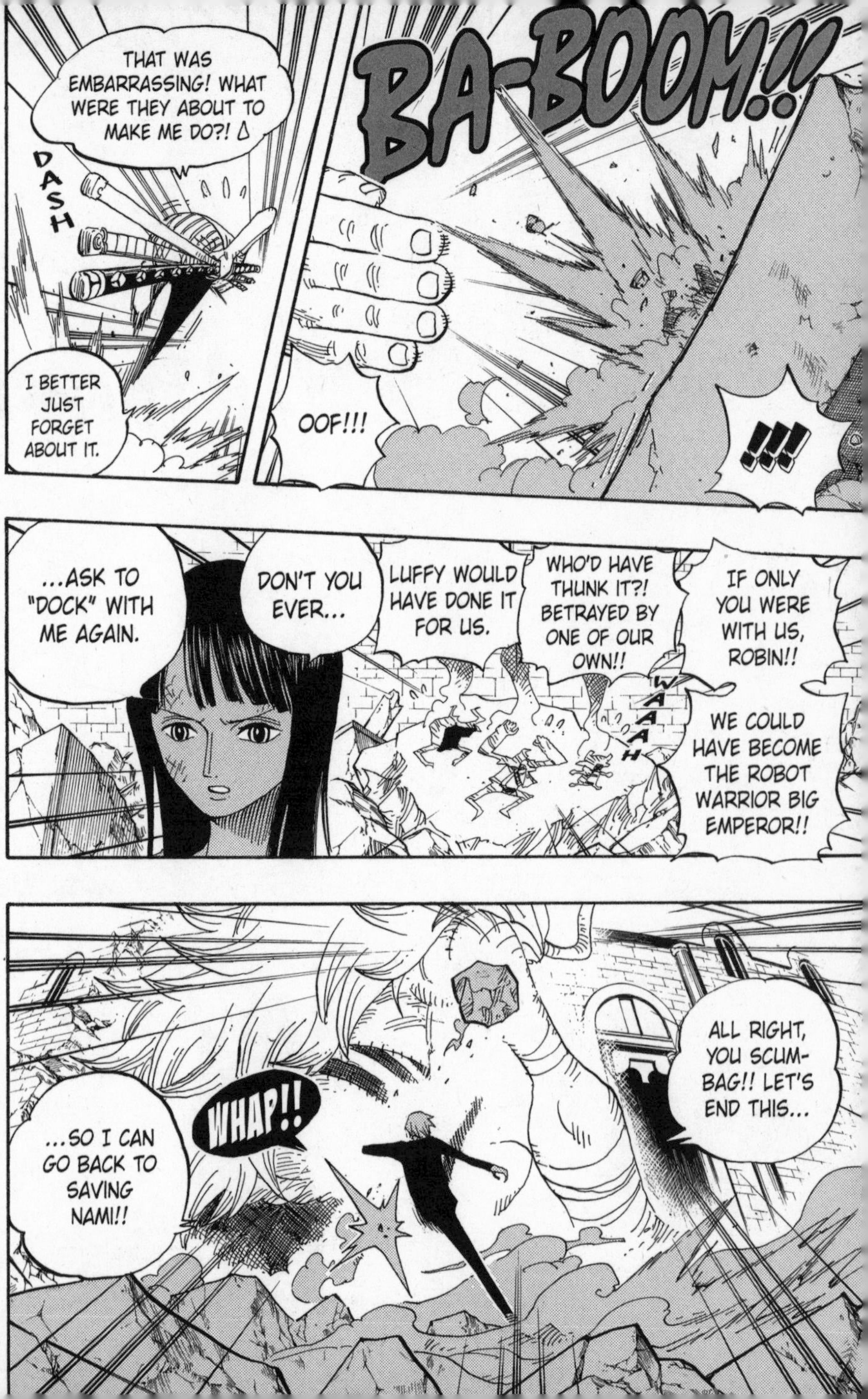
BA-BOOM!!
!!!
OOF!!!
THAT WAS EMBARRASSING! WHAT WERE THEY ABOUT TO MAKE ME DO?!
DASH
I BETTER JUST FORGET ABOUT IT.
IF ONLY YOU WERE WITH US, ROBIN!!
WE COULD HAVE BECOME THE ROBOT WARRIOR BIG EMPEROR!!
WHO'D HAVE THUNK IT?! BETRAYED BY ONE OF OUR OWN!!
WAAAAH
LUFFY WOULD HAVE DONE IT FOR US.
DON'T YOU EVER...
...ASK TO "DOCK" WITH ME AGAIN.
ALL RIGHT, YOU SCUM-BAG!! LET'S END THIS...
WHAP!!
...SO I CAN GO BACK TO SAVING NAMI!!

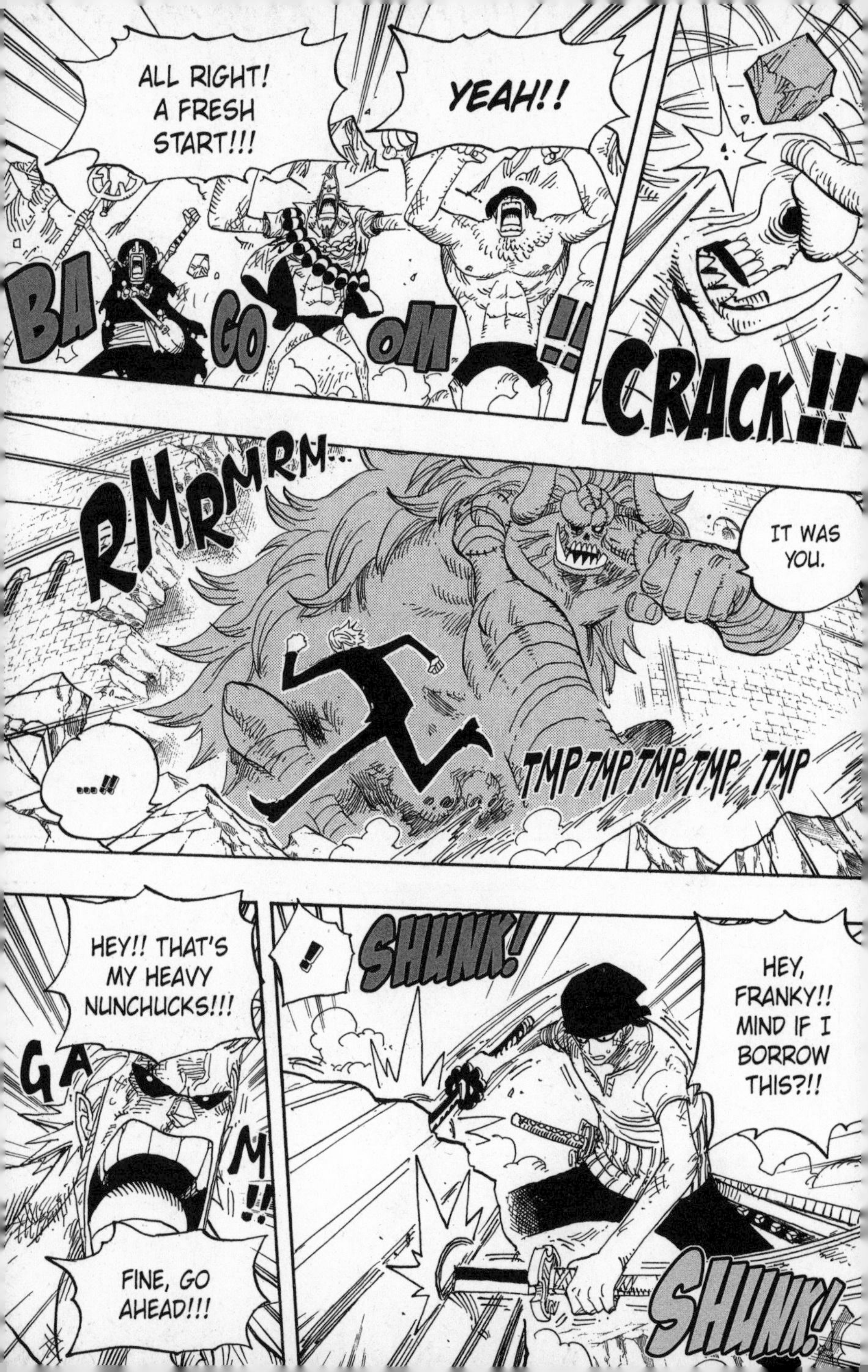
CRACK!!
YEAH!!
ALL RIGHT! A FRESH START!!!
BA GO OM!!
IT WAS YOU.
RMRMRM...
TMP TMP TMP TMP TMP
...!!
HEY, FRANKY!! MIND IF I BORROW THIS?!!
SHUNK!
!
SHUNK!
HEY!! THAT'S MY HEAVY NUNCHUCKS!!!
GAM!!
FINE, GO AHEAD!!!

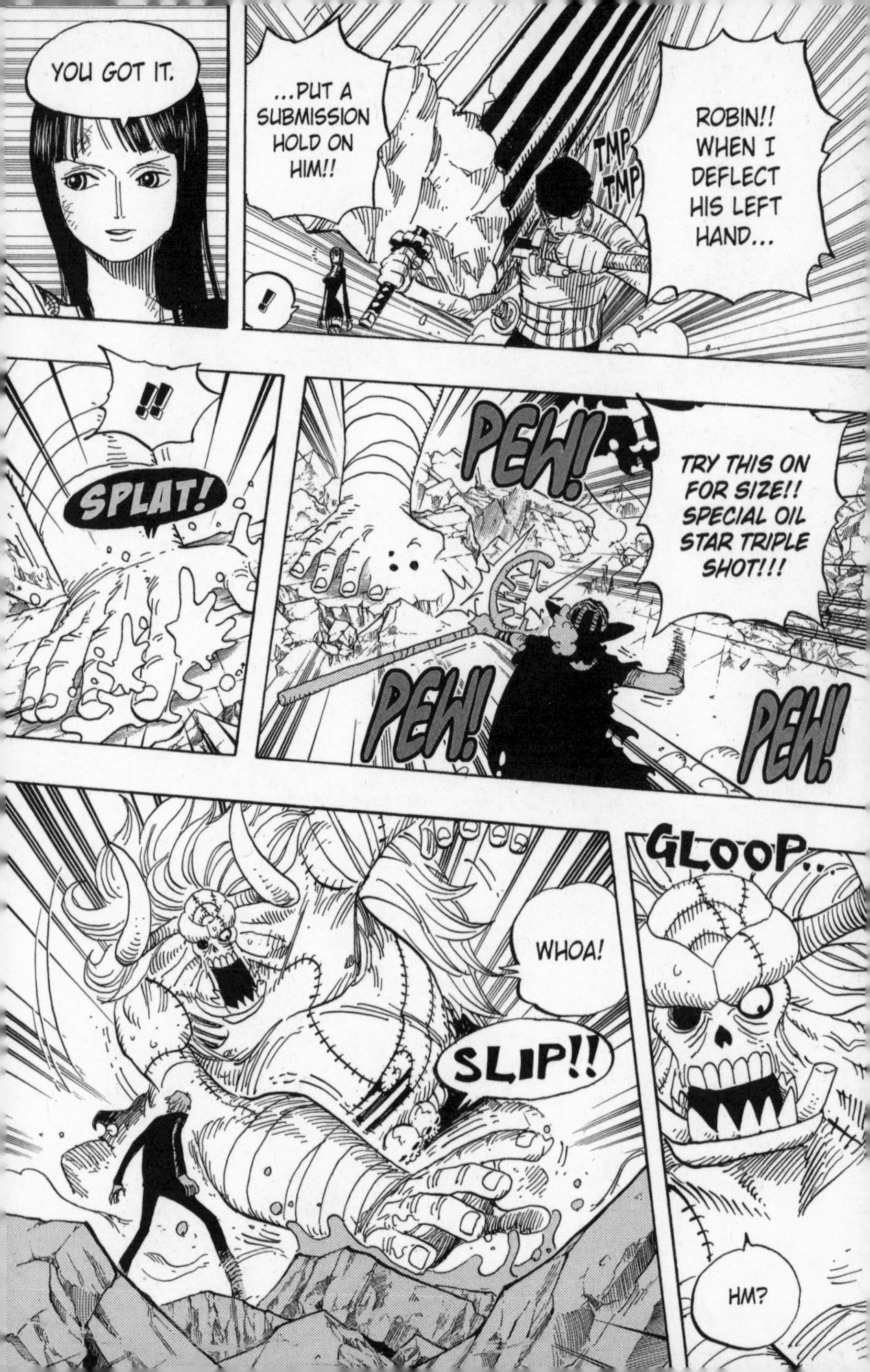
ROBIN!! WHEN I DEFLECT HIS LEFT HAND...
TMP TMP
...PUT A SUBMISSION HOLD ON HIM!!
!
YOU GOT IT.
TRY THIS ON FOR SIZE!! SPECIAL OIL STAR TRIPLE SHOT!!!
PEW!
PEW!
PEW!
!!
SPLAT!
GLOOP..
HM?
WHOA!
SLIP!!

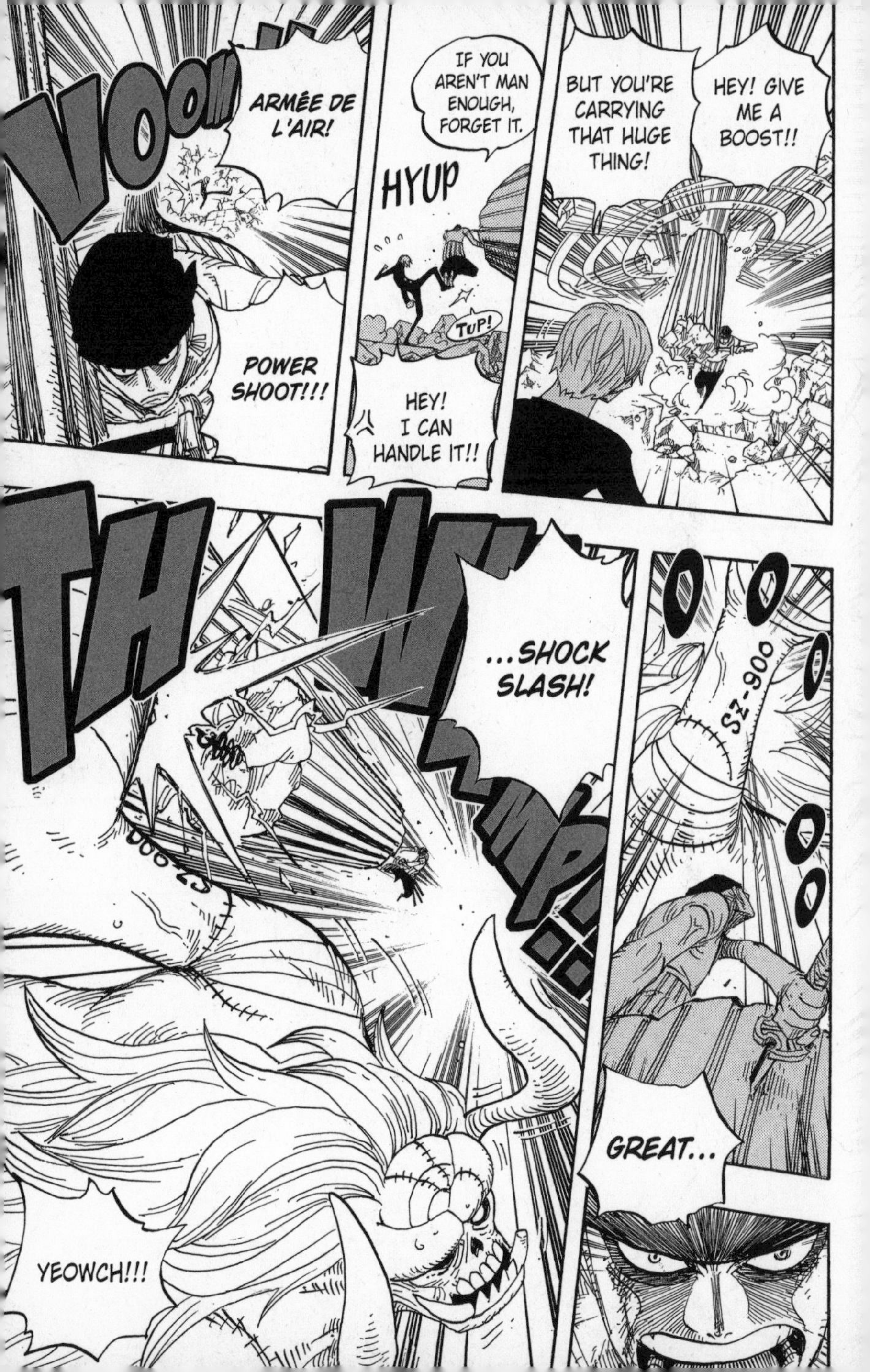
HEY! GIVE ME A BOOST!!
BUT YOU'RE CARRYING THAT HUGE THING!
IF YOU AREN'T MAN ENOUGH, FORGET IT.
HYUP
TUP!
HEY! I CAN HANDLE IT!!
ARMÉE DE L'AIR!
POWER SHOOT!!!
SZ-900
GREAT...
...SHOCK SLASH!
YEOWCH!!!

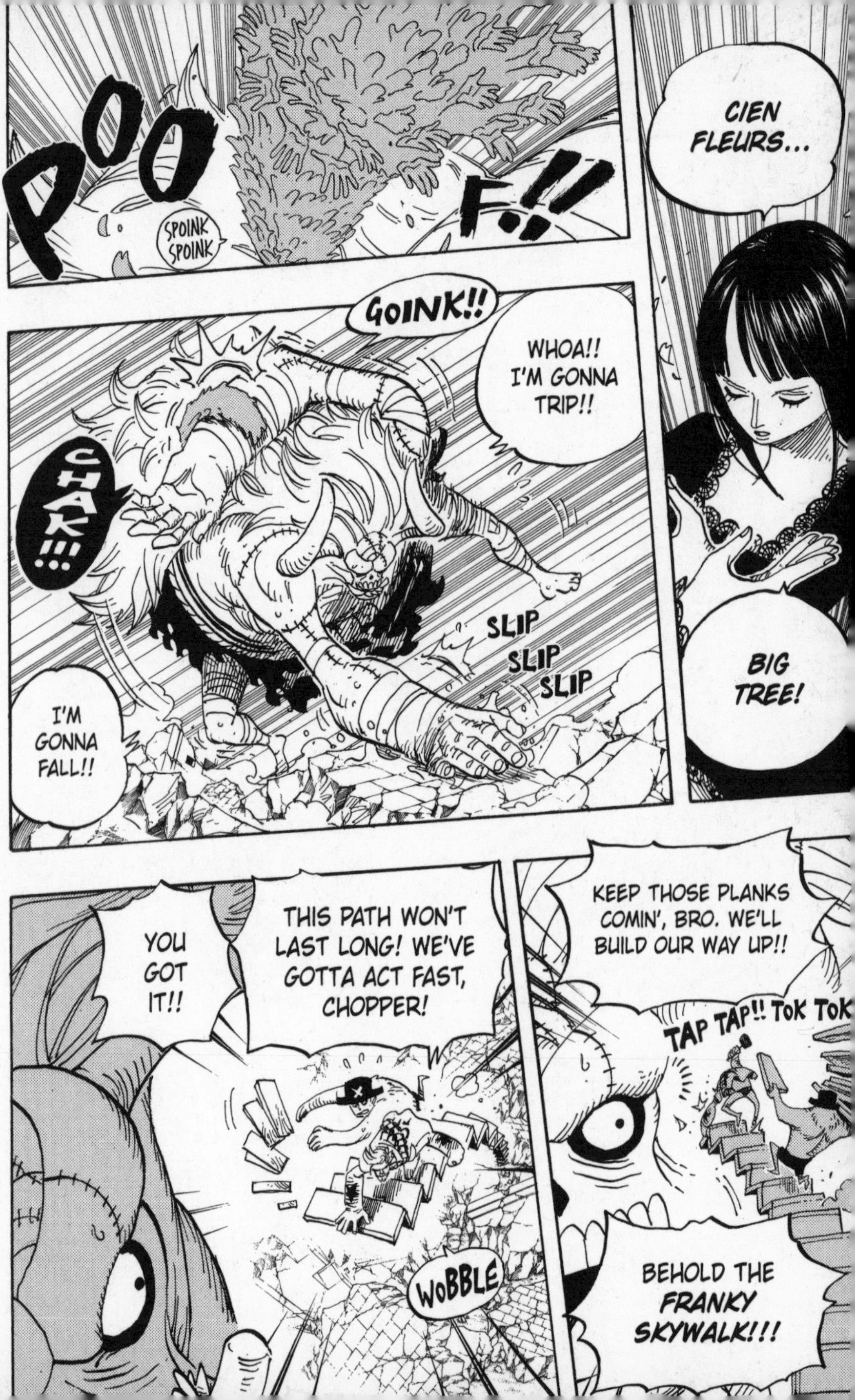
CIEN FLEURS...
BIG TREE!
POOF!!
SPOINK SPOINK
GOINK!!
WHOA!! I'M GONNA TRIP!!
CHAK!!!
SLIP SLIP SLIP
I'M GONNA FALL!!
KEEP THOSE PLANKS COMIN', BRO. WE'LL BUILD OUR WAY UP!!
TAP TAP!! TOK TOK
BEHOLD THE FRANKY SKYWALK!!!
THIS PATH WON'T LAST LONG! WE'VE GOTTA ACT FAST, CHOPPER!
YOU GOT IT!!
WOBBLE

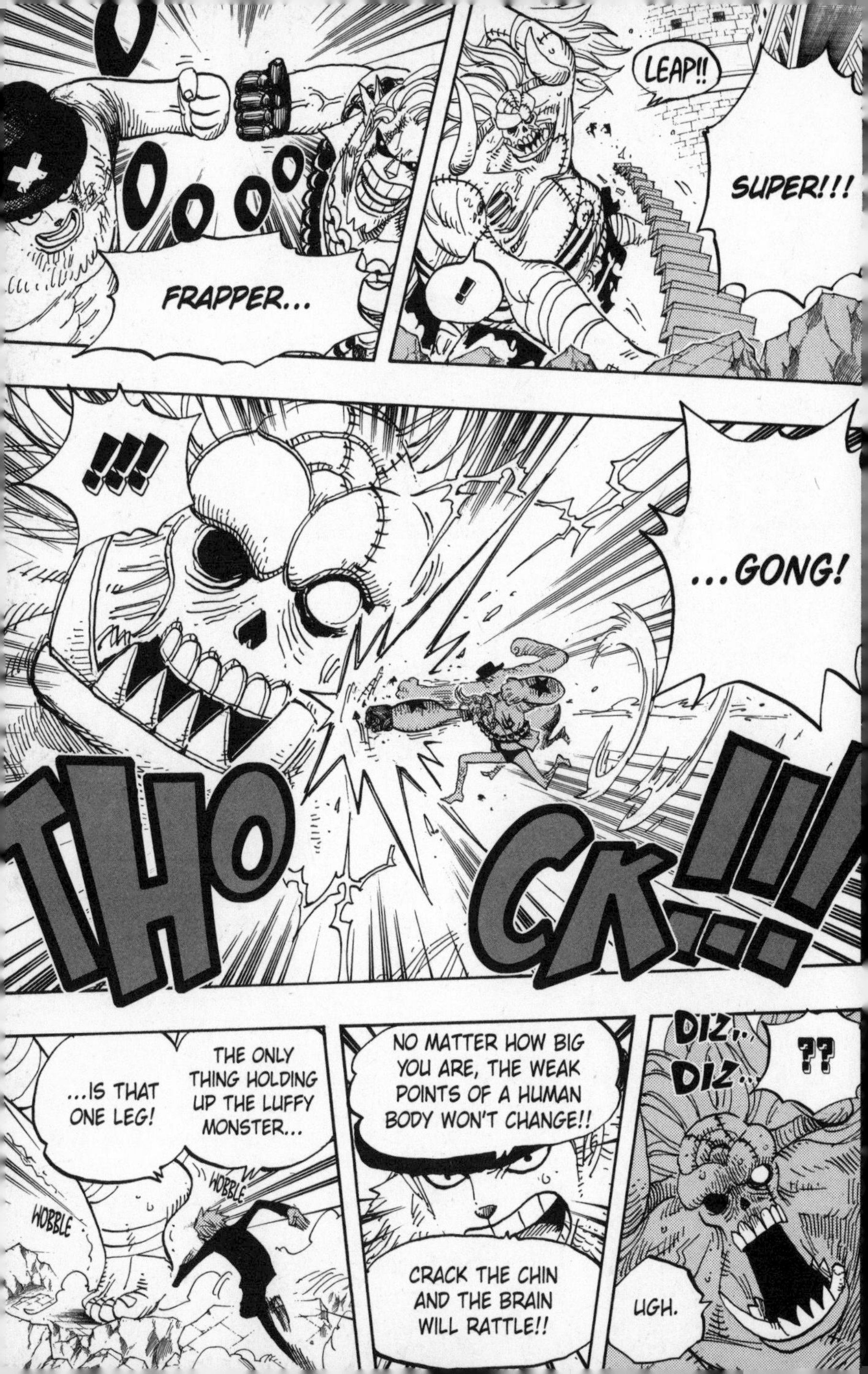
SUPER!!!
LEAP!!
!
FRAPPER...
...GONG!
!!!
THOCK!!!
DIZ..
DIZ..
??
UGH.
NO MATTER HOW BIG YOU ARE, THE WEAK POINTS OF A HUMAN BODY WON'T CHANGE!!
CRACK THE CHIN AND THE BRAIN WILL RATTLE!!
THE ONLY THING HOLDING UP THE LUFFY MONSTER...
...IS THAT ONE LEG!
WOBBLE
WOBBLE

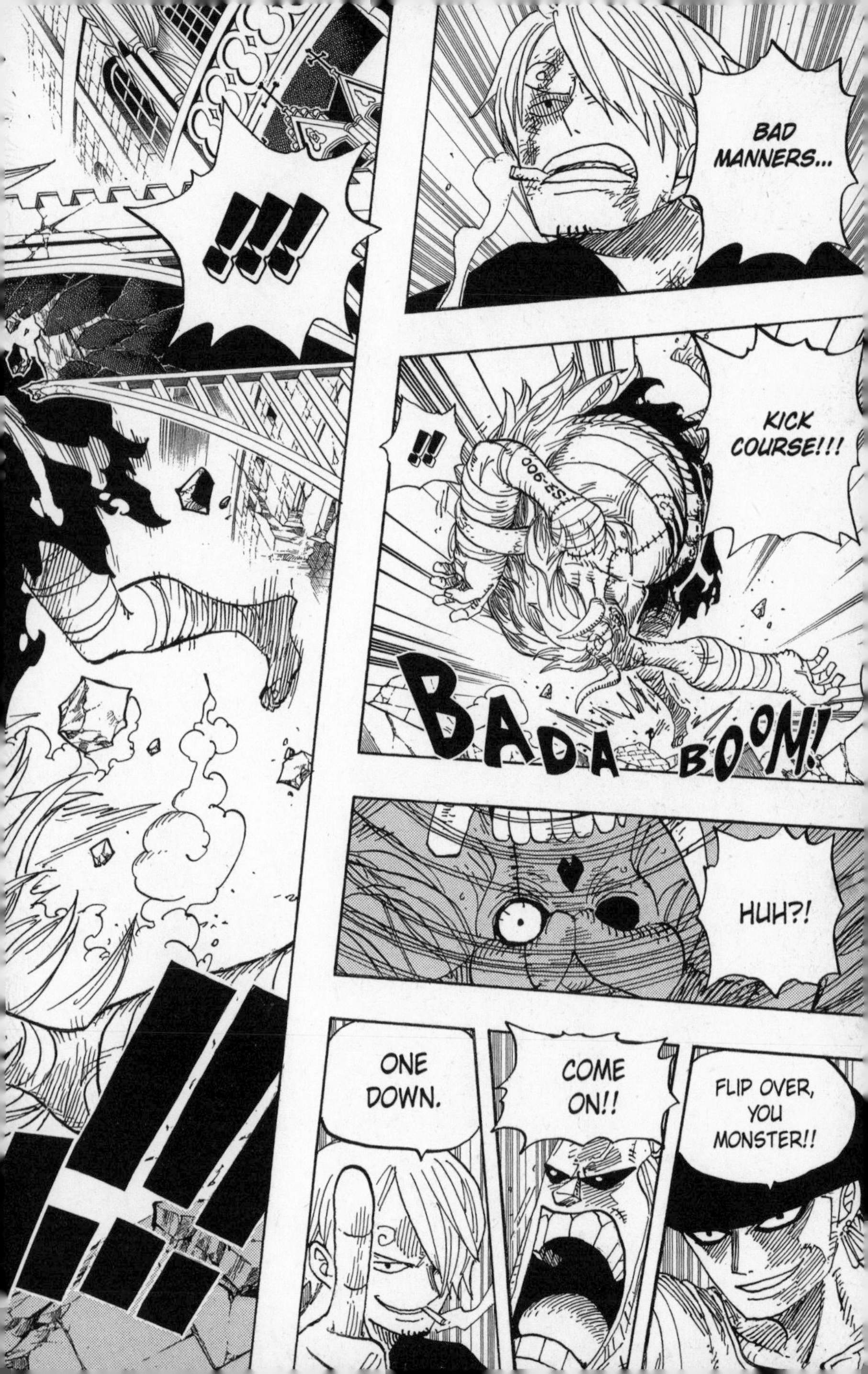
BAD MANNERS...
KICK COURSE!!!
!!
BADA BOOM!
HUH?!
FLIP OVER, YOU MONSTER!!
COME ON!!
ONE DOWN.
!!!
!!!

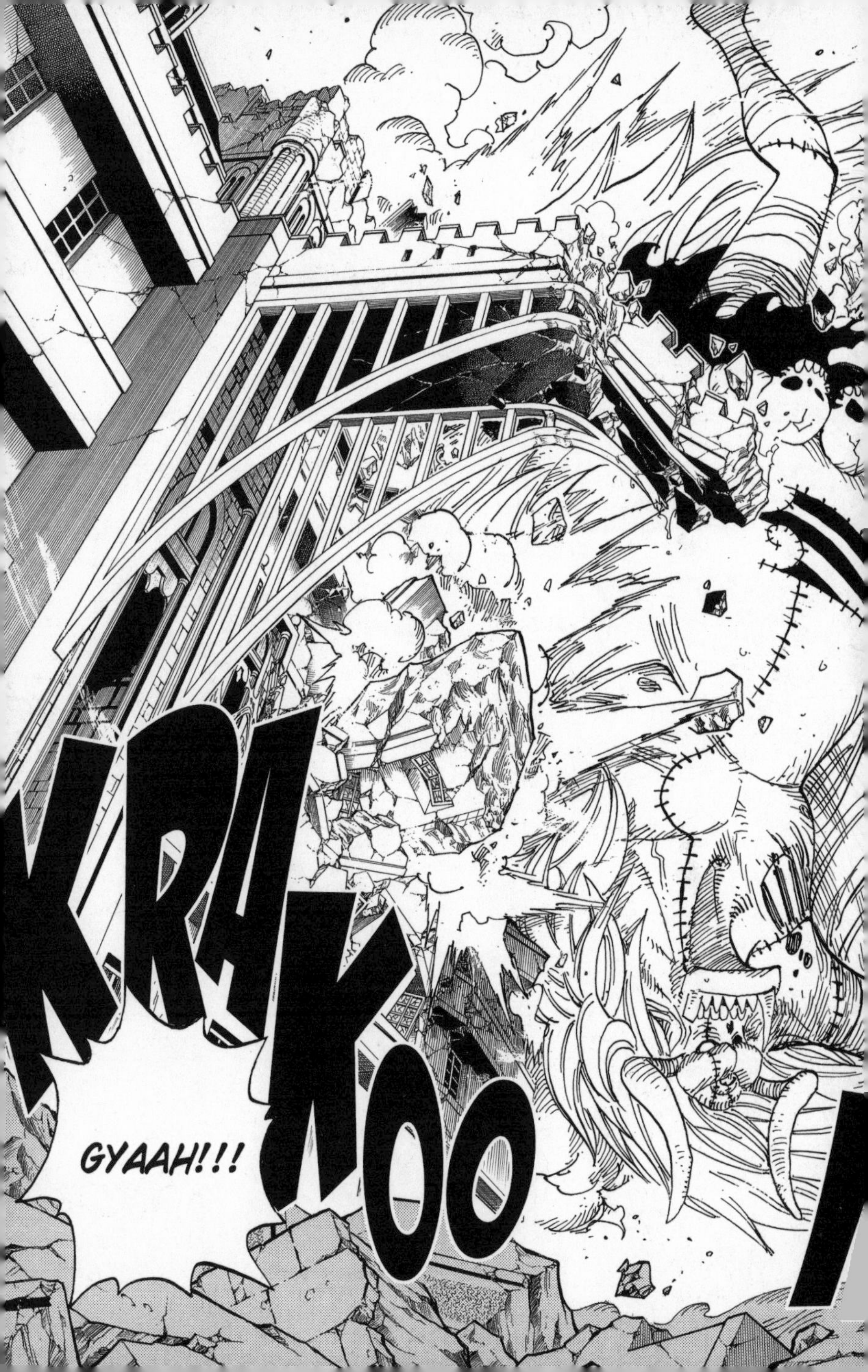
KRAKOO
GYAAH!!!

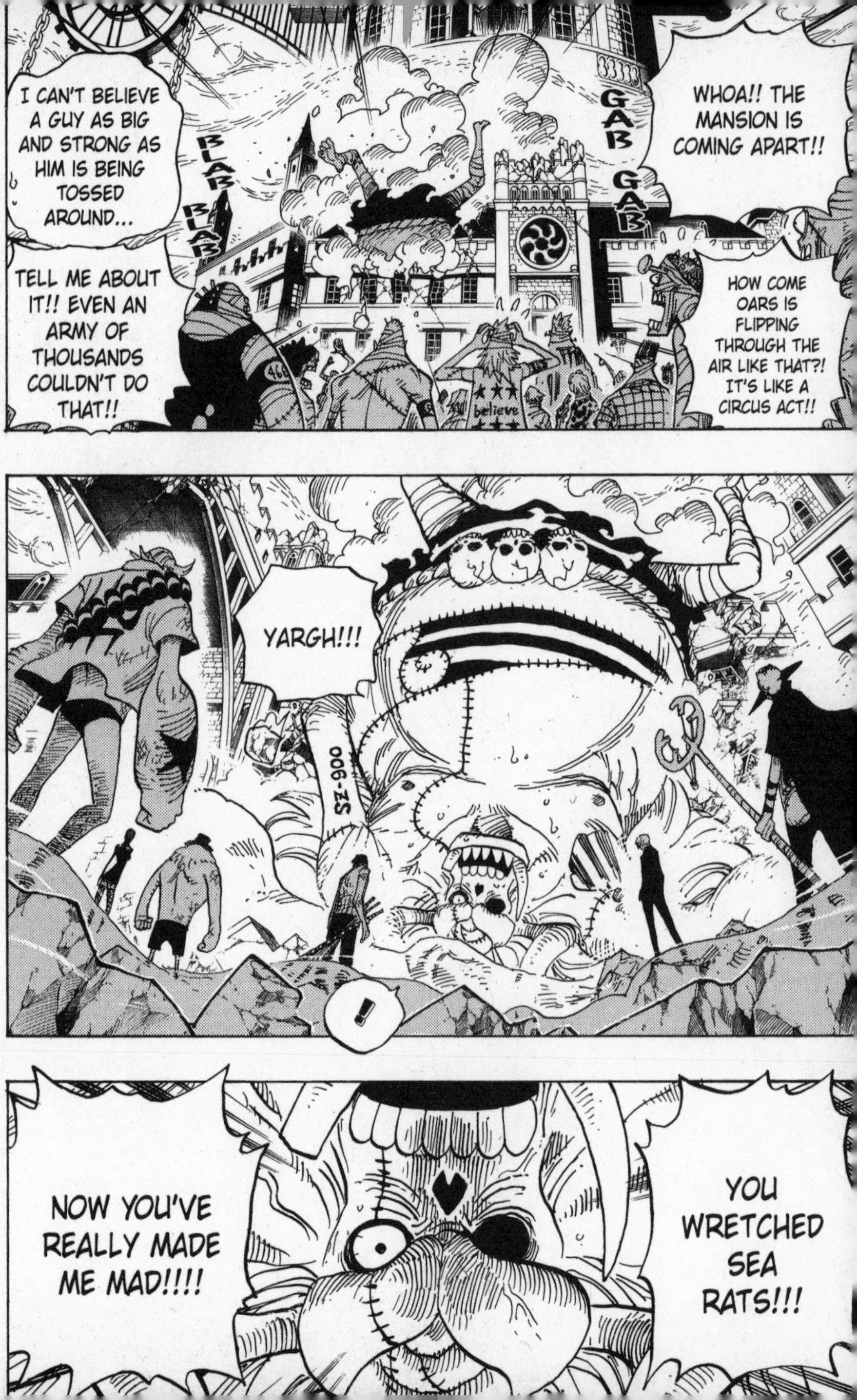
WHOA!! THE MANSION IS COMING APART!!
GAB GAB
HOW COME OARS IS FLIPPING THROUGH THE AIR LIKE THAT?! IT'S LIKE A CIRCUS ACT!!
I CAN'T BELIEVE A GUY AS BIG AND STRONG AS HIM IS BEING TOSSED AROUND...
BLAB BLAB
TELL ME ABOUT IT!! EVEN AN ARMY OF THOUSANDS COULDN'T DO THAT!!
believe
YARGH!!!
SZ-900
!
YOU WRETCHED SEA RATS!!!
NOW YOU'VE REALLY MADE ME MAD!!!!

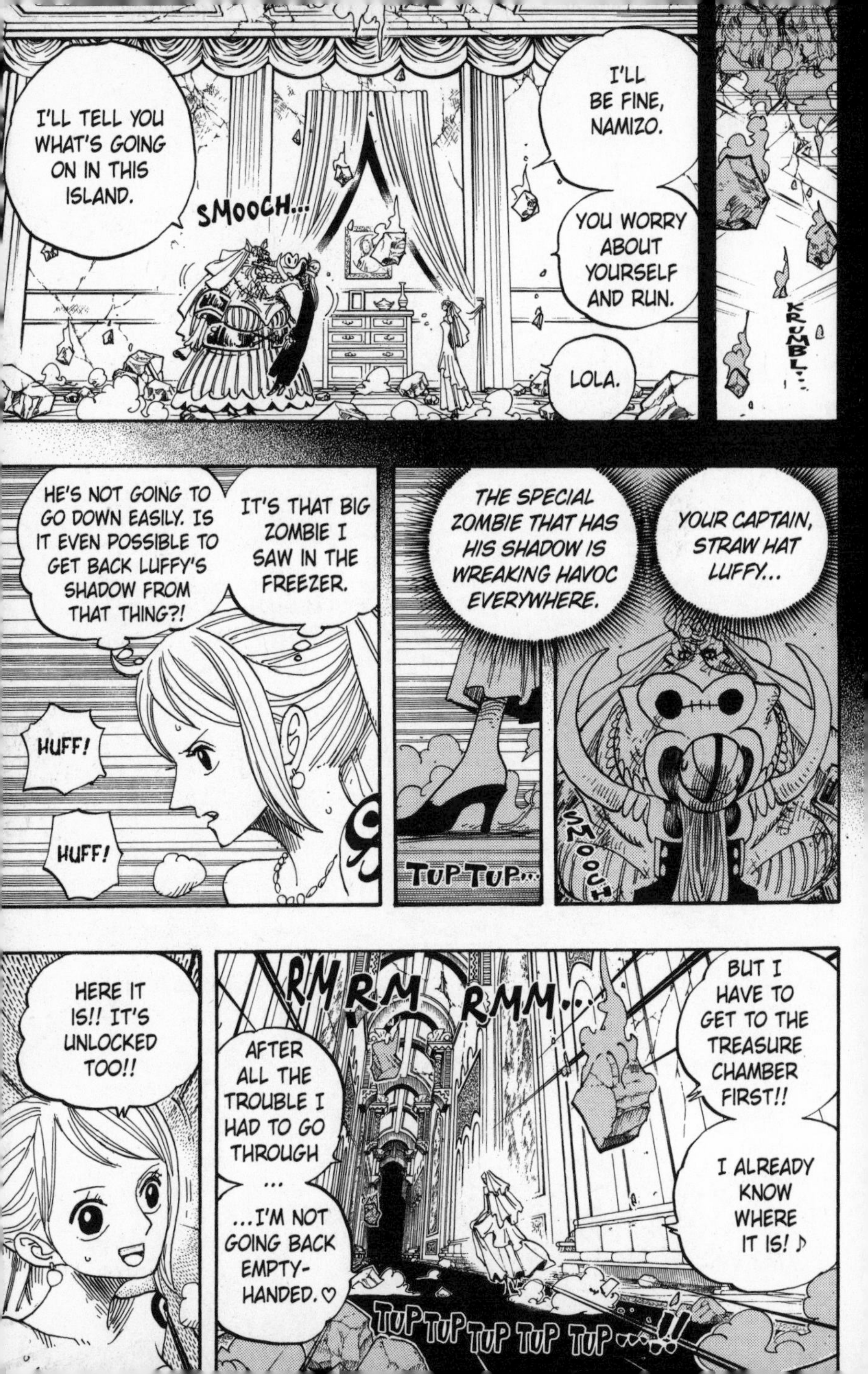
KRUMBL...
I'LL BE FINE, NAMIZO.
YOU WORRY ABOUT YOURSELF AND RUN.
LOLA.
SMOOCH...
I'LL TELL YOU WHAT'S GOING ON IN THIS ISLAND.
YOUR CAPTAIN, STRAW HAT LUFFY...
SMOOCH
THE SPECIAL ZOMBIE THAT HAS HIS SHADOW IS WREAKING HAVOC EVERYWHERE.
TUP TUP...
IT'S THAT BIG ZOMBIE I SAW IN THE FREEZER.
HE'S NOT GOING TO GO DOWN EASILY. IS IT EVEN POSSIBLE TO GET BACK LUFFY'S SHADOW FROM THAT THING?!
HUFF!
HUFF!
RMRM RMM...
BUT I HAVE TO GET TO THE TREASURE CHAMBER FIRST!!
I ALREADY KNOW WHERE IT IS! ♪
AFTER ALL THE TROUBLE I HAD TO GO THROUGH...
...I'M NOT GOING BACK EMPTY-HANDED. ♡
TUP TUP TUP TUP TUP...!!
HERE IT IS!! IT'S UNLOCKED TOO!!

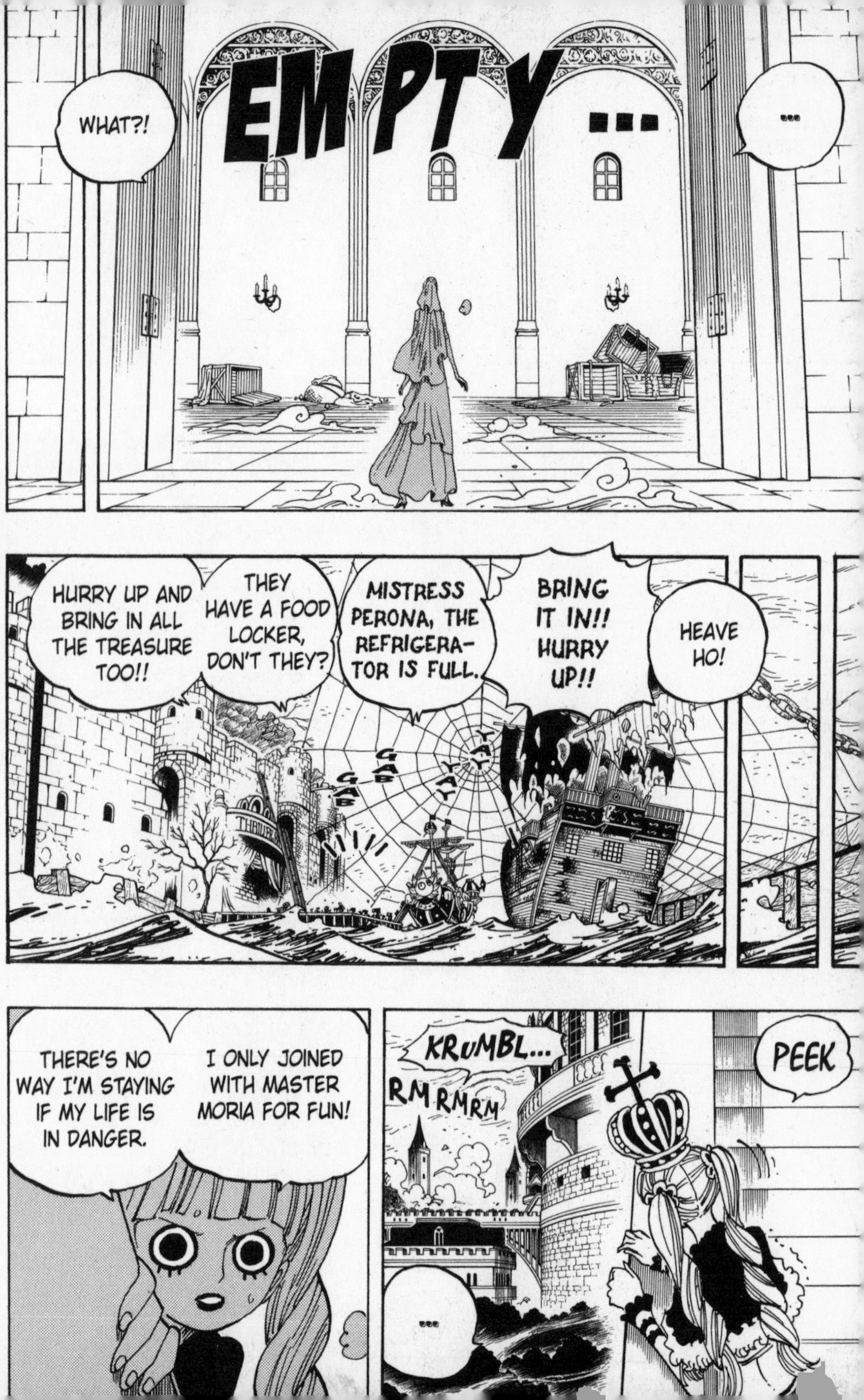
...
EMPTY...
WHAT?!
HEAVE HO!
BRING IT IN!! HURRY UP!!
MISTRESS PERONA, THE REFRIGERATOR IS FULL.
YAY YAY
THEY HAVE A FOOD LOCKER, DON'T THEY?
GAB GAB
HURRY UP AND BRING IN ALL THE TREASURE TOO!!
PEEK
KRUMBL...
RMRMRM
...
I ONLY JOINED WITH MASTER MORIA FOR FUN!
THERE'S NO WAY I'M STAYING IF MY LIFE IS IN DANGER.

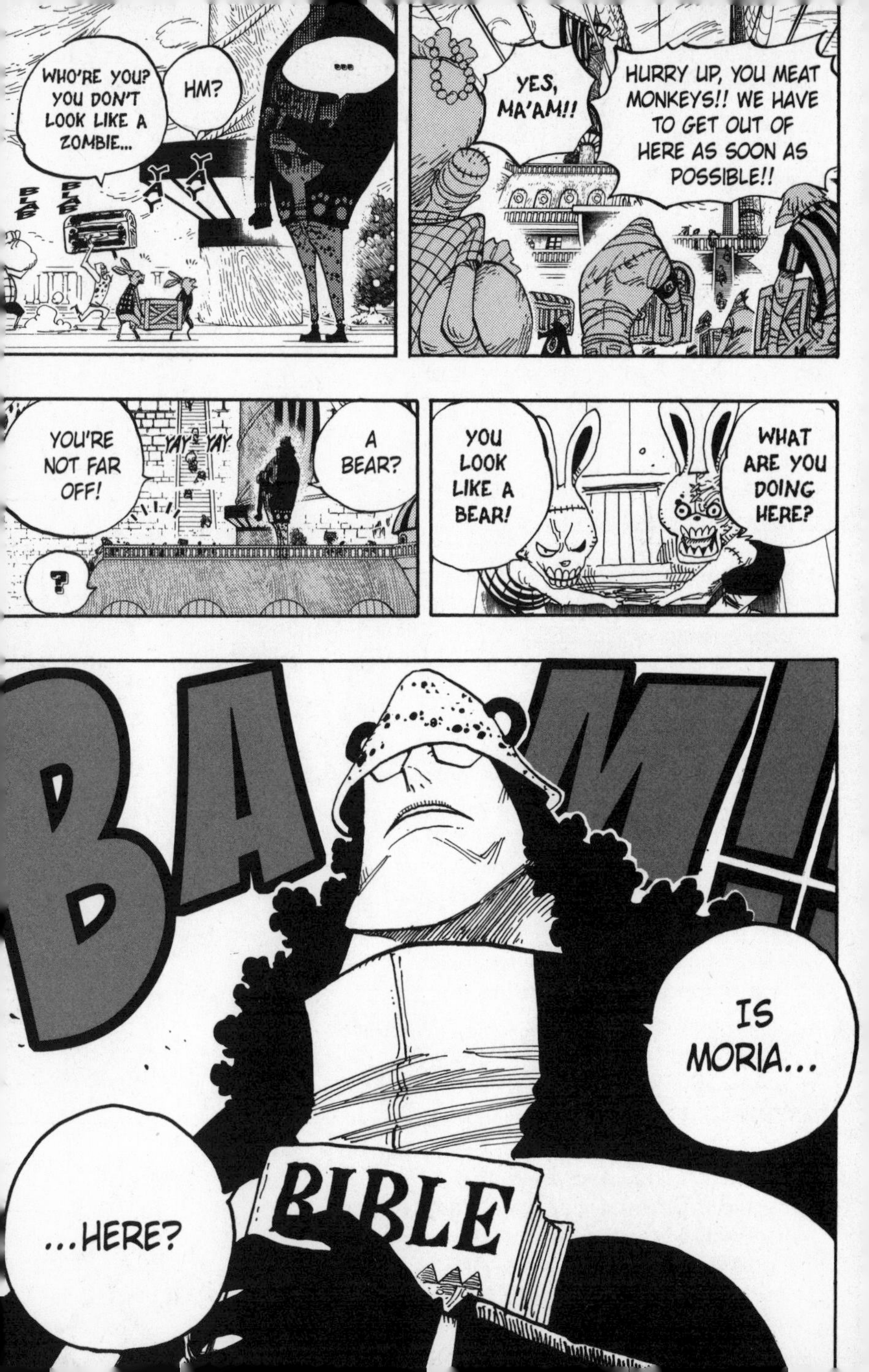
HURRY UP, YOU MEAT MONKEYS!! WE HAVE TO GET OUT OF HERE AS SOON AS POSSIBLE!!
YES, MA'AM!!
...
HM?
WHO'RE YOU? YOU DON'T LOOK LIKE A ZOMBIE...
YAY YAY
BLAB BLAB
WHAT ARE YOU DOING HERE?
YOU LOOK LIKE A BEAR!
A BEAR?
YAY YAY
YOU'RE NOT FAR OFF!
?
BAM!!
IS MORIA...
...HERE?
BIBLE

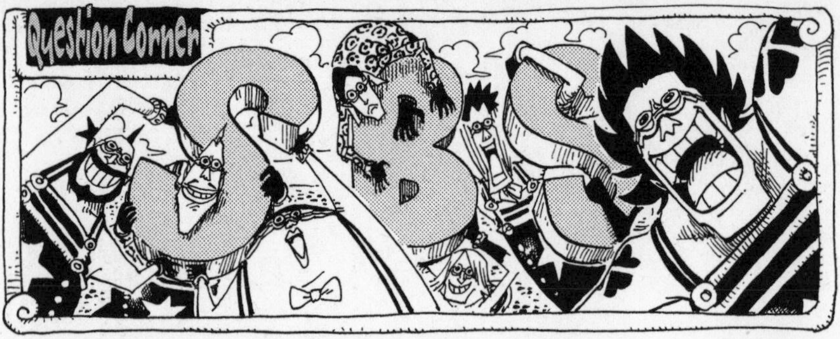
Question Corner
SBS

Q: Mr. Oda! If Kalifa had mistakenly eaten the Ox-Ox Fruit, Giraffe Model, at the Tower of Law, what would she have looked like? --Shiranchon

A: Like this (→). I think this is good in its own way.

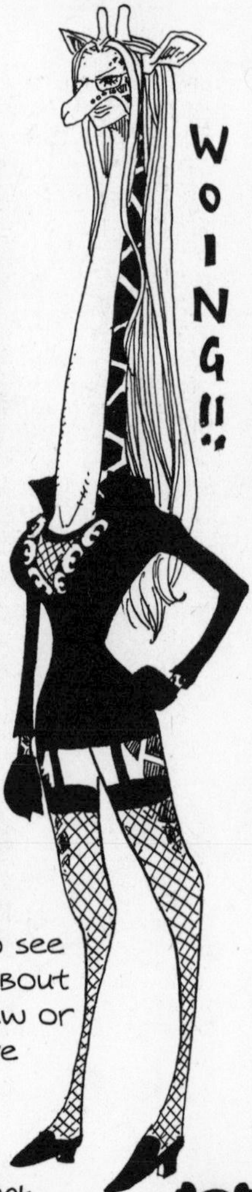
WOING!!

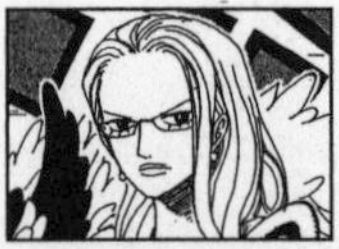

Q: This is my first letter to you! (in the form of a postcard) In chapter 468, during Hogback's flashback, is that teddy bear that Perona's holding actually Kumacy? What did you have to do to make him that huge? --Tonton

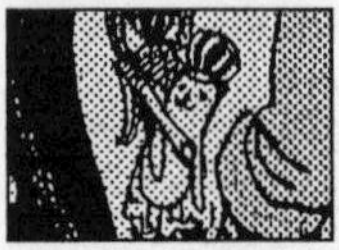

Q: I have a question about the awesomely adorable Perona of Thriller Bark! Around the time of the Skypiea arc, you had the title page story comic, Wapol's Omnivorous Rampage. Within that series, there was a toy hippo that was created at Wapol's Munch Munch factory. Does that have anything to do with Perona's underling, Hippo Gallant? Is Perona a fan of Wapol's toys? --Mitsuki

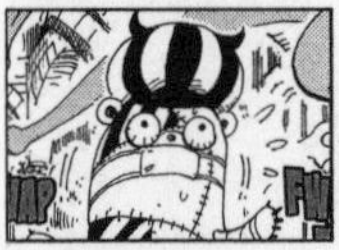

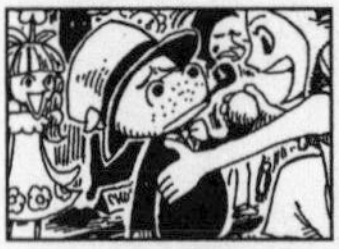

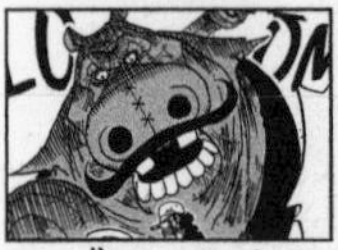

A: These are two very good questions. I'm glad to see that you noticed all of it. Seriously. First off, about the stuffed Kumacy animal, it's not that he grew or anything. One of Perona's pastimes was to have Hogback create zombies that look like her favorite stuffed animals. And it's entirely possible for her to have obtained the stuffed hippo from Wapol from somewhere and Hogback used it for the basis of a new zombie.

Chapter 473:
WARLORD BARTHOLOMEW KUMA APPEARS

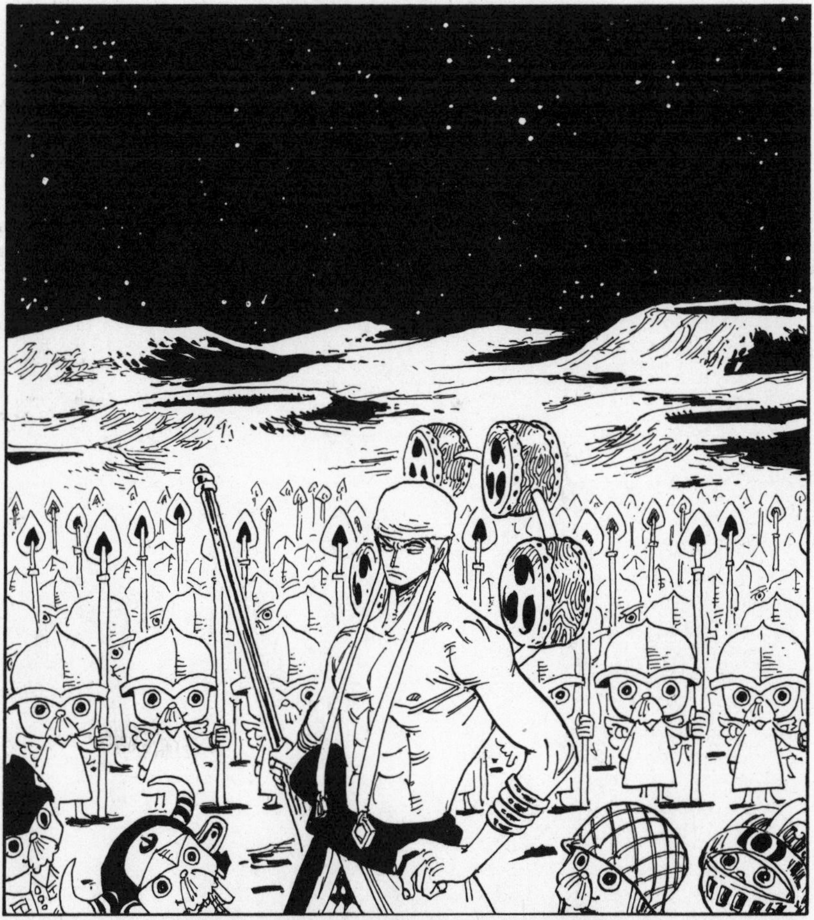

ENERU'S GREAT SPACE MISSION, VOL. 37:
"TURN AROUND AND SEE THE LOYAL SERVANTS AND ENDLESS VARSE!"

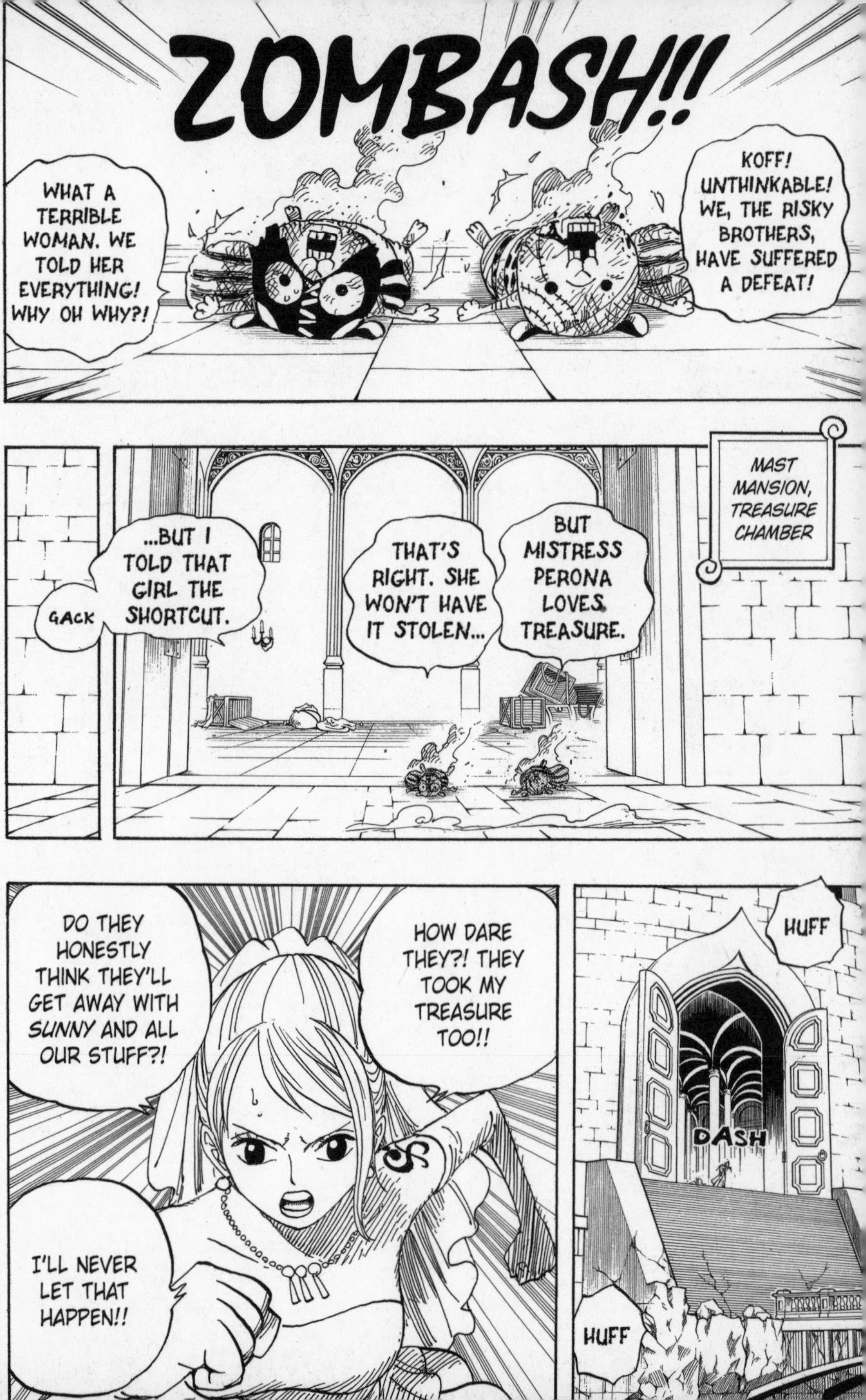
ZOMBASH!!
KOFF! UNTHINKABLE! WE, THE RISKY BROTHERS, HAVE SUFFERED A DEFEAT!
WHAT A TERRIBLE WOMAN. WE TOLD HER EVERYTHING! WHY OH WHY?!
MAST MANSION, TREASURE CHAMBER
BUT MISTRESS PERONA LOVES TREASURE.
THAT'S RIGHT. SHE WON'T HAVE IT STOLEN...
...BUT I TOLD THAT GIRL THE SHORTCUT.
GACK
HUFF
DASH
HUFF
HOW DARE THEY?! THEY TOOK MY TREASURE TOO!!
DO THEY HONESTLY THINK THEY'LL GET AWAY WITH SUNNY AND ALL OUR STUFF?!
I'LL NEVER LET THAT HAPPEN!!

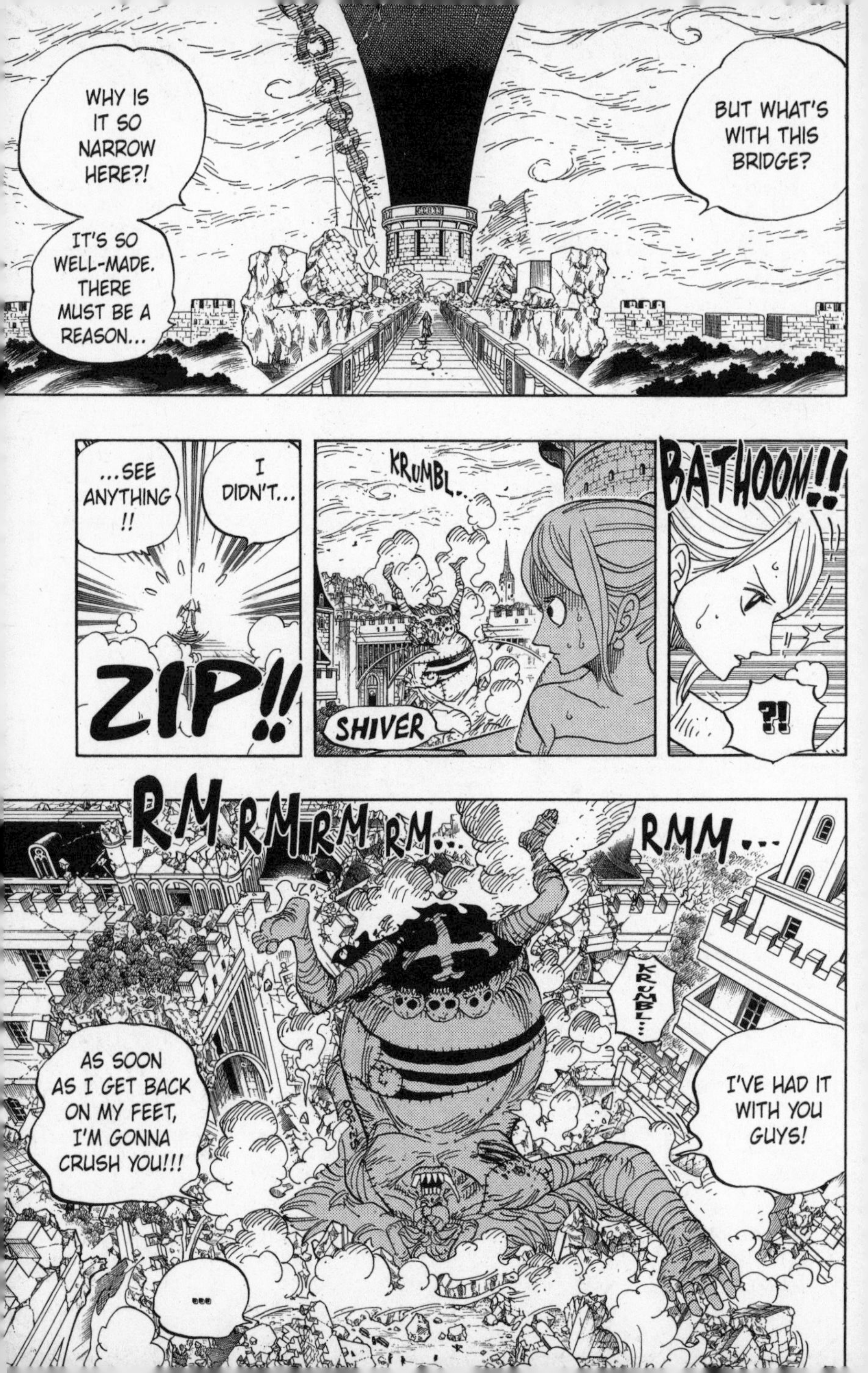
BUT WHAT'S WITH THIS BRIDGE?
WHY IS IT SO NARROW HERE?!
IT'S SO WELL-MADE. THERE MUST BE A REASON...
BATHOOM!!
?!
KRUMBL...
SHIVER
I DIDN'T...
...SEE ANYTHING !!
ZIP!!
RMM...
RM RMRMRM RM...
I'VE HAD IT WITH YOU GUYS!
KRUMBL...
AS SOON AS I GET BACK ON MY FEET, I'M GONNA CRUSH YOU!!!
...

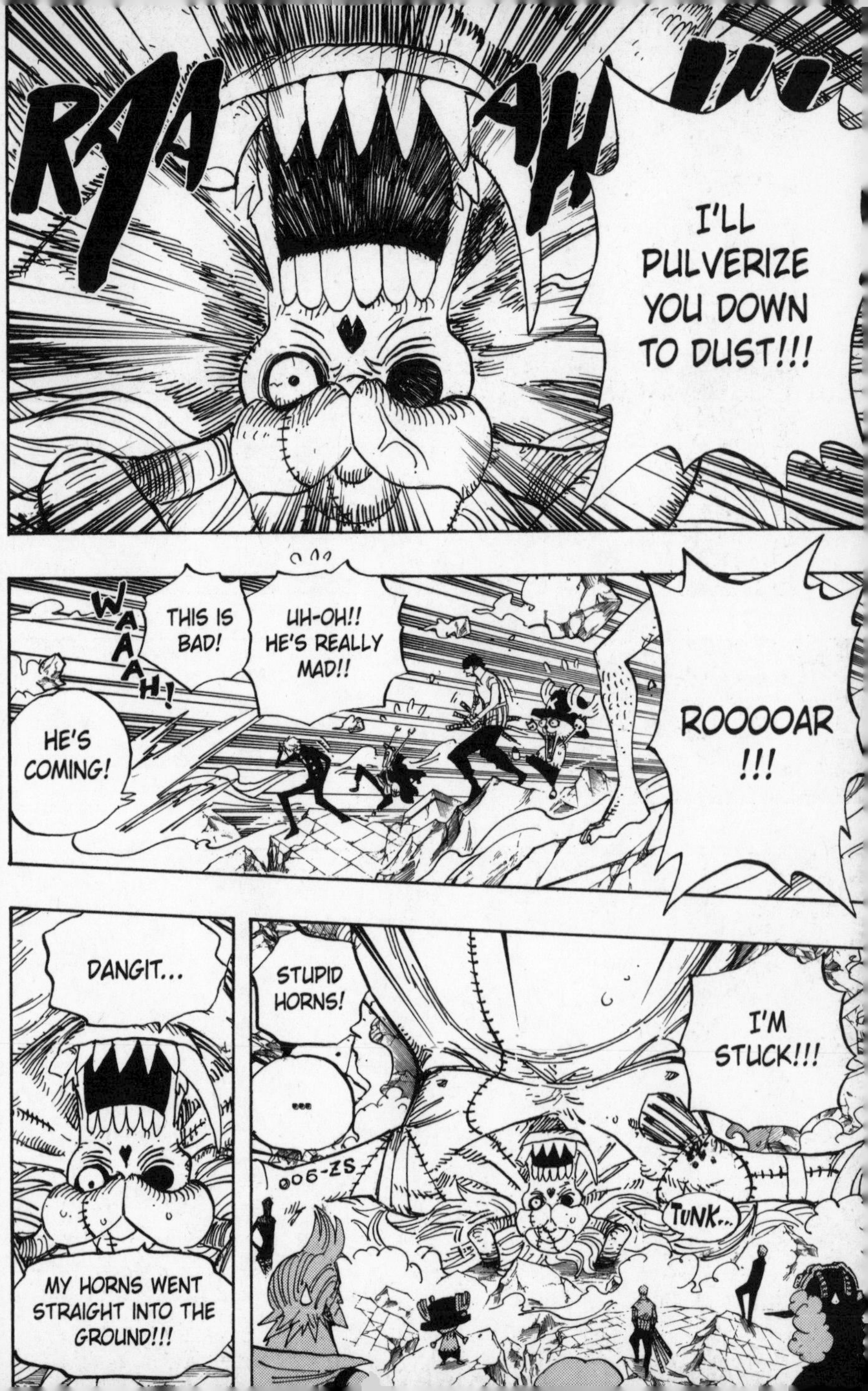
RAA
AH
I'LL PULVERIZE YOU DOWN TO DUST!!!
ROOOOAR !!!
UH-OH!! HE'S REALLY MAD!!
THIS IS BAD!
WAAAH!
HE'S COMING!
I'M STUCK!!!
STUPID HORNS!
...
TUNK...
DANGIT...
MY HORNS WENT STRAIGHT INTO THE GROUND!!!

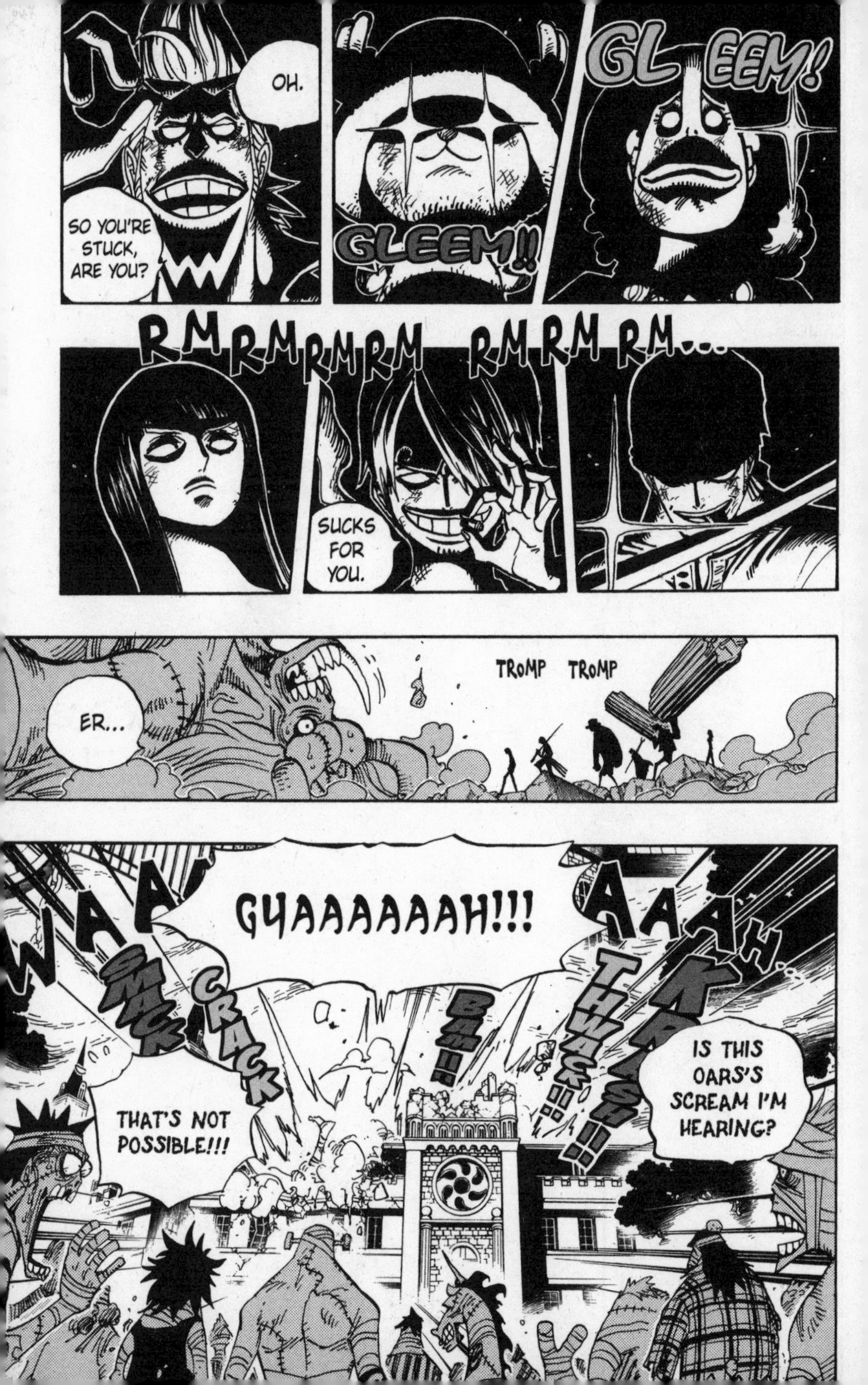
GL EEM!
GLEEM!!
OH.
SO YOU'RE STUCK, ARE YOU?
RMRMRMRM RMRMRM...
SUCKS FOR YOU.
TROMP TROMP
ER...
AAAH...
KRASH!!
THWACK!!
IS THIS OARS'S SCREAM I'M HEARING?
BAM!!
GUAAAAAAH!!!
CRACK
SMACK
WAP
THAT'S NOT POSSIBLE!!!

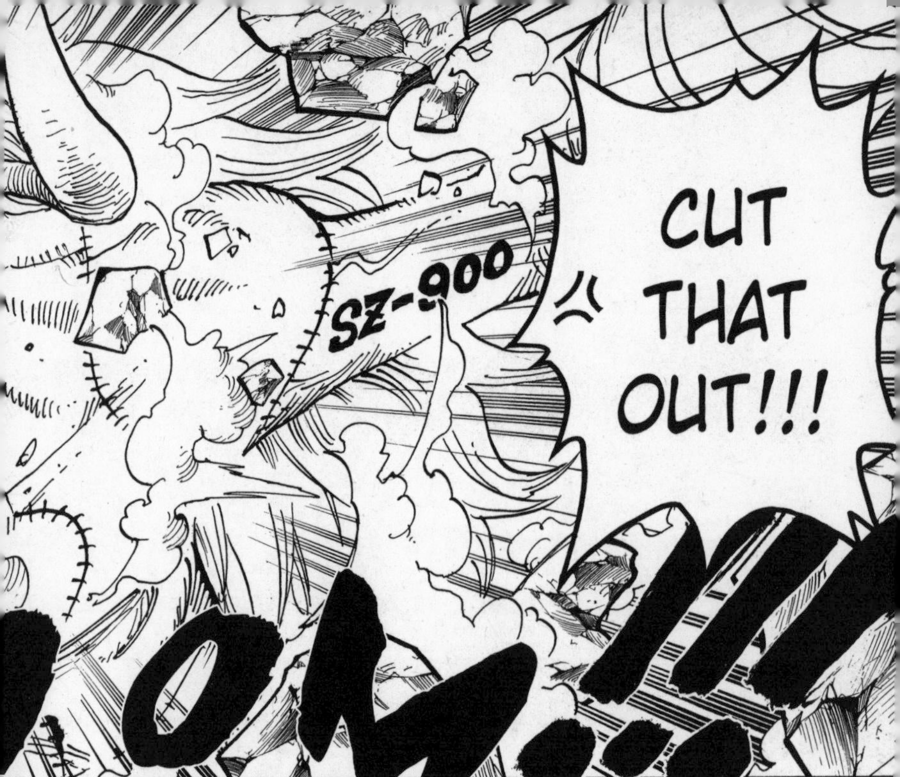
CUT THAT OUT!!!
SZ-900
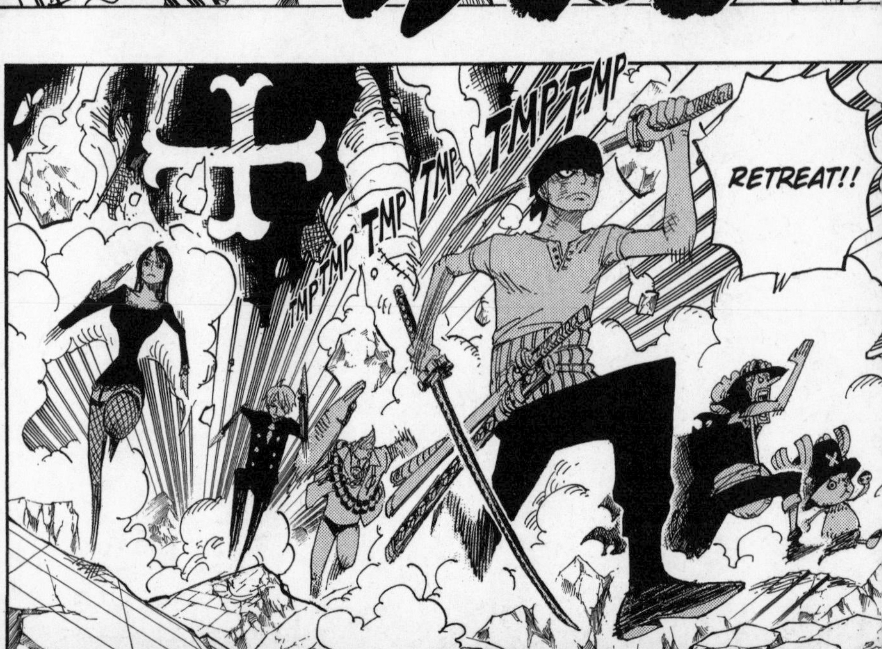
RETREAT!!
TMPTMP
TMP
TMP
TMPTMP

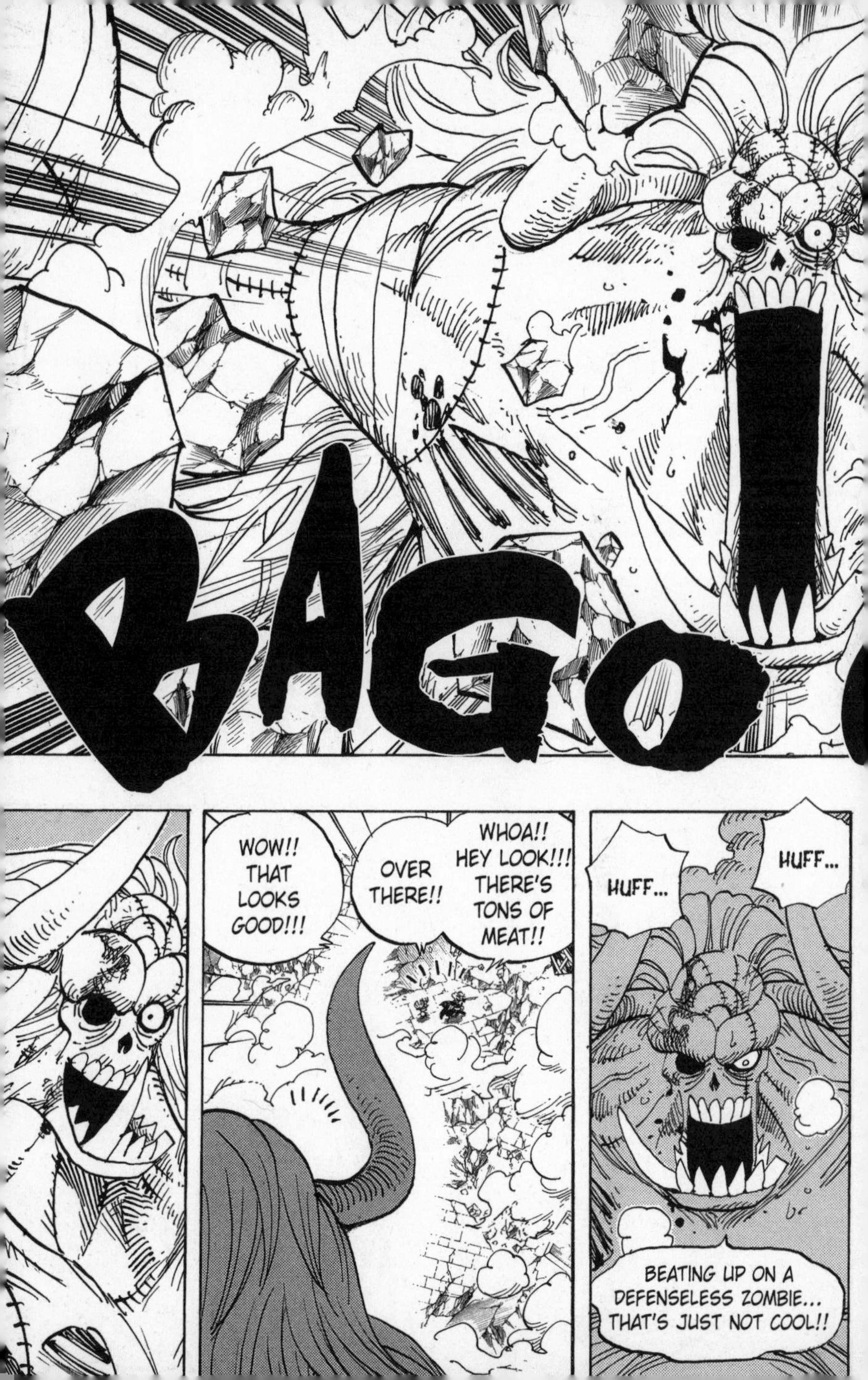
BAGO!
HUFF...
HUFF...
BEATING UP ON A DEFENSELESS ZOMBIE... THAT'S JUST NOT COOL!!
WHOA!! HEY LOOK!!! THERE'S TONS OF MEAT!!
OVER THERE!!
WOW!! THAT LOOKS GOOD!!!

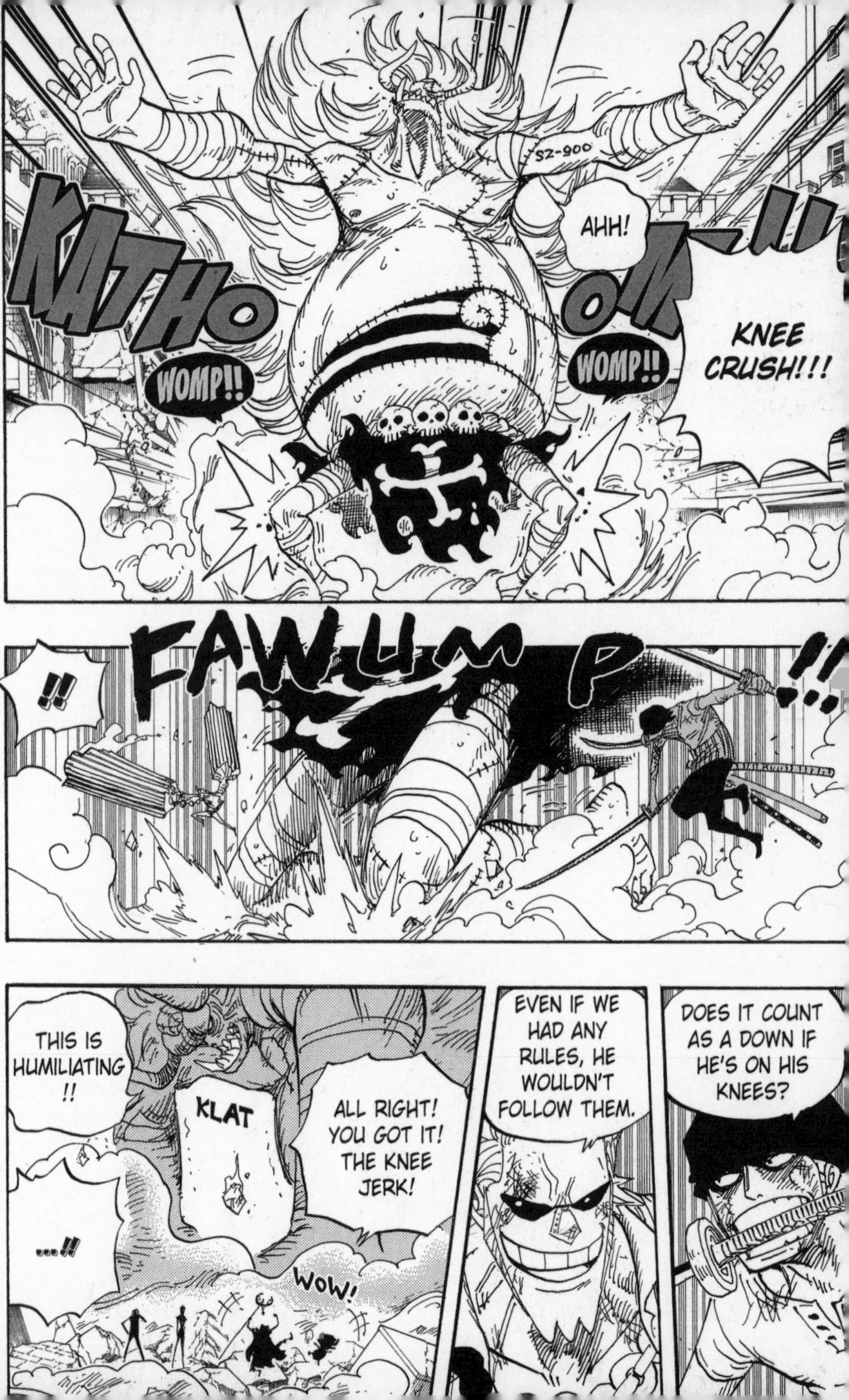
KNEE CRUSH!!!
AHH!
S2-900
OK
WOMP!!
KATHO
WOMP!!
FAWUMP!!
!!
DOES IT COUNT AS A DOWN IF HE'S ON HIS KNEES?
EVEN IF WE HAD ANY RULES, HE WOULDN'T FOLLOW THEM.
THIS IS HUMILIATING!!
KLAT
ALL RIGHT! YOU GOT IT! THE KNEE JERK!
...!!
WOW!

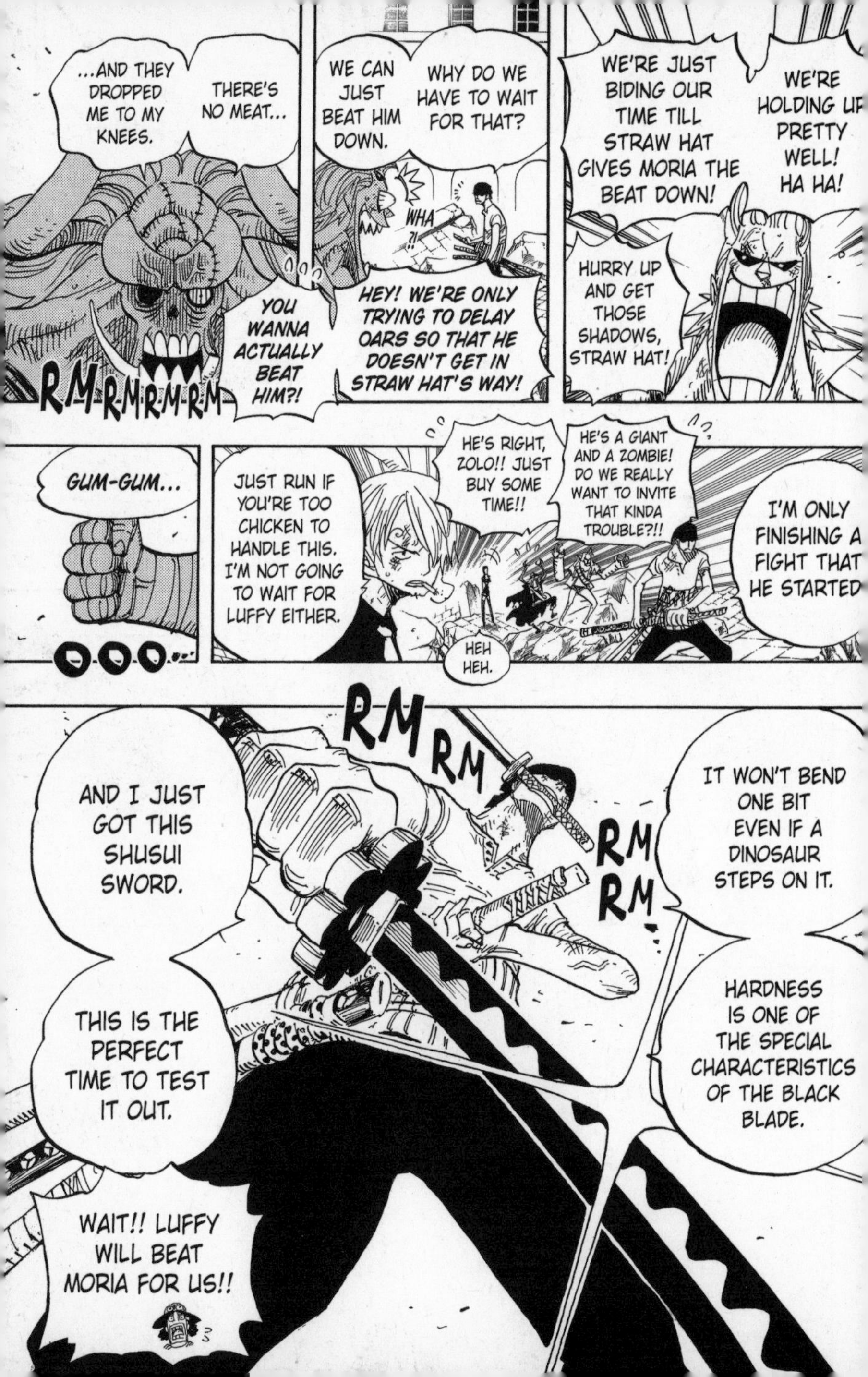
WE'RE HOLDING UP PRETTY WELL! HA HA!
WE'RE JUST BIDING OUR TIME TILL STRAW HAT GIVES MORIA THE BEAT DOWN!
HURRY UP AND GET THOSE SHADOWS, STRAW HAT!
WHY DO WE HAVE TO WAIT FOR THAT?
WE CAN JUST BEAT HIM DOWN.
WHA ?!
HEY! WE'RE ONLY TRYING TO DELAY OARS SO THAT HE DOESN'T GET IN STRAW HAT'S WAY!
YOU WANNA ACTUALLY BEAT HIM?!
THERE'S NO MEAT...
...AND THEY DROPPED ME TO MY KNEES.
RM-RM-RM-RM-RM-RM
I'M ONLY FINISHING A FIGHT THAT HE STARTED
HE'S A GIANT AND A ZOMBIE! DO WE REALLY WANT TO INVITE THAT KINDA TROUBLE?!!
HE'S RIGHT, ZOLO!! JUST BUY SOME TIME!!
JUST RUN IF YOU'RE TOO CHICKEN TO HANDLE THIS. I'M NOT GOING TO WAIT FOR LUFFY EITHER.
HEH HEH.
GUM-GUM...
O-O-O...
IT WON'T BEND ONE BIT EVEN IF A DINOSAUR STEPS ON IT.
HARDNESS IS ONE OF THE SPECIAL CHARACTERISTICS OF THE BLACK BLADE.
RM RM
RM RM
AND I JUST GOT THIS SHUSUI SWORD.
THIS IS THE PERFECT TIME TO TEST IT OUT.
WAIT!! LUFFY WILL BEAT MORIA FOR US!!

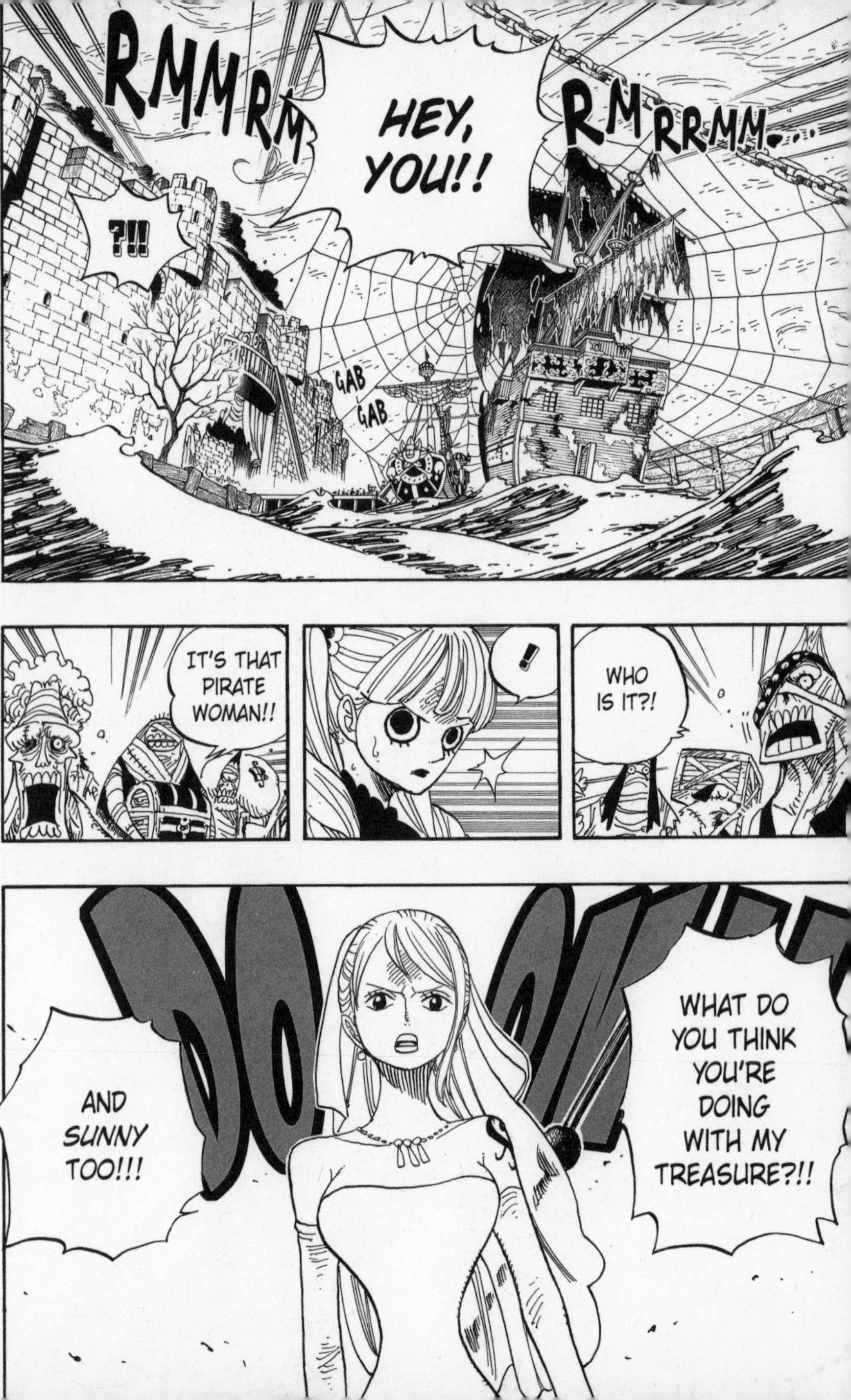
RMRRMM...
HEY, YOU!!
RMMRM
?!!
GAB GAB
WHO IS IT?!
!
IT'S THAT PIRATE WOMAN!!
WHAT DO YOU THINK YOU'RE DOING WITH MY TREASURE?!!
AND SUNNY TOO!!!

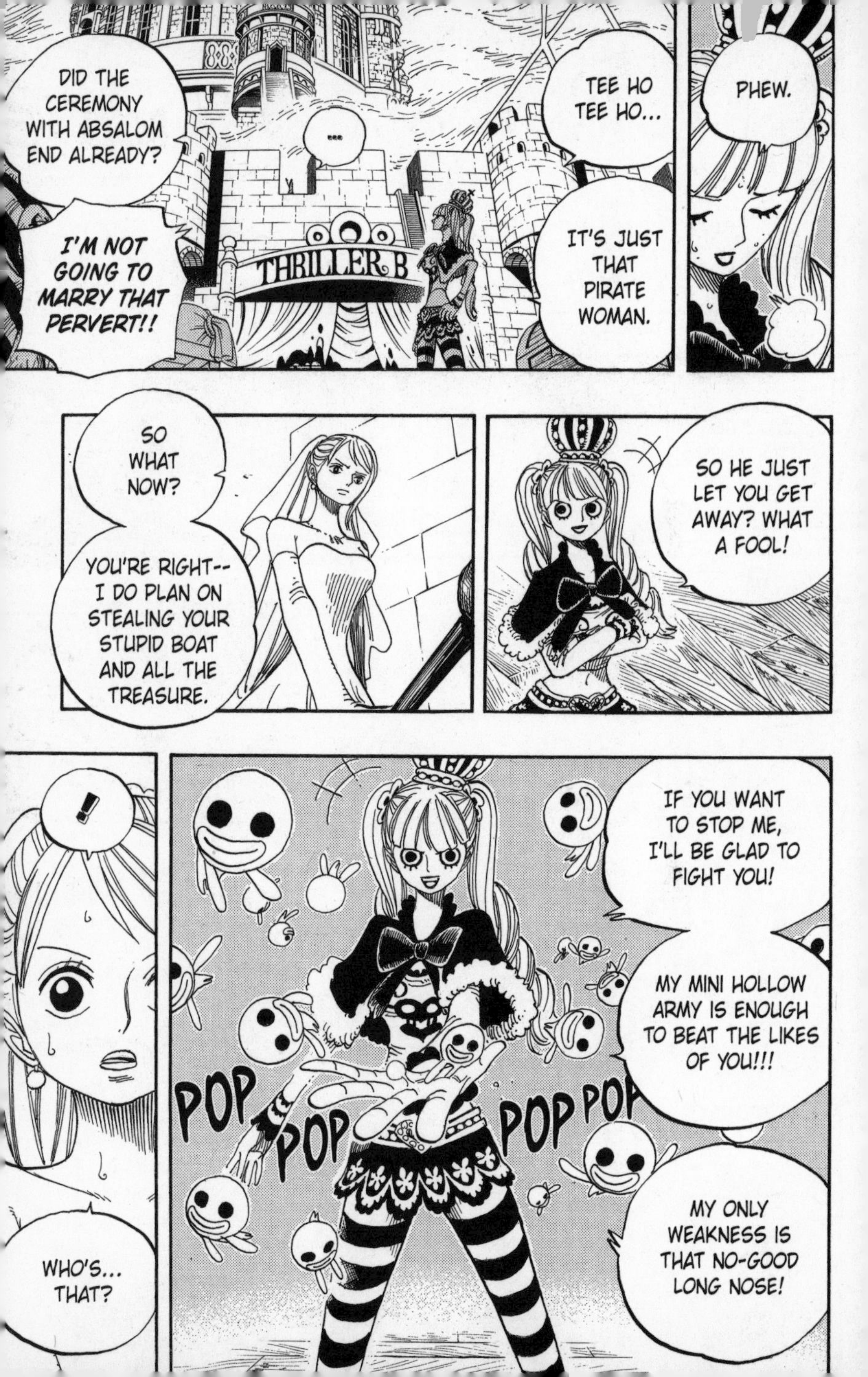
PHEW.
TEE HO TEE HO...
IT'S JUST THAT PIRATE WOMAN.
...
DID THE CEREMONY WITH ABSALOM END ALREADY?
I'M NOT GOING TO MARRY THAT PERVERT!!
THRILLER B
SO HE JUST LET YOU GET AWAY? WHAT A FOOL!
SO WHAT NOW?
YOU'RE RIGHT-- I DO PLAN ON STEALING YOUR STUPID BOAT AND ALL THE TREASURE.
IF YOU WANT TO STOP ME, I'LL BE GLAD TO FIGHT YOU!
MY MINI HOLLOW ARMY IS ENOUGH TO BEAT THE LIKES OF YOU!!!
POP POP
POP
POP POP
MY ONLY WEAKNESS IS THAT NO-GOOD LONG NOSE!
!
WHO'S... THAT?

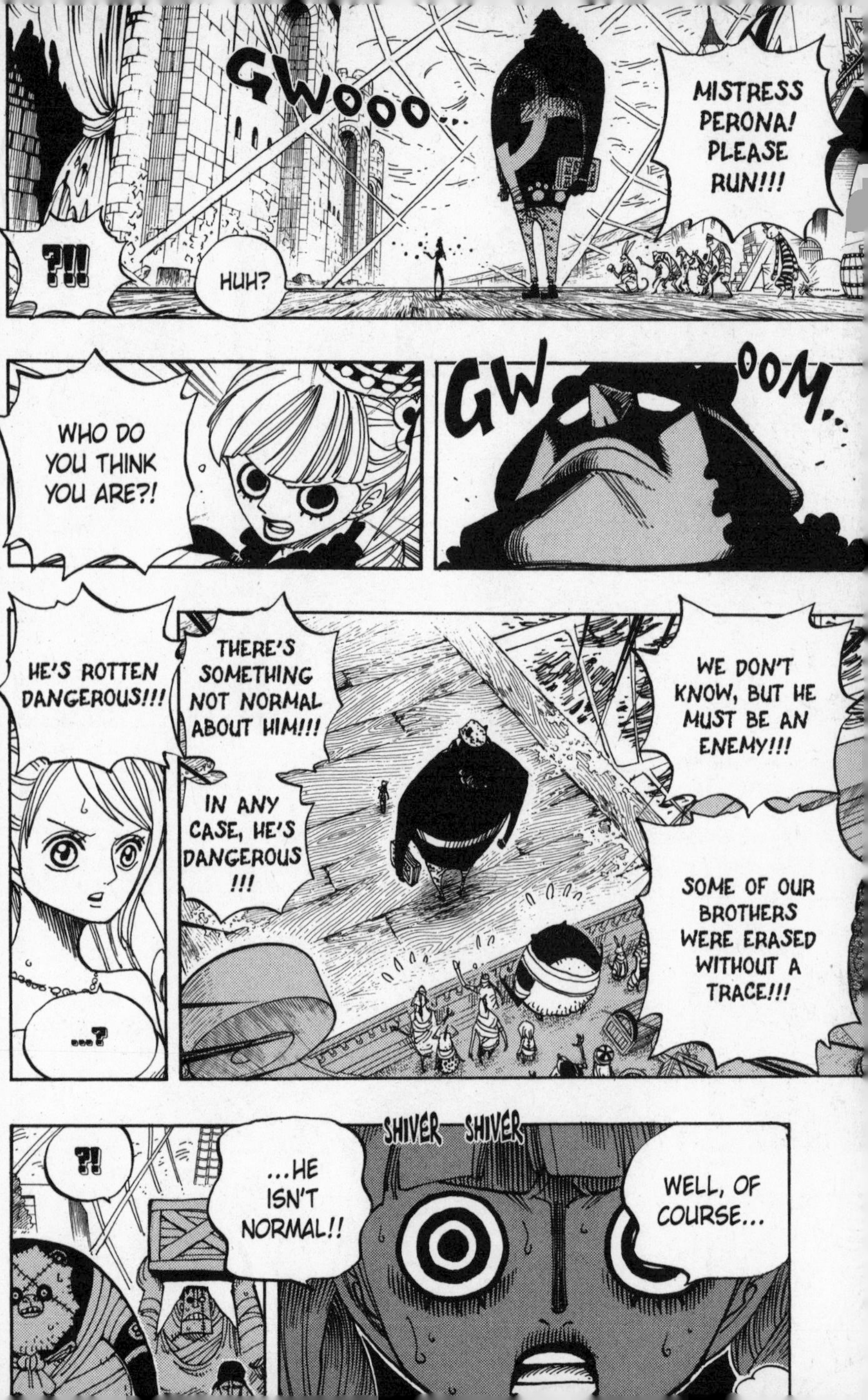
MISTRESS PERONA! PLEASE RUN!!!
GWOOO...
HUH?
?!!
GW
OOM...
WHO DO YOU THINK YOU ARE?!
WE DON'T KNOW, BUT HE MUST BE AN ENEMY!!!
SOME OF OUR BROTHERS WERE ERASED WITHOUT A TRACE!!!
THERE'S SOMETHING NOT NORMAL ABOUT HIM!!!
IN ANY CASE, HE'S DANGEROUS!!!
HE'S ROTTEN DANGEROUS!!!
...?
WELL, OF COURSE...
SHIVER SHIVER
...HE ISN'T NORMAL!!
?!

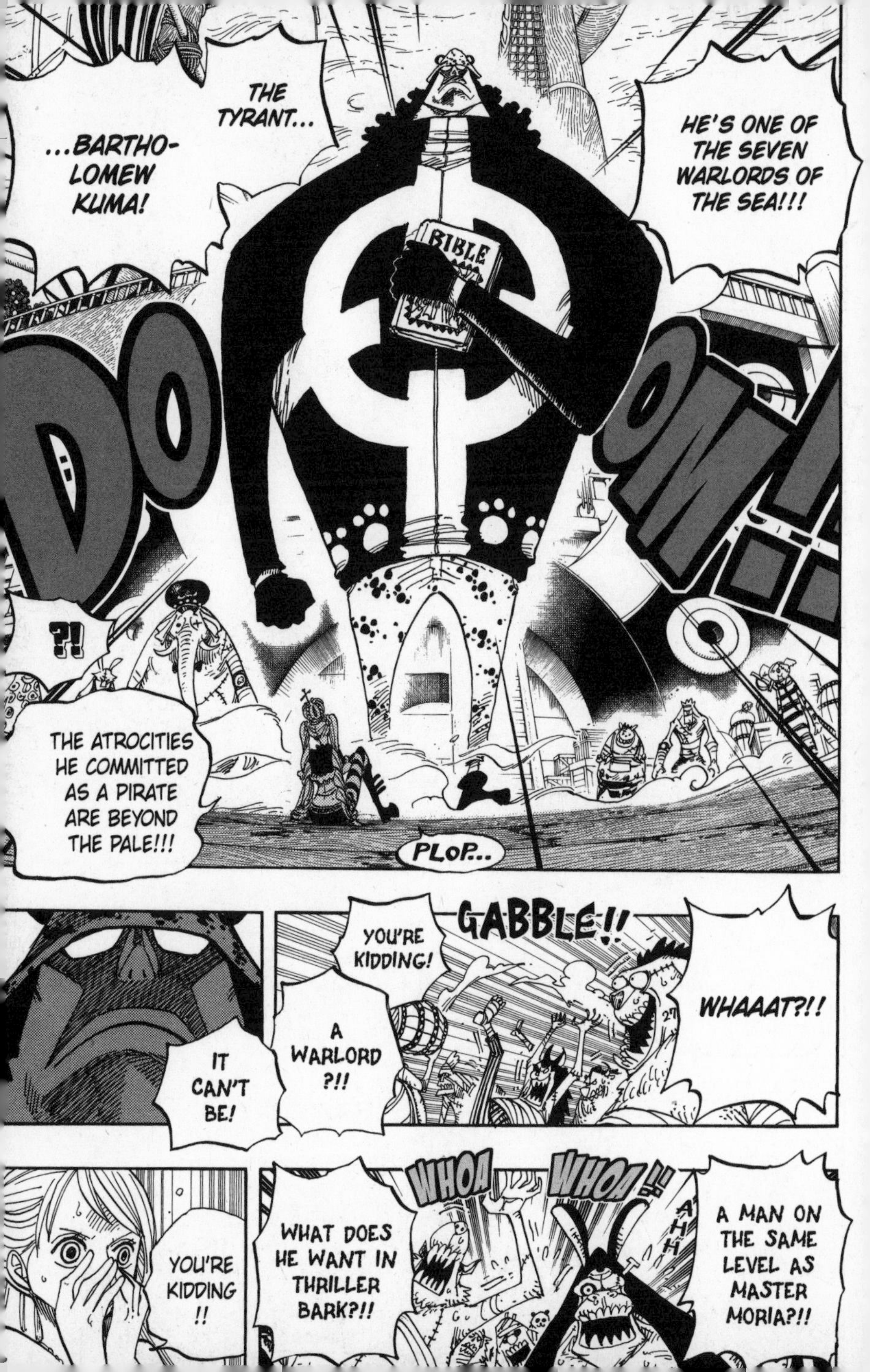
HE'S ONE OF THE SEVEN WARLORDS OF THE SEA!!!
THE TYRANT...
...BARTHO-LOMEW KUMA!
DOON!!
?!
THE ATROCITIES HE COMMITTED AS A PIRATE ARE BEYOND THE PALE!!!
PLOP...
WHAAAT?!!
GABBLE!!
YOU'RE KIDDING!
A WARLORD?!!
IT CAN'T BE!
A MAN ON THE SAME LEVEL AS MASTER MORIA?!!
AHHH
WHOA WHOA!!
WHAT DOES HE WANT IN THRILLER BARK?!!
YOU'RE KIDDING!!

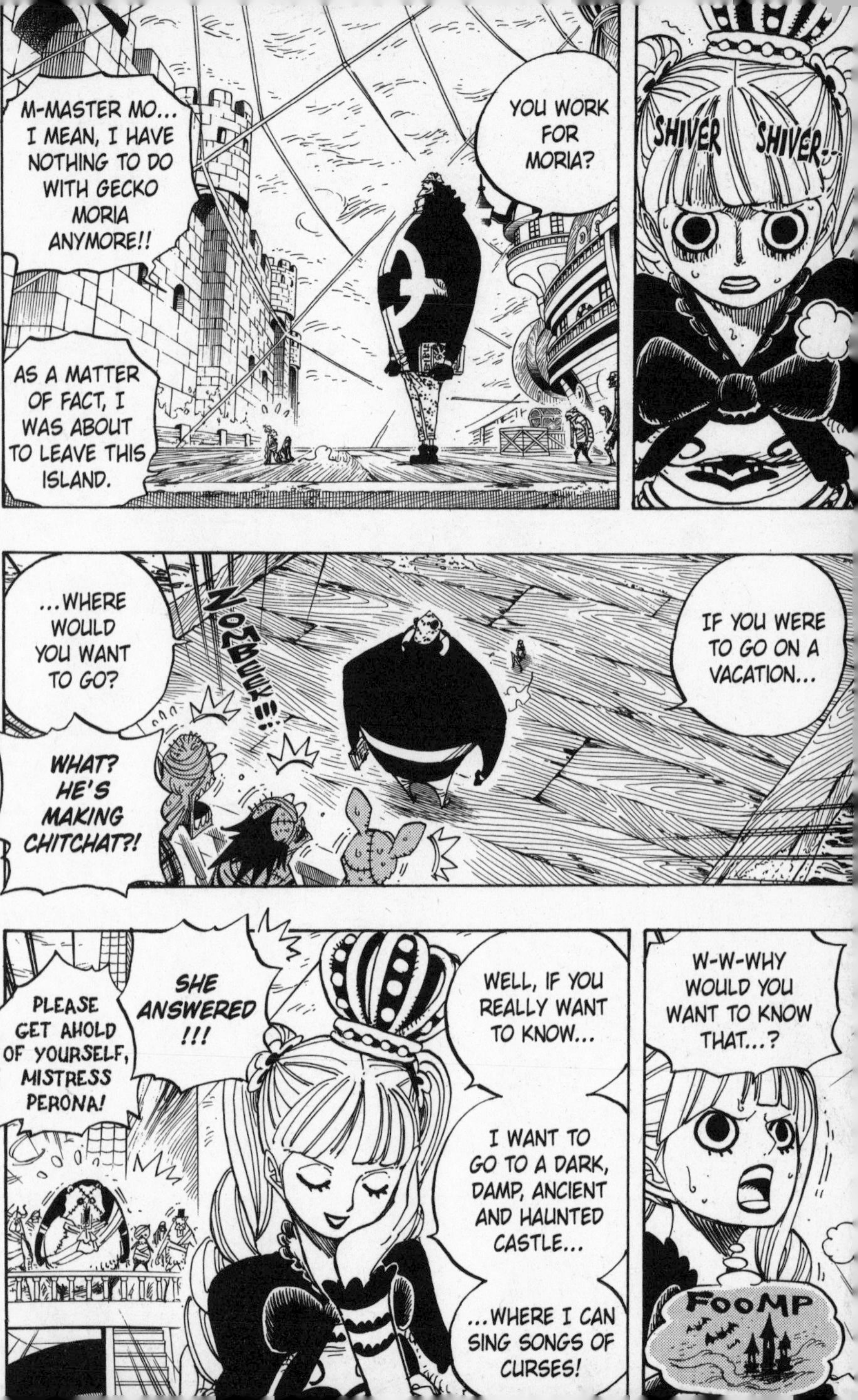
SHIVER SHIVER...
YOU WORK FOR MORIA?
M-MASTER MO... I MEAN, I HAVE NOTHING TO DO WITH GECKO MORIA ANYMORE!!
AS A MATTER OF FACT, I WAS ABOUT TO LEAVE THIS ISLAND.
IF YOU WERE TO GO ON A VACATION...
...WHERE WOULD YOU WANT TO GO?
ZOMBEEK!!!
WHAT? HE'S MAKING CHITCHAT?!
W-W-WHY WOULD YOU WANT TO KNOW THAT...?
FOOMP
WELL, IF YOU REALLY WANT TO KNOW...
SHE ANSWERED!!!
PLEASE GET AHOLD OF YOURSELF, MISTRESS PERONA!
I WANT TO GO TO A DARK, DAMP, ANCIENT AND HAUNTED CASTLE...
...WHERE I CAN SING SONGS OF CURSES!

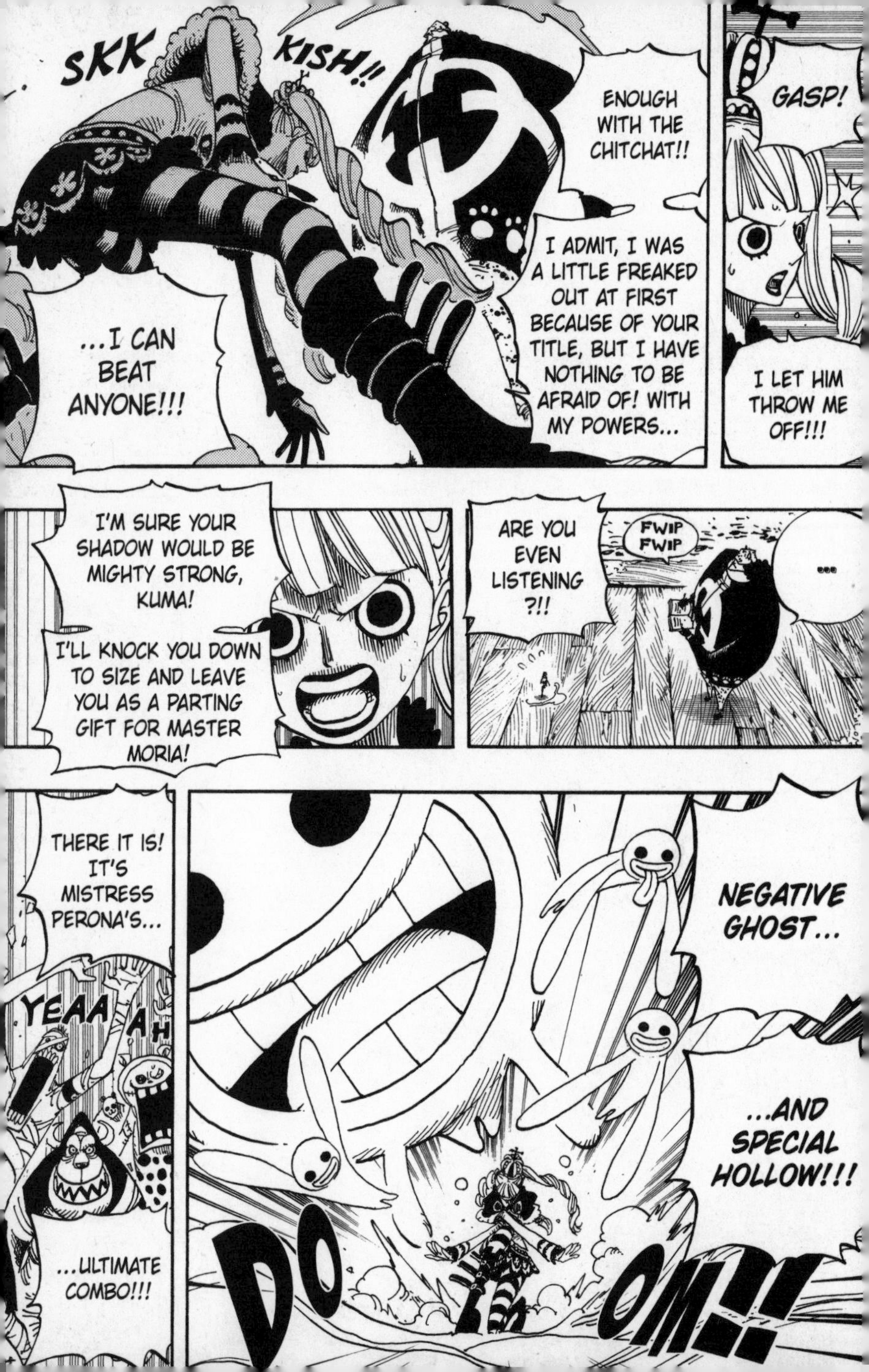
GASP!
I LET HIM THROW ME OFF!!!
SKK KISH!!
ENOUGH WITH THE CHITCHAT!!
I ADMIT, I WAS A LITTLE FREAKED OUT AT FIRST BECAUSE OF YOUR TITLE, BUT I HAVE NOTHING TO BE AFRAID OF! WITH MY POWERS...
...I CAN BEAT ANYONE!!!
...
FWIP FWIP
ARE YOU EVEN LISTENING?!!
I'M SURE YOUR SHADOW WOULD BE MIGHTY STRONG, KUMA!
I'LL KNOCK YOU DOWN TO SIZE AND LEAVE YOU AS A PARTING GIFT FOR MASTER MORIA!
NEGATIVE GHOST...
...AND SPECIAL HOLLOW!!!
DOOM!!
THERE IT IS! IT'S MISTRESS PERONA'S...
YEAAAH
...ULTIMATE COMBO!!!

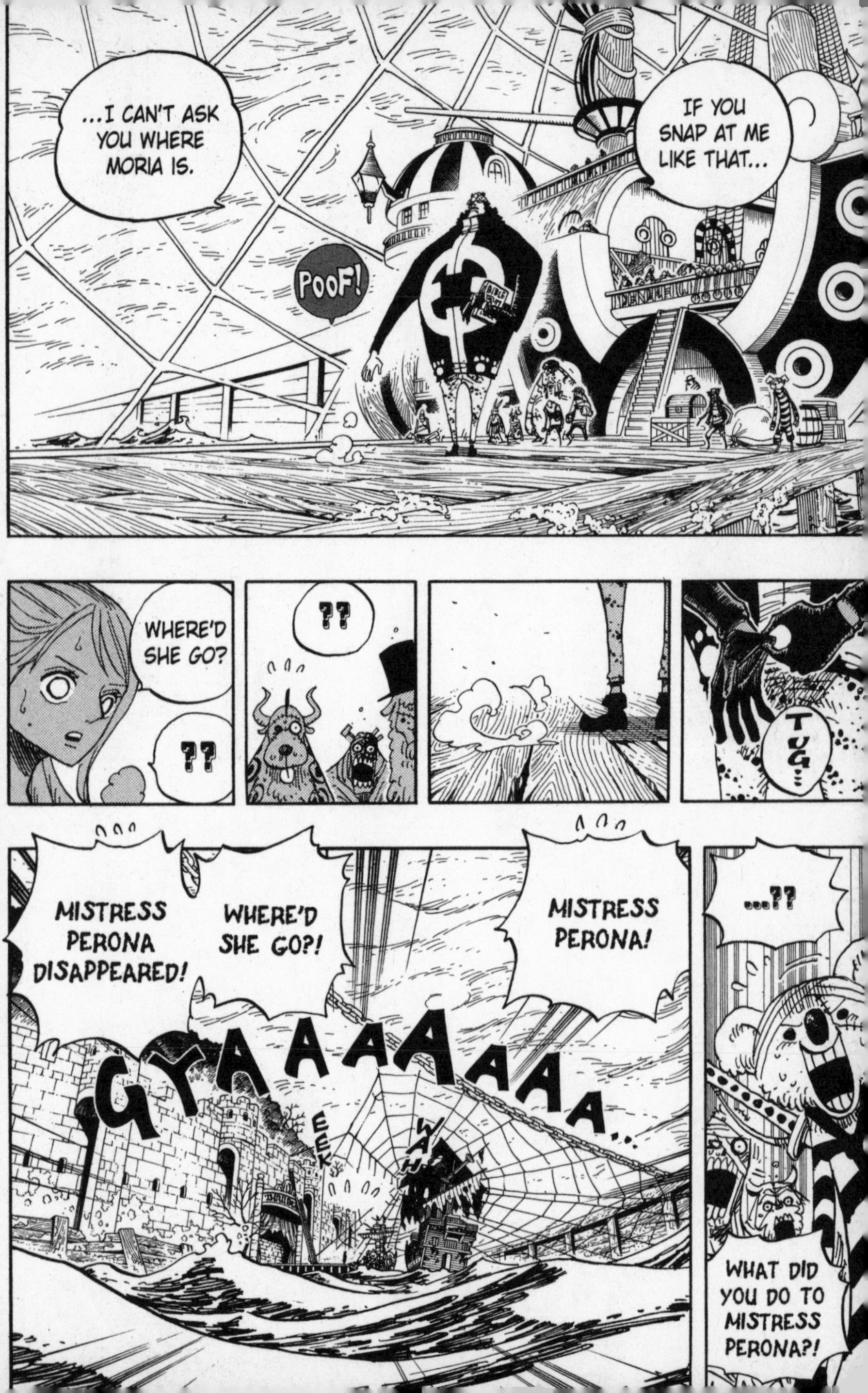
IF YOU SNAP AT ME LIKE THAT...
...I CAN'T ASK YOU WHERE MORIA IS.
POOF!
TUG...
??
WHERE'D SHE GO?
??
...??
WHAT DID YOU DO TO MISTRESS PERONA?!
MISTRESS PERONA!
WHERE'D SHE GO?!
MISTRESS PERONA DISAPPEARED!
GYAAAAAAA...
EEK
WAH

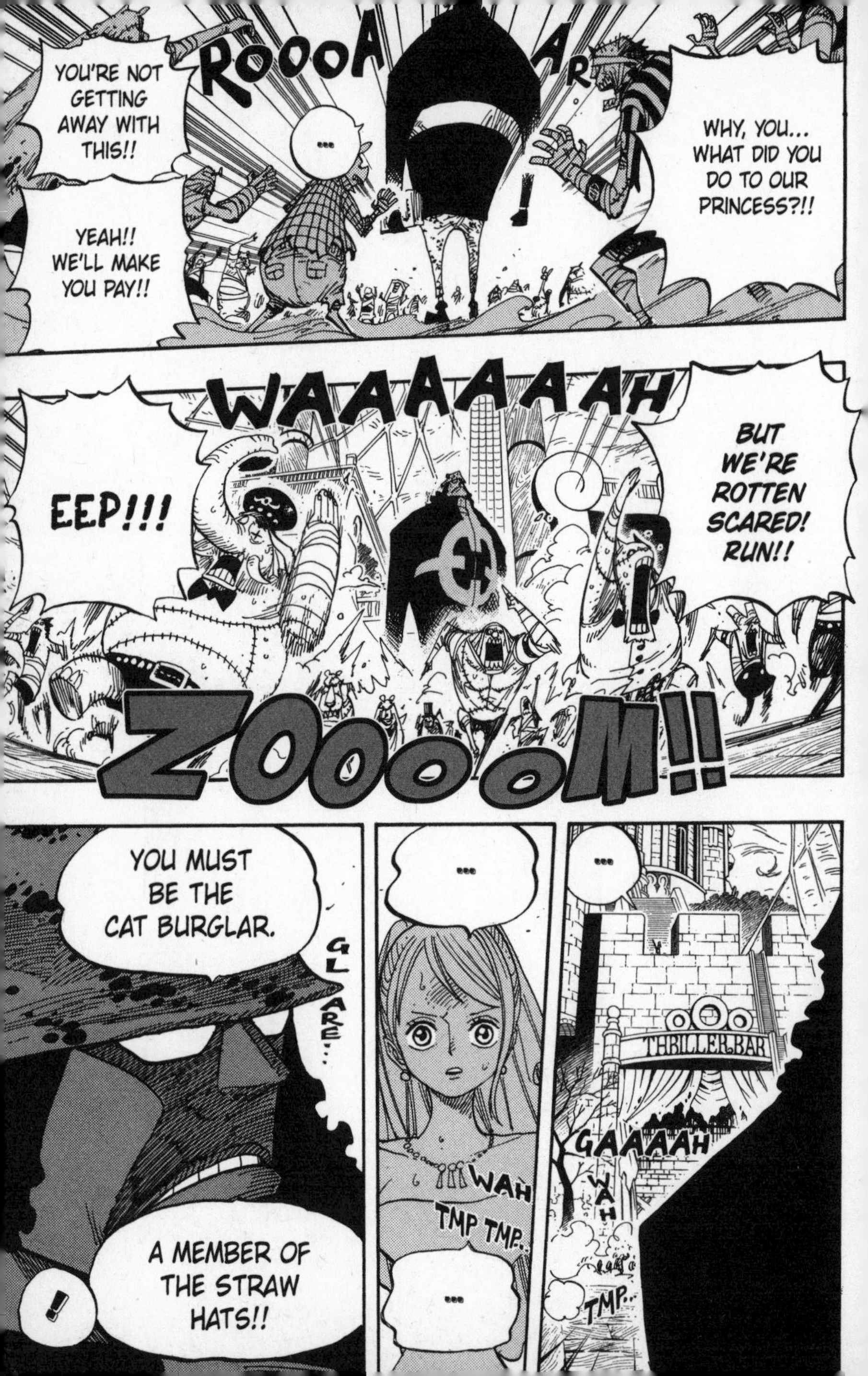
ROOOA AR
WHY, YOU... WHAT DID YOU DO TO OUR PRINCESS?!!
!
...
YOU'RE NOT GETTING AWAY WITH THIS!!
YEAH!! WE'LL MAKE YOU PAY!!
BUT WE'RE ROTTEN SCARED! RUN!!
WAAAAAAH
EEP!!!
ZOOOOM!!
...
THRILLER BAR
GAAAAH
WAH
TMP..
...
WAH
TMP TMP..
...
YOU MUST BE THE CAT BURGLAR.
GLARE..
A MEMBER OF THE STRAW HATS!!
!

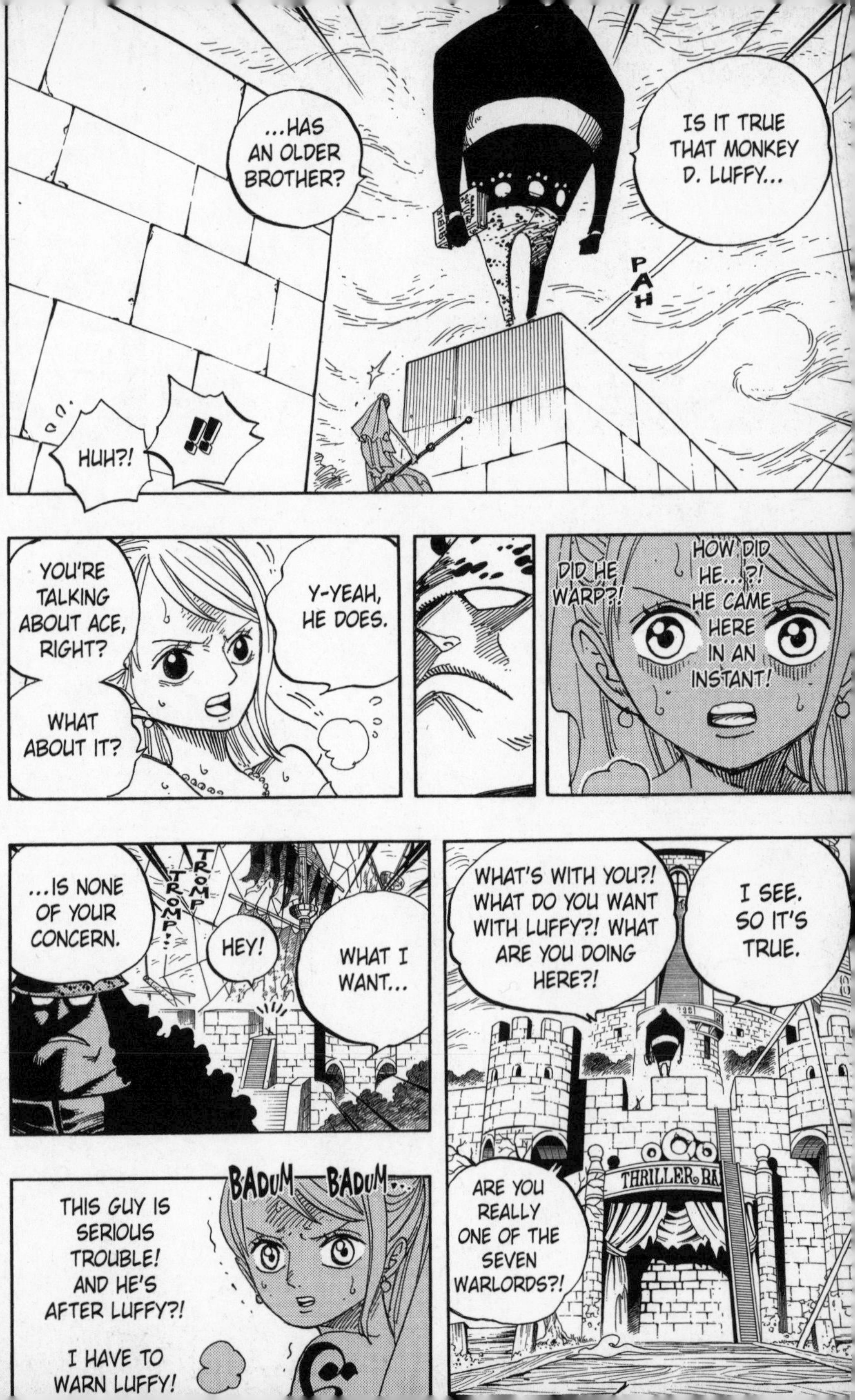
IS IT TRUE THAT MONKEY D. LUFFY...
PAH
...HAS AN OLDER BROTHER?
!!
HUH?!
HOW DID HE...?! HE CAME HERE IN AN INSTANT!
DID HE WARP?!
Y-YEAH, HE DOES.
YOU'RE TALKING ABOUT ACE, RIGHT?
WHAT ABOUT IT?
I SEE. SO IT'S TRUE.
WHAT'S WITH YOU?! WHAT DO YOU WANT WITH LUFFY?! WHAT ARE YOU DOING HERE?!
THRILLER BA
ARE YOU REALLY ONE OF THE SEVEN WARLORDS?!
WHAT I WANT...
HEY!
TROMP TROMP
TROMP
...IS NONE OF YOUR CONCERN.
BADUM BADUM...
THIS GUY IS SERIOUS TROUBLE! AND HE'S AFTER LUFFY?!
I HAVE TO WARN LUFFY!

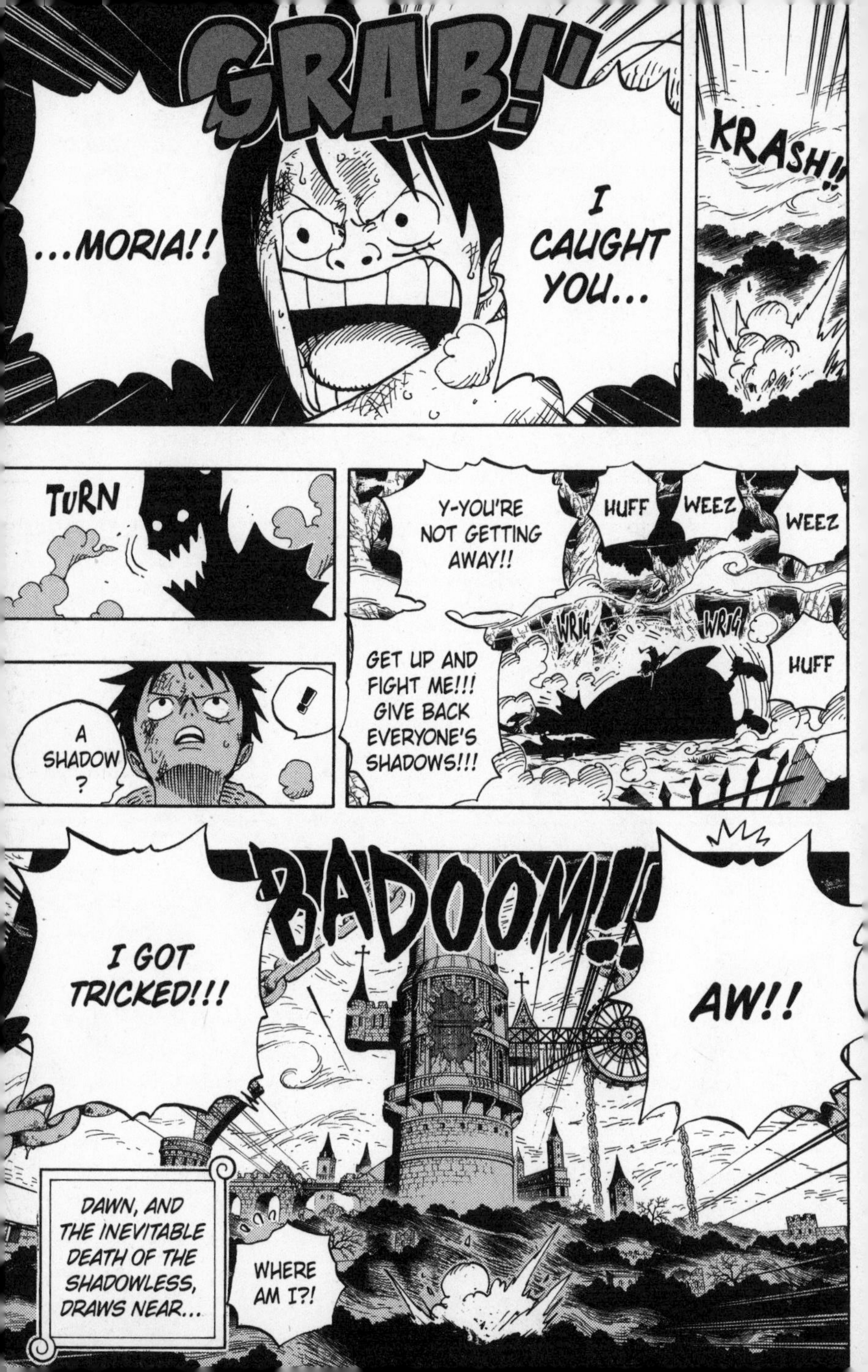
KRASH!!
GRAB!!
I CAUGHT YOU...
...MORIA!!
WEEZ
WEEZ
HUFF
Y-YOU'RE NOT GETTING AWAY!!
WRIG
WRIG
HUFF
GET UP AND FIGHT ME!!! GIVE BACK EVERYONE'S SHADOWS!!!
TURN
!
A SHADOW?
BADOOM!!
AW!!
I GOT TRICKED!!!
WHERE AM I?!
DAWN, AND THE INEVITABLE DEATH OF THE SHADOWLESS, DRAWS NEAR...

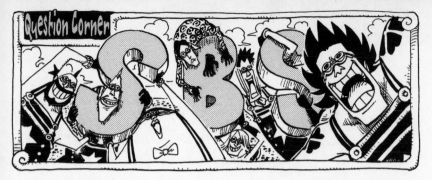

Question Corner

Q: I opened up a very nice soba restaurant. --Kimuchi-maru

A: Get out of here! 人 (RAGE!) Huff...Huff... I'm sorry. That was very immature of me.

Q: Oda Sensei, I have a very serious question. Shanks was an apprentice on Gold Roger's ship, so in volume 3, the person that punched Buggy and Shanks for fighting... Was he the ship's captain? Or some other high-ranking person? --Sonoe

A: Regarding the flashback with Buggy and Shanks as apprentices, the captain of their ship would be Gold Roger. The person that punished those two is the first mate. At the time, I had already decided on this arrangement, so I made sure the anime staff members didn't call that person "captain" by mistake.

Q: Hello, Oda Sensei! I have a question. Oars seems to be really big, but is he a giant? If he's a giant, is he a warrior of Elbaph? Please tell me! --Naranara

A: I'm guessing that there's probably an especially tall person in your class. Oars is a giant, all right, but he's also like that especially tall person. He's not a warrior of Elbaph. In the world of One Piece, there are many different islands where giants live. Born in a village of giants, he's biggest of all! That's who Oars is.

Chapter 474:
WE HAVE TO DO IT!

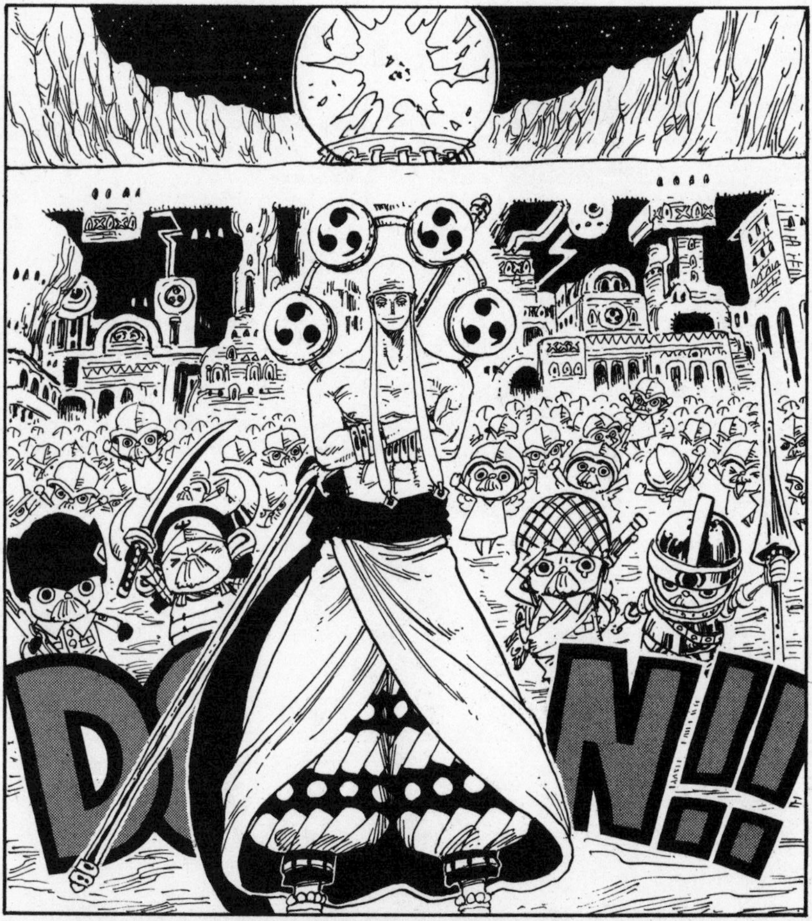
DON!!

ENERU'S GREAT SPACE MISSION, FINAL VOLUME:
"FULL POWER! THE ENERU ARMY STANDS TALL!"

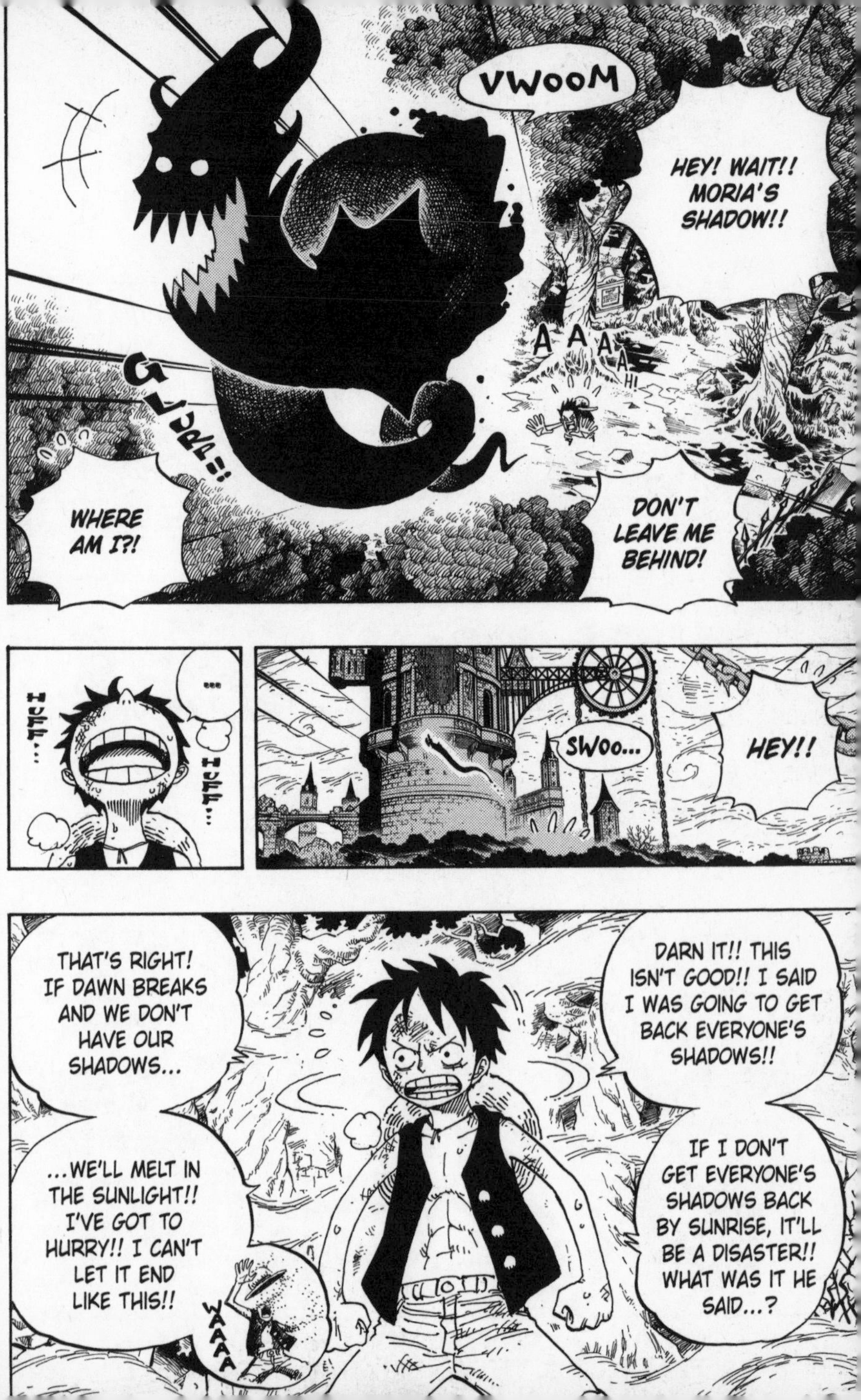
HEY! WAIT!! MORIA'S SHADOW!!
VWOOM
AAAAAH!
DON'T LEAVE ME BEHIND!
GLURP!!
WHERE AM I?!
HEY!!
SWOO...
...
HUFF... HUFF...
DARN IT!! THIS ISN'T GOOD!! I SAID I WAS GOING TO GET BACK EVERYONE'S SHADOWS!!
IF I DON'T GET EVERYONE'S SHADOWS BACK BY SUNRISE, IT'LL BE A DISASTER!! WHAT WAS IT HE SAID...?
THAT'S RIGHT! IF DAWN BREAKS AND WE DON'T HAVE OUR SHADOWS...
...WE'LL MELT IN THE SUNLIGHT!! I'VE GOT TO HURRY!! I CAN'T LET IT END LIKE THIS!!
WAAAA

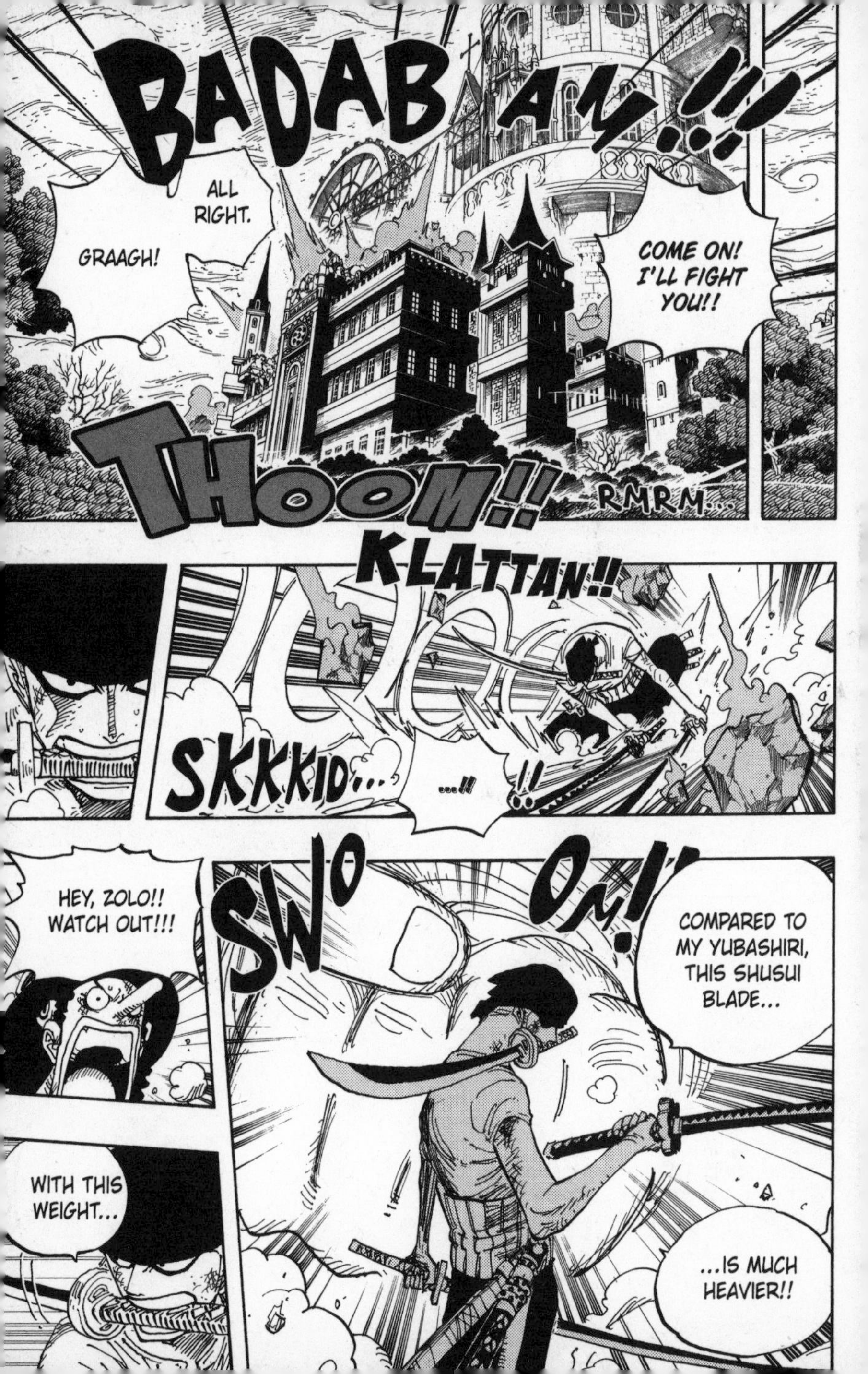
BADABAM!!!
COME ON! I'LL FIGHT YOU!!
ALL RIGHT.
GRAAGH!
THOOM!!
RMRM...
KLATTAN!!
SKKKID...
...!!
!!
SWOOM!!
COMPARED TO MY YUBASHIRI, THIS SHUSUI BLADE...
...IS MUCH HEAVIER!!
HEY, ZOLO!! WATCH OUT!!!
WITH THIS WEIGHT...

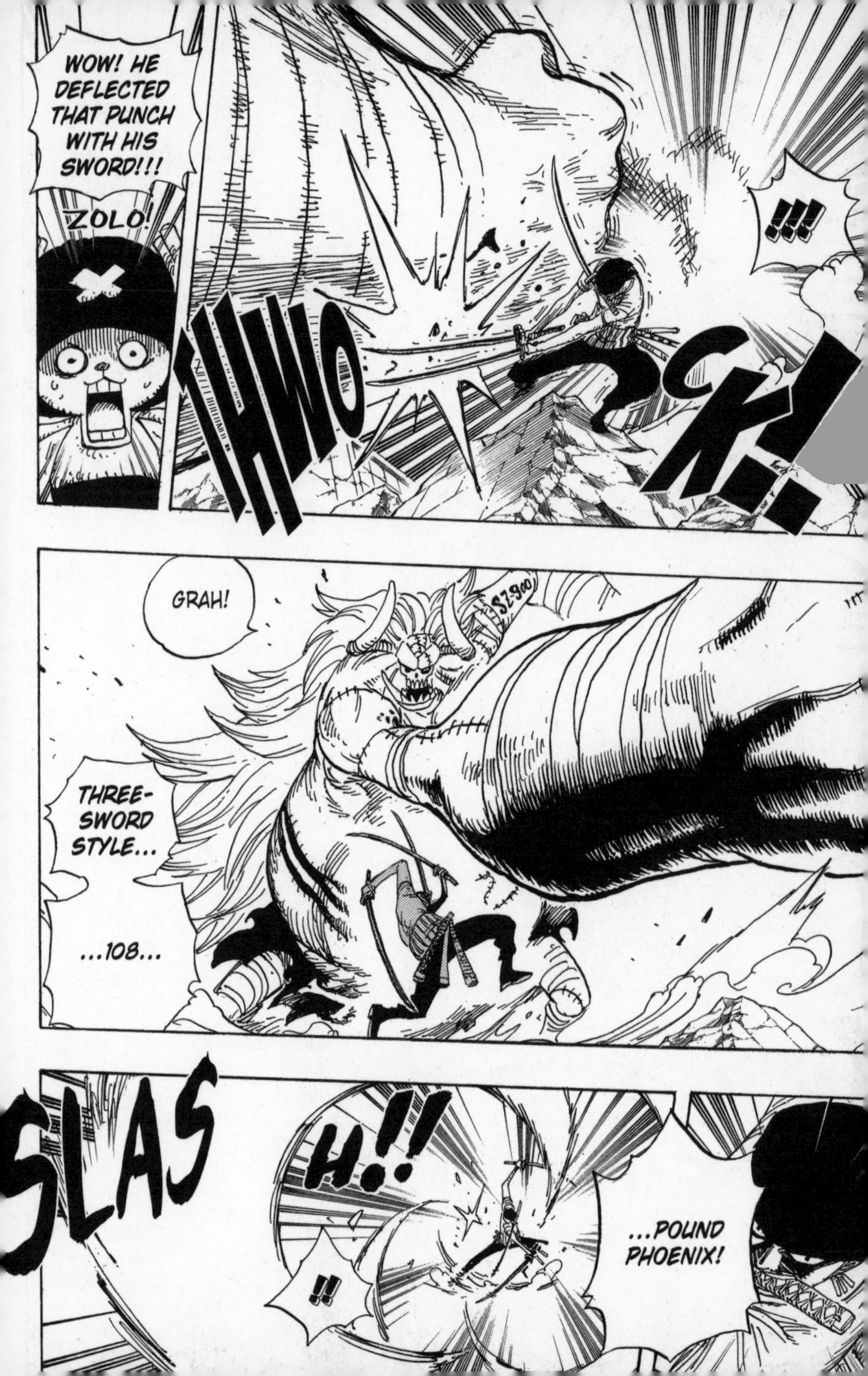
!!!
THWOCK!!
WOW! HE DEFLECTED THAT PUNCH WITH HIS SWORD!!!
ZOLO!
GRAH!
THREE-SWORD STYLE...
...108...
...POUND PHOENIX!
SLASH!!
!!

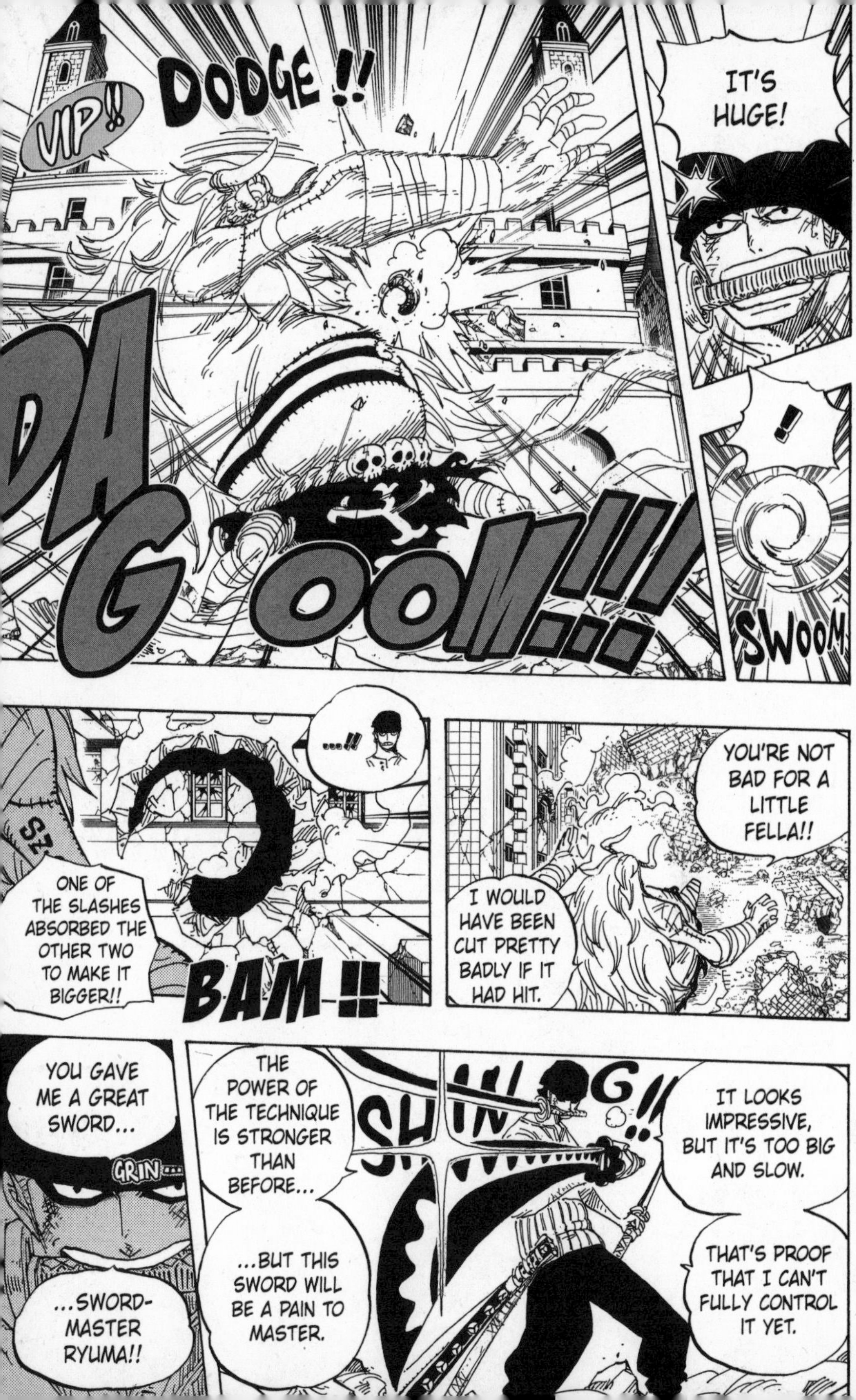
IT'S HUGE!
!
SWOOM
VIP!!
DODGE!!
DA GOOM!!
YOU'RE NOT BAD FOR A LITTLE FELLA!!
I WOULD HAVE BEEN CUT PRETTY BADLY IF IT HAD HIT.
...!!
ONE OF THE SLASHES ABSORBED THE OTHER TWO TO MAKE IT BIGGER!!
BAM!!
IT LOOKS IMPRESSIVE, BUT IT'S TOO BIG AND SLOW.
SHING!!
THE POWER OF THE TECHNIQUE IS STRONGER THAN BEFORE...
THAT'S PROOF THAT I CAN'T FULLY CONTROL IT YET.
...BUT THIS SWORD WILL BE A PAIN TO MASTER.
YOU GAVE ME A GREAT SWORD...
GRIN...
...SWORD-MASTER RYUMA!!

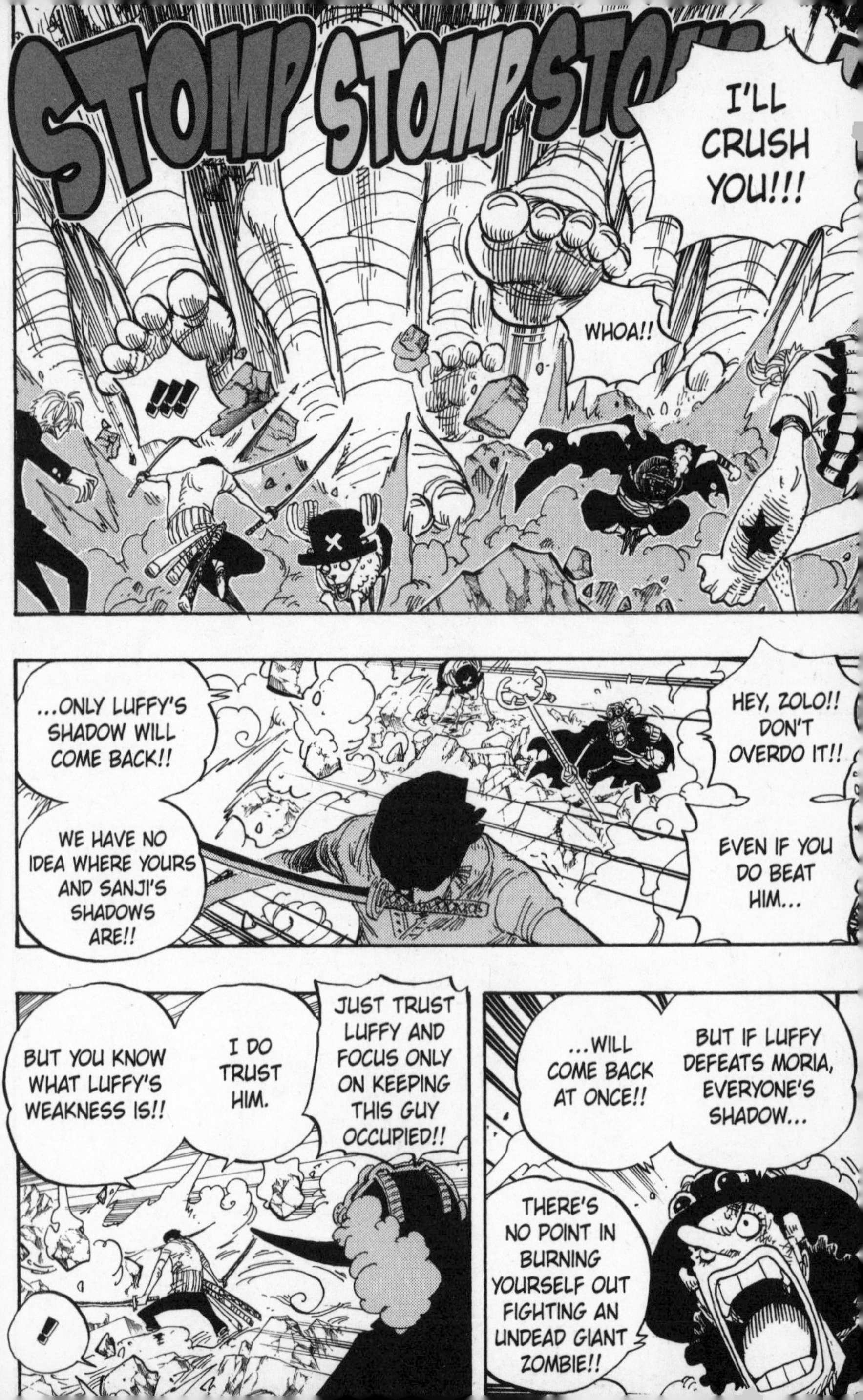
I'LL CRUSH YOU!!!
STOMP STOMP STO
WHOA!!
!!!
HEY, ZOLO!! DON'T OVERDO IT!!
EVEN IF YOU DO BEAT HIM...
...ONLY LUFFY'S SHADOW WILL COME BACK!!
WE HAVE NO IDEA WHERE YOURS AND SANJI'S SHADOWS ARE!!
BUT IF LUFFY DEFEATS MORIA, EVERYONE'S SHADOW...
...WILL COME BACK AT ONCE!!
THERE'S NO POINT IN BURNING YOURSELF OUT FIGHTING AN UNDEAD GIANT ZOMBIE!!
JUST TRUST LUFFY AND FOCUS ONLY ON KEEPING THIS GUY OCCUPIED!!
I DO TRUST HIM.
BUT YOU KNOW WHAT LUFFY'S WEAKNESS IS!!
!

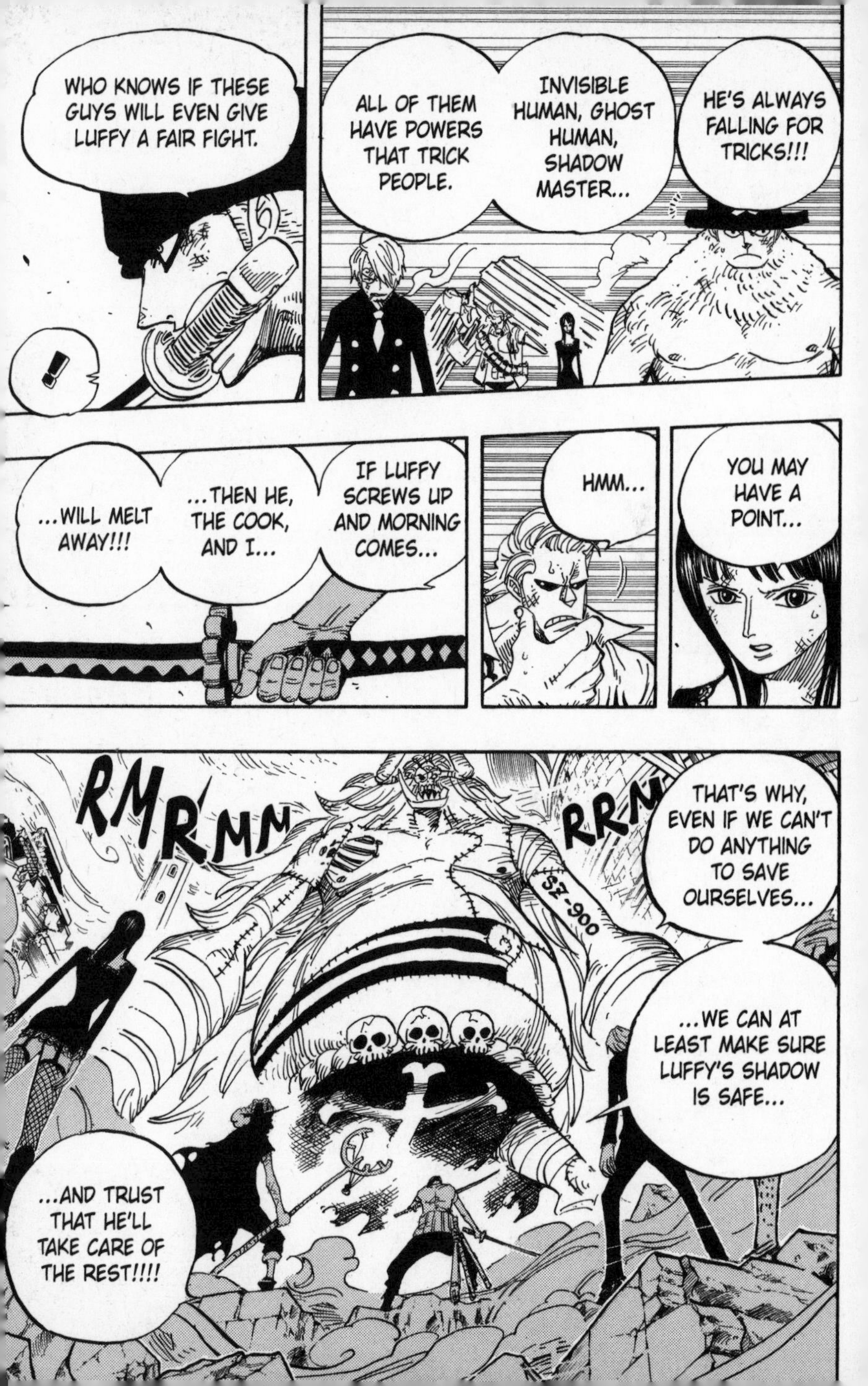
HE'S ALWAYS FALLING FOR TRICKS!!!
INVISIBLE HUMAN, GHOST HUMAN, SHADOW MASTER...
ALL OF THEM HAVE POWERS THAT TRICK PEOPLE.
WHO KNOWS IF THESE GUYS WILL EVEN GIVE LUFFY A FAIR FIGHT.
!
YOU MAY HAVE A POINT...
HMM...
IF LUFFY SCREWS UP AND MORNING COMES...
...THEN HE, THE COOK, AND I...
...WILL MELT AWAY!!!
THAT'S WHY, EVEN IF WE CAN'T DO ANYTHING TO SAVE OURSELVES...
RRM
RMRMM
...WE CAN AT LEAST MAKE SURE LUFFY'S SHADOW IS SAFE...
...AND TRUST THAT HE'LL TAKE CARE OF THE REST!!!!

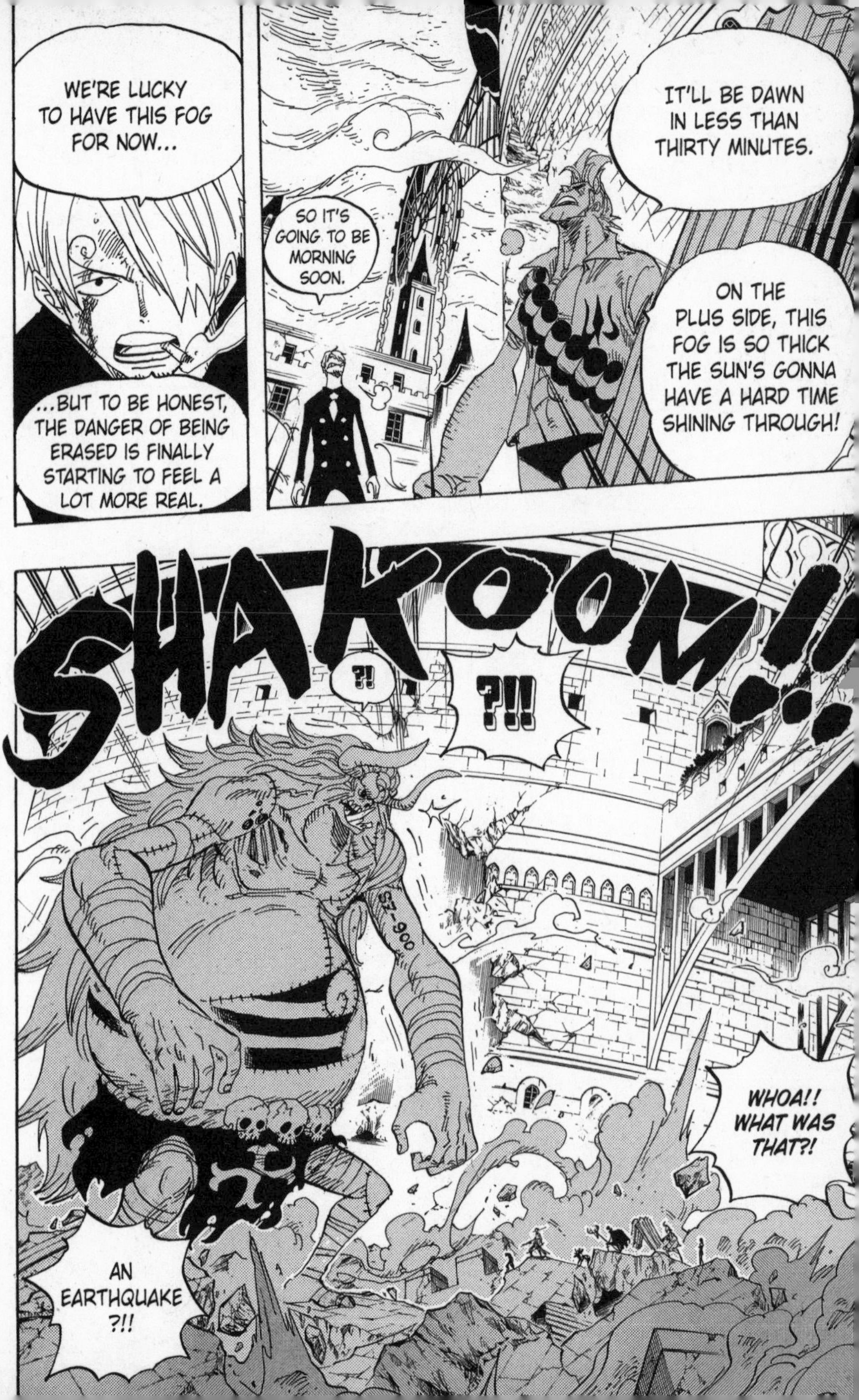

IT'LL BE DAWN IN LESS THAN THIRTY MINUTES.
SO IT'S GOING TO BE MORNING SOON.
ON THE PLUS SIDE, THIS FOG IS SO THICK THE SUN'S GONNA HAVE A HARD TIME SHINING THROUGH!
WE'RE LUCKY TO HAVE THIS FOG FOR NOW...
...BUT TO BE HONEST, THE DANGER OF BEING ERASED IS FINALLY STARTING TO FEEL A LOT MORE REAL.
SHAKOOM!!
?!!
?!
WHOA!! WHAT WAS THAT?!
AN EARTHQUAKE ?!!

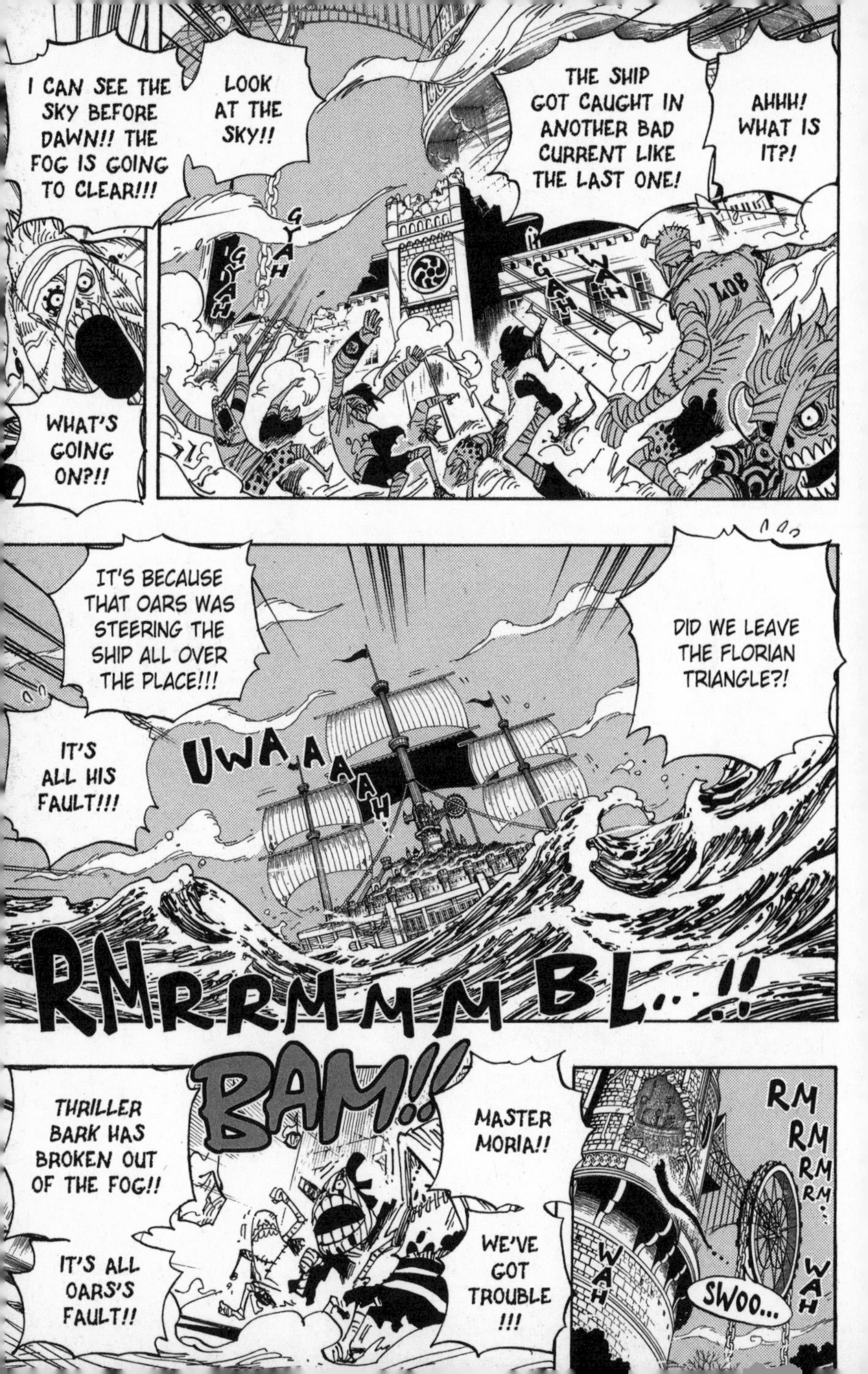
AHHH! WHAT IS IT?!
THE SHIP GOT CAUGHT IN ANOTHER BAD CURRENT LIKE THE LAST ONE!
LOOK AT THE SKY!!
I CAN SEE THE SKY BEFORE DAWN!! THE FOG IS GOING TO CLEAR!!!
WAH
GYAH
GYAH
GYAH
WHAT'S GOING ON?!!
DID WE LEAVE THE FLORIAN TRIANGLE?!
IT'S BECAUSE THAT OARS WAS STEERING THE SHIP ALL OVER THE PLACE!!!
IT'S ALL HIS FAULT!!!
UWAAAAAH
RMRRRMMM BL...!!
RM RM RM RM RM
WAH
SWOO...
WAH
MASTER MORIA!!
WE'VE GOT TROUBLE!!!
BAM!!
THRILLER BARK HAS BROKEN OUT OF THE FOG!!
IT'S ALL OARS'S FAULT!!

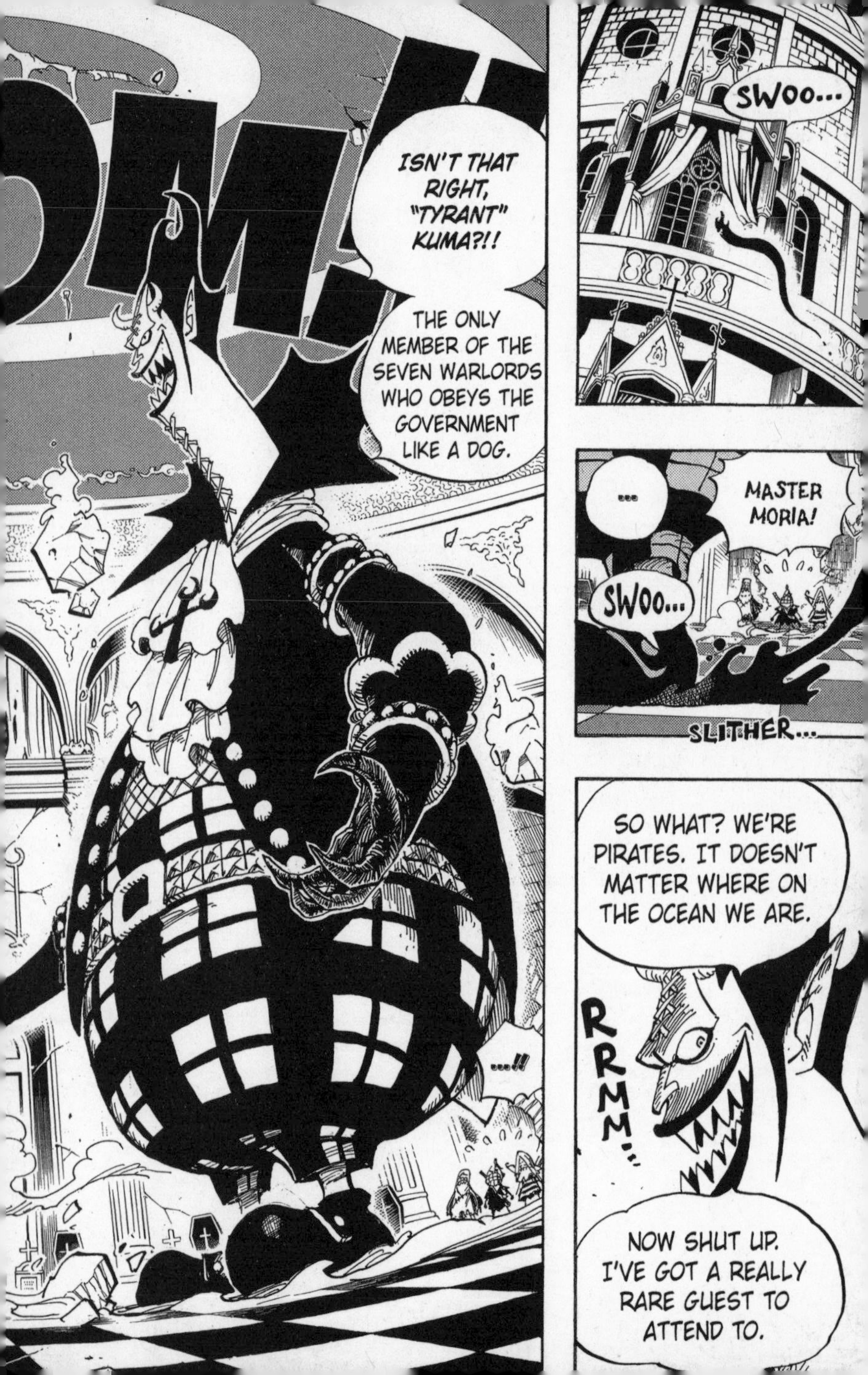
SWOO...
MASTER MORIA!
...
SWOO...
SLITHER...
SO WHAT? WE'RE PIRATES. IT DOESN'T MATTER WHERE ON THE OCEAN WE ARE.
RRMM..
NOW SHUT UP. I'VE GOT A REALLY RARE GUEST TO ATTEND TO.
ISN'T THAT RIGHT, "TYRANT" KUMA?!!
THE ONLY MEMBER OF THE SEVEN WARLORDS WHO OBEYS THE GOVERNMENT LIKE A DOG.
...!!

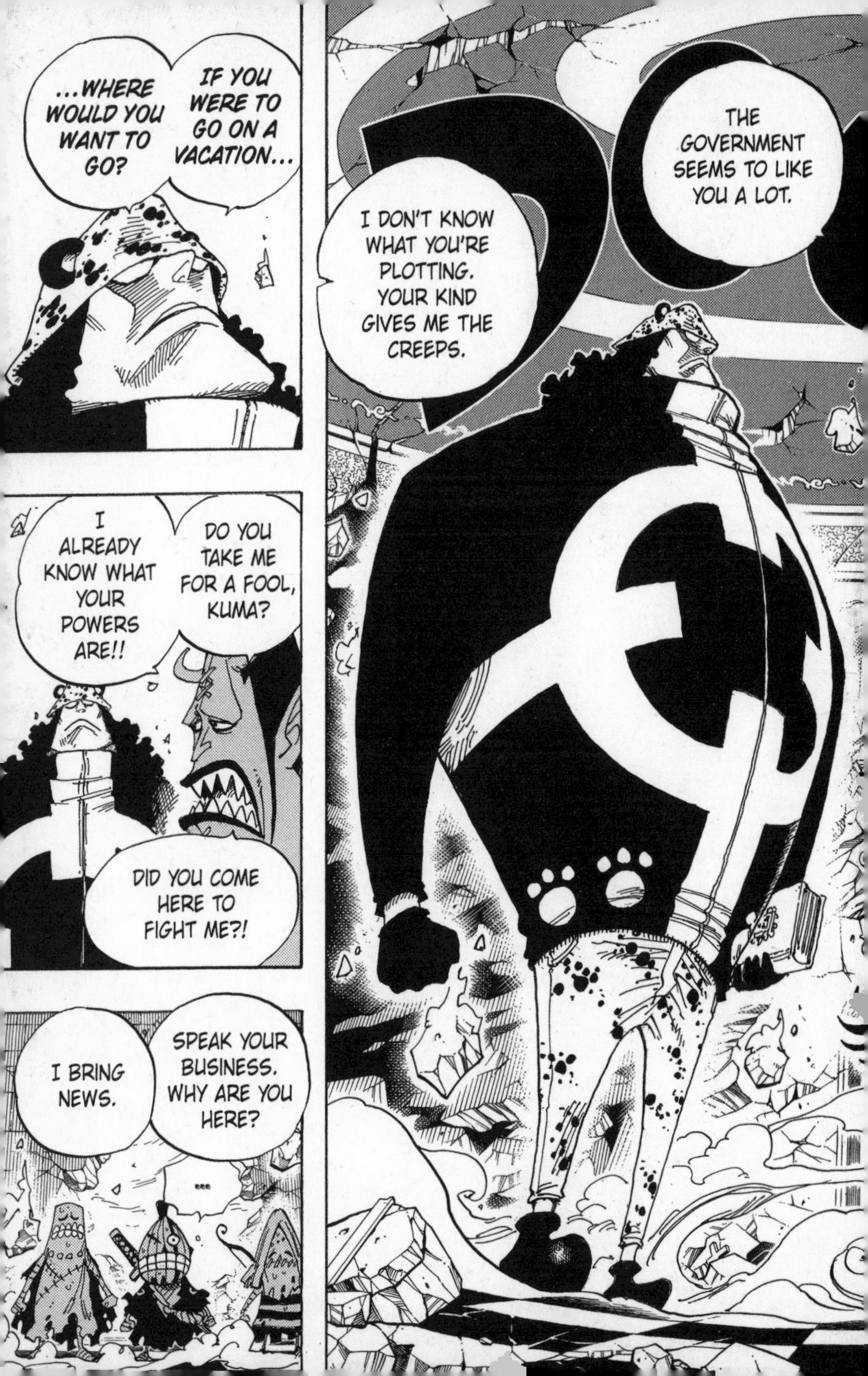
THE GOVERNMENT SEEMS TO LIKE YOU A LOT.
I DON'T KNOW WHAT YOU'RE PLOTTING. YOUR KIND GIVES ME THE CREEPS.
IF YOU WERE TO GO ON A VACATION...
...WHERE WOULD YOU WANT TO GO?
DO YOU TAKE ME FOR A FOOL, KUMA?
I ALREADY KNOW WHAT YOUR POWERS ARE!!
DID YOU COME HERE TO FIGHT ME?!
SPEAK YOUR BUSINESS. WHY ARE YOU HERE?
I BRING NEWS.
...

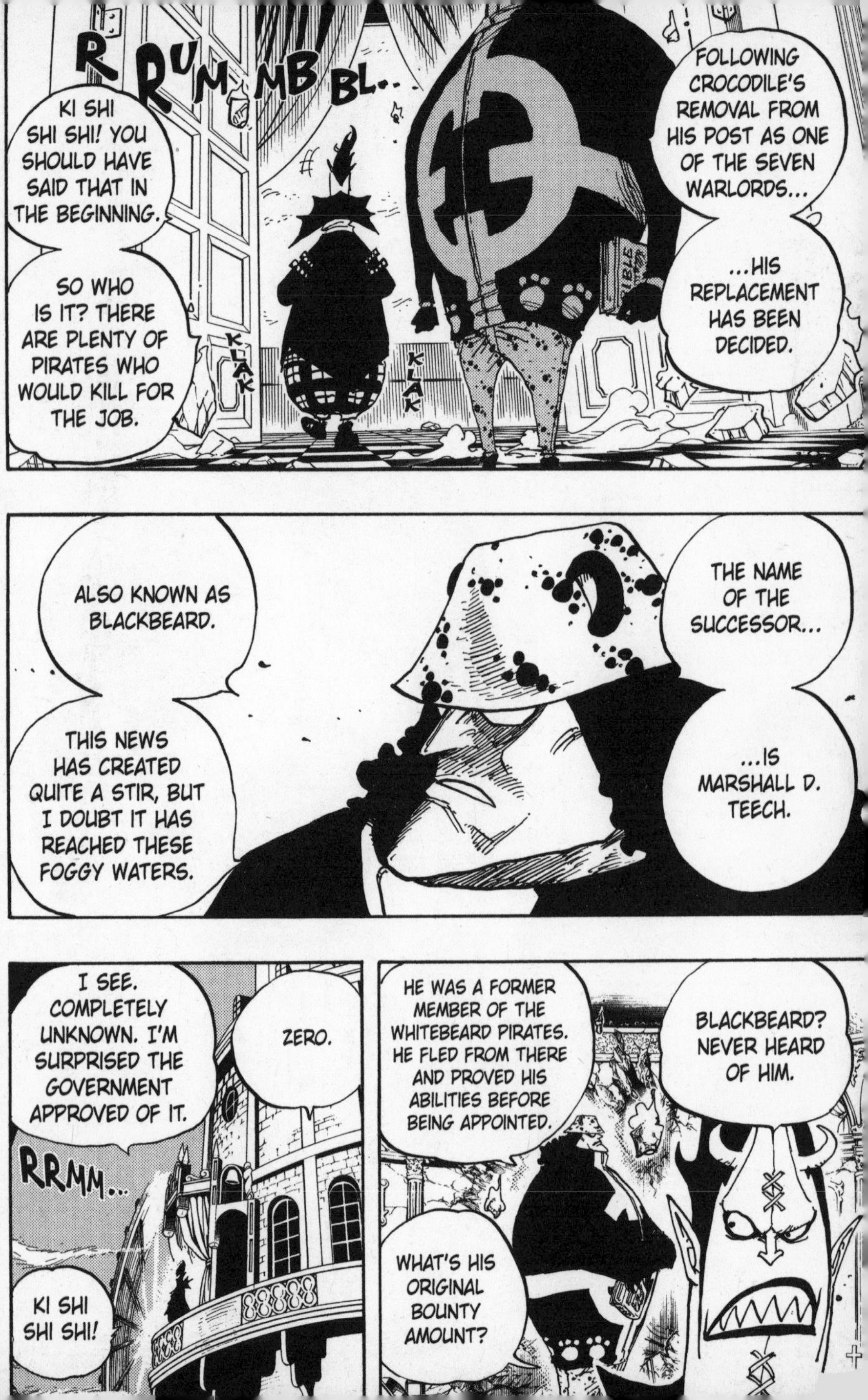
FOLLOWING CROCODILE'S REMOVAL FROM HIS POST AS ONE OF THE SEVEN WARLORDS...
...HIS REPLACEMENT HAS BEEN DECIDED.
RRUMMBBL...
KI SHI SHI SHI! YOU SHOULD HAVE SAID THAT IN THE BEGINNING.
SO WHO IS IT? THERE ARE PLENTY OF PIRATES WHO WOULD KILL FOR THE JOB.
KLAK
KLAK
THE NAME OF THE SUCCESSOR...
...IS MARSHALL D. TEECH.
ALSO KNOWN AS BLACKBEARD.
THIS NEWS HAS CREATED QUITE A STIR, BUT I DOUBT IT HAS REACHED THESE FOGGY WATERS.
BLACKBEARD? NEVER HEARD OF HIM.
HE WAS A FORMER MEMBER OF THE WHITEBEARD PIRATES. HE FLED FROM THERE AND PROVED HIS ABILITIES BEFORE BEING APPOINTED.
WHAT'S HIS ORIGINAL BOUNTY AMOUNT?
ZERO.
I SEE. COMPLETELY UNKNOWN. I'M SURPRISED THE GOVERNMENT APPROVED OF IT.
RRMM...
KI SHI SHI SHI!

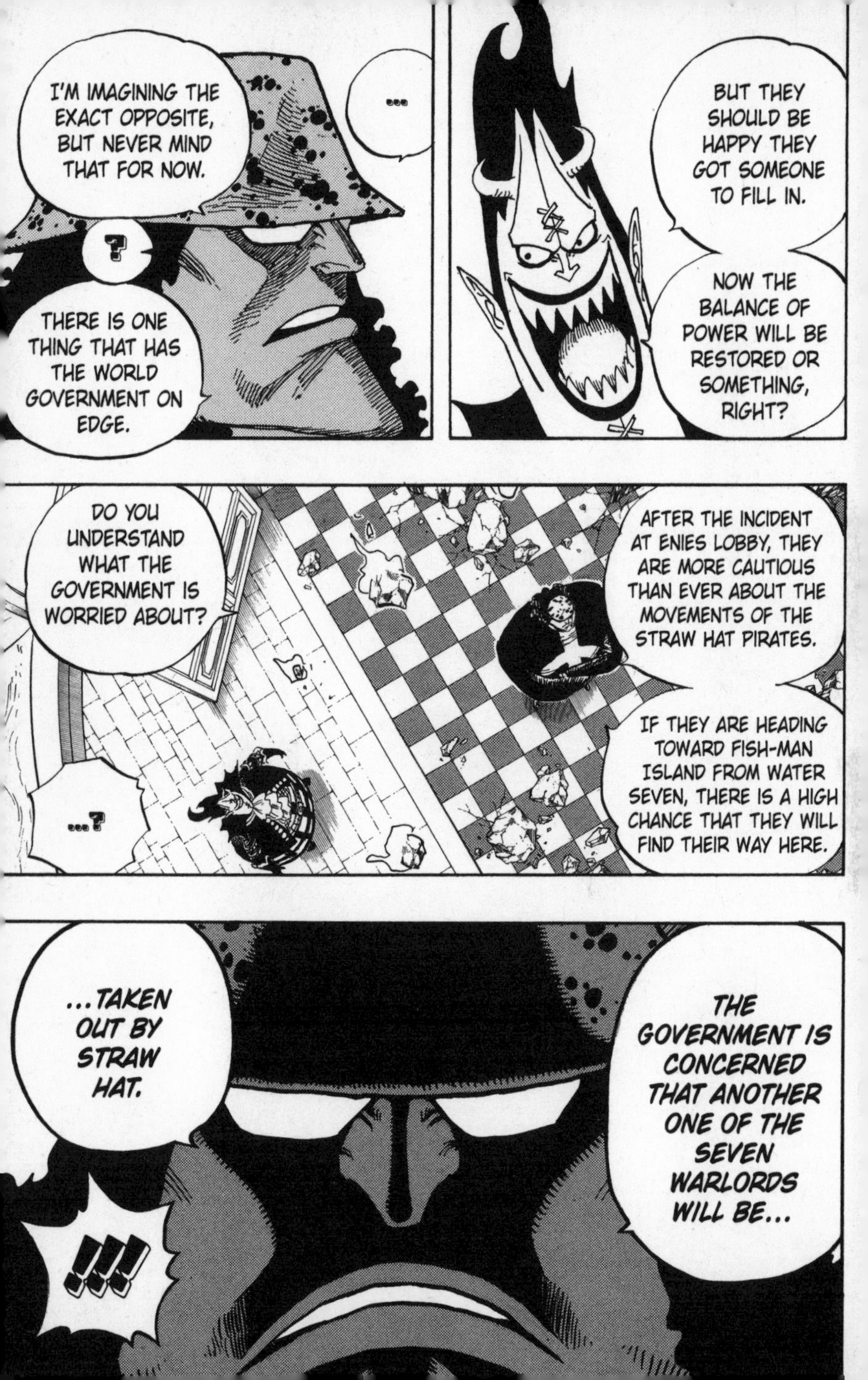
BUT THEY SHOULD BE HAPPY THEY GOT SOMEONE TO FILL IN.
NOW THE BALANCE OF POWER WILL BE RESTORED OR SOMETHING, RIGHT?
...
I'M IMAGINING THE EXACT OPPOSITE, BUT NEVER MIND THAT FOR NOW.
?
THERE IS ONE THING THAT HAS THE WORLD GOVERNMENT ON EDGE.
AFTER THE INCIDENT AT ENIES LOBBY, THEY ARE MORE CAUTIOUS THAN EVER ABOUT THE MOVEMENTS OF THE STRAW HAT PIRATES.
IF THEY ARE HEADING TOWARD FISH-MAN ISLAND FROM WATER SEVEN, THERE IS A HIGH CHANCE THAT THEY WILL FIND THEIR WAY HERE.
DO YOU UNDERSTAND WHAT THE GOVERNMENT IS WORRIED ABOUT?
...?
THE GOVERNMENT IS CONCERNED THAT ANOTHER ONE OF THE SEVEN WARLORDS WILL BE...
...TAKEN OUT BY STRAW HAT.
!!!

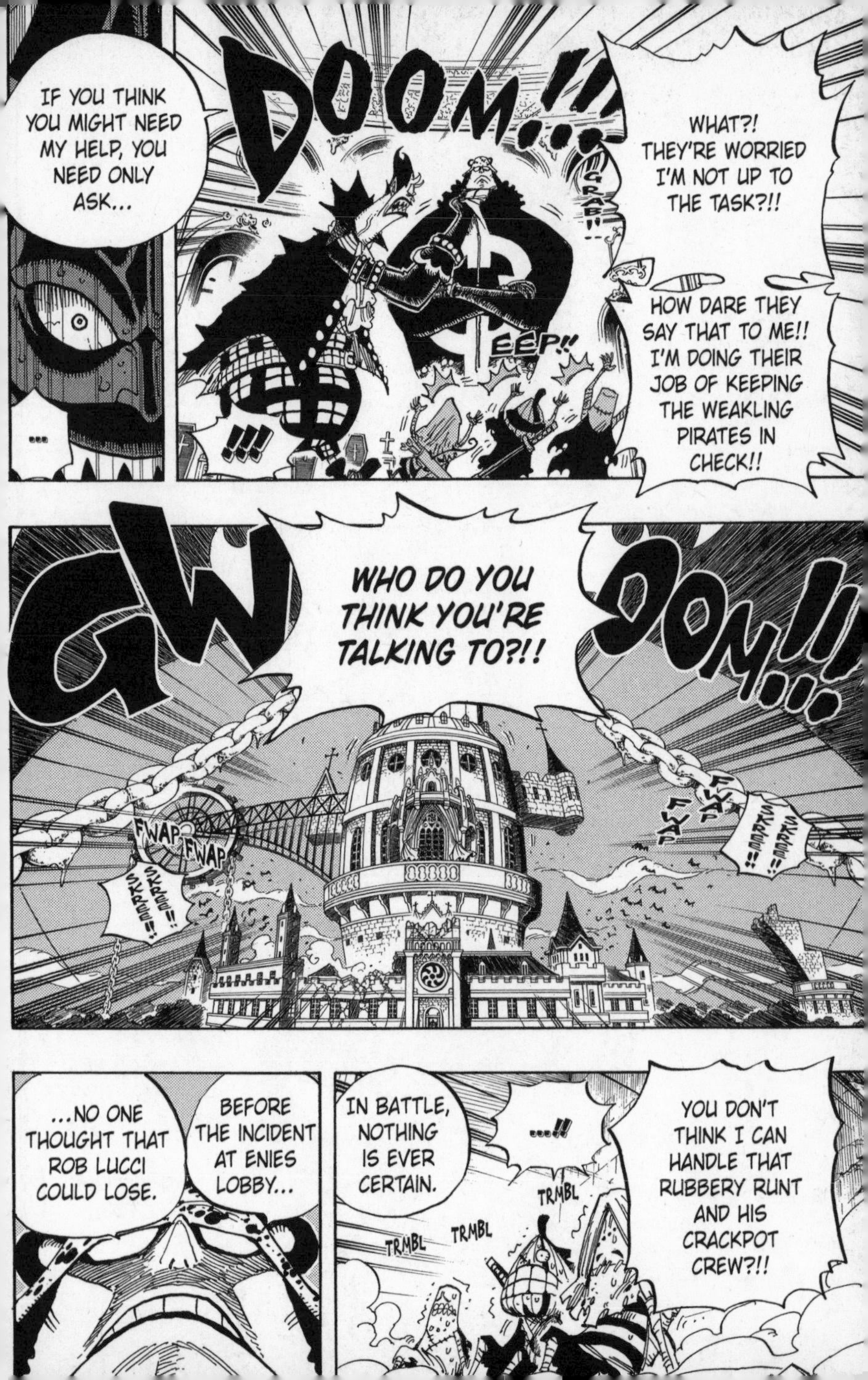
WHAT?! THEY'RE WORRIED I'M NOT UP TO THE TASK?!!
HOW DARE THEY SAY THAT TO ME!! I'M DOING THEIR JOB OF KEEPING THE WEAKLING PIRATES IN CHECK!!
DOOM...!!
GRAB!!
EEP!!
!!!
IF YOU THINK YOU MIGHT NEED MY HELP, YOU NEED ONLY ASK...
...
GW
WHO DO YOU THINK YOU'RE TALKING TO?!!
OON...!!
FWAP FWAP
SKREE!! SKREE!!
FWAP FWAP
SKREE!! SKREE!!
YOU DON'T THINK I CAN HANDLE THAT RUBBERY RUNT AND HIS CRACKPOT CREW?!!
...!!
TRMBL
TRMBL
TRMBL
IN BATTLE, NOTHING IS EVER CERTAIN.
BEFORE THE INCIDENT AT ENIES LOBBY...
...NO ONE THOUGHT THAT ROB LUCCI COULD LOSE.

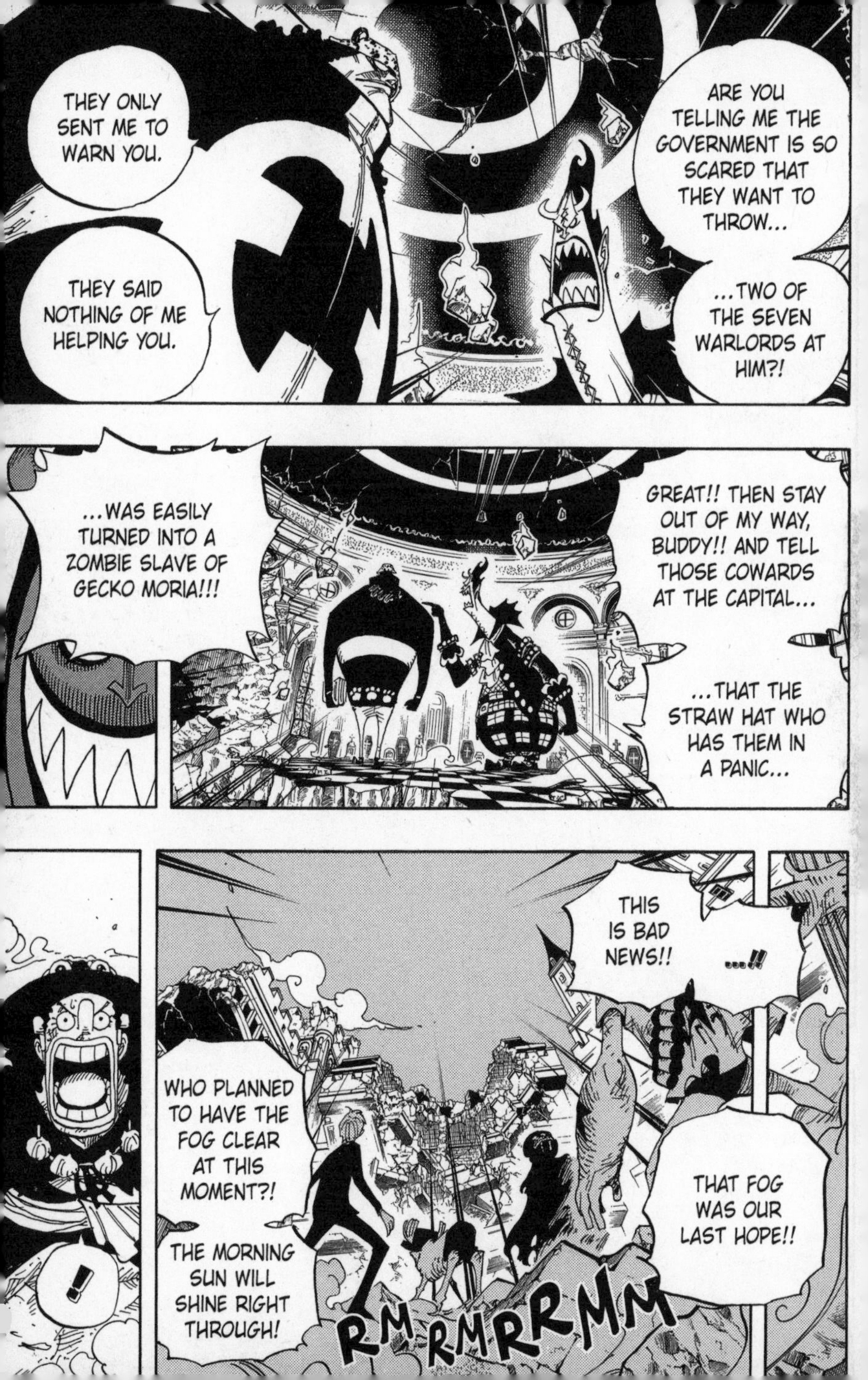
ARE YOU TELLING ME THE GOVERNMENT IS SO SCARED THAT THEY WANT TO THROW...
...TWO OF THE SEVEN WARLORDS AT HIM?!
THEY ONLY SENT ME TO WARN YOU.
THEY SAID NOTHING OF ME HELPING YOU.
GREAT!! THEN STAY OUT OF MY WAY, BUDDY!! AND TELL THOSE COWARDS AT THE CAPITAL...
...THAT THE STRAW HAT WHO HAS THEM IN A PANIC...
...WAS EASILY TURNED INTO A ZOMBIE SLAVE OF GECKO MORIA!!!
THIS IS BAD NEWS!!
...!!
THAT FOG WAS OUR LAST HOPE!!
WHO PLANNED TO HAVE THE FOG CLEAR AT THIS MOMENT?!
THE MORNING SUN WILL SHINE RIGHT THROUGH!
RMMRMRRMM
!

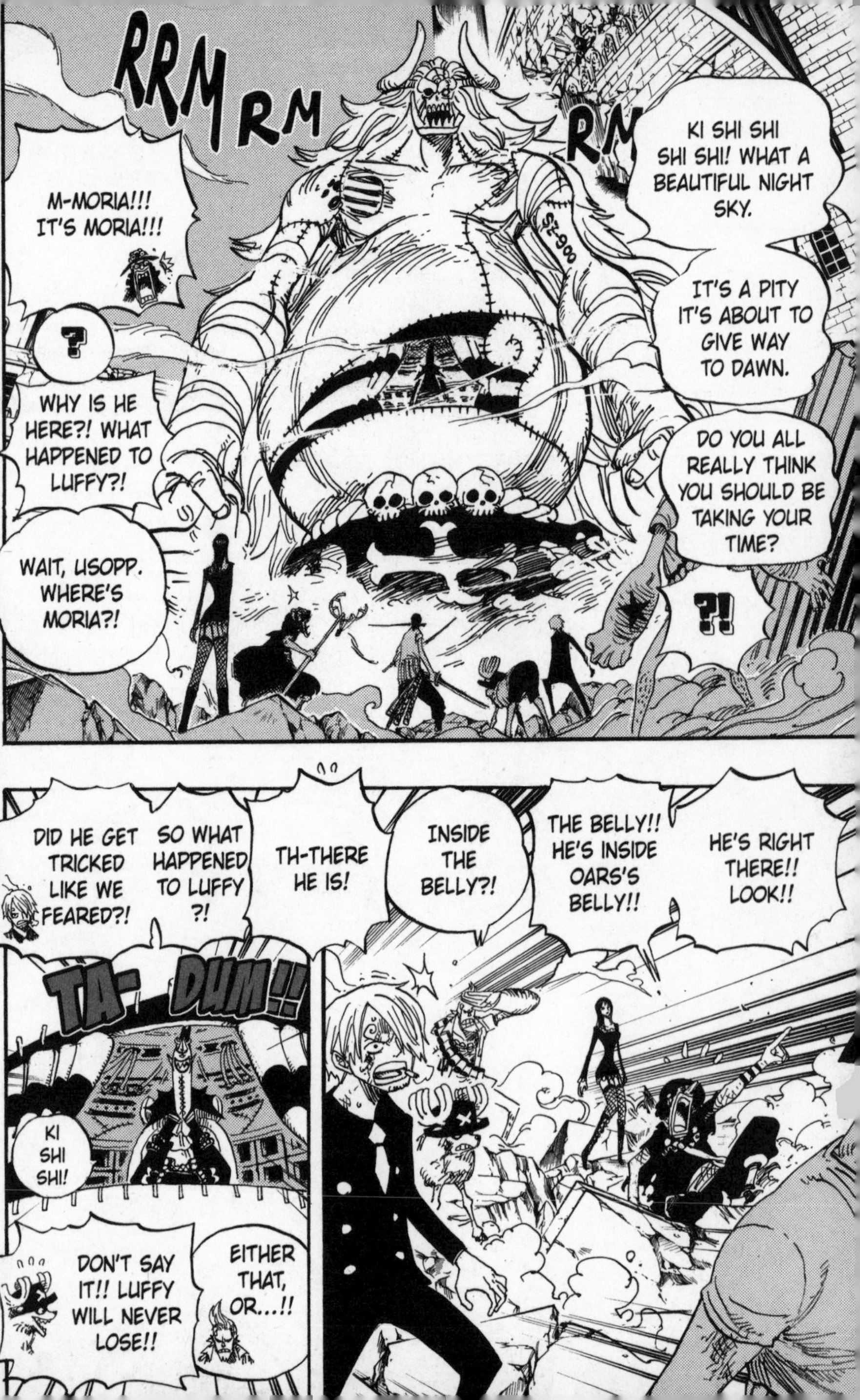
KI SHI SHI SHI SHI! WHAT A BEAUTIFUL NIGHT SKY.
RN
IT'S A PITY IT'S ABOUT TO GIVE WAY TO DAWN.
DO YOU ALL REALLY THINK YOU SHOULD BE TAKING YOUR TIME?
?!
RRM RM
M-MORIA!!! IT'S MORIA!!!
?
WHY IS HE HERE?! WHAT HAPPENED TO LUFFY?!
WAIT, USOPP. WHERE'S MORIA?!
HE'S RIGHT THERE!! LOOK!!
THE BELLY!! HE'S INSIDE OARS'S BELLY!!
INSIDE THE BELLY?!
TH-THERE HE IS!
SO WHAT HAPPENED TO LUFFY?!
DID HE GET TRICKED LIKE WE FEARED?!
TA- DUM!!
KI SHI SHI!
EITHER THAT, OR...!!
DON'T SAY IT!! LUFFY WILL NEVER LOSE!!

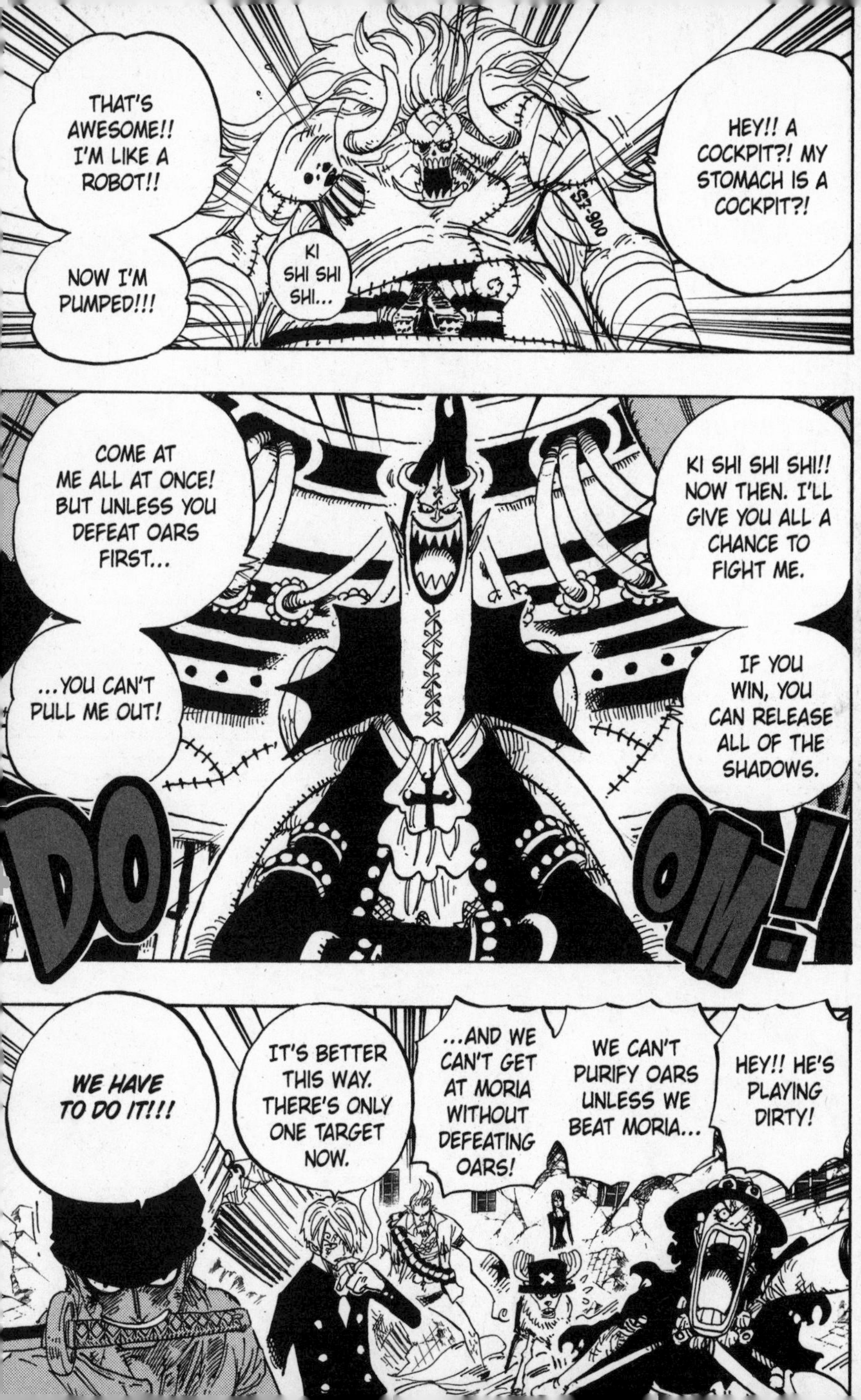
HEY!! A COCKPIT?! MY STOMACH IS A COCKPIT?!
KI SHI SHI SHI...
THAT'S AWESOME!! I'M LIKE A ROBOT!!
NOW I'M PUMPED!!!
KI SHI SHI SHI!! NOW THEN. I'LL GIVE YOU ALL A CHANCE TO FIGHT ME.
IF YOU WIN, YOU CAN RELEASE ALL OF THE SHADOWS.
COME AT ME ALL AT ONCE! BUT UNLESS YOU DEFEAT OARS FIRST...
...YOU CAN'T PULL ME OUT!
DOOM!!
HEY!! HE'S PLAYING DIRTY!
WE CAN'T PURIFY OARS UNLESS WE BEAT MORIA...
...AND WE CAN'T GET AT MORIA WITHOUT DEFEATING OARS!
IT'S BETTER THIS WAY. THERE'S ONLY ONE TARGET NOW.
WE HAVE TO DO IT!!!

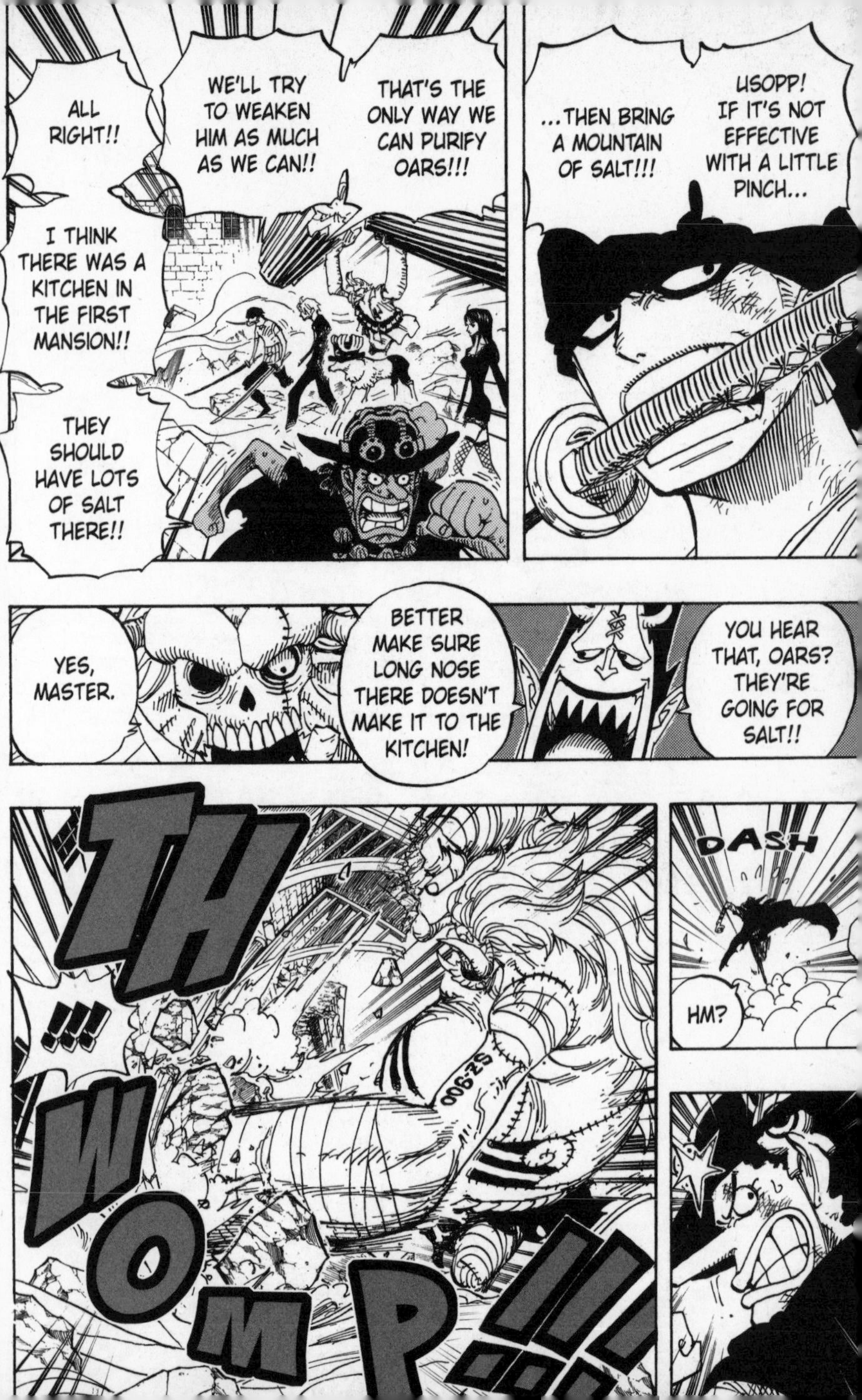
USOPP! IF IT'S NOT EFFECTIVE WITH A LITTLE PINCH...
...THEN BRING A MOUNTAIN OF SALT!!!
THAT'S THE ONLY WAY WE CAN PURIFY OARS!!!
WE'LL TRY TO WEAKEN HIM AS MUCH AS WE CAN!!
ALL RIGHT!!
I THINK THERE WAS A KITCHEN IN THE FIRST MANSION!!
THEY SHOULD HAVE LOTS OF SALT THERE!!
YOU HEAR THAT, OARS? THEY'RE GOING FOR SALT!!
BETTER MAKE SURE LONG NOSE THERE DOESN'T MAKE IT TO THE KITCHEN!
YES, MASTER.
DASH
HM?
TH!!! WOMP!!!

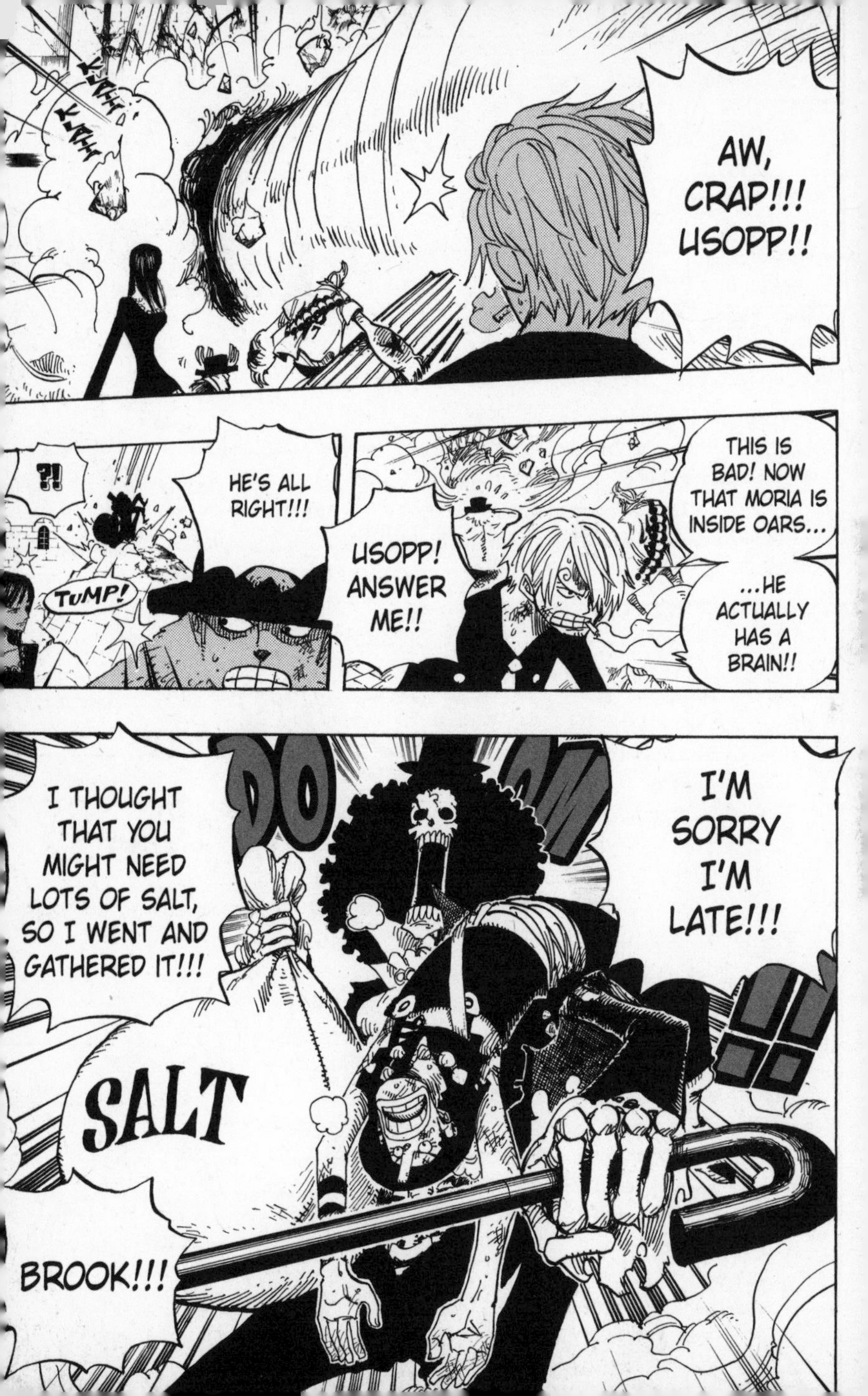
AW, CRAP!!! USOPP!!
THIS IS BAD! NOW THAT MORIA IS INSIDE OARS...
...HE ACTUALLY HAS A BRAIN!!
USOPP! ANSWER ME!!
HE'S ALL RIGHT!!!
?!
TUMP!
I'M SORRY I'M LATE!!!
I THOUGHT THAT YOU MIGHT NEED LOTS OF SALT, SO I WENT AND GATHERED IT!!!
SALT
BROOK!!!

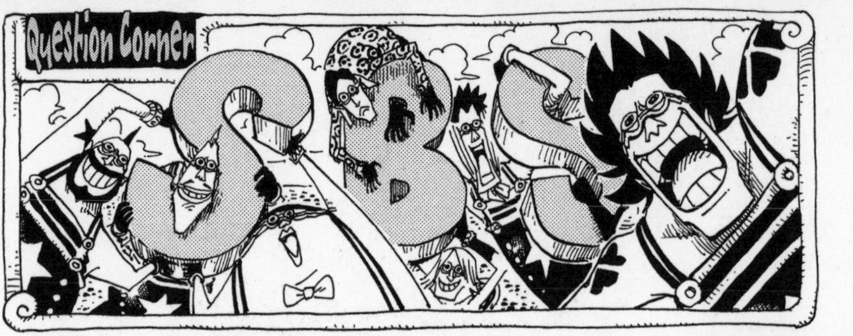
Question Corner
SBS

Q: In Chopper's movie (Miraculous Cherry Blossom in Winter), wasn't Franky cold? --Polar Bear Plunge Tani

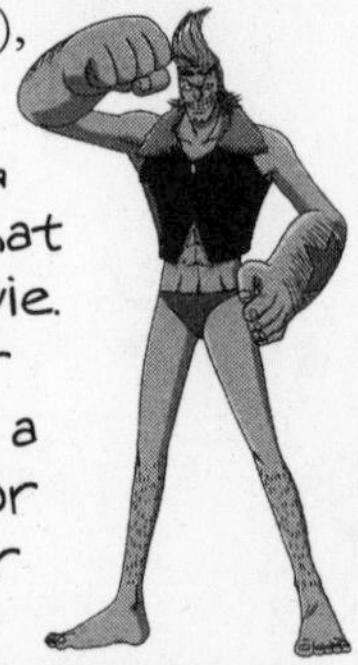

A: Hmm. You thought about that while watching the movie, right? I was also thinking about that when I saw the concept sketches for the movie. I didn't know if I should have pointed it out or just left it as is. In the end, I decided that for a guy like Franky, it doesn't matter if it's cold or not! It's about if it's weird or not! To answer you, yes, the way he looks gives me the chills.
*He may be a cyborg, but he does feel cold.

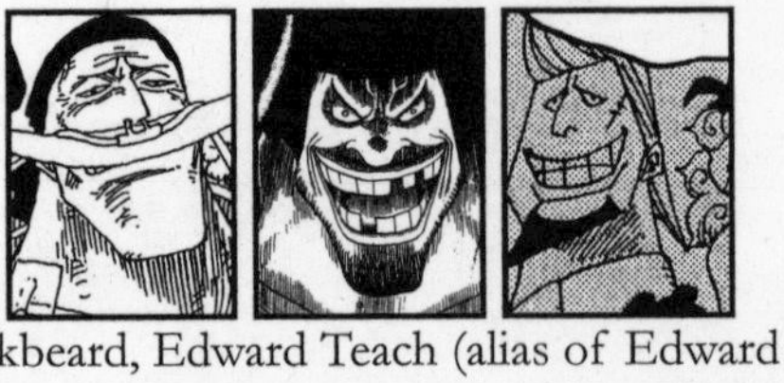

Q: I have a question! Whitebeard Edward Newgate, Blackbeard Marshall D. Teech, and 4th Squad Commander Thatch! All three of them seem to be based on the 18th century pirate of the Caribbean, Blackbeard, Edward Teach (alias of Edward Thatch). Is that true? Please tell me more about that person. --G-On King

A: Yes, all three of them are inspired by him. Whitebeard and Thatch only have their names based on him, but the Blackbeard in this comic is actually modeled after the real Blackbeard. The real Blackbeard had a lot of names. One of them is Thatch. Others include Drummond and Thache. He braided his long black beard, had lots of smoking match cords hanging from his hat, carried six pistols and three swords, all of which made people say that he looked like the devil. To show who was boss, he would sometimes shoot his own crew-mates without warning. There are countless stories like that. There are legends that his hidden treasure still hasn't been found. Now's your chance to find it!

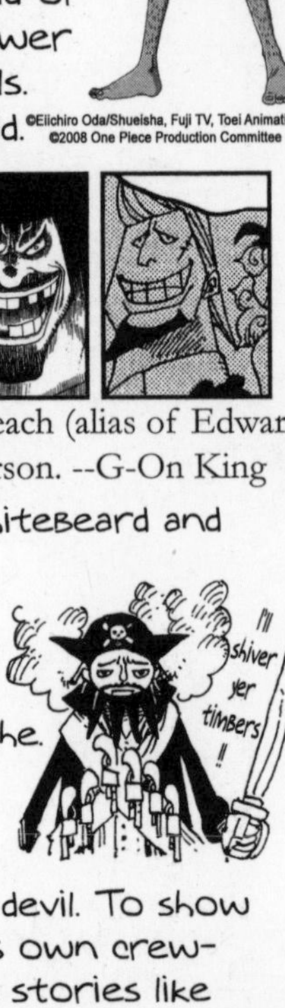
I'll shiver yer timbers!!

Chapter 475:
PIRATES OF THE FOREST

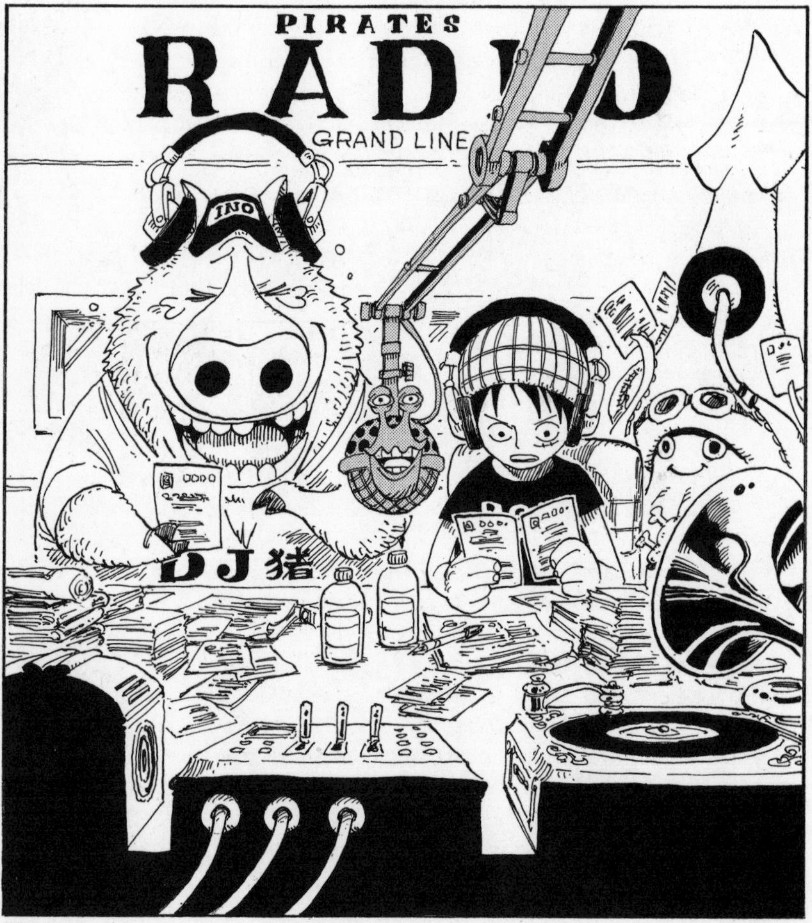
PIRATES
GRAND LINE
INO
DJ 猪

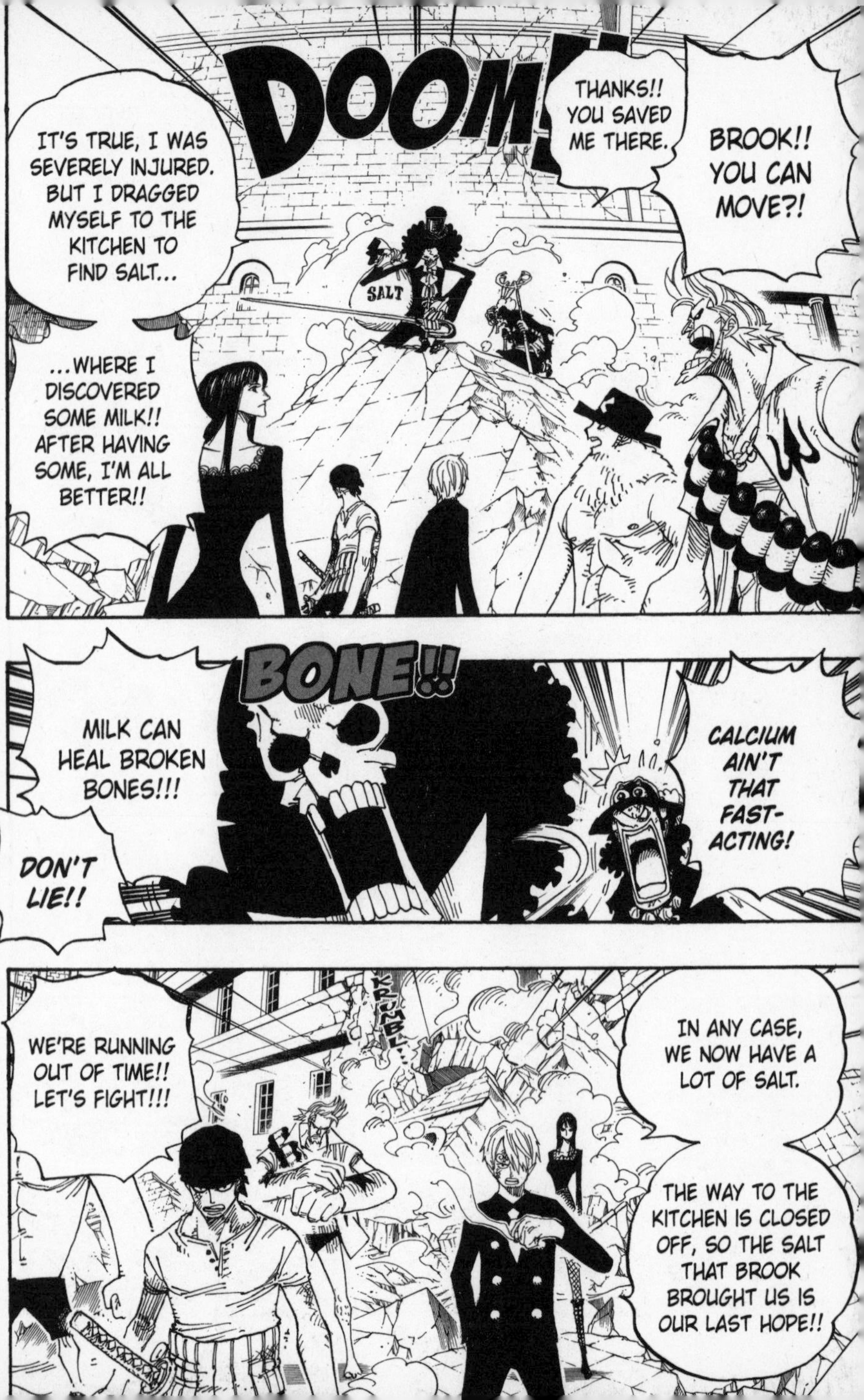
BROOK!! YOU CAN MOVE?!
THANKS!! YOU SAVED ME THERE.
DOOM!
IT'S TRUE, I WAS SEVERELY INJURED. BUT I DRAGGED MYSELF TO THE KITCHEN TO FIND SALT...
SALT
...WHERE I DISCOVERED SOME MILK!! AFTER HAVING SOME, I'M ALL BETTER!!
BONE!!
MILK CAN HEAL BROKEN BONES!!!
CALCIUM AIN'T THAT FAST-ACTING!
DON'T LIE!!
IN ANY CASE, WE NOW HAVE A LOT OF SALT.
THE WAY TO THE KITCHEN IS CLOSED OFF, SO THE SALT THAT BROOK BROUGHT US IS OUR LAST HOPE!!
KRUMBL...
WE'RE RUNNING OUT OF TIME!! LET'S FIGHT!!!

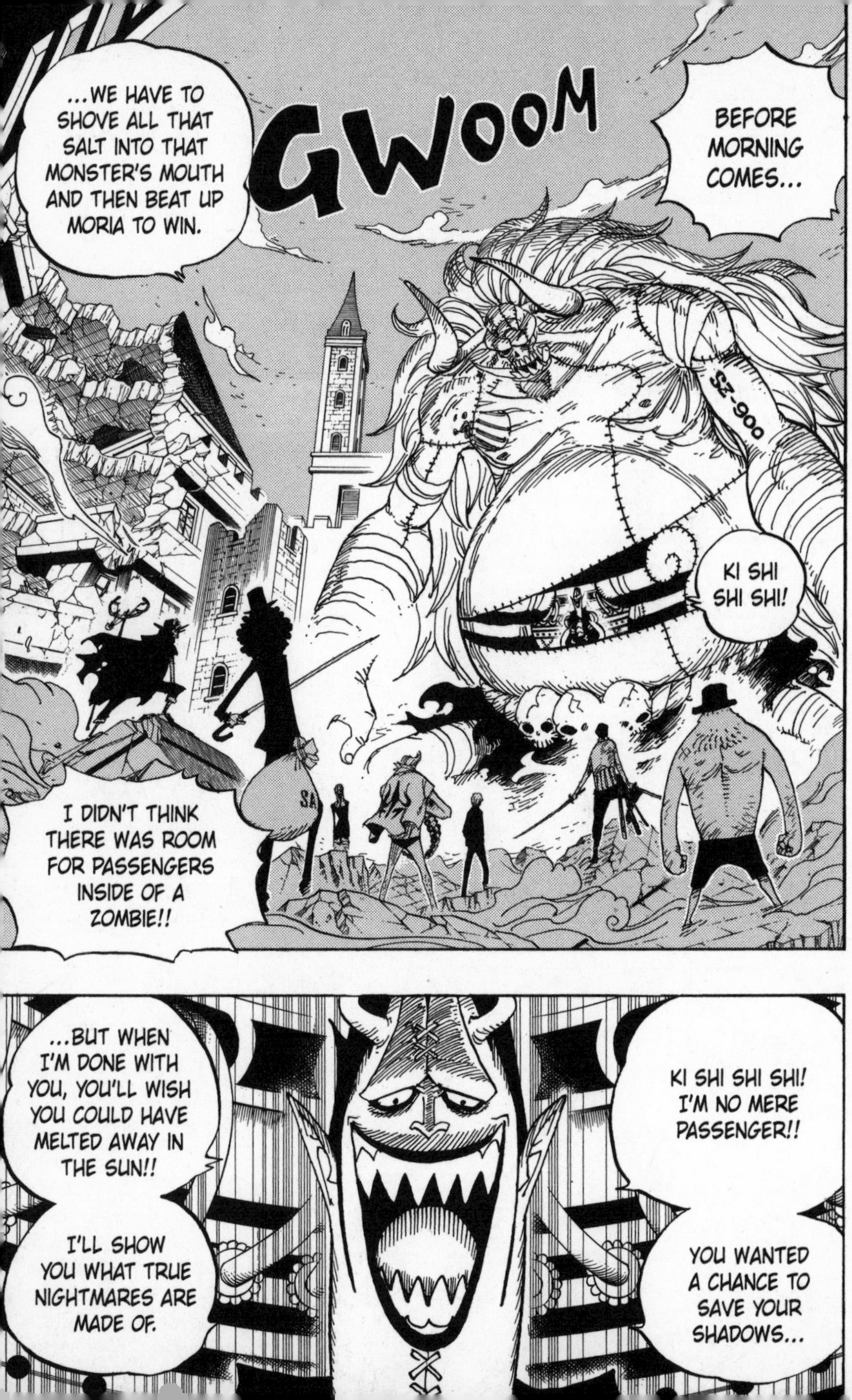
BEFORE MORNING COMES...
GWOOM
...WE HAVE TO SHOVE ALL THAT SALT INTO THAT MONSTER'S MOUTH AND THEN BEAT UP MORIA TO WIN.
KI SHI SHI SHI!
I DIDN'T THINK THERE WAS ROOM FOR PASSENGERS INSIDE OF A ZOMBIE!!
KI SHI SHI SHI! I'M NO MERE PASSENGER!!
YOU WANTED A CHANCE TO SAVE YOUR SHADOWS...
...BUT WHEN I'M DONE WITH YOU, YOU'LL WISH YOU COULD HAVE MELTED AWAY IN THE SUN!!
I'LL SHOW YOU WHAT TRUE NIGHTMARES ARE MADE OF.

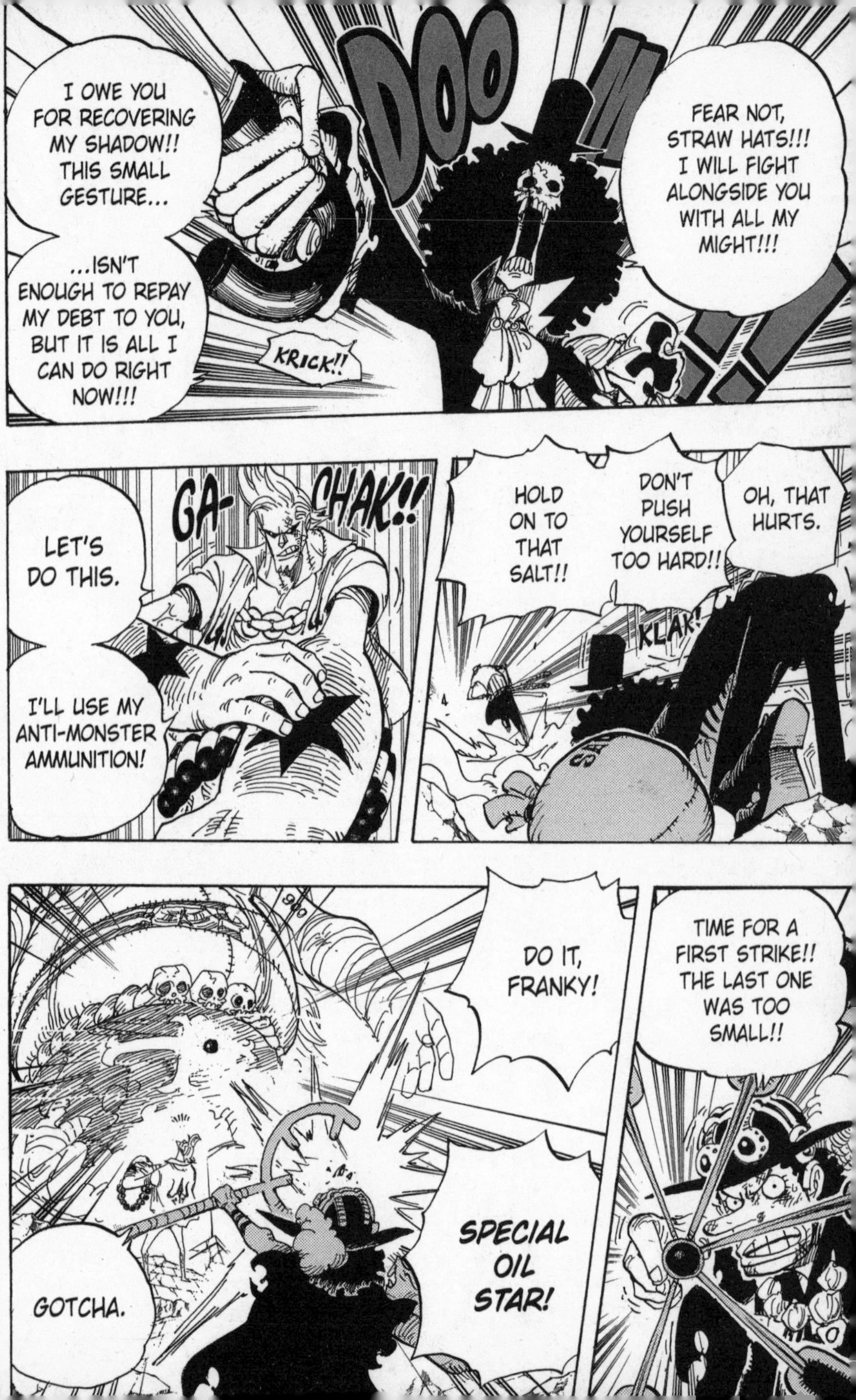
FEAR NOT, STRAW HATS!!! I WILL FIGHT ALONGSIDE YOU WITH ALL MY MIGHT!!!
DOOM
I OWE YOU FOR RECOVERING MY SHADOW!! THIS SMALL GESTURE...
...ISN'T ENOUGH TO REPAY MY DEBT TO YOU, BUT IT IS ALL I CAN DO RIGHT NOW!!!
KRICK!!
OH, THAT HURTS.
DON'T PUSH YOURSELF TOO HARD!!
HOLD ON TO THAT SALT!!
KLAK!
GA-CHAK!!
LET'S DO THIS.
I'LL USE MY ANTI-MONSTER AMMUNITION!
TIME FOR A FIRST STRIKE!! THE LAST ONE WAS TOO SMALL!!
DO IT, FRANKY!
SPECIAL OIL STAR!
GOTCHA.

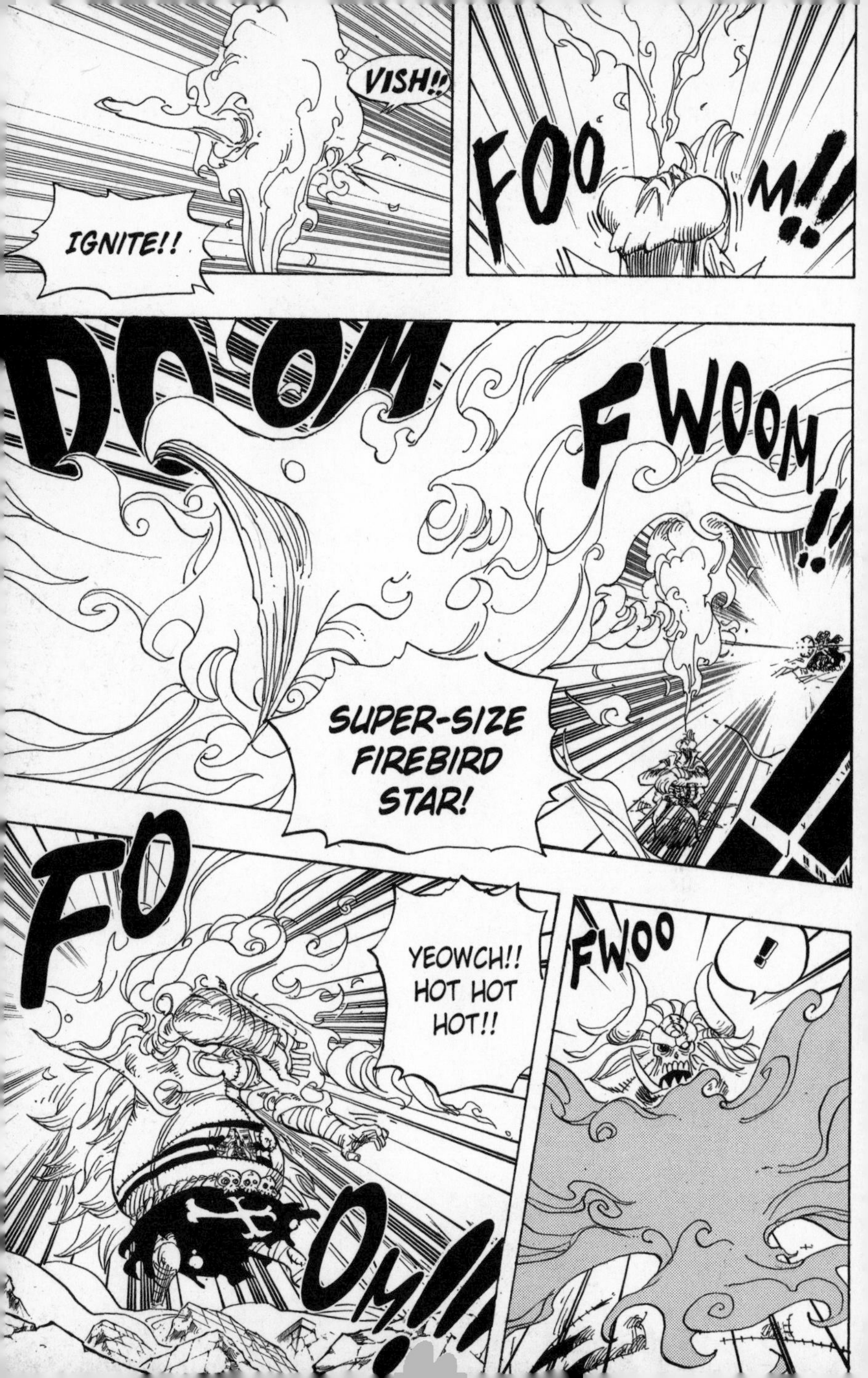
FOO M!!
VISH!!
IGNITE!!
FWOOM!!
DOOM
SUPER-SIZE FIREBIRD STAR!
FWOO !
FO OM!!!
YEOWCH!! HOT HOT HOT!!

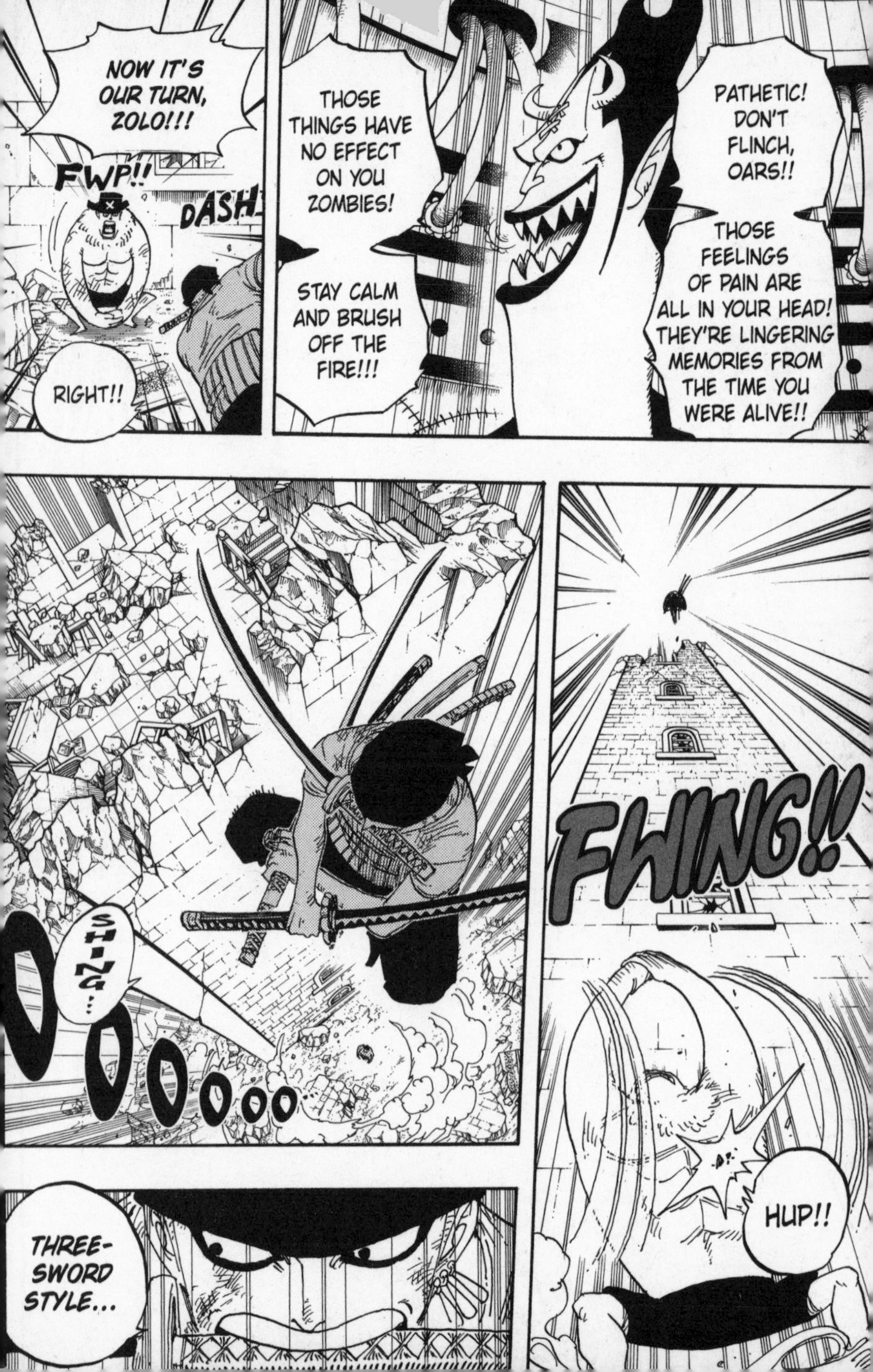
PATHETIC! DON'T FLINCH, OARS!!
THOSE FEELINGS OF PAIN ARE ALL IN YOUR HEAD! THEY'RE LINGERING MEMORIES FROM THE TIME YOU WERE ALIVE!!
THOSE THINGS HAVE NO EFFECT ON YOU ZOMBIES!
STAY CALM AND BRUSH OFF THE FIRE!!!
NOW IT'S OUR TURN, ZOLO!!!
FWP!!
DASH
RIGHT!!
FWING!!
HUP!!
SHING...
THREE-SWORD STYLE...

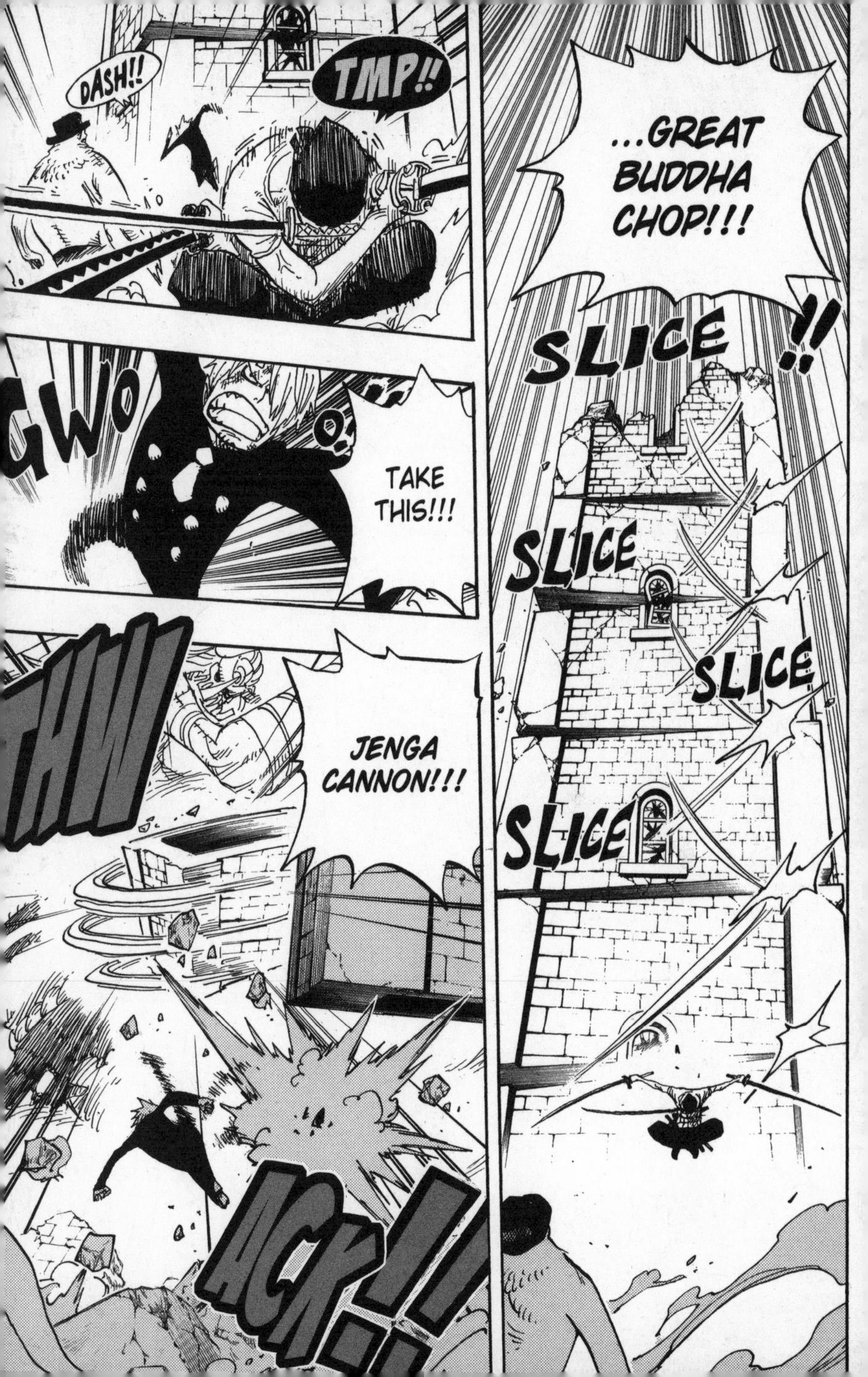
...GREAT BUDDHA CHOP!!!
SLICE!!
SLICE
SLICE
SLICE
TMP!!
DASH!!
GWO
TAKE THIS!!!
THW
JENGA CANNON!!!
ACK!!

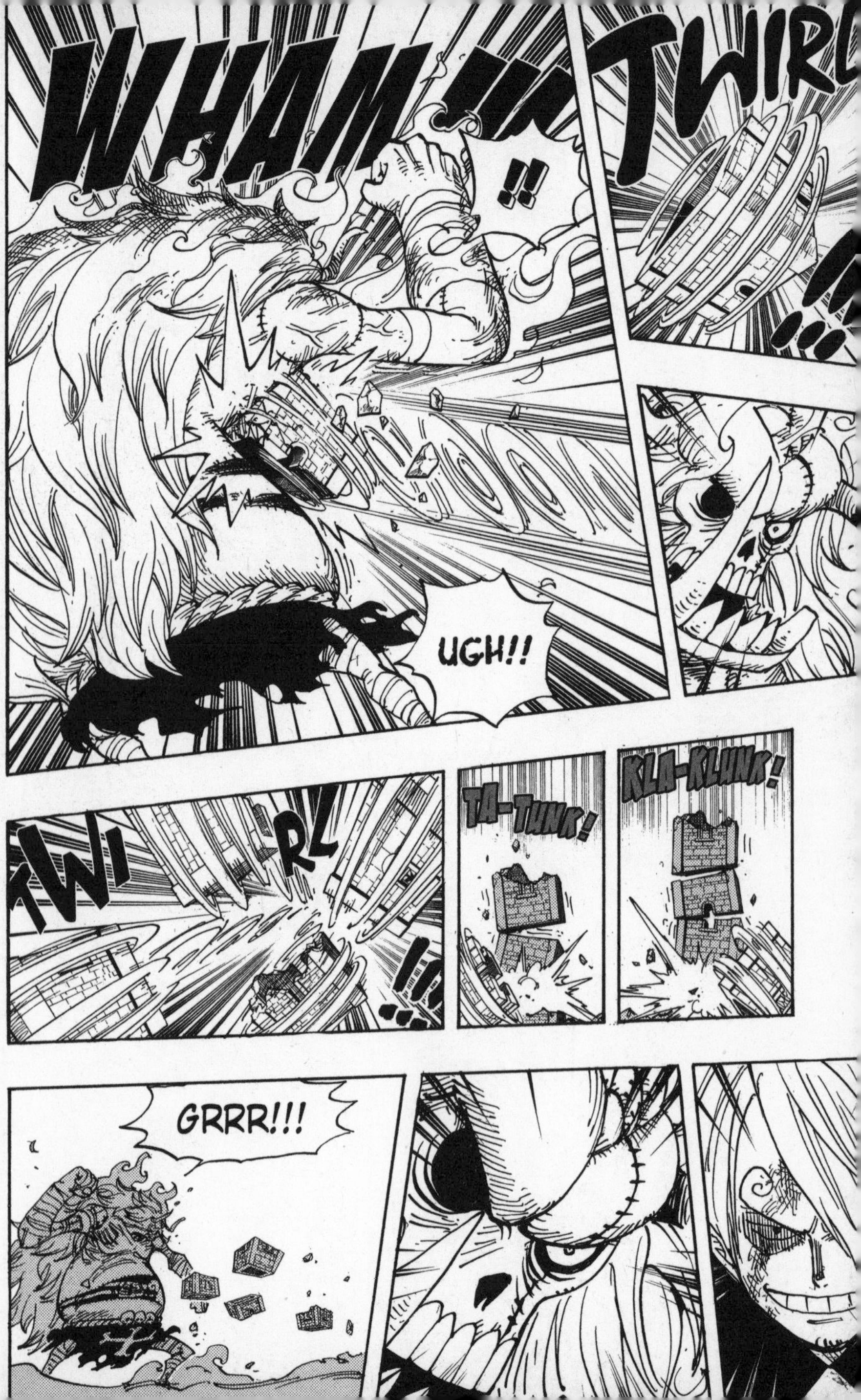
TWIRL
WHAM!!
UGH!!
KLA-KLUNK!
TA-TUNK!
TWIRL
GRRR!!!

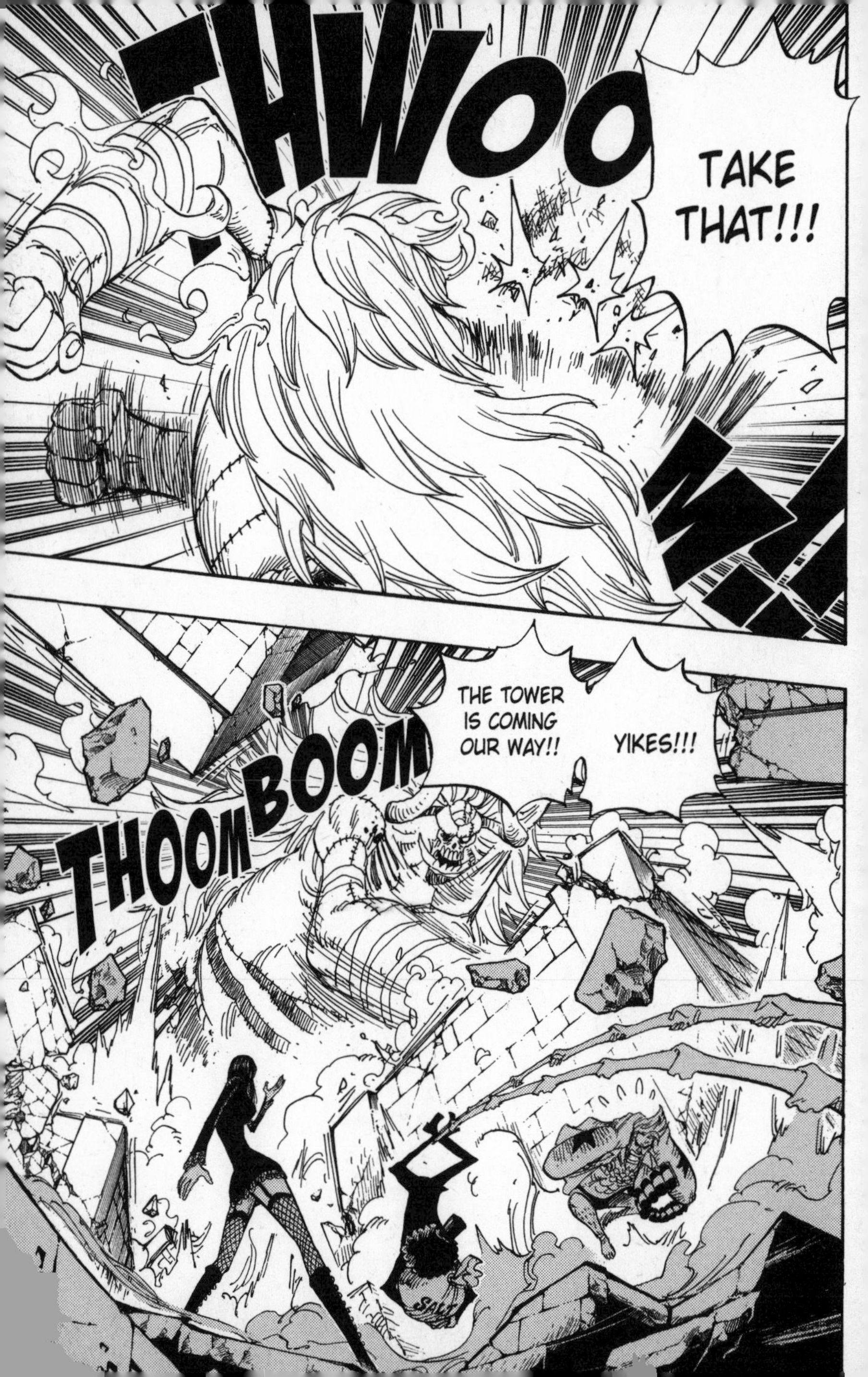
THWOO
TAKE THAT!!!
YIKES!!!
THE TOWER IS COMING OUR WAY!!
THOOMBOOM

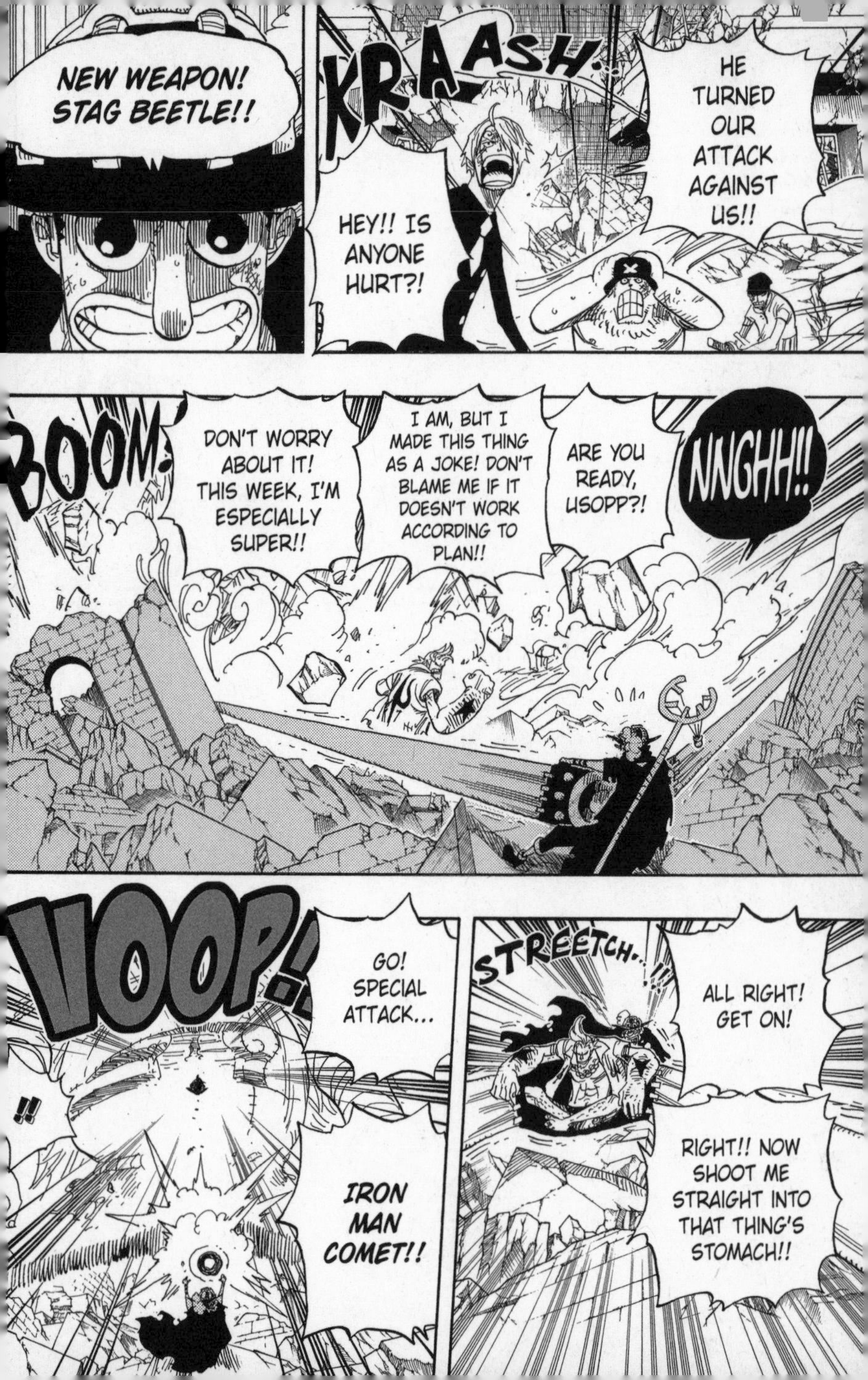
HE TURNED OUR ATTACK AGAINST US!!
KRAASH
HEY!! IS ANYONE HURT?!
NEW WEAPON! STAG BEETLE!!
NNGHH!!
ARE YOU READY, USOPP?!
I AM, BUT I MADE THIS THING AS A JOKE! DON'T BLAME ME IF IT DOESN'T WORK ACCORDING TO PLAN!!
DON'T WORRY ABOUT IT! THIS WEEK, I'M ESPECIALLY SUPER!!
BOOM
ALL RIGHT! GET ON!
STREETCH
RIGHT!! NOW SHOOT ME STRAIGHT INTO THAT THING'S STOMACH!!
VOOP
GO! SPECIAL ATTACK...
IRON MAN COMET!!

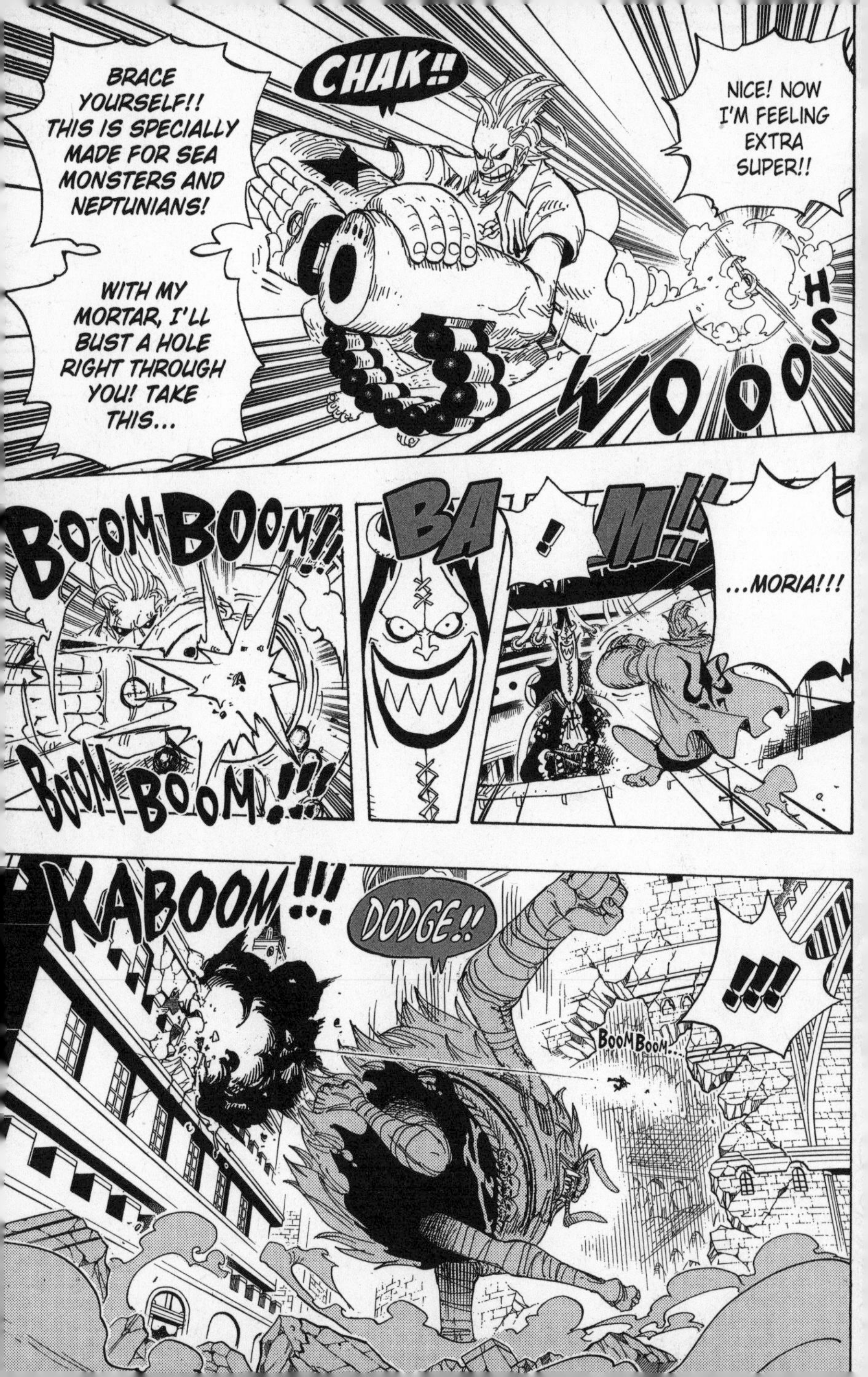

NICE! NOW I'M FEELING EXTRA SUPER!!
CHAK!!
BRACE YOURSELF!! THIS IS SPECIALLY MADE FOR SEA MONSTERS AND NEPTUNIANS!
WOOOSH
WITH MY MORTAR, I'LL BUST A HOLE RIGHT THROUGH YOU! TAKE THIS...
...MORIA!!!
BAM!!
BOOMBOOM!!
BOOM BOOM!!!
!!!
BOOMBOOM...
DODGE!!
KABOOM!!!

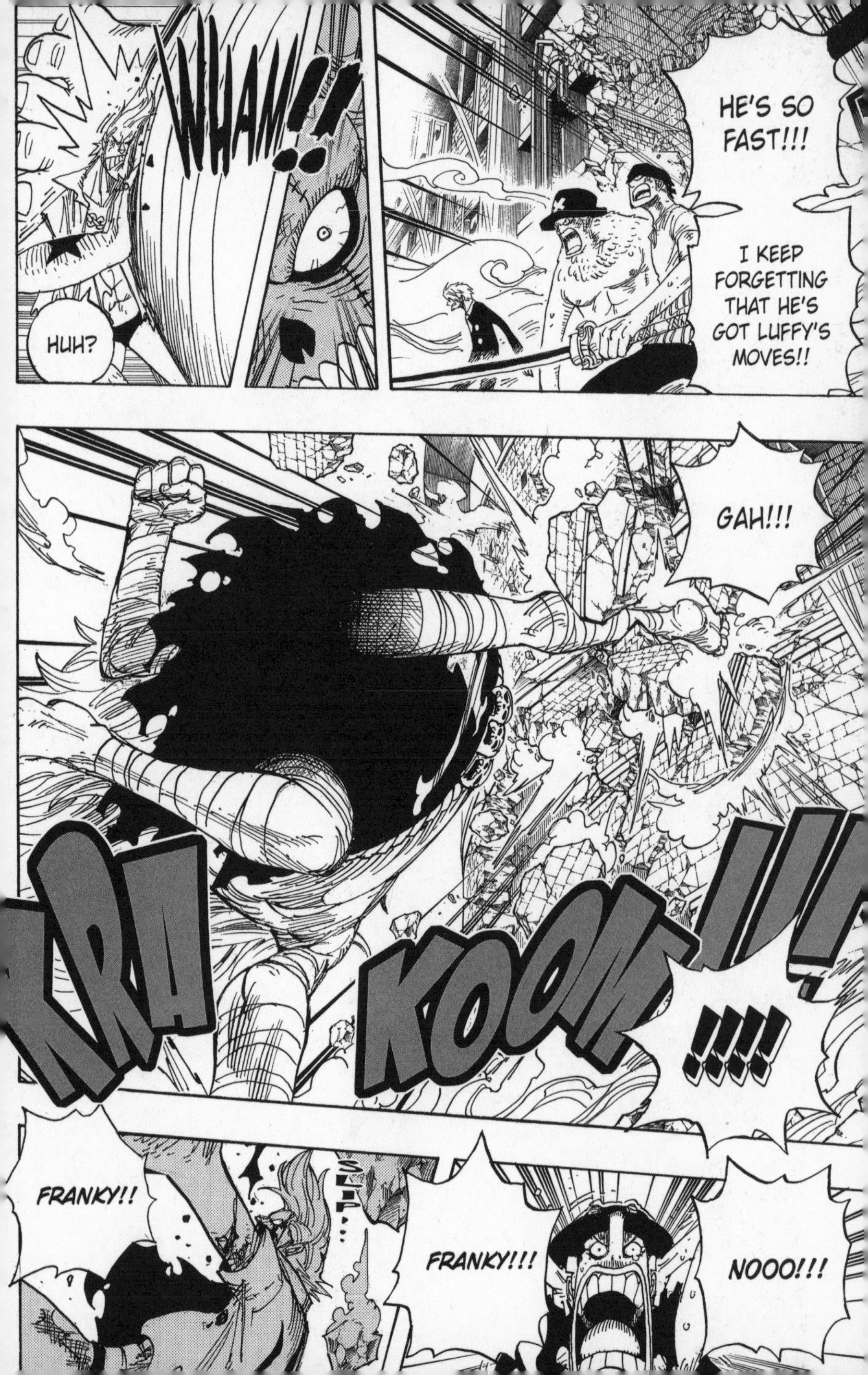

HE'S SO FAST!!!
I KEEP FORGETTING THAT HE'S GOT LUFFY'S MOVES!!
WHAM!!
HUH?
GAH!!!
KRAKOOM!!!!
NOOO!!!
FRANKY!!!
SLIP...
FRANKY!!

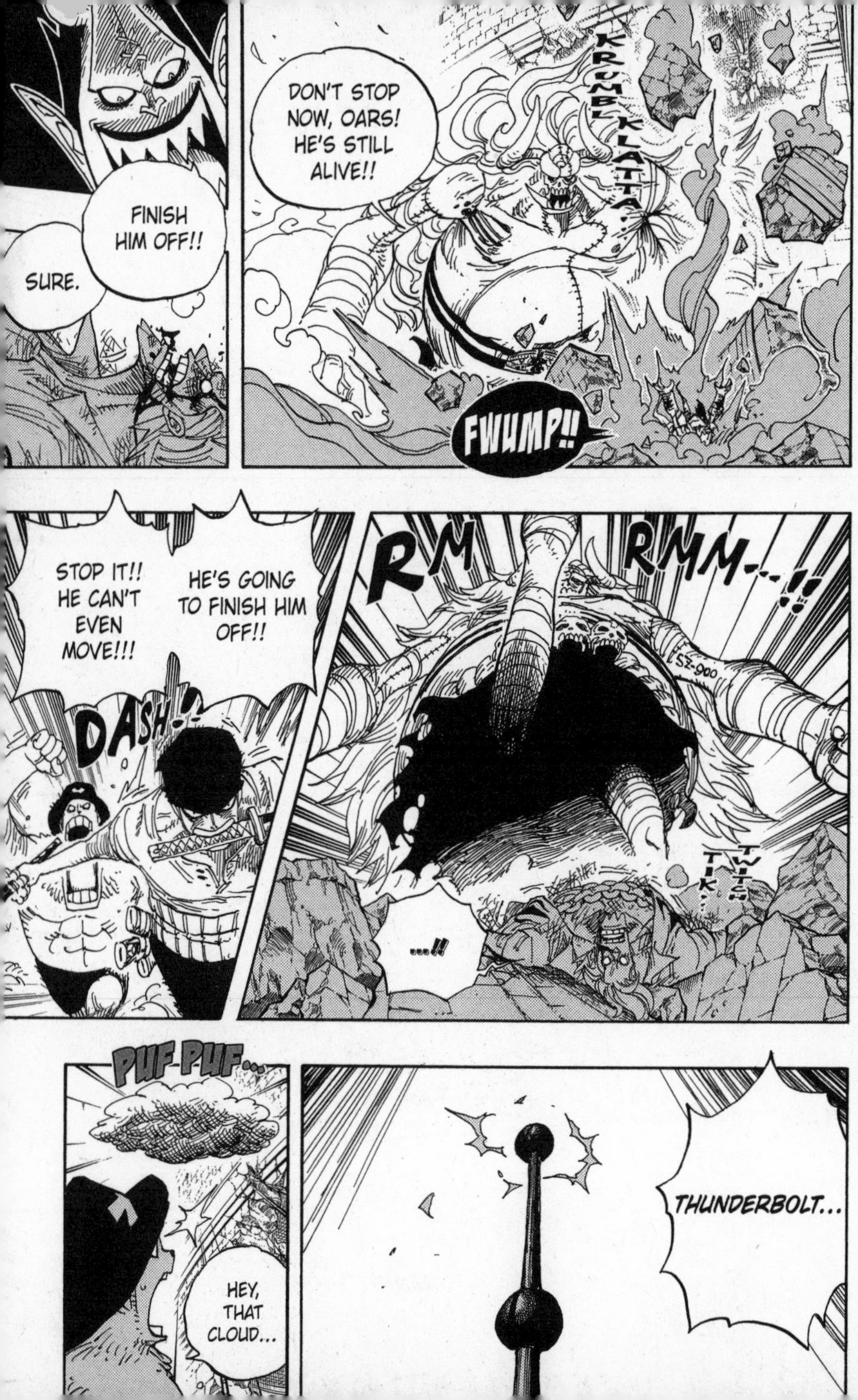
DON'T STOP NOW, OARS! HE'S STILL ALIVE!!
KRUMBL KLATTA
FWUMP!!
FINISH HIM OFF!!
SURE.
RM RMM...!!
TWITCH
TIK...
...!!
HE'S GOING TO FINISH HIM OFF!!
STOP IT!! HE CAN'T EVEN MOVE!!!
DASH!!
THUNDERBOLT...
PUF-PUF...
HEY, THAT CLOUD...

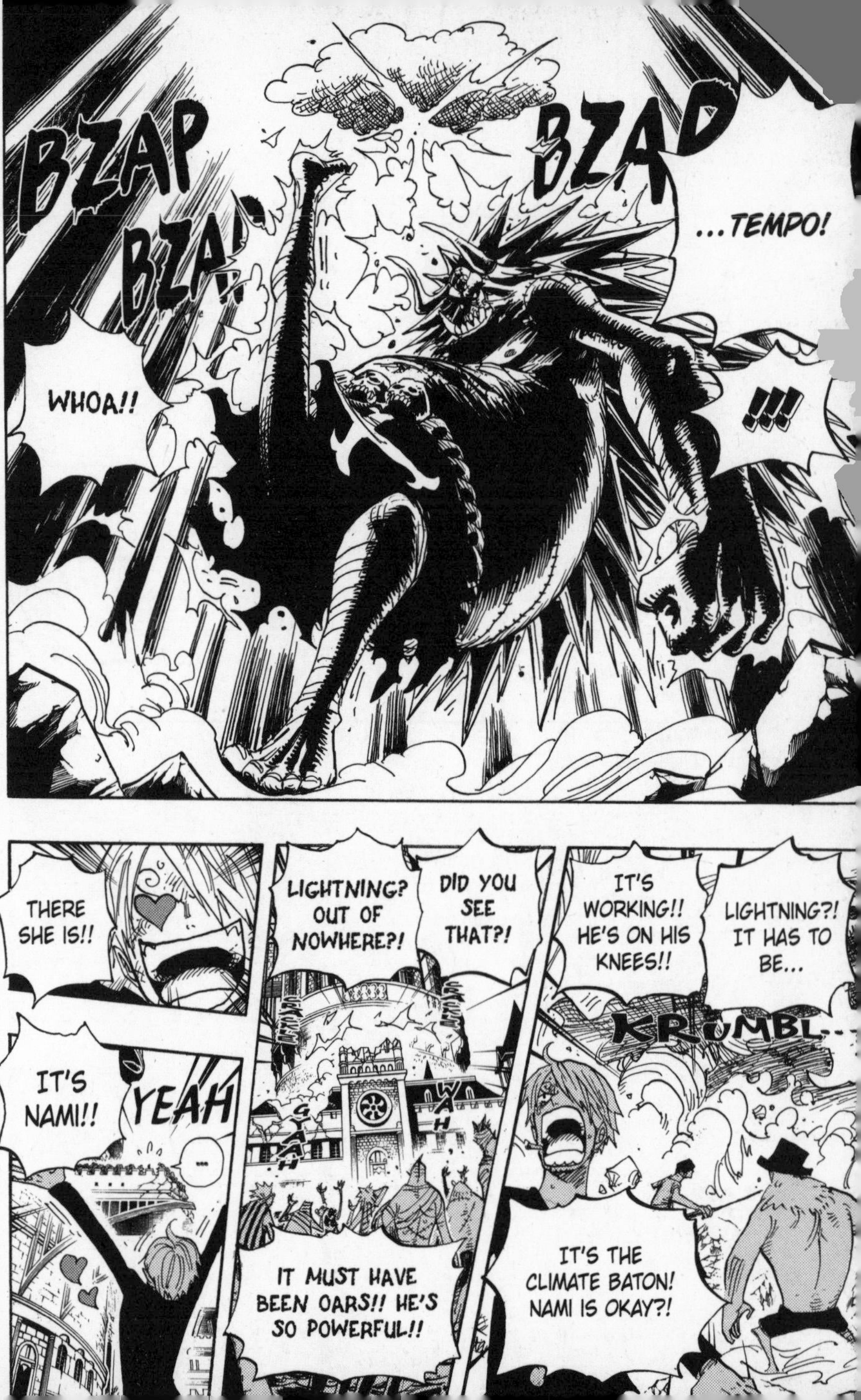
BZAD
...TEMPO!
!!!
BZAP
BZA!!
WHOA!!
LIGHTNING?! IT HAS TO BE...
IT'S WORKING!! HE'S ON HIS KNEES!!
KRUMBL...
IT'S THE CLIMATE BATON! NAMI IS OKAY?!
DID YOU SEE THAT?!
LIGHTNING? OUT OF NOWHERE?!
IT MUST HAVE BEEN OARS!! HE'S SO POWERFUL!!
THERE SHE IS!!
IT'S NAMI!!
YEAH
...

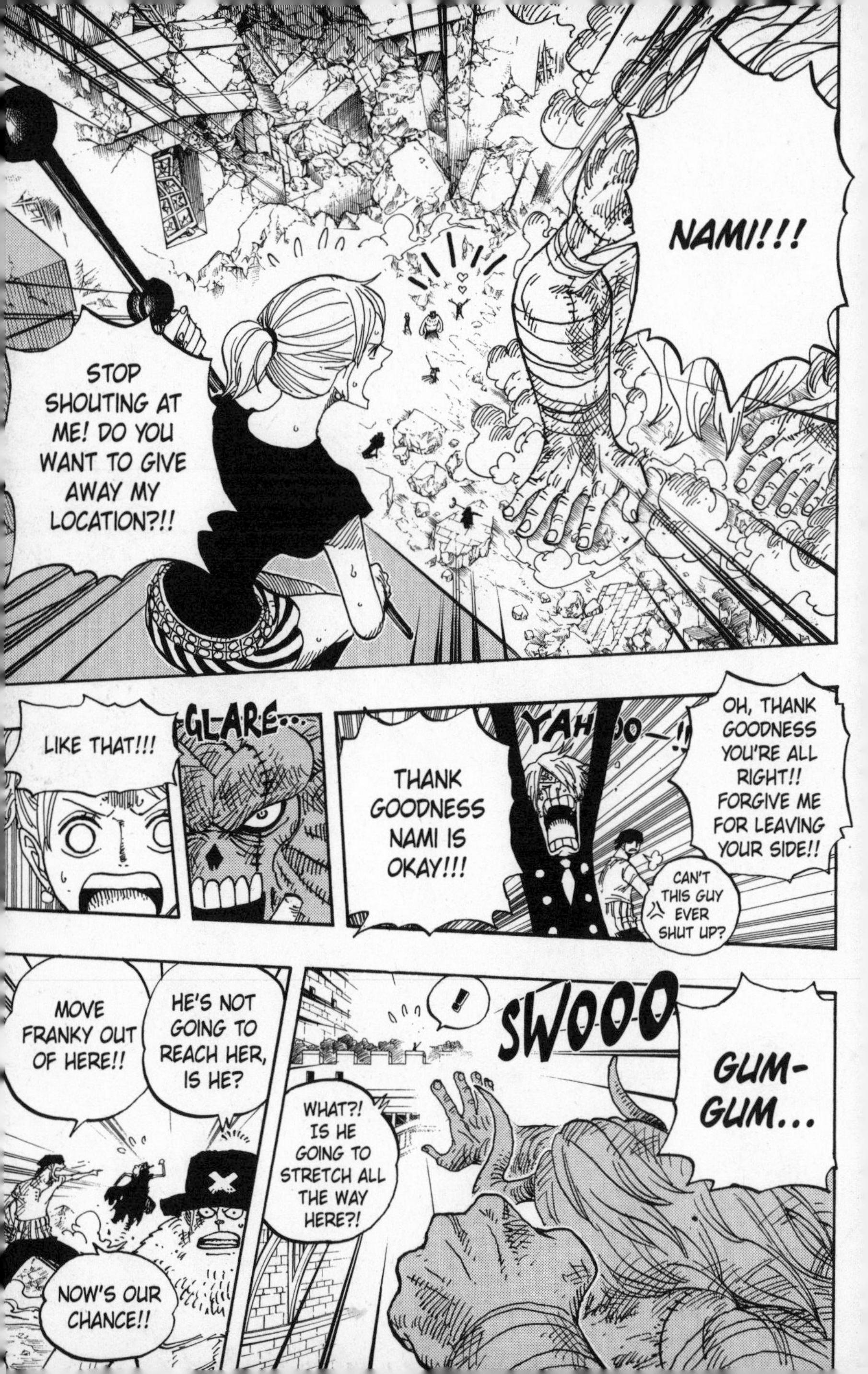
NAMI!!!
STOP SHOUTING AT ME! DO YOU WANT TO GIVE AWAY MY LOCATION?!!
OH, THANK GOODNESS YOU'RE ALL RIGHT!! FORGIVE ME FOR LEAVING YOUR SIDE!!
CAN'T THIS GUY EVER SHUT UP?
YAH OO—!!
THANK GOODNESS NAMI IS OKAY!!!
GLARE...
LIKE THAT!!!
GUM-GUM...
SWOOO
!
WHAT?! IS HE GOING TO STRETCH ALL THE WAY HERE?!
HE'S NOT GOING TO REACH HER, IS HE?
MOVE FRANKY OUT OF HERE!!
NOW'S OUR CHANCE!!

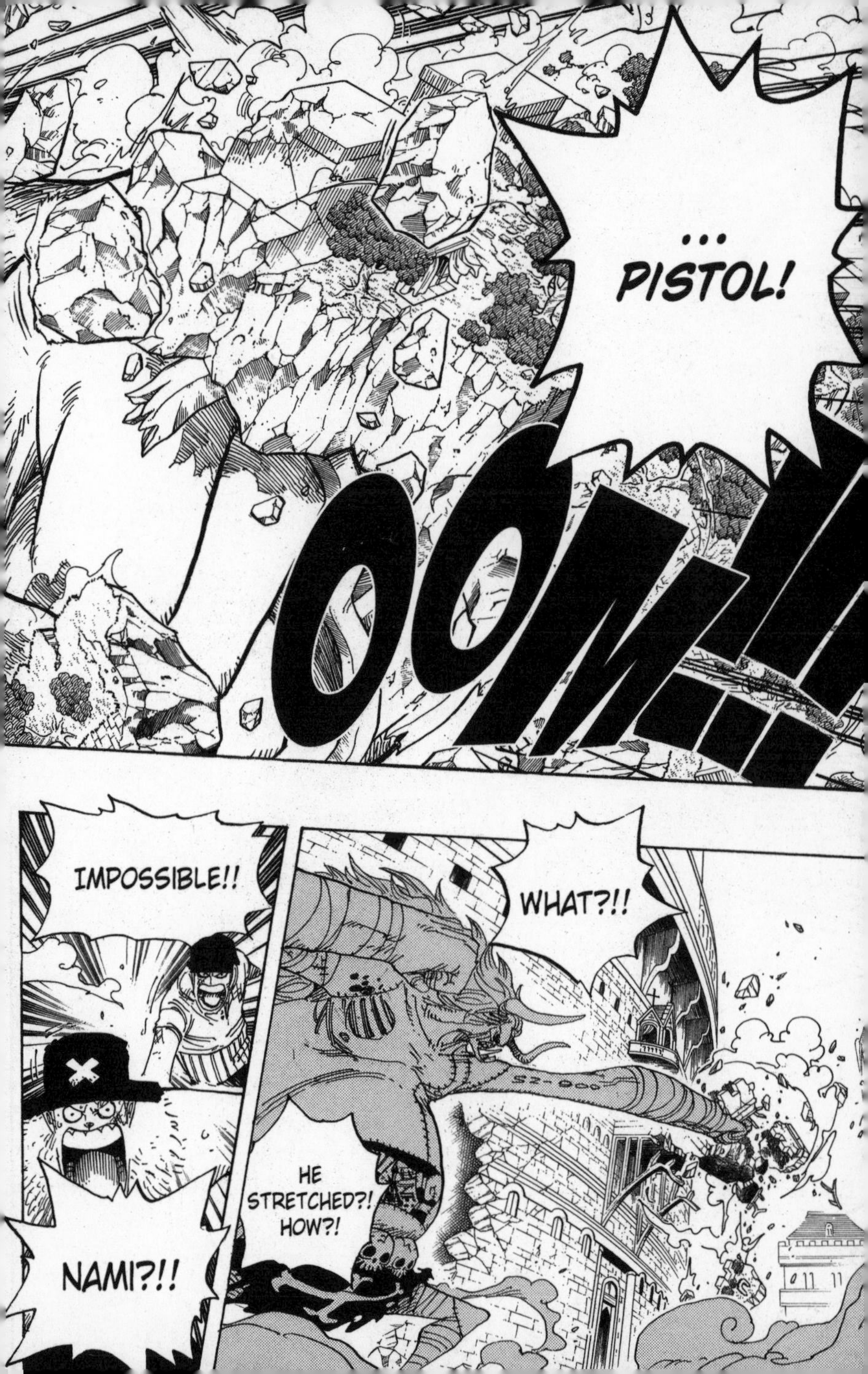
... PISTOL!
WHAT?!!
HE STRETCHED?! HOW?!
IMPOSSIBLE!!
NAMI?!!

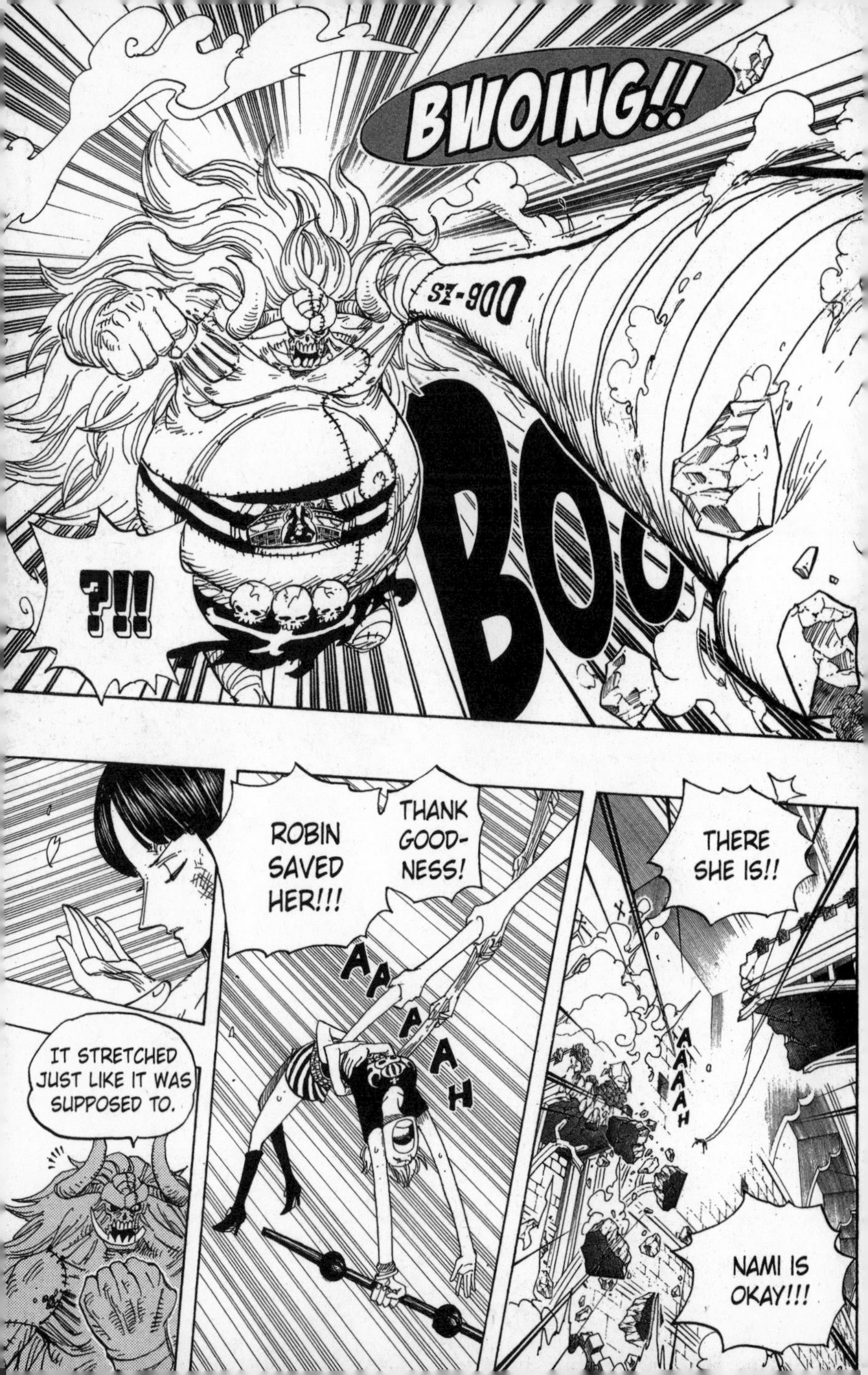
BWOING!!
BOO
?!!
THERE SHE IS!!
AAAAH
NAMI IS OKAY!!!
THANK GOODNESS!
ROBIN SAVED HER!!!
AAAAAH
IT STRETCHED JUST LIKE IT WAS SUPPOSED TO.

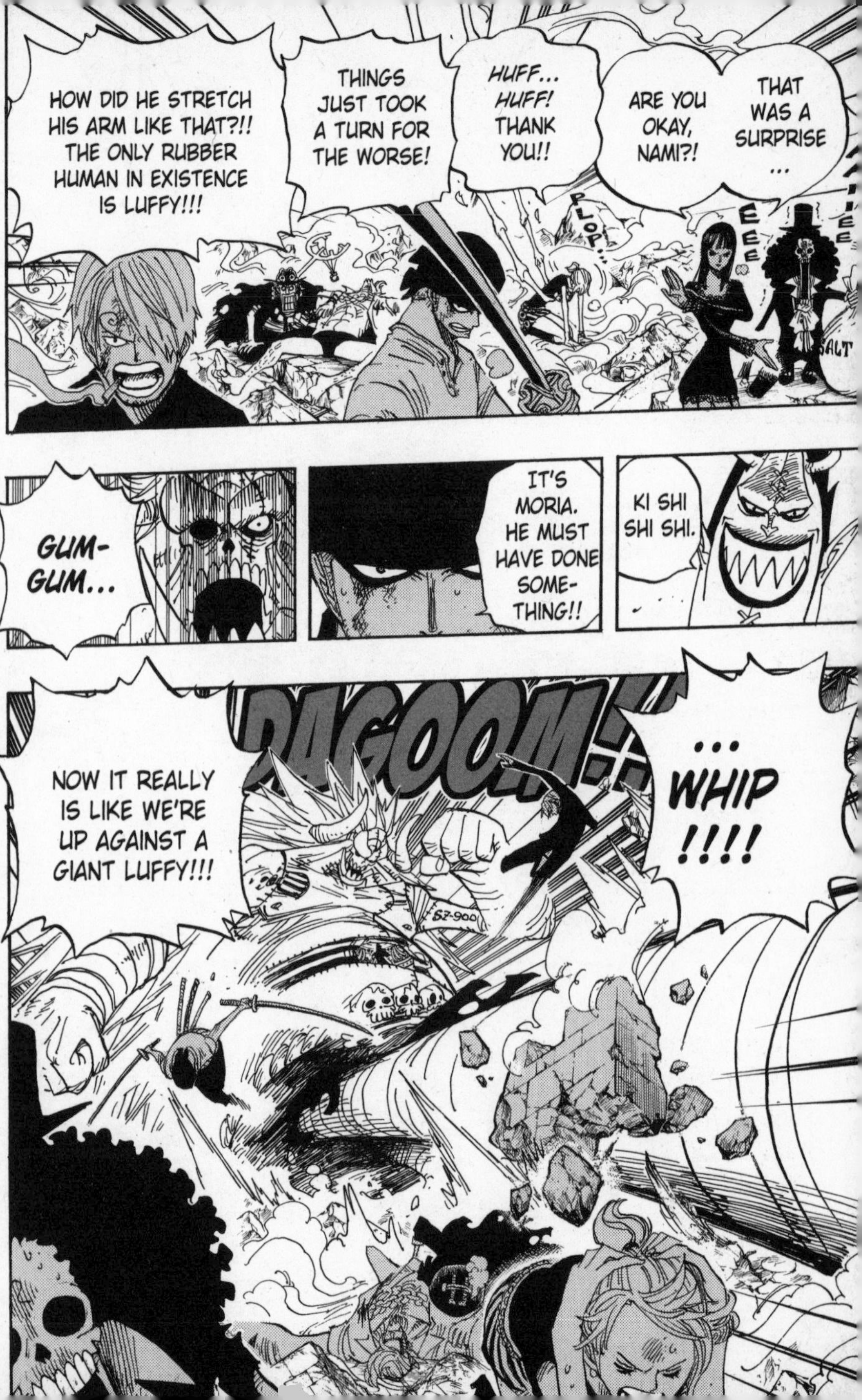
THAT WAS A SURPRISE ...
ARE YOU OKAY, NAMI?!
HUFF... HUFF! THANK YOU!!
PLOP...
THINGS JUST TOOK A TURN FOR THE WORSE!
HOW DID HE STRETCH HIS ARM LIKE THAT?!! THE ONLY RUBBER HUMAN IN EXISTENCE IS LUFFY!!!
SALT
KI SHI SHI SHI.
IT'S MORIA. HE MUST HAVE DONE SOME-THING!!
GUM-GUM...
... WHIP !!!!
DAGOOM!!
NOW IT REALLY IS LIKE WE'RE UP AGAINST A GIANT LUFFY!!!

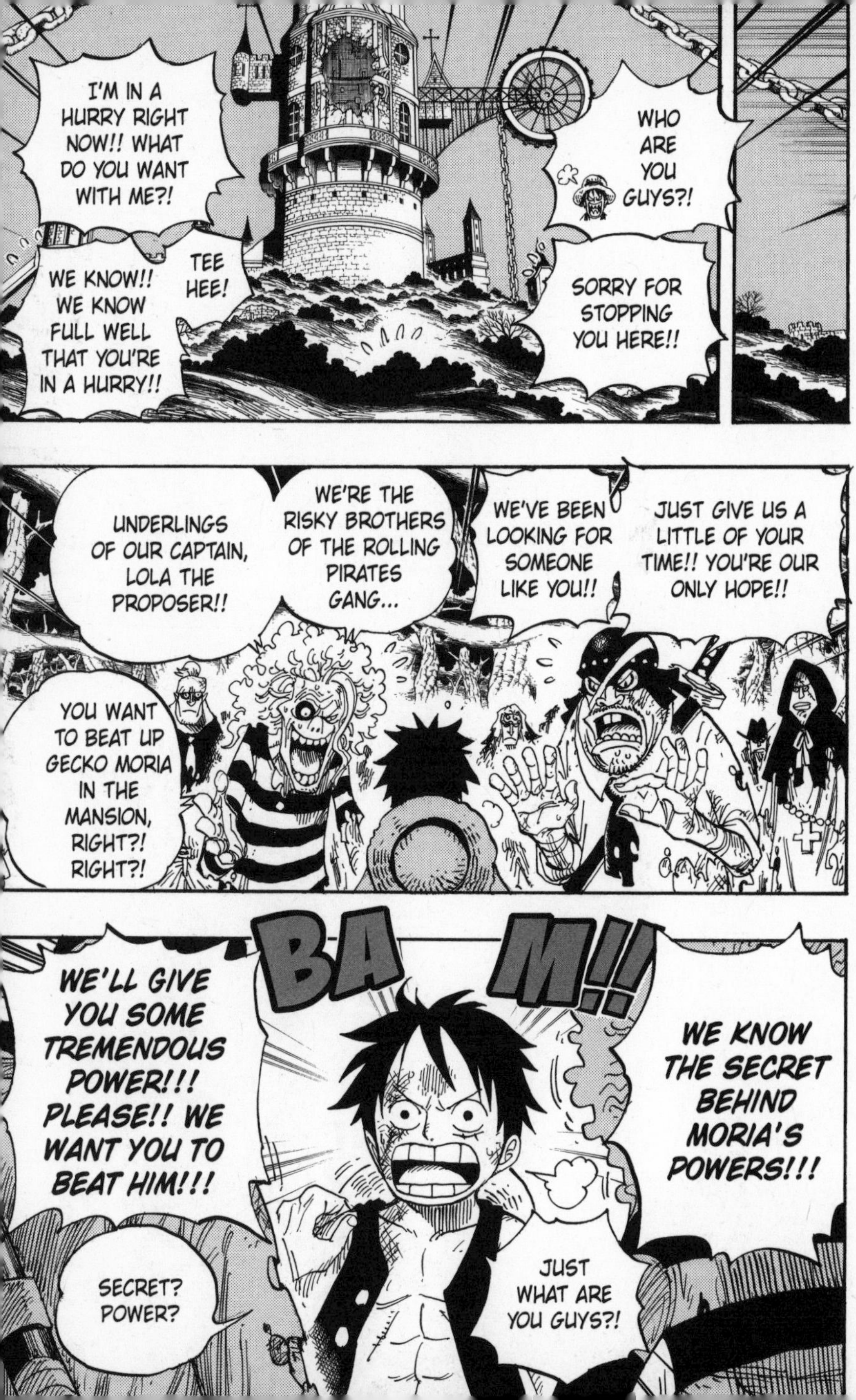
WHO ARE YOU GUYS?!
SORRY FOR STOPPING YOU HERE!!
I'M IN A HURRY RIGHT NOW!! WHAT DO YOU WANT WITH ME?!
TEE HEE!
WE KNOW!! WE KNOW FULL WELL THAT YOU'RE IN A HURRY!!
JUST GIVE US A LITTLE OF YOUR TIME!! YOU'RE OUR ONLY HOPE!!
WE'VE BEEN LOOKING FOR SOMEONE LIKE YOU!!
WE'RE THE RISKY BROTHERS OF THE ROLLING PIRATES GANG...
UNDERLINGS OF OUR CAPTAIN, LOLA THE PROPOSER!!
YOU WANT TO BEAT UP GECKO MORIA IN THE MANSION, RIGHT?! RIGHT?!
BAM!!
WE KNOW THE SECRET BEHIND MORIA'S POWERS!!!
WE'LL GIVE YOU SOME TREMENDOUS POWER!!! PLEASE!! WE WANT YOU TO BEAT HIM!!!
JUST WHAT ARE YOU GUYS?!
SECRET? POWER?

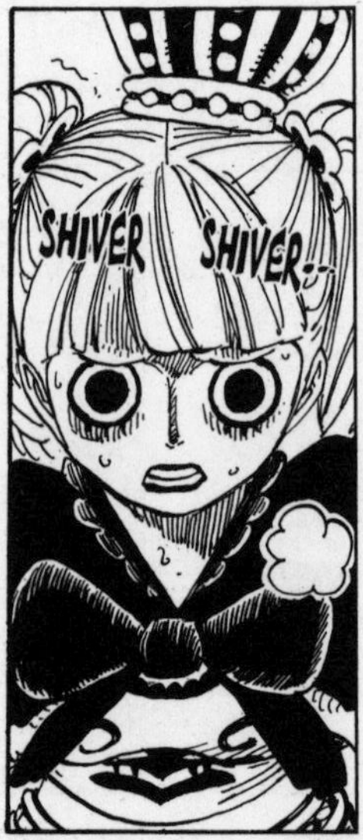
SHIVER SHIVER...

Chapter 476:
NIGHTMARE LUFFY

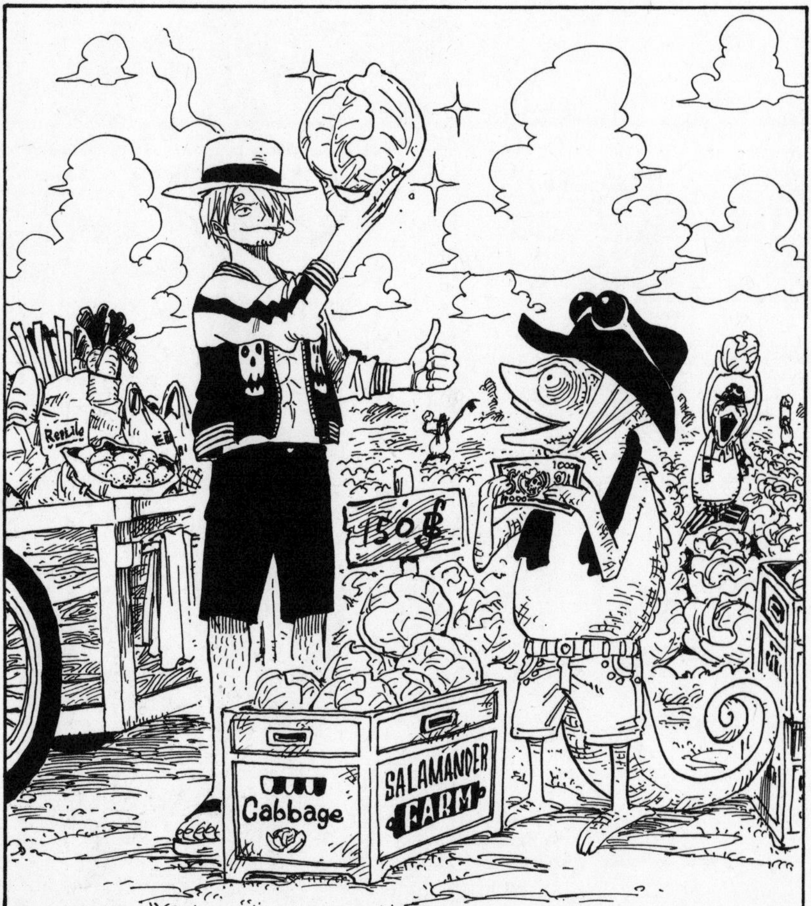
150
SALAMANDER
FARM
Cabbage

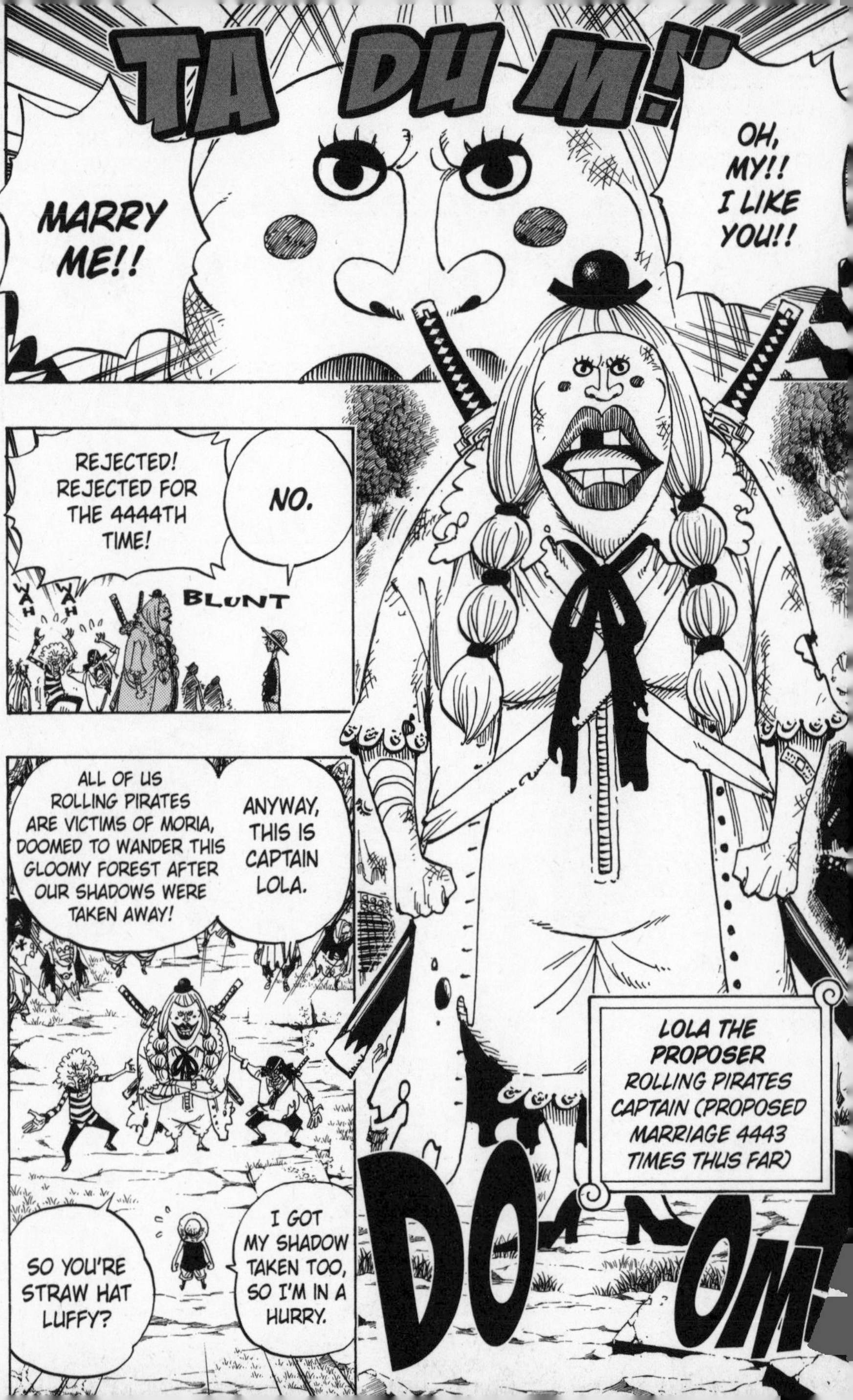
TA DU M!!
OH, MY!! I LIKE YOU!!
MARRY ME!!
LOLA THE PROPOSER
ROLLING PIRATES CAPTAIN (PROPOSED MARRIAGE 4443 TIMES THUS FAR)
DO OM
NO.
REJECTED! REJECTED FOR THE 4444TH TIME!
BLUNT
WAH WAH
ANYWAY, THIS IS CAPTAIN LOLA.
ALL OF US ROLLING PIRATES ARE VICTIMS OF MORIA, DOOMED TO WANDER THIS GLOOMY FOREST AFTER OUR SHADOWS WERE TAKEN AWAY!
I GOT MY SHADOW TAKEN TOO, SO I'M IN A HURRY.
SO YOU'RE STRAW HAT LUFFY?

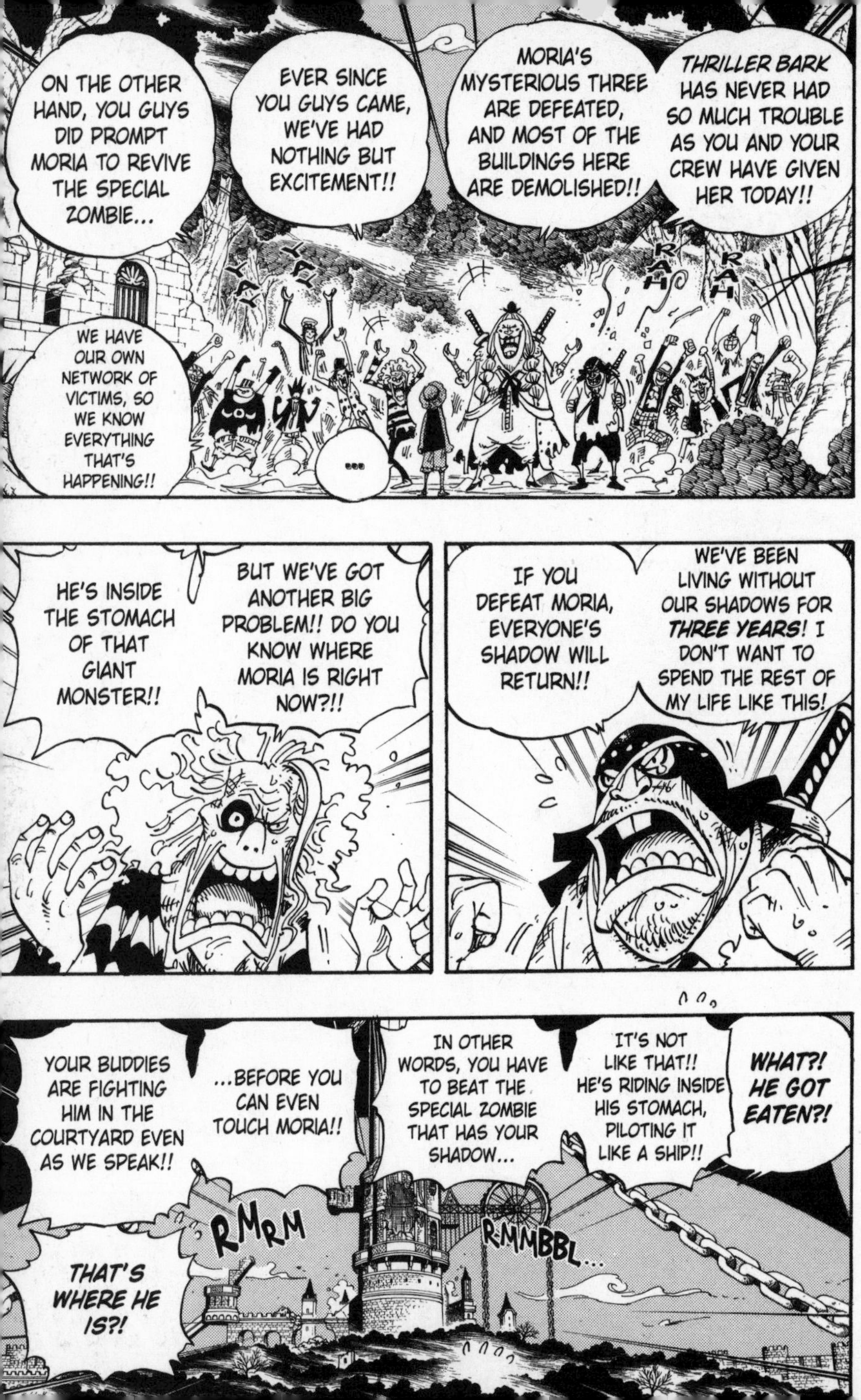
THRILLER BARK HAS NEVER HAD SO MUCH TROUBLE AS YOU AND YOUR CREW HAVE GIVEN HER TODAY!!
MORIA'S MYSTERIOUS THREE ARE DEFEATED, AND MOST OF THE BUILDINGS HERE ARE DEMOLISHED!!
EVER SINCE YOU GUYS CAME, WE'VE HAD NOTHING BUT EXCITEMENT!!
ON THE OTHER HAND, YOU GUYS DID PROMPT MORIA TO REVIVE THE SPECIAL ZOMBIE...
RAH
RAH
WE HAVE OUR OWN NETWORK OF VICTIMS, SO WE KNOW EVERYTHING THAT'S HAPPENING!!
...
WE'VE BEEN LIVING WITHOUT OUR SHADOWS FOR THREE YEARS! I DON'T WANT TO SPEND THE REST OF MY LIFE LIKE THIS!
IF YOU DEFEAT MORIA, EVERYONE'S SHADOW WILL RETURN!!
BUT WE'VE GOT ANOTHER BIG PROBLEM!! DO YOU KNOW WHERE MORIA IS RIGHT NOW?!!
HE'S INSIDE THE STOMACH OF THAT GIANT MONSTER!!
WHAT?! HE GOT EATEN?!
IT'S NOT LIKE THAT!! HE'S RIDING INSIDE HIS STOMACH, PILOTING IT LIKE A SHIP!!
IN OTHER WORDS, YOU HAVE TO BEAT THE SPECIAL ZOMBIE THAT HAS YOUR SHADOW...
...BEFORE YOU CAN EVEN TOUCH MORIA!!
YOUR BUDDIES ARE FIGHTING HIM IN THE COURTYARD EVEN AS WE SPEAK!!
R-MMBBL...
RMRM
THAT'S WHERE HE IS?!

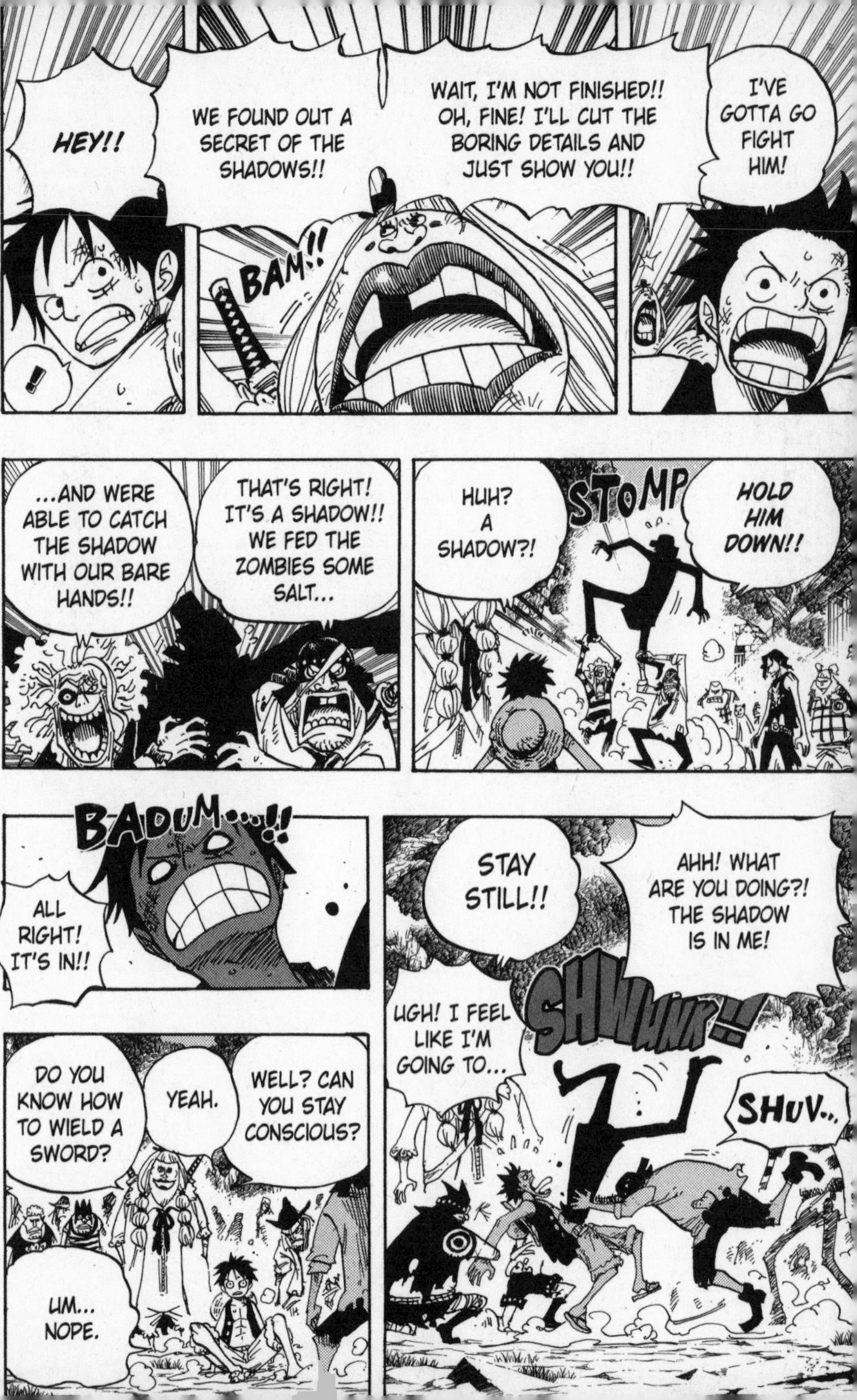
I'VE GOTTA GO FIGHT HIM!
WAIT, I'M NOT FINISHED!! OH, FINE! I'LL CUT THE BORING DETAILS AND JUST SHOW YOU!!
WE FOUND OUT A SECRET OF THE SHADOWS!!
BAM!!
HEY!!
!
HOLD HIM DOWN!!
STOMP
HUH? A SHADOW?!
THAT'S RIGHT! IT'S A SHADOW!! WE FED THE ZOMBIES SOME SALT...
...AND WERE ABLE TO CATCH THE SHADOW WITH OUR BARE HANDS!!
AHH! WHAT ARE YOU DOING?! THE SHADOW IS IN ME!
STAY STILL!!
SHWUNK!!
SHUV..
UGH! I FEEL LIKE I'M GOING TO...
BADUM...!!
ALL RIGHT! IT'S IN!!
WELL? CAN YOU STAY CONSCIOUS?
YEAH.
DO YOU KNOW HOW TO WIELD A SWORD?
UM... NOPE.

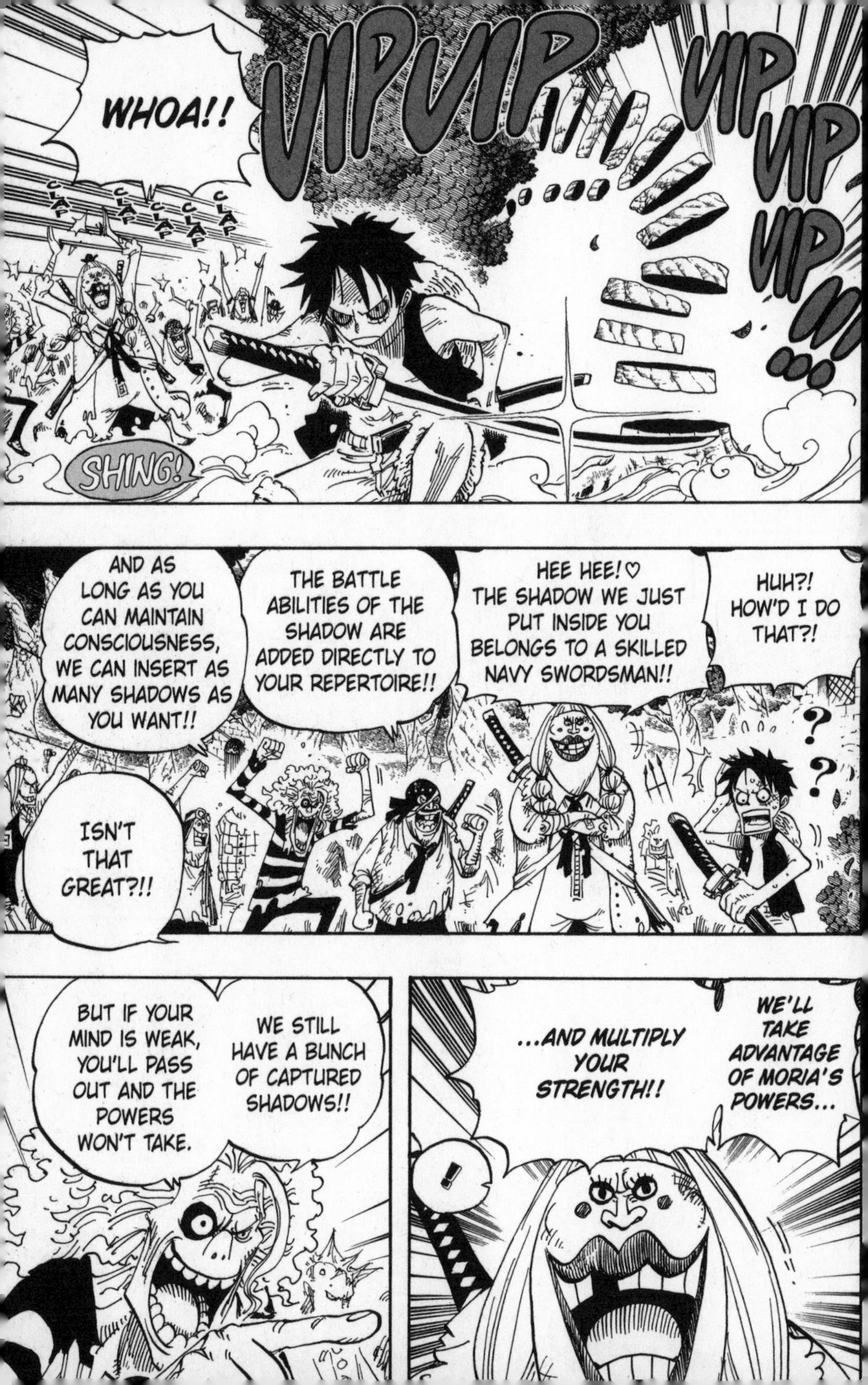
VIP VIP VIP!!!
VIPVIP
WHOA!!
CLAP CLAP CLAP CLAP CLAP
SHING!
HUH?! HOW'D I DO THAT?!
??
HEE HEE! ♡ THE SHADOW WE JUST PUT INSIDE YOU BELONGS TO A SKILLED NAVY SWORDSMAN!!
THE BATTLE ABILITIES OF THE SHADOW ARE ADDED DIRECTLY TO YOUR REPERTOIRE!!
AND AS LONG AS YOU CAN MAINTAIN CONSCIOUSNESS, WE CAN INSERT AS MANY SHADOWS AS YOU WANT!!
ISN'T THAT GREAT?!!
WE'LL TAKE ADVANTAGE OF MORIA'S POWERS...
...AND MULTIPLY YOUR STRENGTH!!
!
WE STILL HAVE A BUNCH OF CAPTURED SHADOWS!!
BUT IF YOUR MIND IS WEAK, YOU'LL PASS OUT AND THE POWERS WON'T TAKE.

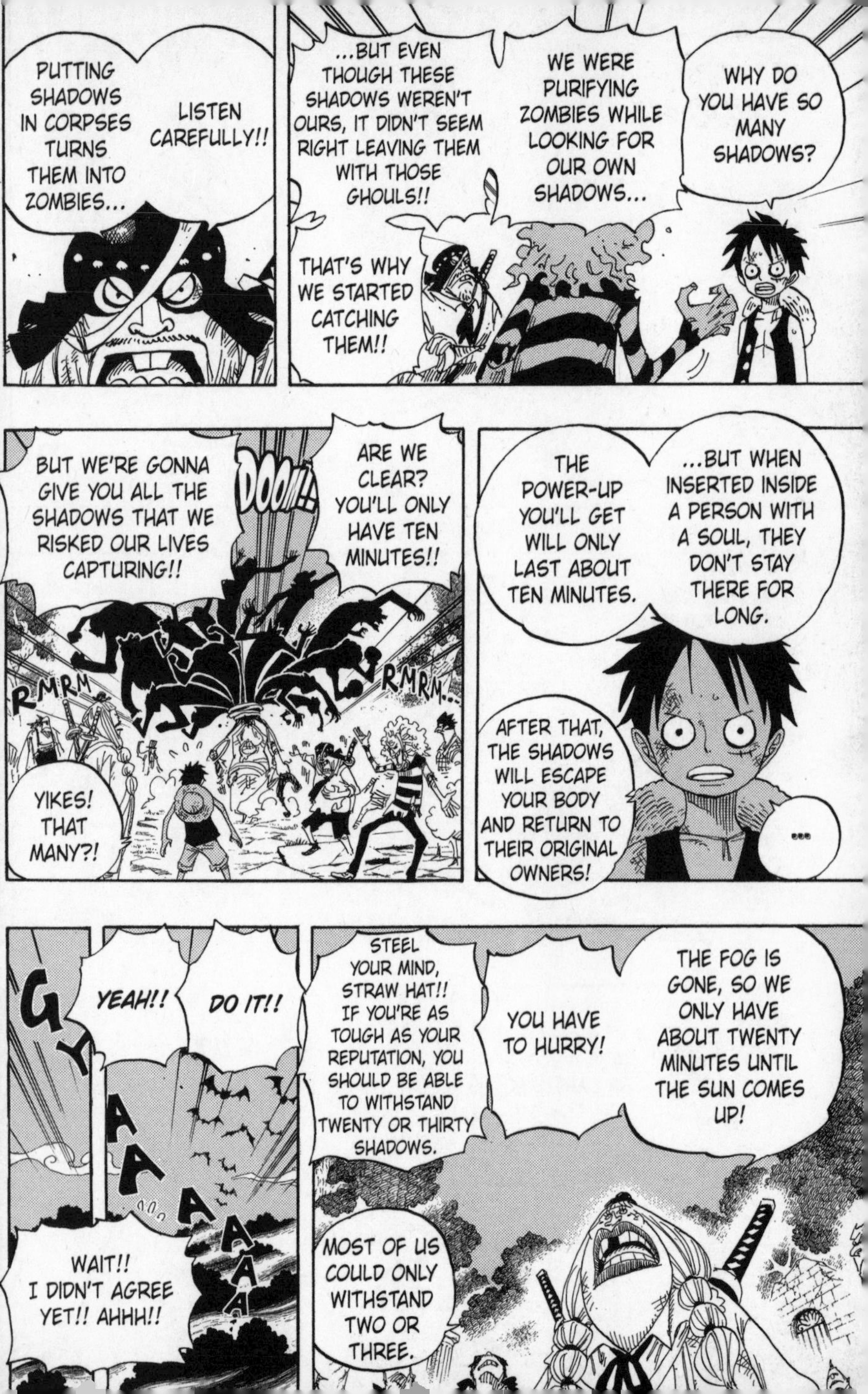
WHY DO YOU HAVE SO MANY SHADOWS?
WE WERE PURIFYING ZOMBIES WHILE LOOKING FOR OUR OWN SHADOWS...
...BUT EVEN THOUGH THESE SHADOWS WEREN'T OURS, IT DIDN'T SEEM RIGHT LEAVING THEM WITH THOSE GHOULS!!
THAT'S WHY WE STARTED CATCHING THEM!!
LISTEN CAREFULLY!!
PUTTING SHADOWS IN CORPSES TURNS THEM INTO ZOMBIES...
...BUT WHEN INSERTED INSIDE A PERSON WITH A SOUL, THEY DON'T STAY THERE FOR LONG.
THE POWER-UP YOU'LL GET WILL ONLY LAST ABOUT TEN MINUTES.
...
AFTER THAT, THE SHADOWS WILL ESCAPE YOUR BODY AND RETURN TO THEIR ORIGINAL OWNERS!
ARE WE CLEAR? YOU'LL ONLY HAVE TEN MINUTES!!
DOOM!!
BUT WE'RE GONNA GIVE YOU ALL THE SHADOWS THAT WE RISKED OUR LIVES CAPTURING!!
RMRM...
RMRM
YIKES! THAT MANY?!
THE FOG IS GONE, SO WE ONLY HAVE ABOUT TWENTY MINUTES UNTIL THE SUN COMES UP!
YOU HAVE TO HURRY!
STEEL YOUR MIND, STRAW HAT!! IF YOU'RE AS TOUGH AS YOUR REPUTATION, YOU SHOULD BE ABLE TO WITHSTAND TWENTY OR THIRTY SHADOWS.
MOST OF US COULD ONLY WITHSTAND TWO OR THREE.
DO IT!!
YEAH!!
GYAAAAAAA
WAIT!! I DIDN'T AGREE YET!! AHHH!!

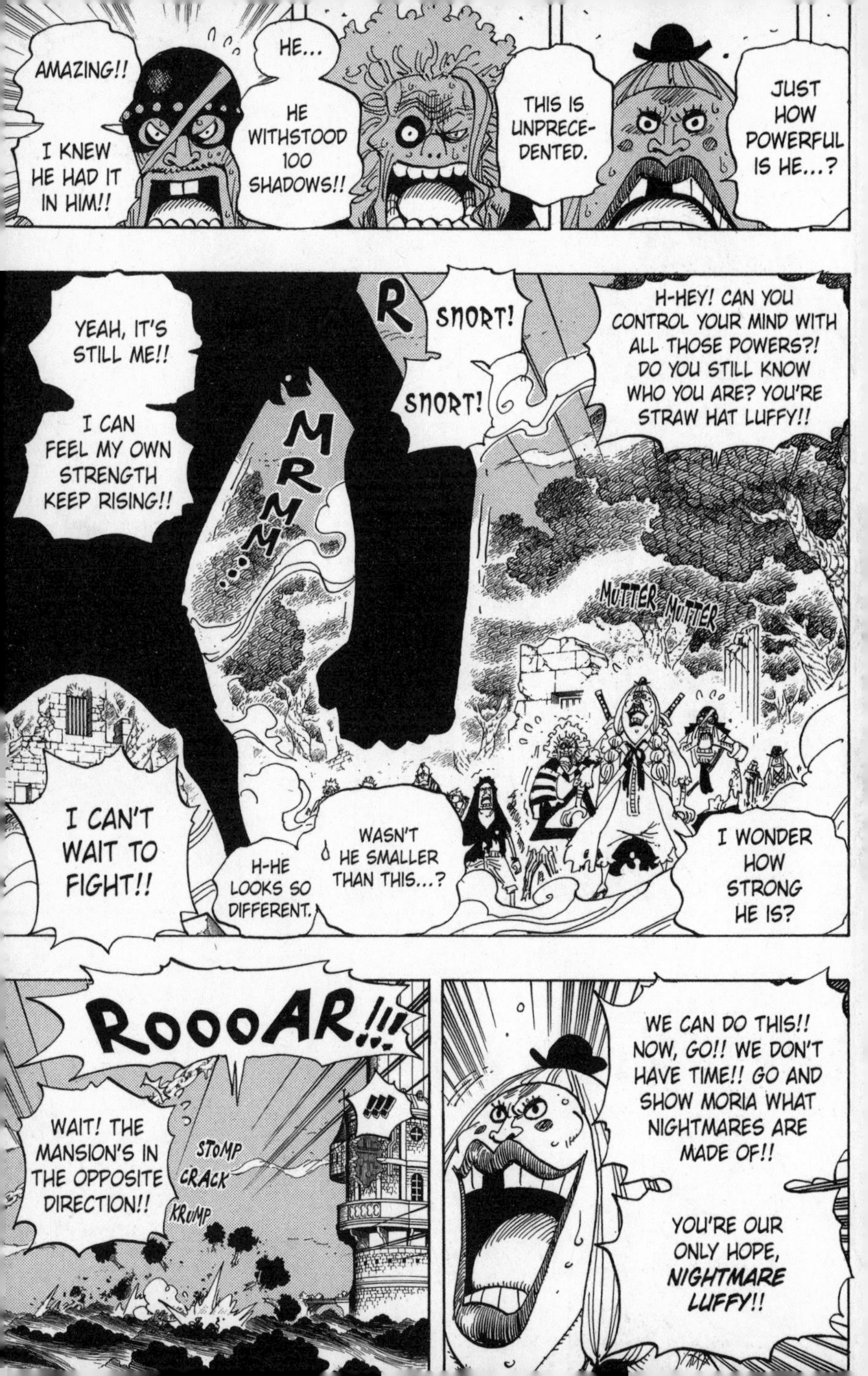
JUST HOW POWERFUL IS HE...?
THIS IS UNPRECE-DENTED.
HE...
HE WITHSTOOD 100 SHADOWS!!
AMAZING!!
I KNEW HE HAD IT IN HIM!!
H-HEY! CAN YOU CONTROL YOUR MIND WITH ALL THOSE POWERS?! DO YOU STILL KNOW WHO YOU ARE? YOU'RE STRAW HAT LUFFY!!
SNORT!
SNORT!
R
MRMM...
YEAH, IT'S STILL ME!!
I CAN FEEL MY OWN STRENGTH KEEP RISING!!
MUTTER MUTTER
I WONDER HOW STRONG HE IS?
WASN'T HE SMALLER THAN THIS...?
H-HE LOOKS SO DIFFERENT.
I CAN'T WAIT TO FIGHT!!
WE CAN DO THIS!! NOW, GO!! WE DON'T HAVE TIME!! GO AND SHOW MORIA WHAT NIGHTMARES ARE MADE OF!!
YOU'RE OUR ONLY HOPE, *NIGHTMARE LUFFY*!!
ROOOAR!!!
!!!
WAIT! THE MANSION'S IN THE OPPOSITE DIRECTION!!
STOMP
CRACK
KRUMP

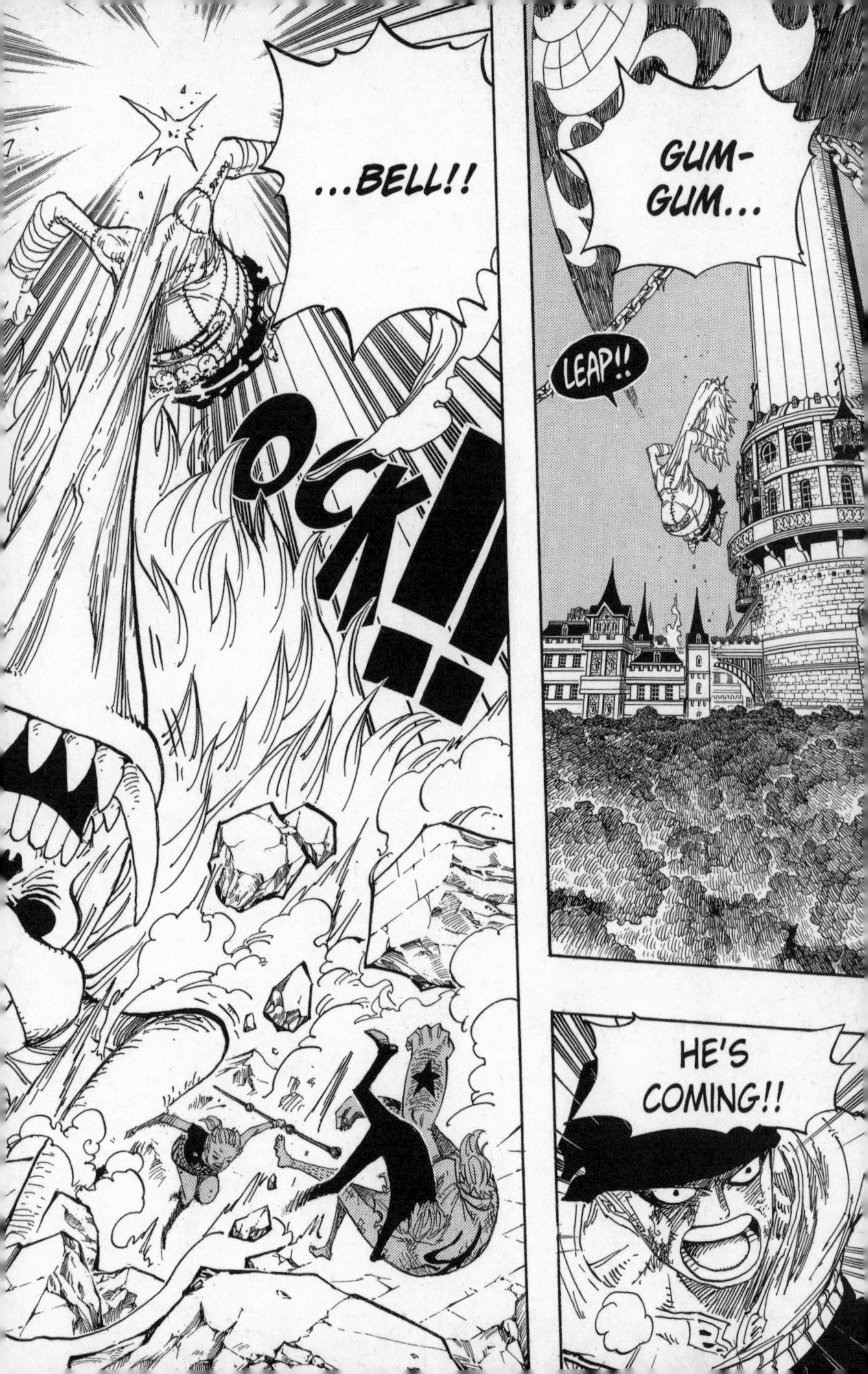
GUM-
GUM...
LEAP!!
HE'S
COMING!!
...BELL!!
OCK!!

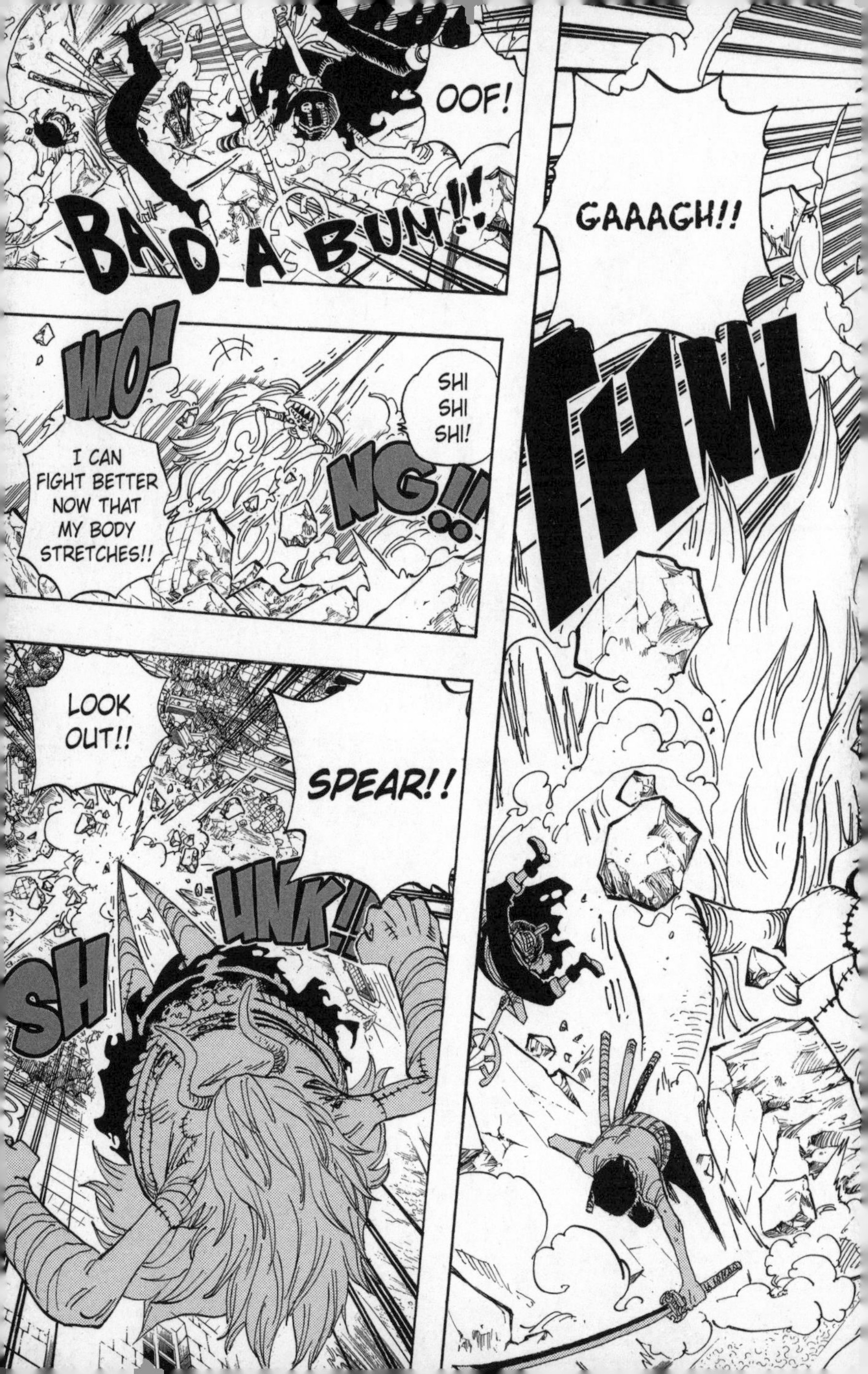
GAAAGH!!
THW
OOF!
BADABUM!!
SHI SHI SHI!
WO
NG!!
I CAN FIGHT BETTER NOW THAT MY BODY STRETCHES!!
LOOK OUT!!
SPEAR!!
UNK!!
SH

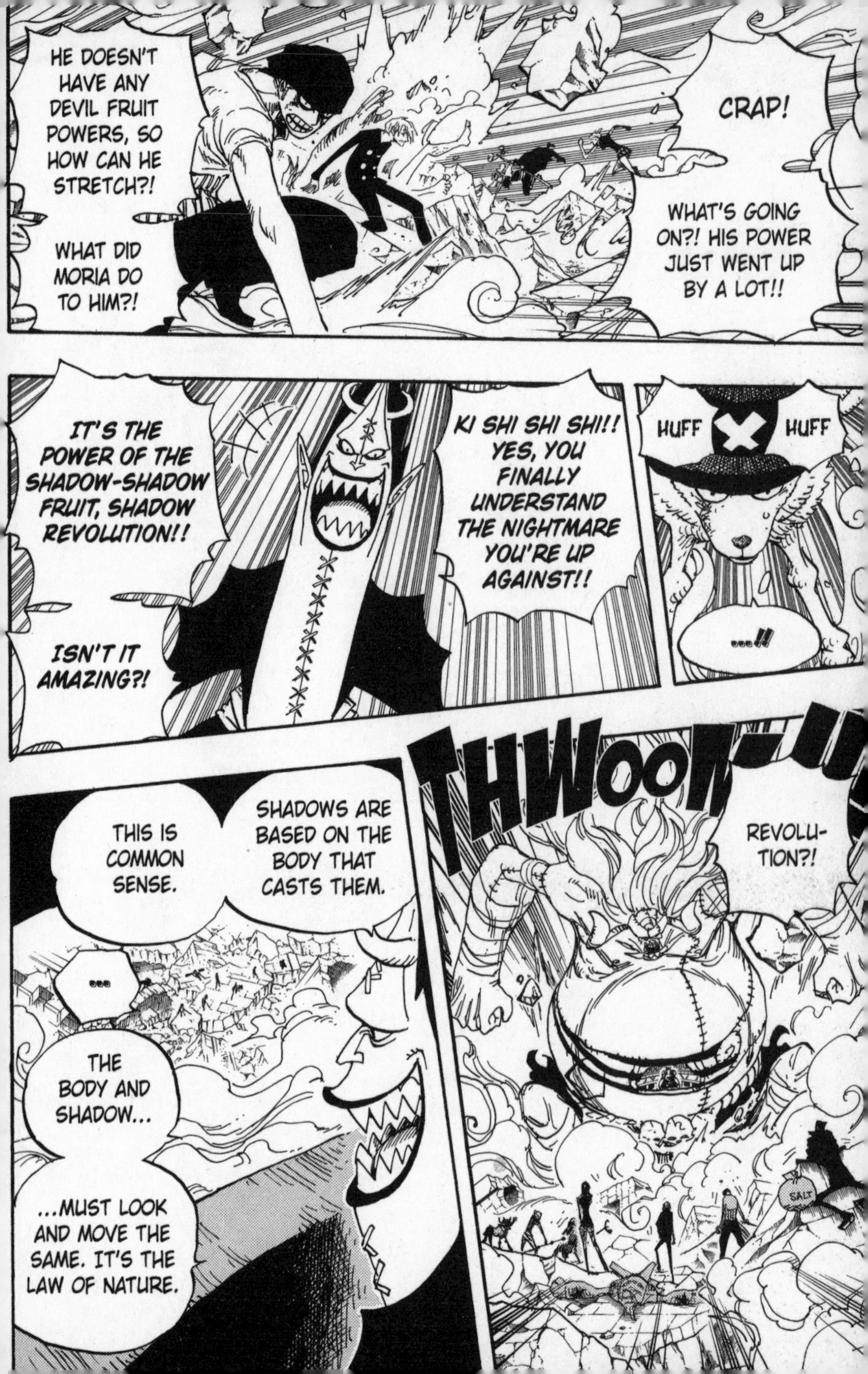

CRAP!
WHAT'S GOING ON?! HIS POWER JUST WENT UP BY A LOT!!
HE DOESN'T HAVE ANY DEVIL FRUIT POWERS, SO HOW CAN HE STRETCH?!
WHAT DID MORIA DO TO HIM?!
HUFF
HUFF
...!!
KI SHI SHI SHI!! YES, YOU FINALLY UNDERSTAND THE NIGHTMARE YOU'RE UP AGAINST!!
IT'S THE POWER OF THE SHADOW-SHADOW FRUIT, SHADOW REVOLUTION!!
ISN'T IT AMAZING?!
THWOOM
REVOLU-TION?!
SHADOWS ARE BASED ON THE BODY THAT CASTS THEM.
THIS IS COMMON SENSE.
...
THE BODY AND SHADOW...
...MUST LOOK AND MOVE THE SAME. IT'S THE LAW OF NATURE.

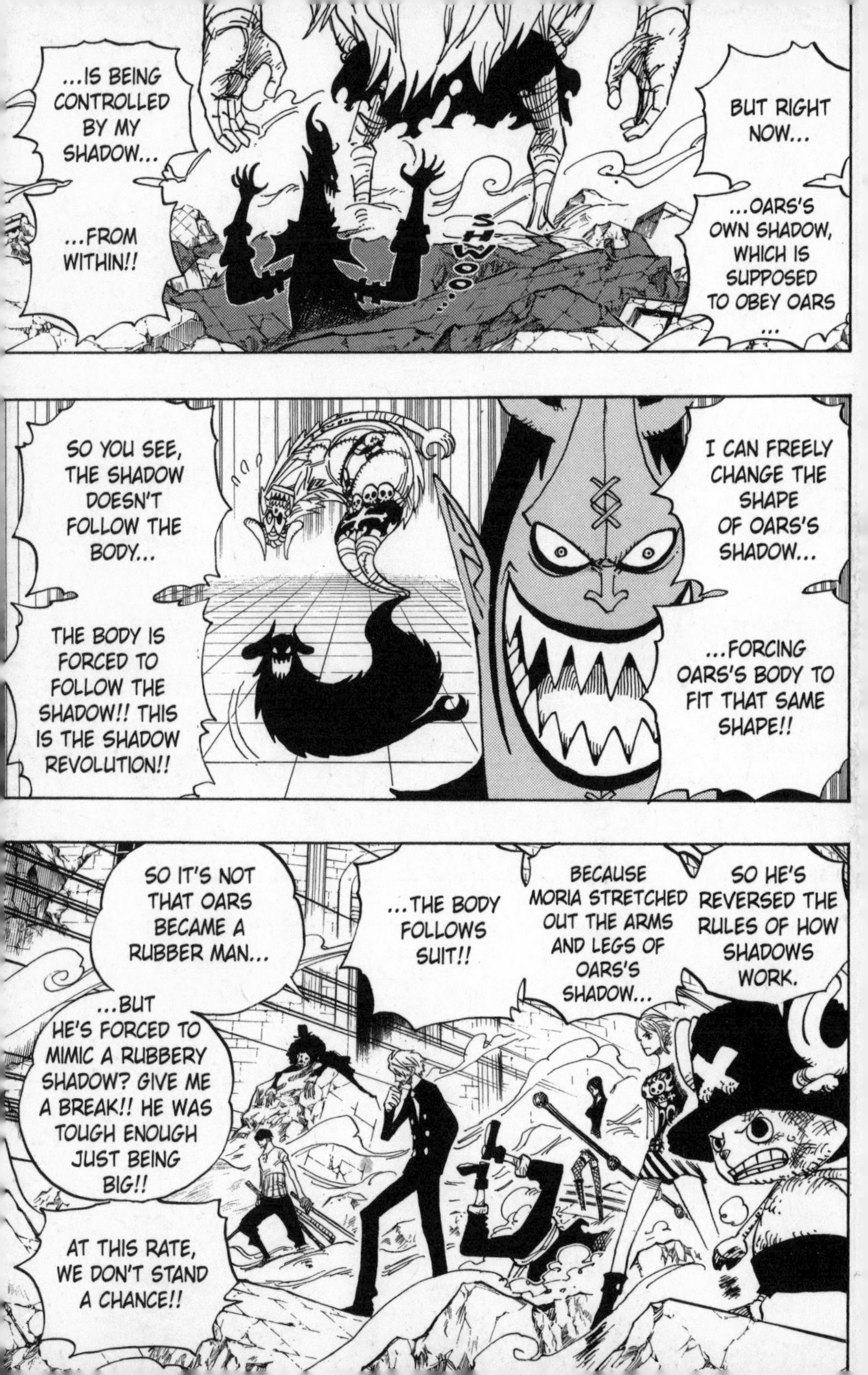
BUT RIGHT NOW...
...OARS'S OWN SHADOW, WHICH IS SUPPOSED TO OBEY OARS ...
SHWOOO...
...IS BEING CONTROLLED BY MY SHADOW...
...FROM WITHIN!!
I CAN FREELY CHANGE THE SHAPE OF OARS'S SHADOW...
...FORCING OARS'S BODY TO FIT THAT SAME SHAPE!!
SO YOU SEE, THE SHADOW DOESN'T FOLLOW THE BODY...
THE BODY IS FORCED TO FOLLOW THE SHADOW!! THIS IS THE SHADOW REVOLUTION!!
SO HE'S REVERSED THE RULES OF HOW SHADOWS WORK.
BECAUSE MORIA STRETCHED OUT THE ARMS AND LEGS OF OARS'S SHADOW...
...THE BODY FOLLOWS SUIT!!
SO IT'S NOT THAT OARS BECAME A RUBBER MAN...
...BUT HE'S FORCED TO MIMIC A RUBBERY SHADOW? GIVE ME A BREAK!! HE WAS TOUGH ENOUGH JUST BEING BIG!!
AT THIS RATE, WE DON'T STAND A CHANCE!!

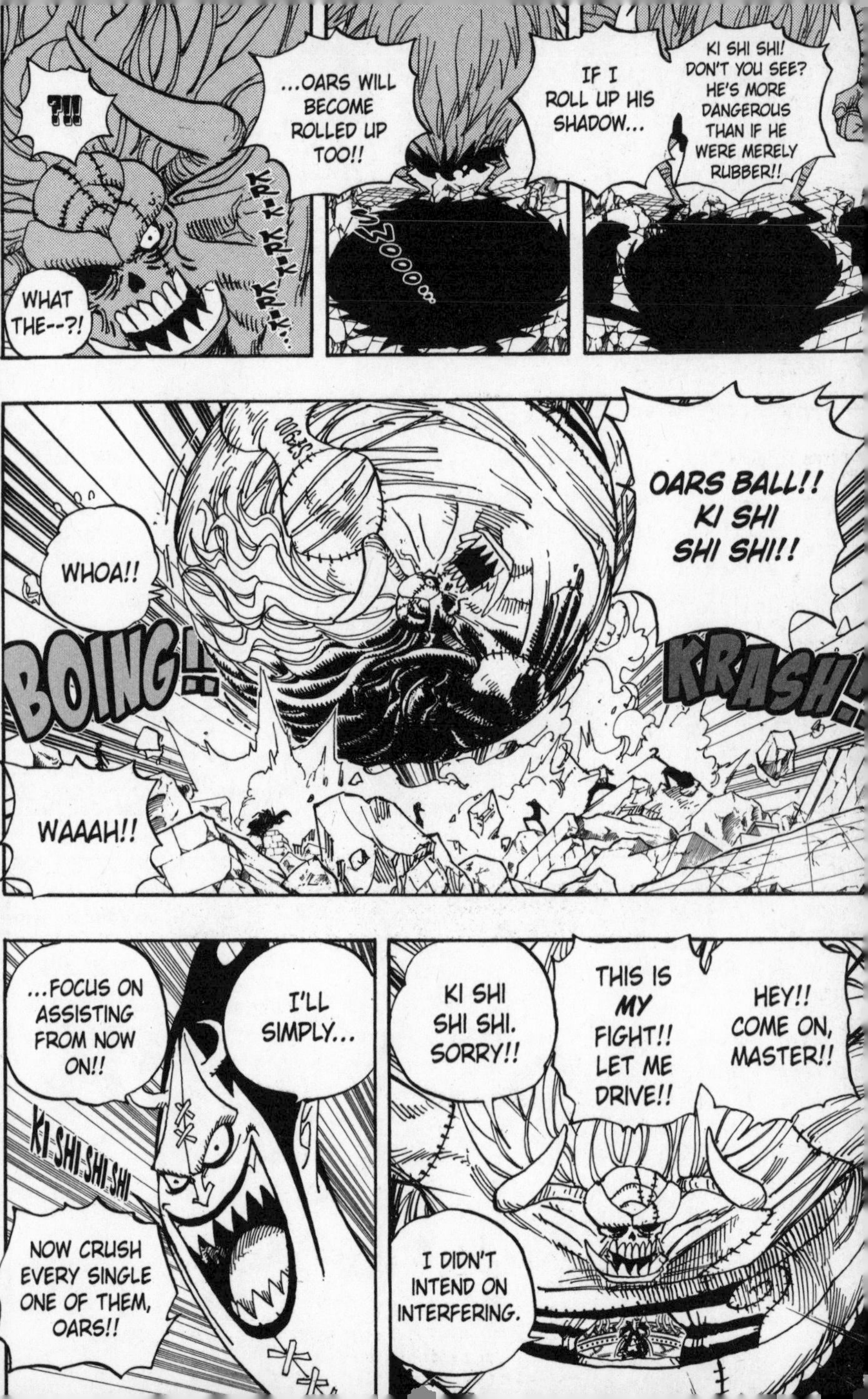
KI SHI SHI! DON'T YOU SEE? HE'S MORE DANGEROUS THAN IF HE WERE MERELY RUBBER!!
IF I ROLL UP HIS SHADOW...
...OARS WILL BECOME ROLLED UP TOO!!
?!!
KRIK KRIK KRIK KRIK...
WHAT THE--?!
OARS BALL!! KI SHI SHI SHI!!
KRASH!!
WHOA!!
BOING!!
WAAAH!!
HEY!! COME ON, MASTER!!
THIS IS *MY* FIGHT!! LET ME DRIVE!!
KI SHI SHI SHI. SORRY!!
I DIDN'T INTEND ON INTERFERING.
I'LL SIMPLY...
...FOCUS ON ASSISTING FROM NOW ON!!
KI-SHI-SHI-SHI
NOW CRUSH EVERY SINGLE ONE OF THEM, OARS!!

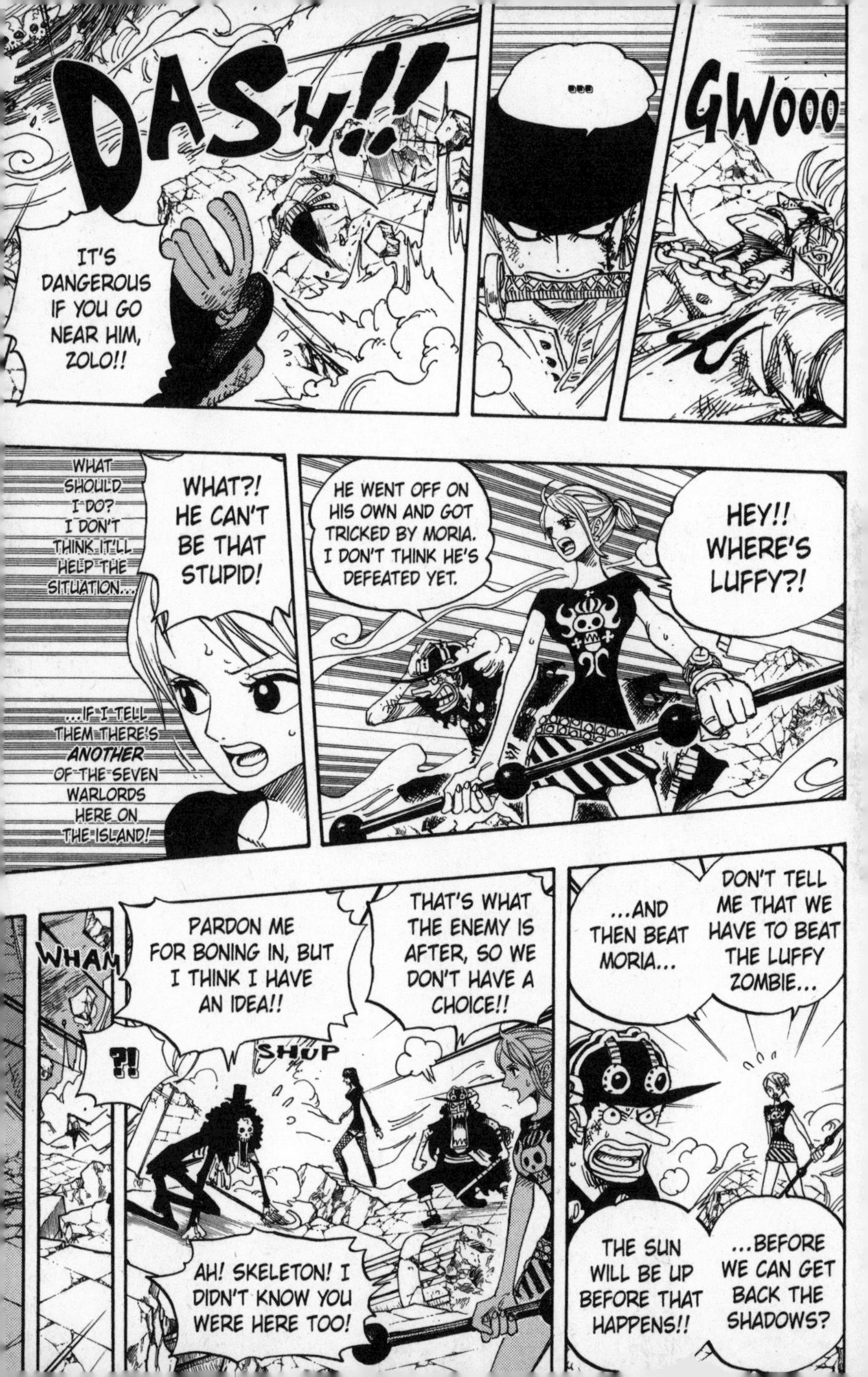
GWOOO
...
DASH!!
IT'S DANGEROUS IF YOU GO NEAR HIM, ZOLO!!
HEY!! WHERE'S LUFFY?!
HE WENT OFF ON HIS OWN AND GOT TRICKED BY MORIA. I DON'T THINK HE'S DEFEATED YET.
WHAT?! HE CAN'T BE THAT STUPID!
WHAT SHOULD I DO? I DON'T THINK IT'LL HELP THE SITUATION...
...IF I TELL THEM THERE'S ANOTHER OF THE SEVEN WARLORDS HERE ON THE ISLAND!
DON'T TELL ME THAT WE HAVE TO BEAT THE LUFFY ZOMBIE...
...AND THEN BEAT MORIA...
...BEFORE WE CAN GET BACK THE SHADOWS?
THE SUN WILL BE UP BEFORE THAT HAPPENS!!
THAT'S WHAT THE ENEMY IS AFTER, SO WE DON'T HAVE A CHOICE!!
PARDON ME FOR BONING IN, BUT I THINK I HAVE AN IDEA!!
WHAM
SHUP
?!
AH! SKELETON! I DIDN'T KNOW YOU WERE HERE TOO!

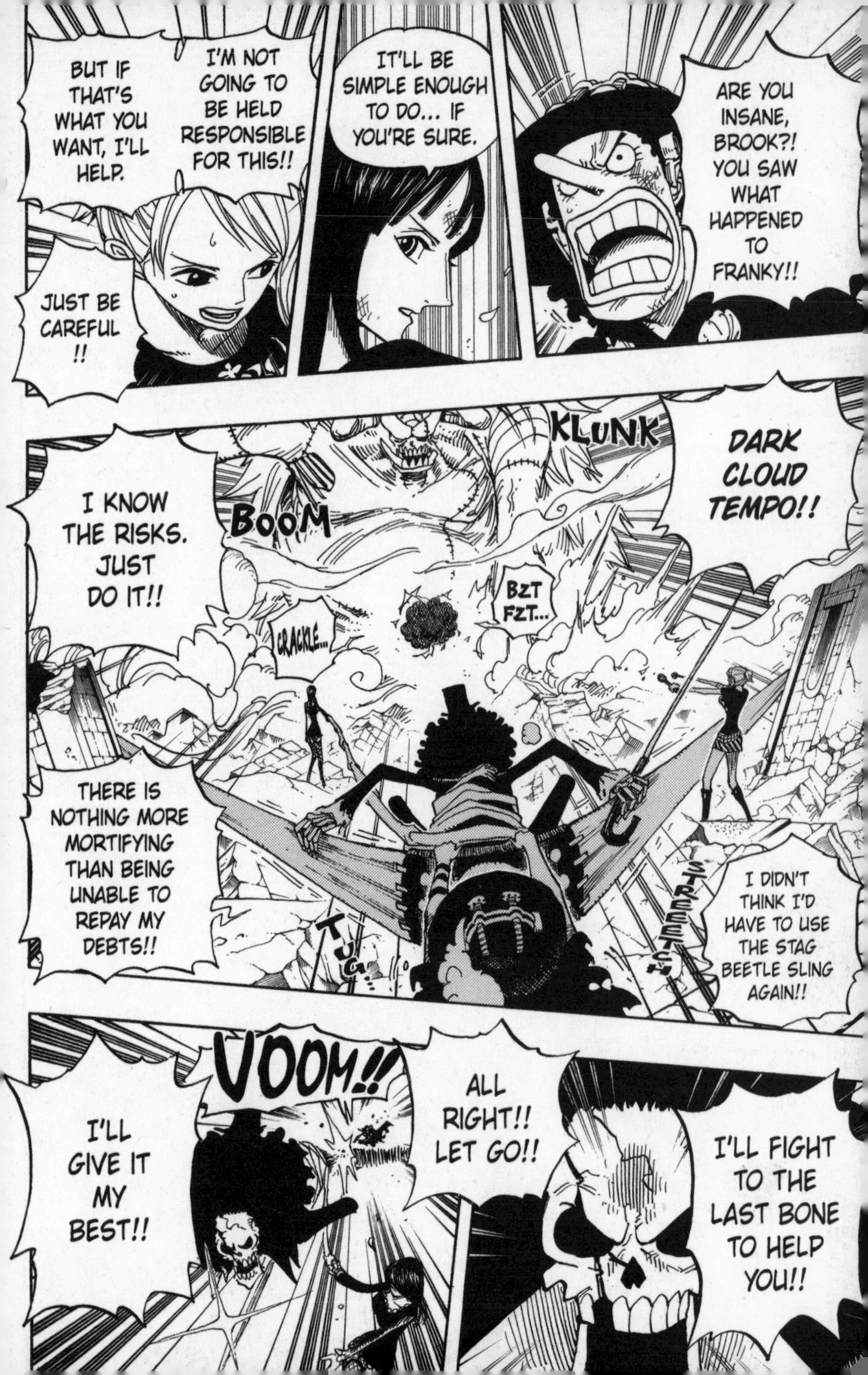
ARE YOU INSANE, BROOK?! YOU SAW WHAT HAPPENED TO FRANKY!!
IT'LL BE SIMPLE ENOUGH TO DO... IF YOU'RE SURE.
I'M NOT GOING TO BE HELD RESPONSIBLE FOR THIS!!
BUT IF THAT'S WHAT YOU WANT, I'LL HELP.
JUST BE CAREFUL !!
DARK CLOUD TEMPO!!
KLUNK
I KNOW THE RISKS. JUST DO IT!!
BOOM
BZT FZT...
CRACKLE...
I DIDN'T THINK I'D HAVE TO USE THE STAG BEETLE SLING AGAIN!!
STREEETCH
THERE IS NOTHING MORE MORTIFYING THAN BEING UNABLE TO REPAY MY DEBTS!!
TUG...
I'LL FIGHT TO THE LAST BONE TO HELP YOU!!
ALL RIGHT!! LET GO!!
VOOM!!
I'LL GIVE IT MY BEST!!

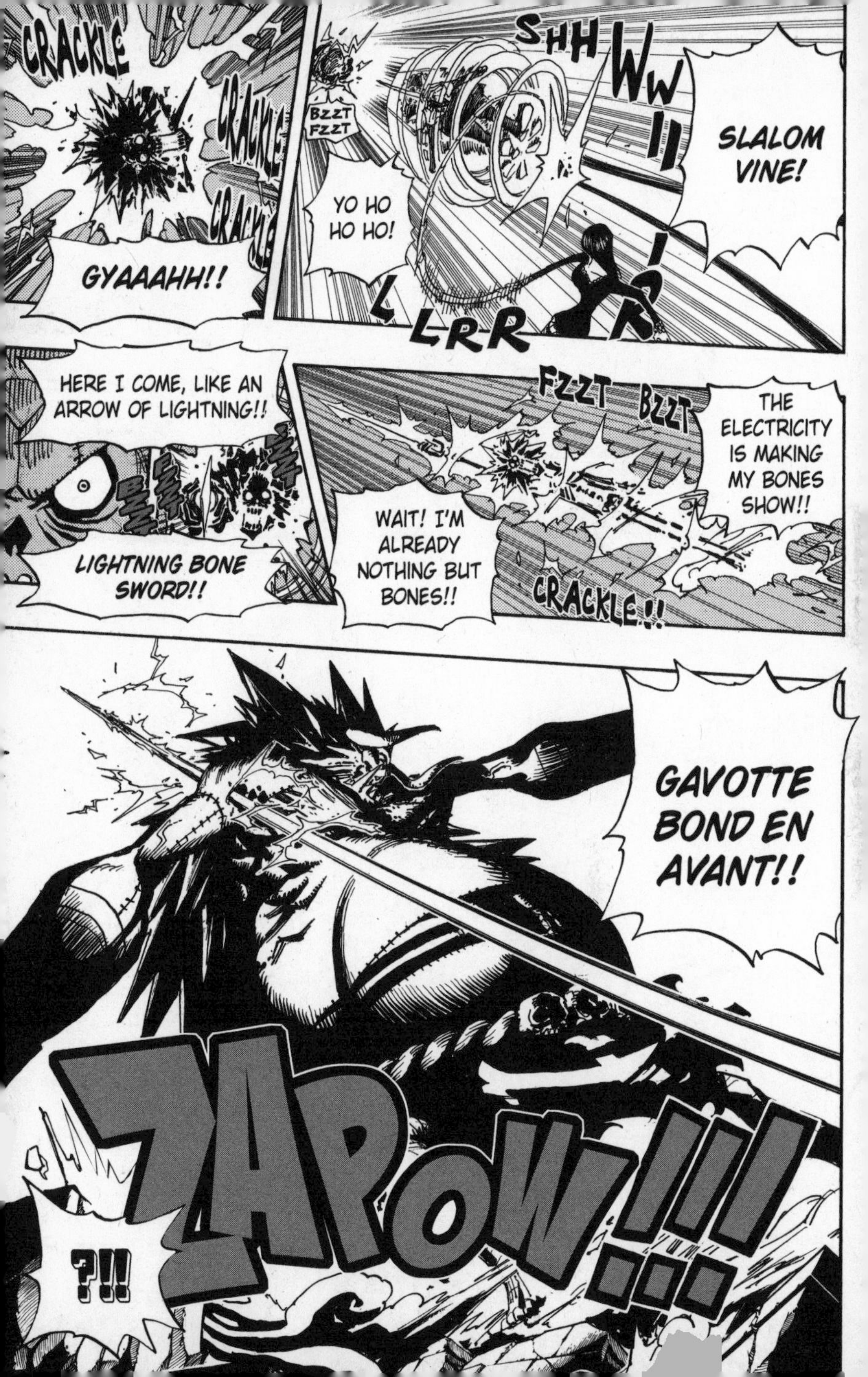
SLALOM VINE!
YO HO HO HO!
BZZT FZZT
CRACKLE
CRACKLE
CRACKLE
GYAAAHH!!
THE ELECTRICITY IS MAKING MY BONES SHOW!!
FZZT BZZT
WAIT! I'M ALREADY NOTHING BUT BONES!!
CRACKLE!!
HERE I COME, LIKE AN ARROW OF LIGHTNING!!
LIGHTNING BONE SWORD!!
GAVOTTE BOND EN AVANT!!
ZAPOW!!!
?!!

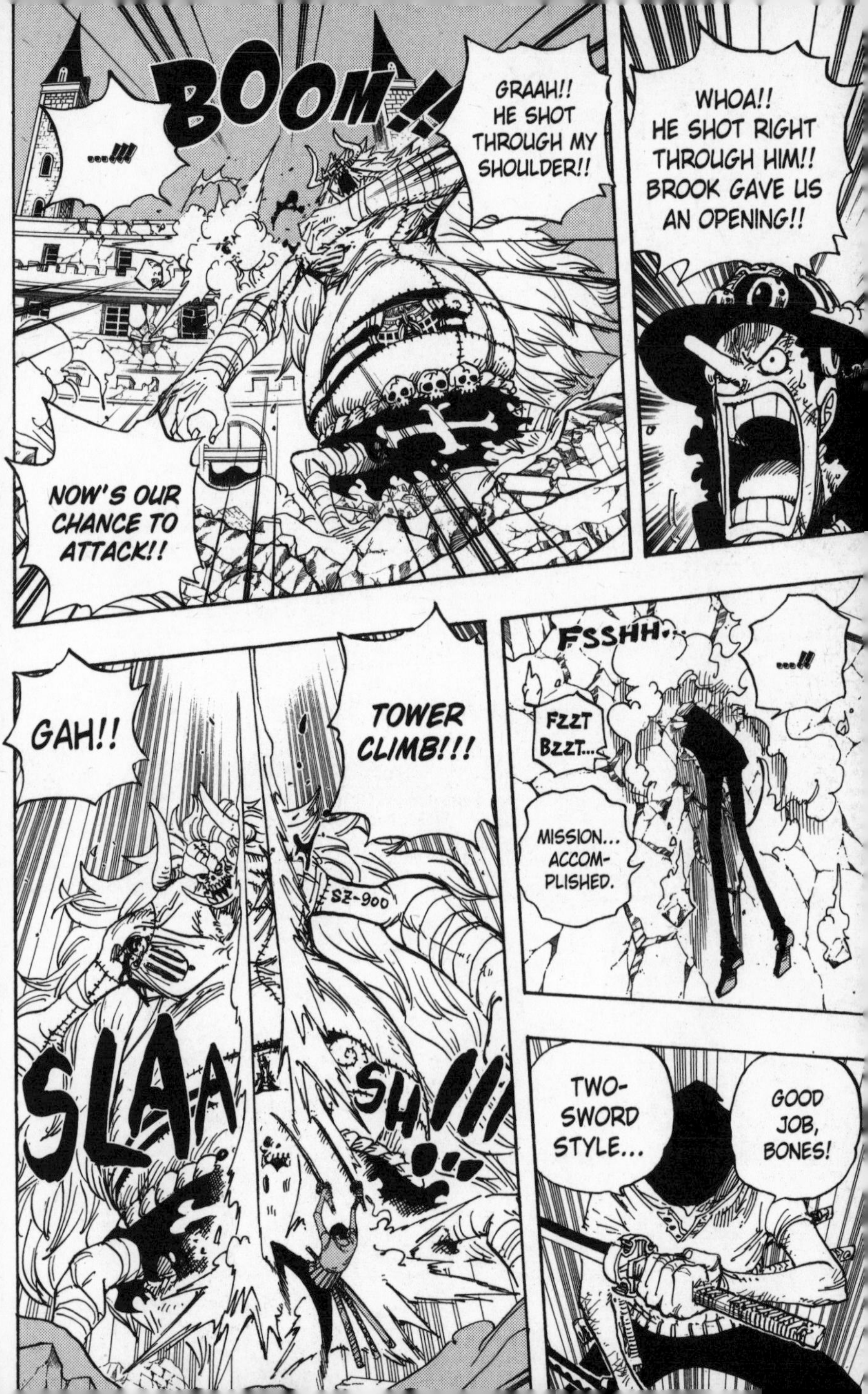
WHOA!! HE SHOT RIGHT THROUGH HIM!! BROOK GAVE US AN OPENING!!
GRAAH!! HE SHOT THROUGH MY SHOULDER!!
BOOM!!
...!!!
NOW'S OUR CHANCE TO ATTACK!!
...!!
FSSHH...
FZZT BZZT...
MISSION... ACCOMPLISHED.
GOOD JOB, BONES!
TWO-SWORD STYLE...
TOWER CLIMB!!!
GAH!!
SZ-900
SLAASH!!!

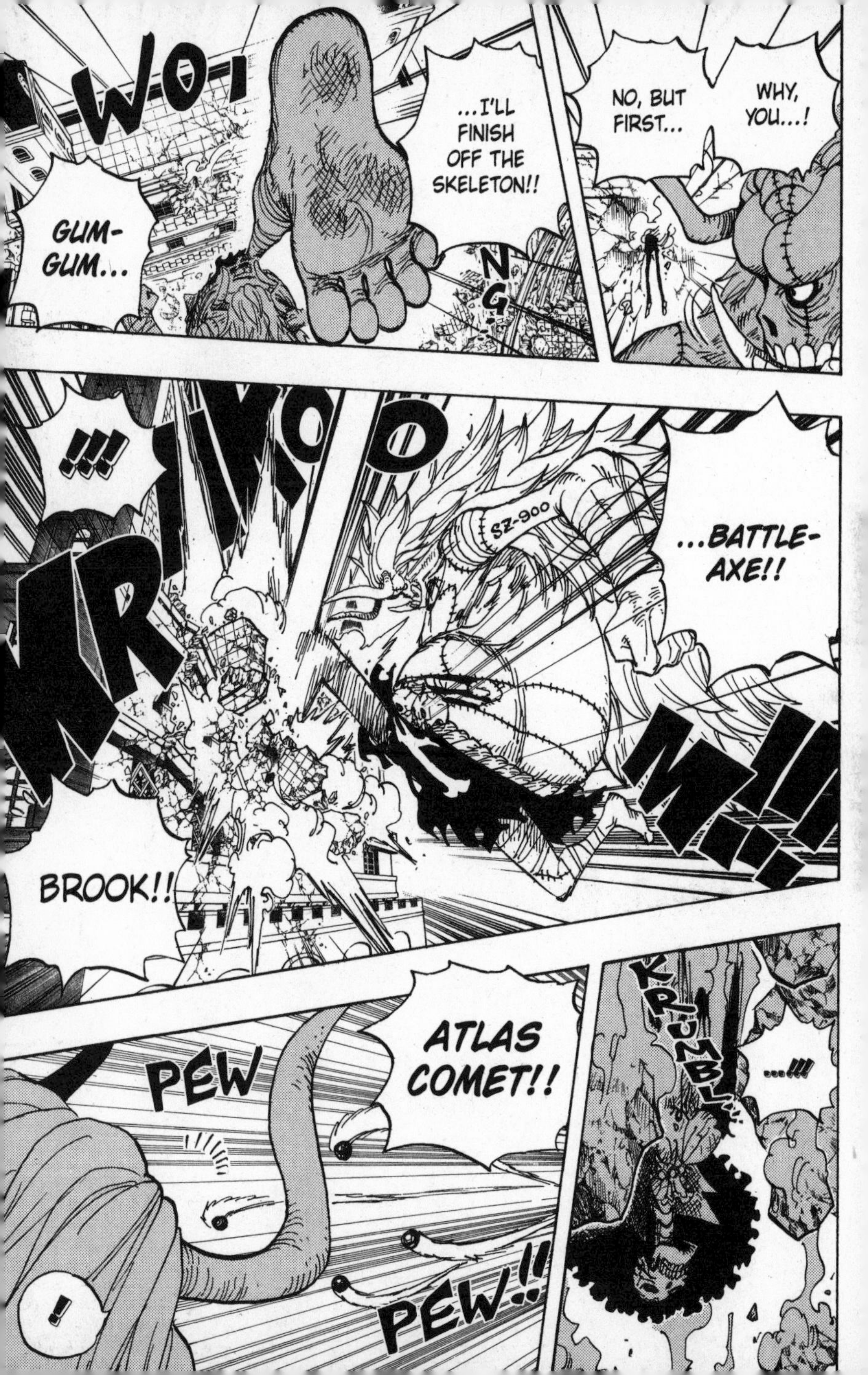
WHY, YOU...!
NO, BUT FIRST...
...I'LL FINISH OFF THE SKELETON!!
WOI
NG
GUM-GUM...
...BATTLE-AXE!!
!!!
BROOK!!
KRUMBL
...!!!
ATLAS COMET!!
PEW
PEW!!
!

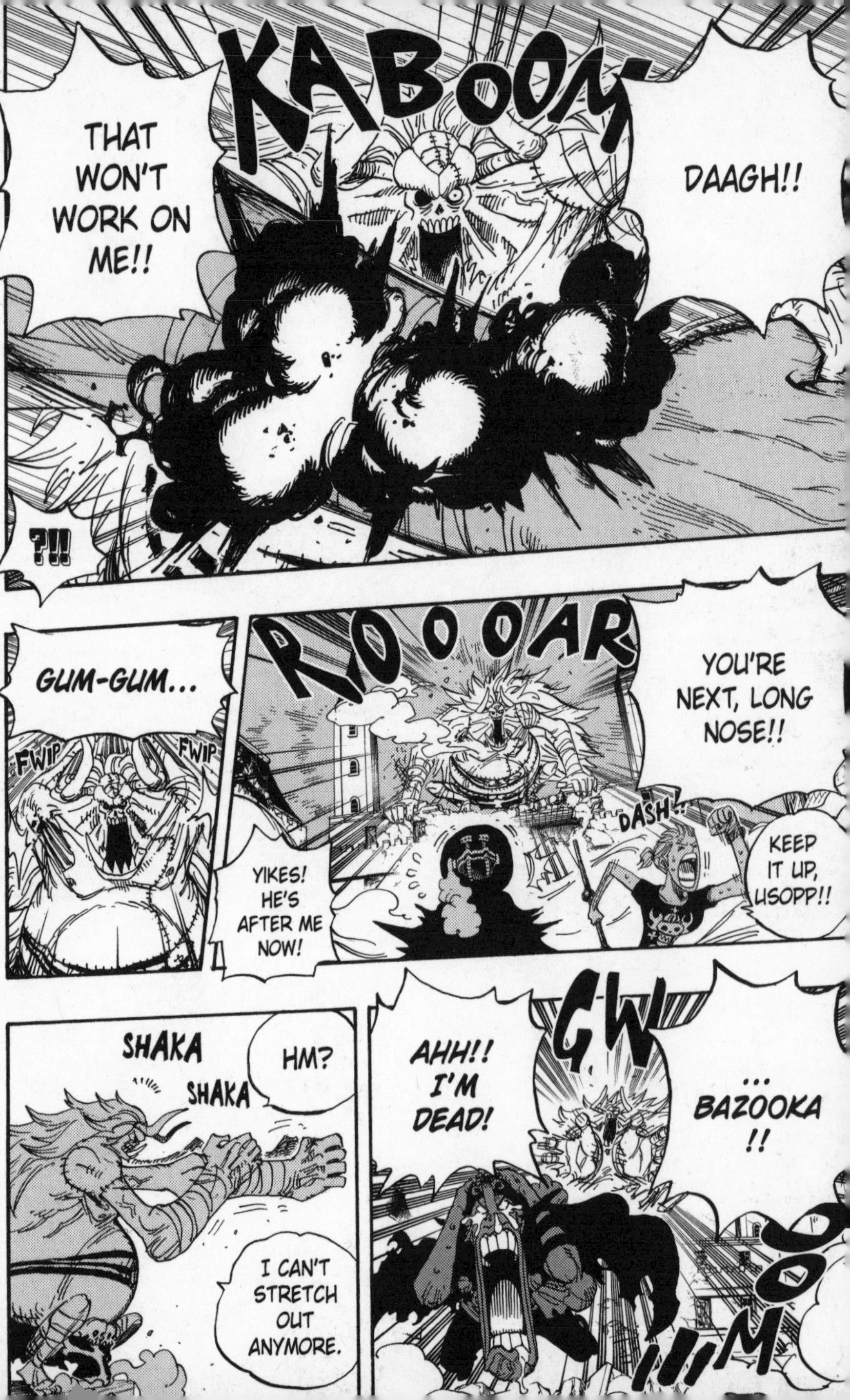
KABOOM
DAAGH!!
THAT WON'T WORK ON ME!!
?!!
ROOOAR
YOU'RE NEXT, LONG NOSE!!
KEEP IT UP, USOPP!!
DASH
YIKES! HE'S AFTER ME NOW!
GUM-GUM...
FWIP
FWIP
GW
... BAZOOKA !!
AHH!! I'M DEAD!
OOM
HM?
SHAKA
SHAKA
I CAN'T STRETCH OUT ANYMORE.

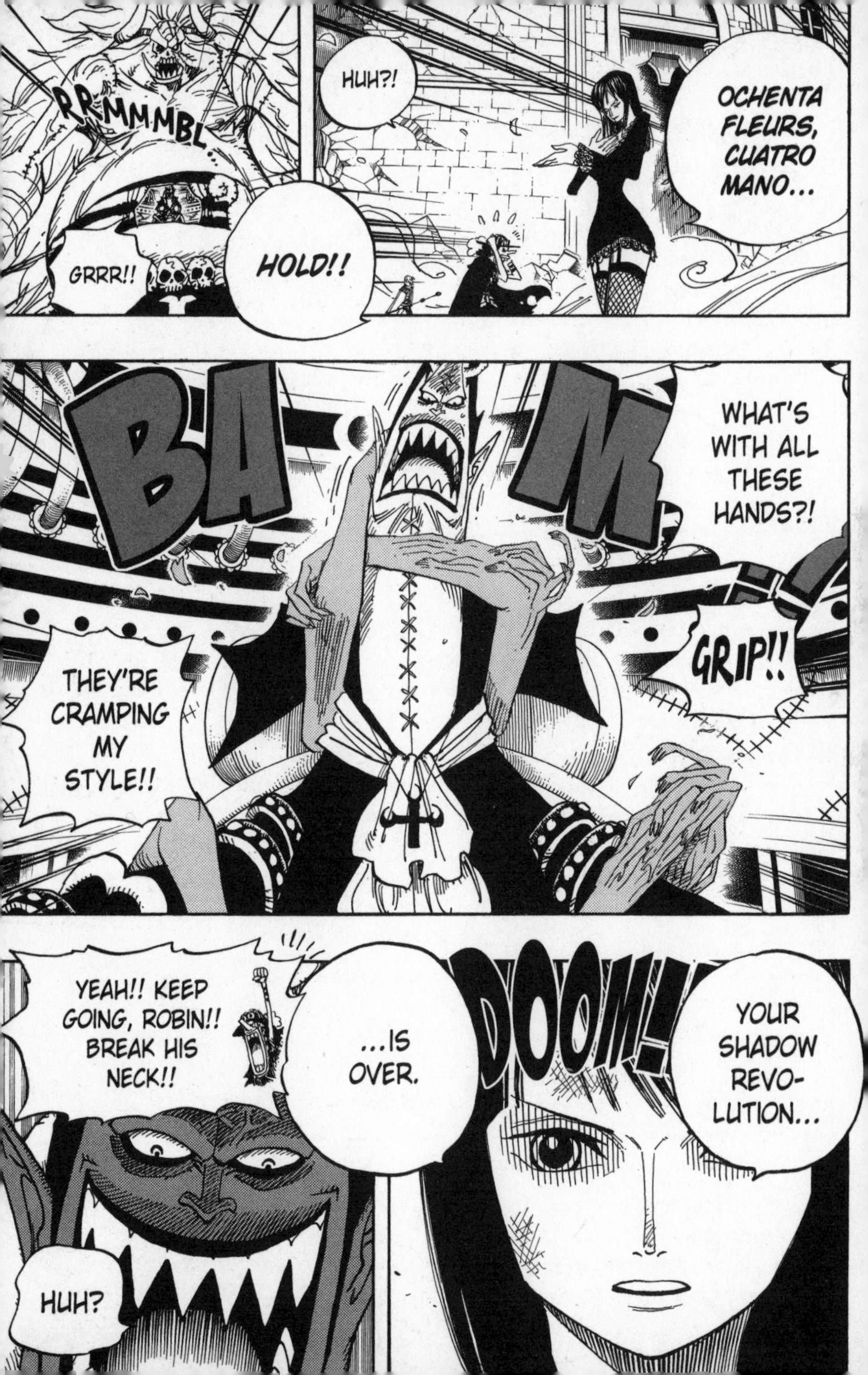
OCHENTA FLEURS, CUATRO MANO...
HUH?!
HOLD!!
RRMMMMBL
GRRR!!
WHAT'S WITH ALL THESE HANDS?!
BAM
GRIP!!
THEY'RE CRAMPING MY STYLE!!
YOUR SHADOW REVO-LUTION...
DOOM!!
...IS OVER.
YEAH!! KEEP GOING, ROBIN!! BREAK HIS NECK!!
HUH?

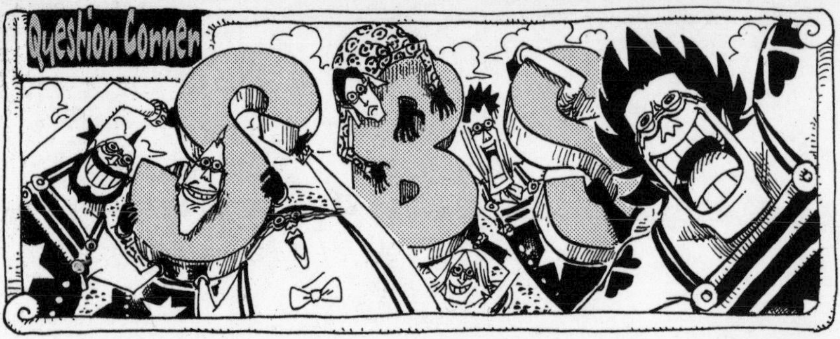
Question Corner
SBS

Q: I made a huge discovery! Despite needing to study for my exams, I read through volumes 1-48 of *One Piece* again! And the thing I discovered was that in volume 25, chapter 233: "The World's Greatest Power," there was a scene where Buggy was looking for Captain John's treasure. And in volume 47, we see Captain John appear in chapter 451, "Perona's Wonder Garden!" This is the discovery of the century! Who exactly is Captain John?! And how exactly was he cruel? Tell me, Ei-Chan!! --Dosa Boy

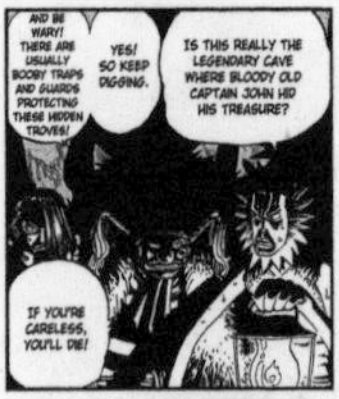
IS THIS REALLY THE LEGENDARY CAVE WHERE BLOODY OLD CAPTAIN JOHN HID HIS TREASURE?
YES! SO KEEP DIGGING.
AND BE WARY! THERE ARE USUALLY BOOBY TRAPS AND GUARDS PROTECTING THESE HIDDEN TROVES!
IF YOU'RE CARELESS, YOU'LL DIE!

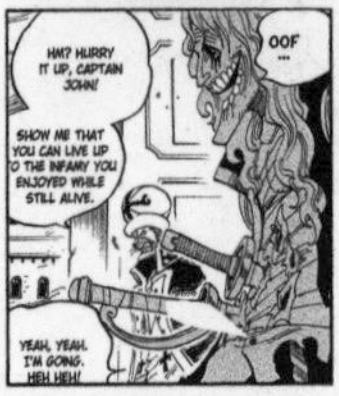
OOF ...
HM? HURRY IT UP, CAPTAIN JOHN!
SHOW ME THAT YOU CAN LIVE UP TO THE INFAMY YOU ENJOYED WHILE STILL ALIVE.
YEAH, YEAH. I'M GOING. HEH HEH!

A: I'm surprised that you found it. You're right. The treasure that Buggy and his crew were looking for belonged to a man who's already a zombie in Thriller Bark. Look carefully at the stomach of the zombie of Captain John. He has many stab wounds and still has two swords stuck in his stomach. John tried to keep all the treasure for himself, and his own crew killed him. After John died, his treasure became the stuff of legend.

Q: Don't mind me. Just move on to the next question. --15

A: Okay.

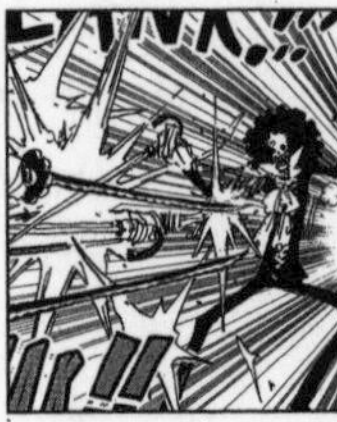

Q: The battle between Brook and Ryuma in chapter 462: "Adventures of Oars" looks like fencing! I learned some fencing back in high school, so I can tell. And as I kept reading, I see Coup Droit, Bond en Avant, Remise, and many other fencing terms! As a fencing lover, I was overjoyed! So Brook was a fencer! His height and slim build is perfect for fencing! (You'll die if you don't wear a mask!!) --G-chan

A: That's right. He's a fencer! (So that's what you call them) Yes, he's a fencer! Guess what everyone, Brook is a fencer! And about the Question Corner, I'll be fencing it off (ending) here! See you next volume!!

Chapter 477: 3/8

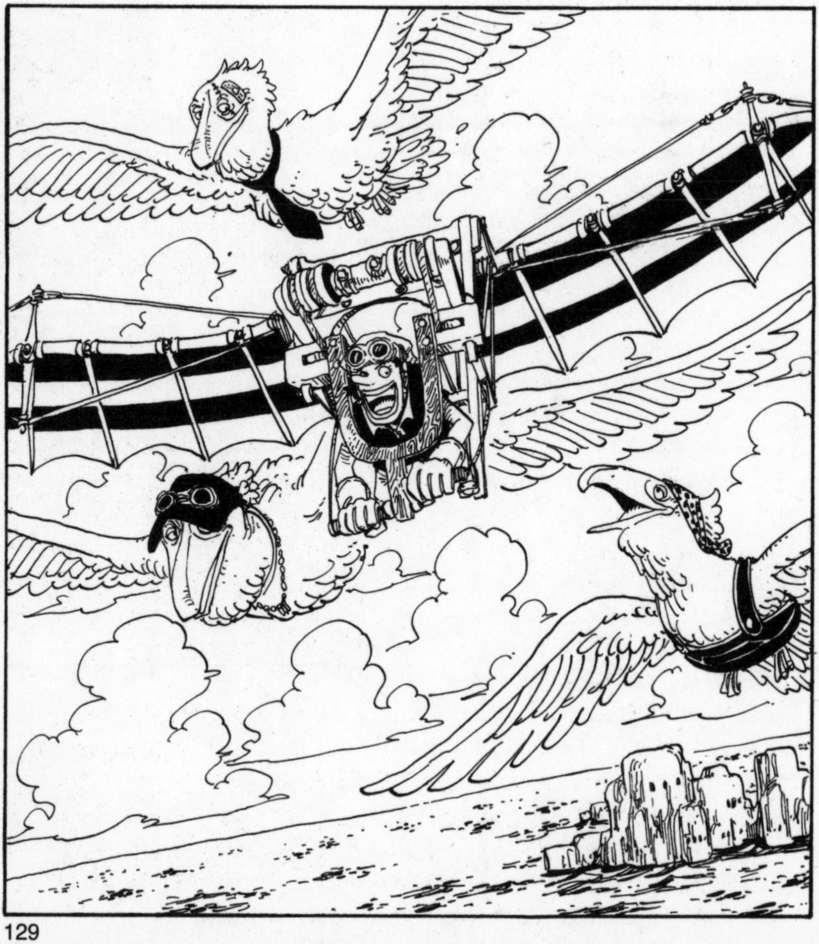

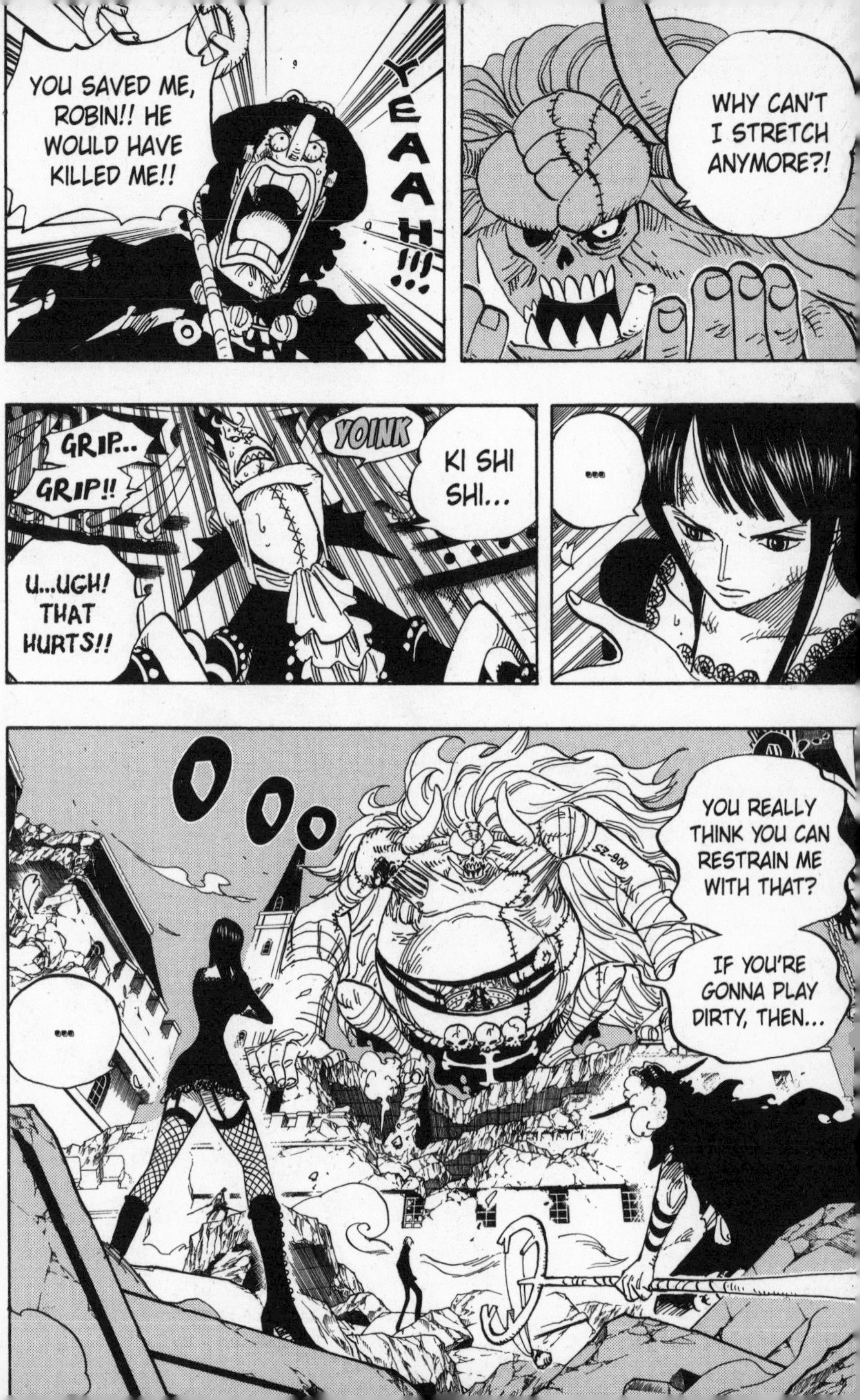
WHY CAN'T I STRETCH ANYMORE?!
YOU SAVED ME, ROBIN!! HE WOULD HAVE KILLED ME!!
YEAAH!!!
...
YOINK
KI SHI SHI...
GRIP...
GRIP!!
U...UGH! THAT HURTS!!
YOU REALLY THINK YOU CAN RESTRAIN ME WITH THAT?
IF YOU'RE GONNA PLAY DIRTY, THEN...
...

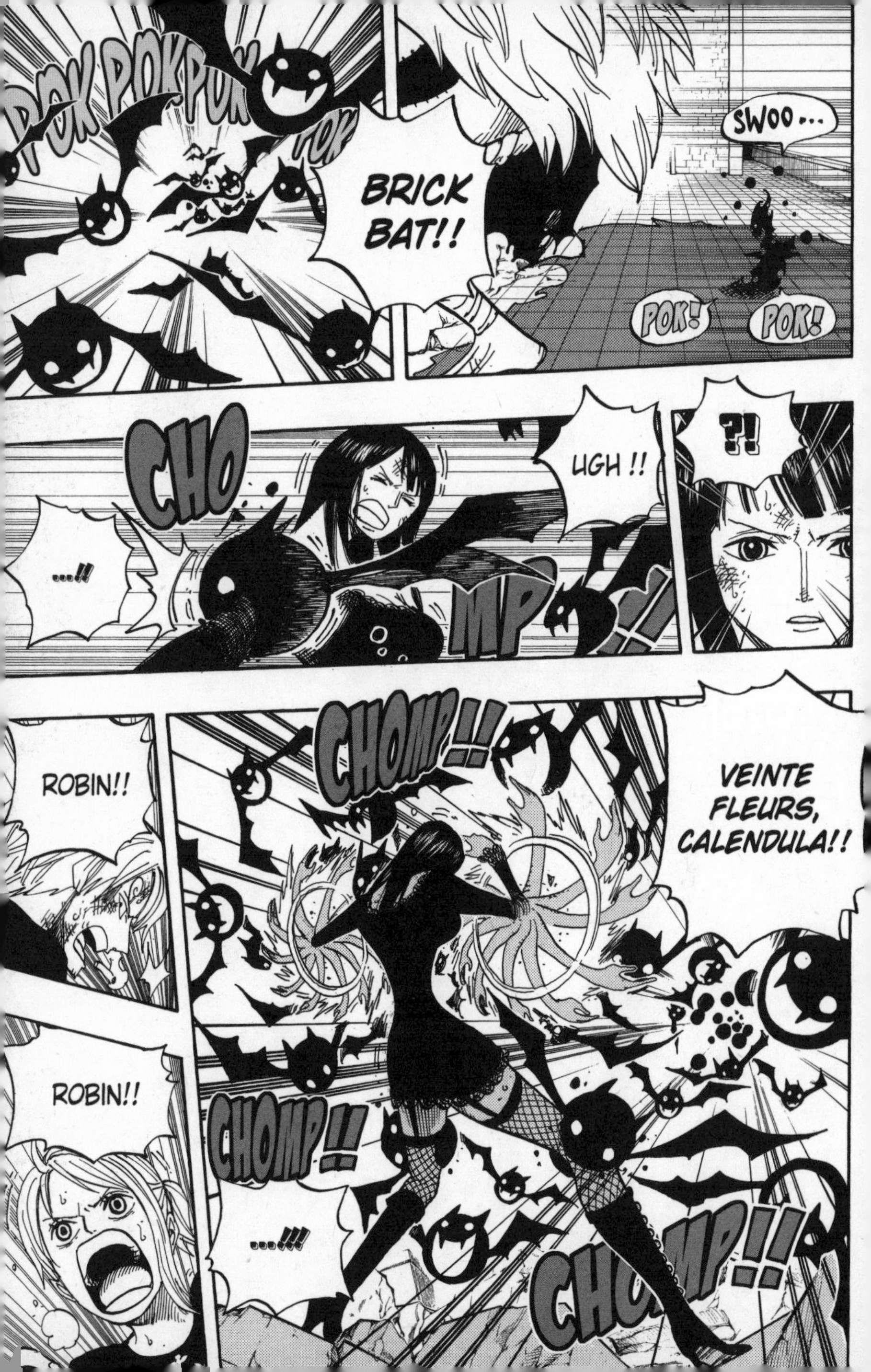
SWOO...
POK!
POK!
BRICK BAT!!
POK POK POK POK
?!
UGH !!
CHOMP!!
...!!
VEINTE FLEURS, CALENDULA!!
CHOMP!!
CHOMP!!
...!!!
CHOMP!!
ROBIN!!
ROBIN!!

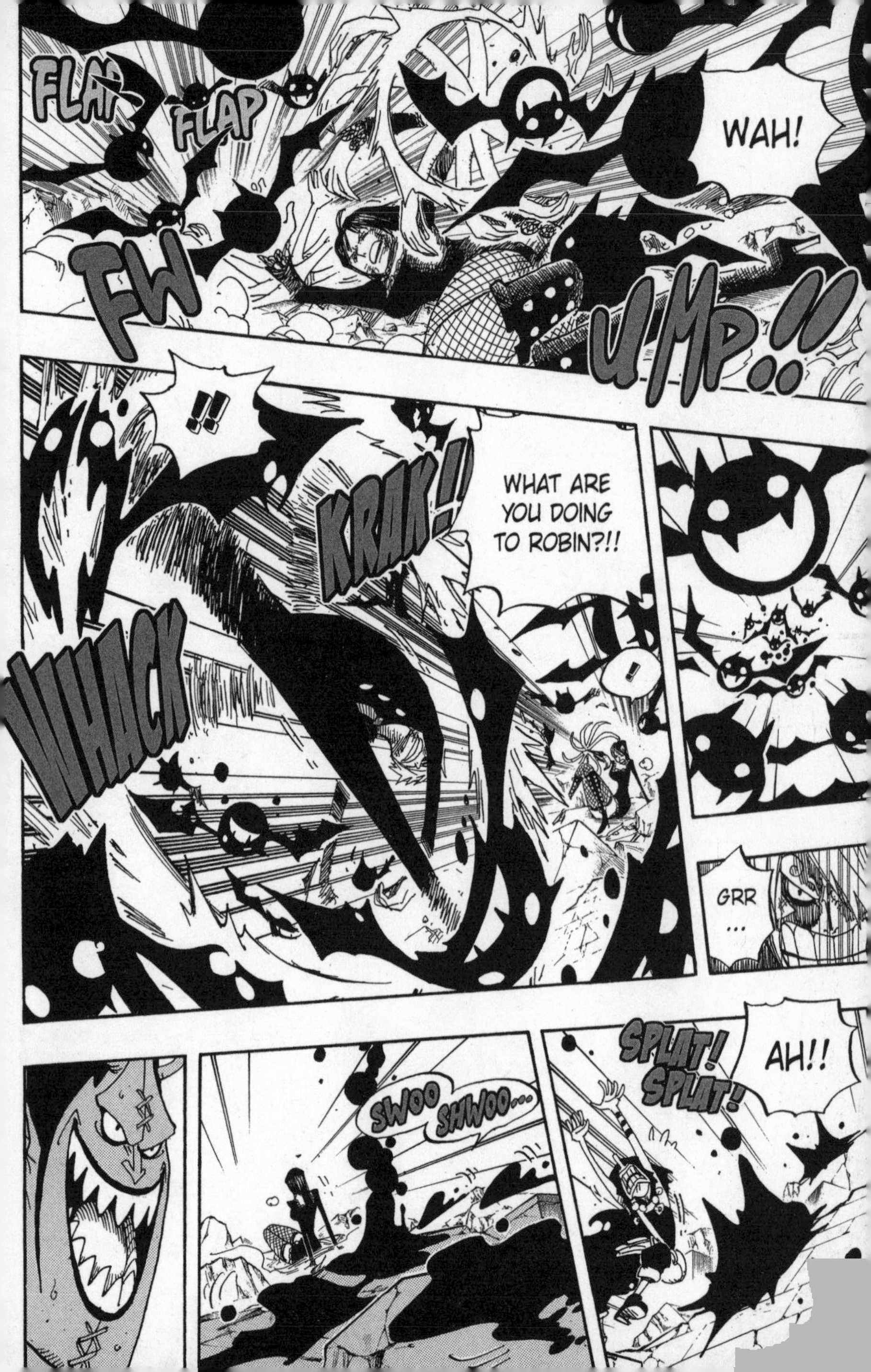
WAH!
FLAP
FLAP
FWUMP!!
GRR...
WHAT ARE YOU DOING TO ROBIN?!!
!!
KRAK!!
WHACK
!
AH!!
SPLAT! SPLAT!
SWOO SHWOO...

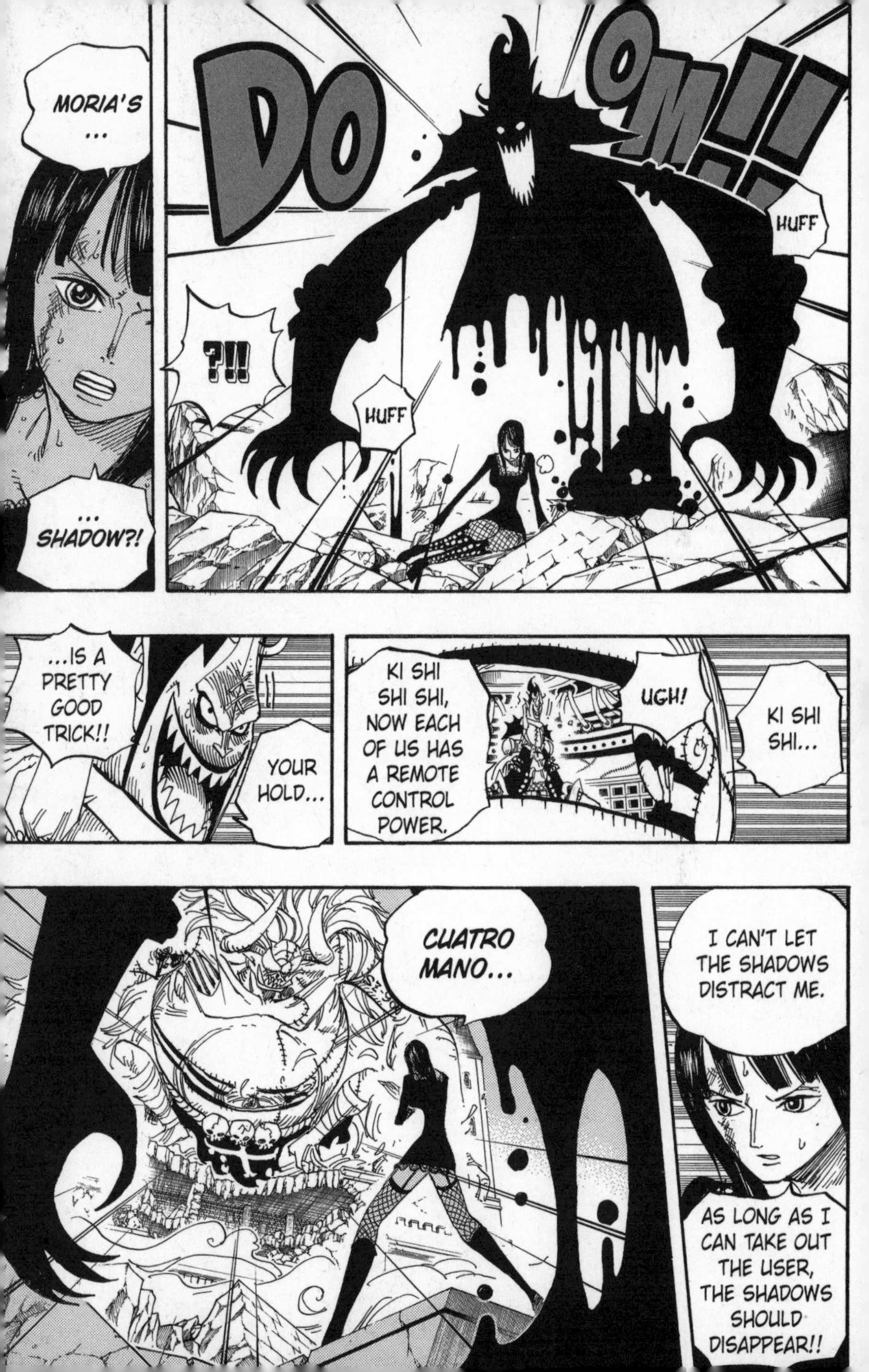
DO
OM!!
HUFF
?!!
HUFF
MORIA'S ...
... SHADOW?!
KI SHI SHI...
UGH!
KI SHI SHI SHI, NOW EACH OF US HAS A REMOTE CONTROL POWER.
YOUR HOLD...
...IS A PRETTY GOOD TRICK!!
I CAN'T LET THE SHADOWS DISTRACT ME.
AS LONG AS I CAN TAKE OUT THE USER, THE SHADOWS SHOULD DISAPPEAR!!
CUATRO MANO...

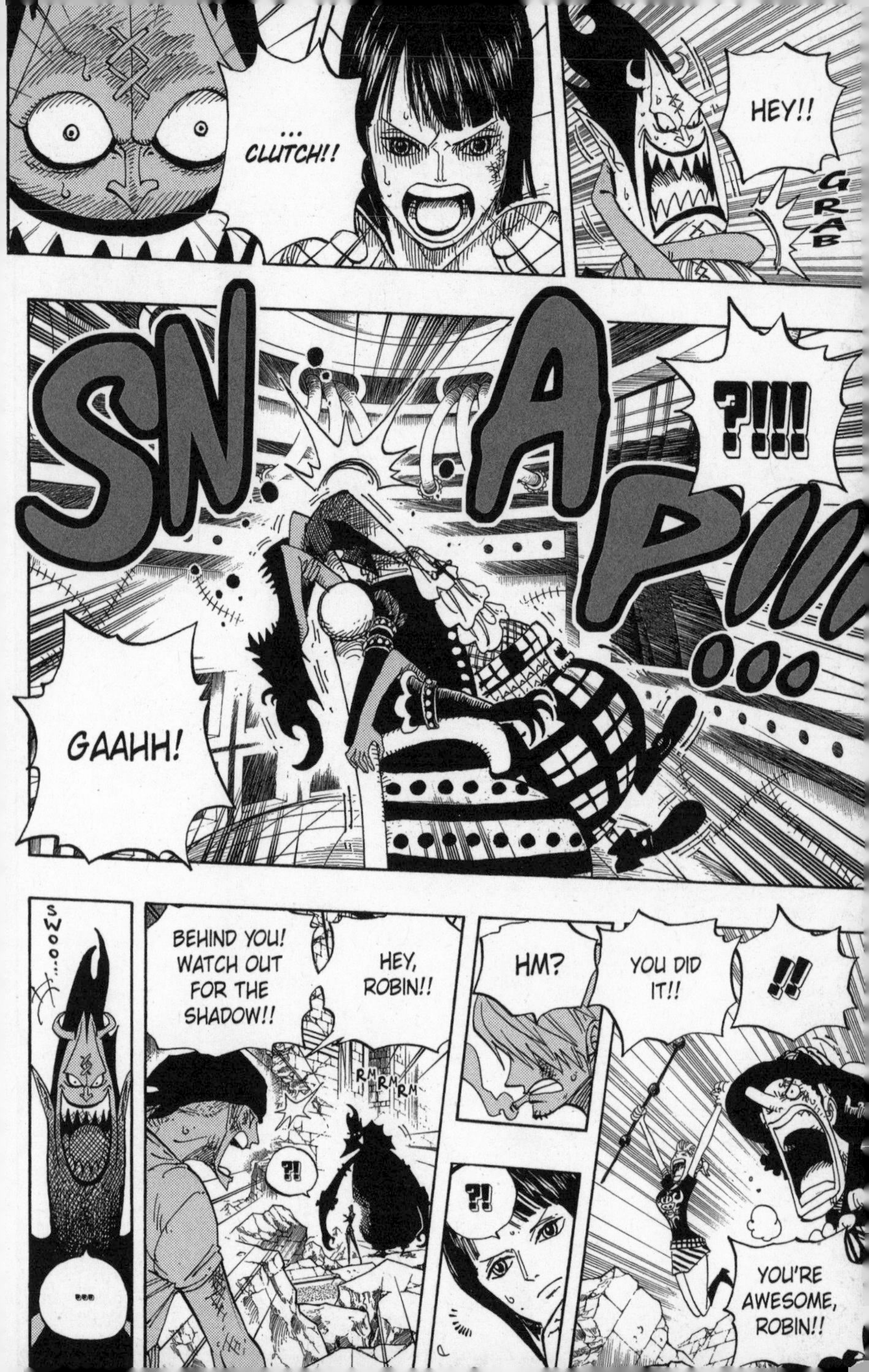
HEY!!
GRAB
... CLUTCH!!
?!!!
SNAP!!!...
GAAHH!
!!
YOU DID IT!!
YOU'RE AWESOME, ROBIN!!
HM?
?!
HEY, ROBIN!!
BEHIND YOU! WATCH OUT FOR THE SHADOW!!
?!
SWOO...
...

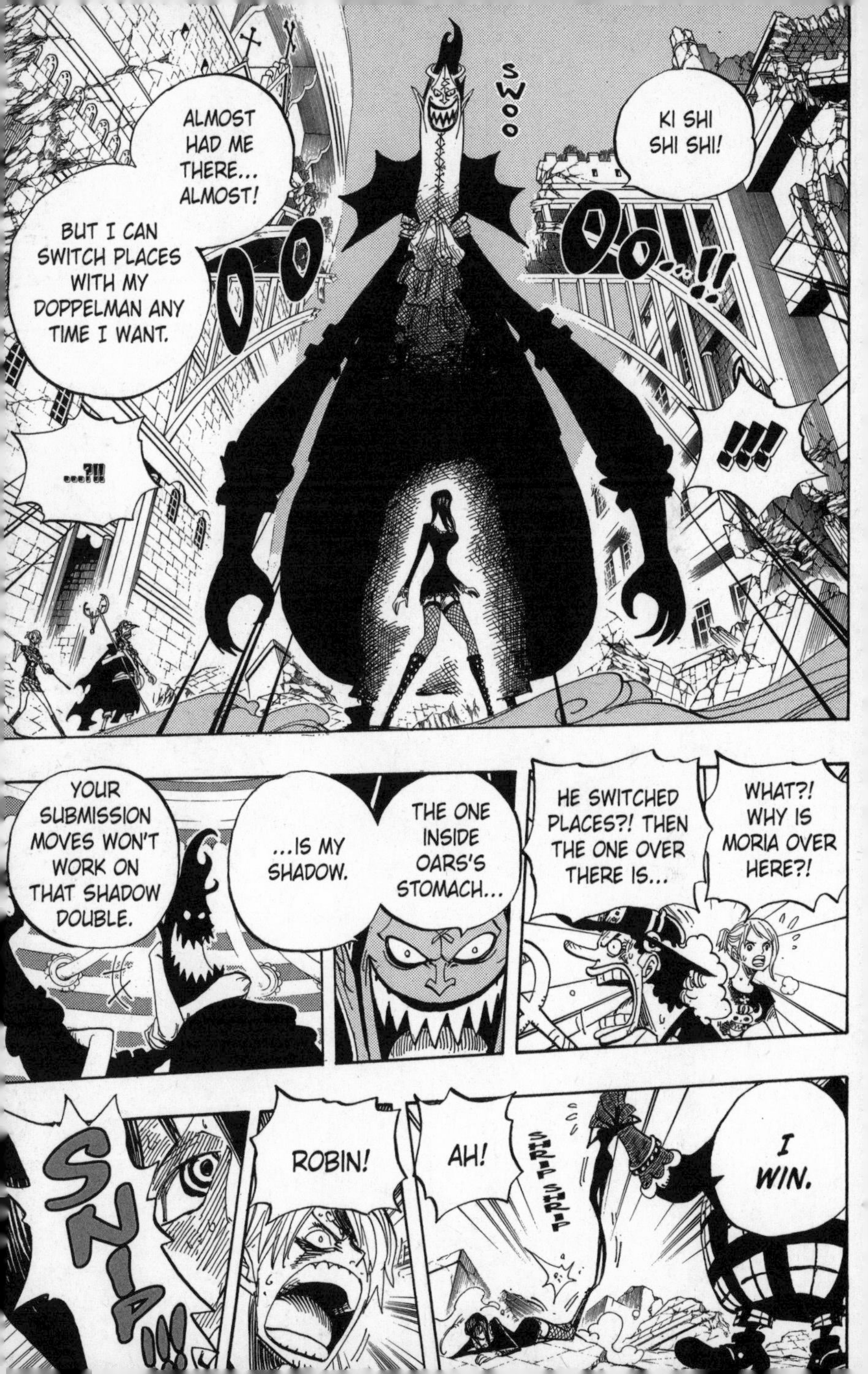
KI SHI SHI SHI!
SWOO
OO...!!
OOO
ALMOST HAD ME THERE... ALMOST!
BUT I CAN SWITCH PLACES WITH MY DOPPELMAN ANY TIME I WANT.
!!!
...?!!
WHAT?! WHY IS MORIA OVER HERE?!
HE SWITCHED PLACES?! THEN THE ONE OVER THERE IS...
THE ONE INSIDE OARS'S STOMACH...
...IS MY SHADOW.
YOUR SUBMISSION MOVES WON'T WORK ON THAT SHADOW DOUBLE.
I WIN.
SHRIP SHRIP
AH!
ROBIN!
SNIP!!!

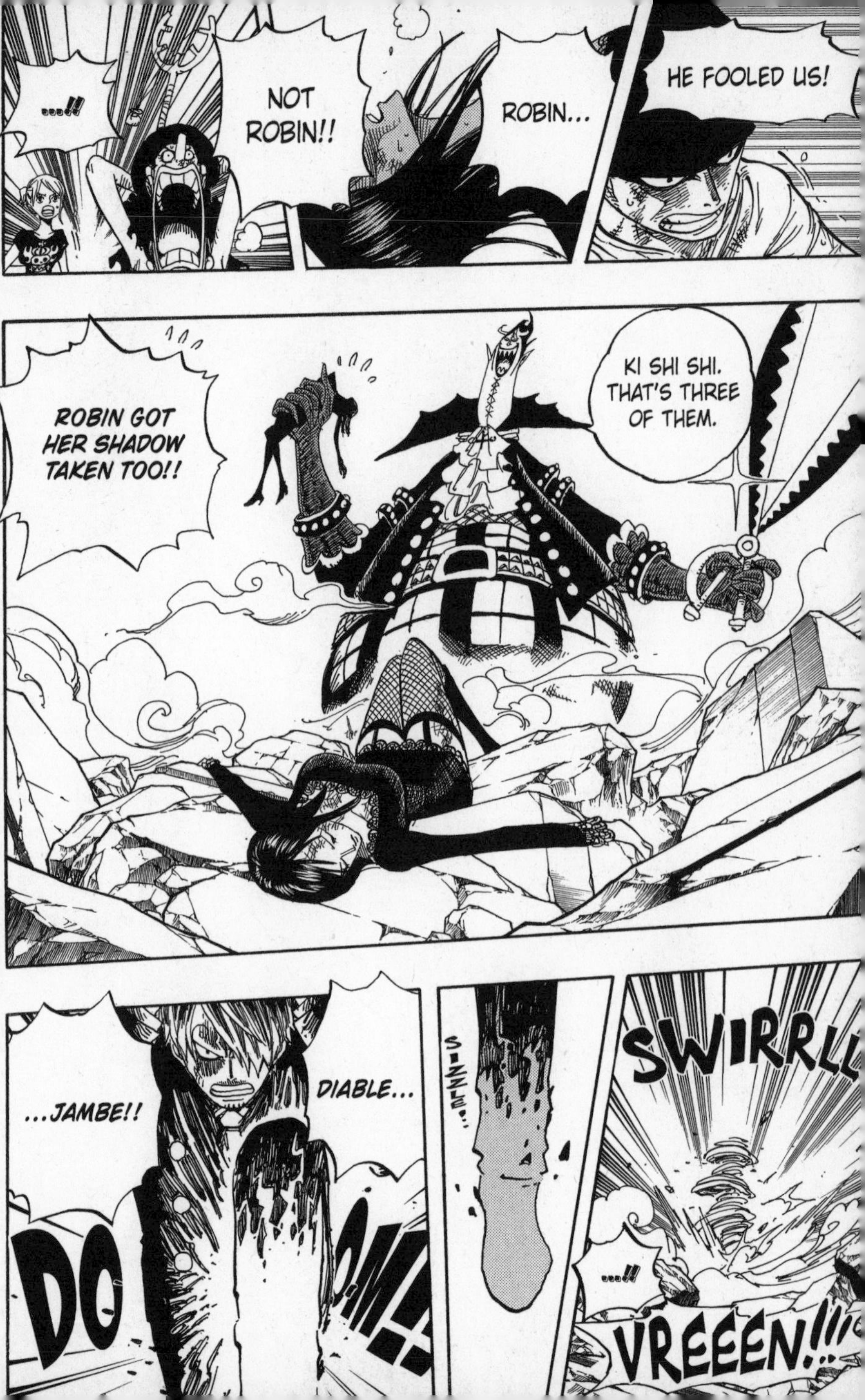
HE FOOLED US!
ROBIN...
NOT ROBIN!!
...!!
KI SHI SHI. THAT'S THREE OF THEM.
ROBIN GOT HER SHADOW TAKEN TOO!!
SWIRRLL
...!!
VREEEN!!!
SIZZLE..
DIABLE...
...JAMBE!!
DO
OM!!

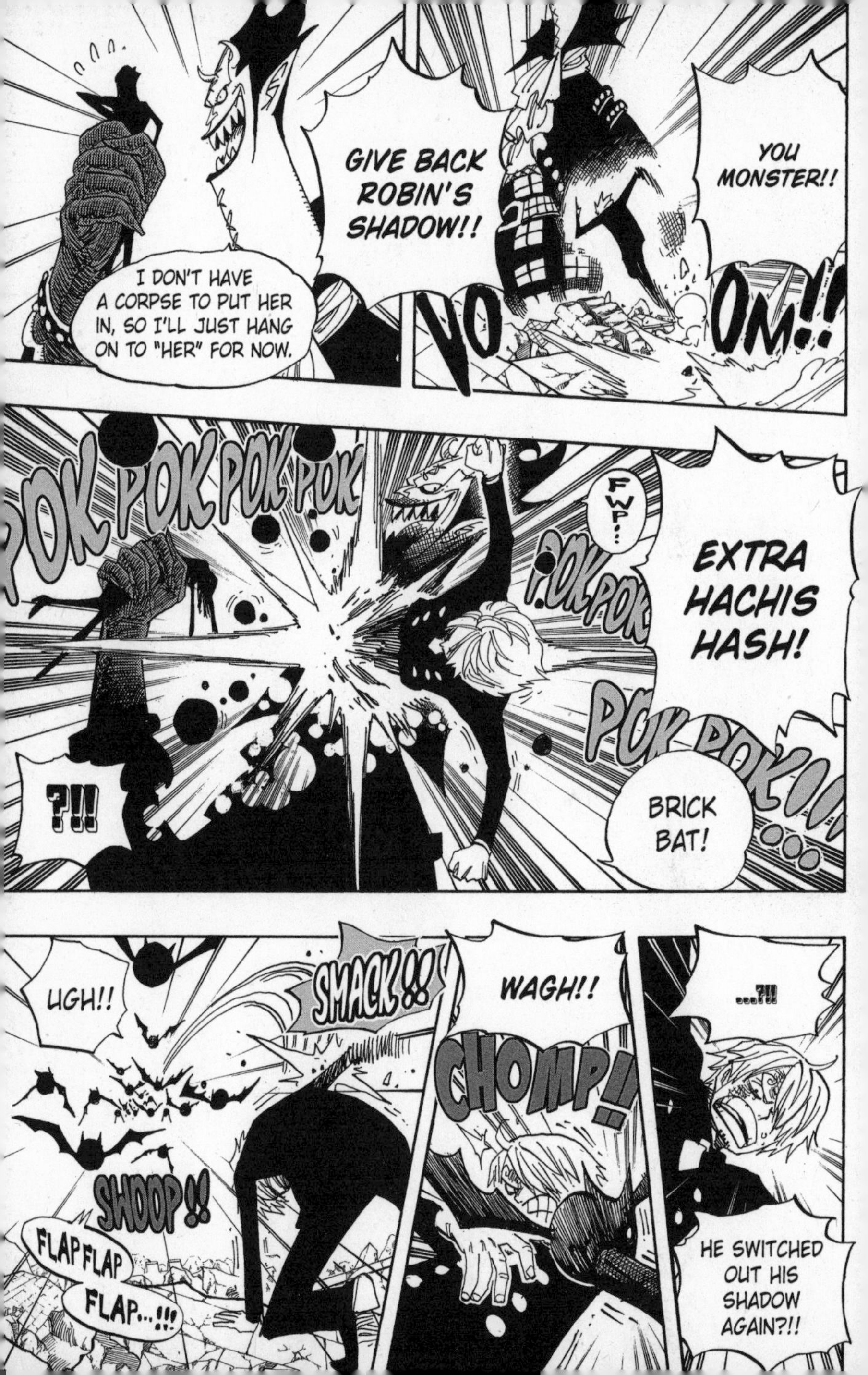
YOU MONSTER!!
GIVE BACK ROBIN'S SHADOW!!
VO OM!!
I DON'T HAVE A CORPSE TO PUT HER IN, SO I'LL JUST HANG ON TO "HER" FOR NOW.
EXTRA HACHIS HASH!
FWP...
POK POK
POK POK
BRICK BAT!
POK POK POK POK
?!!
...?!!
HE SWITCHED OUT HIS SHADOW AGAIN?!!
WAGH!!
CHOMP!!
SMACK!!
UGH!!
SHOOP!!
FLAP FLAP
FLAP...!!!

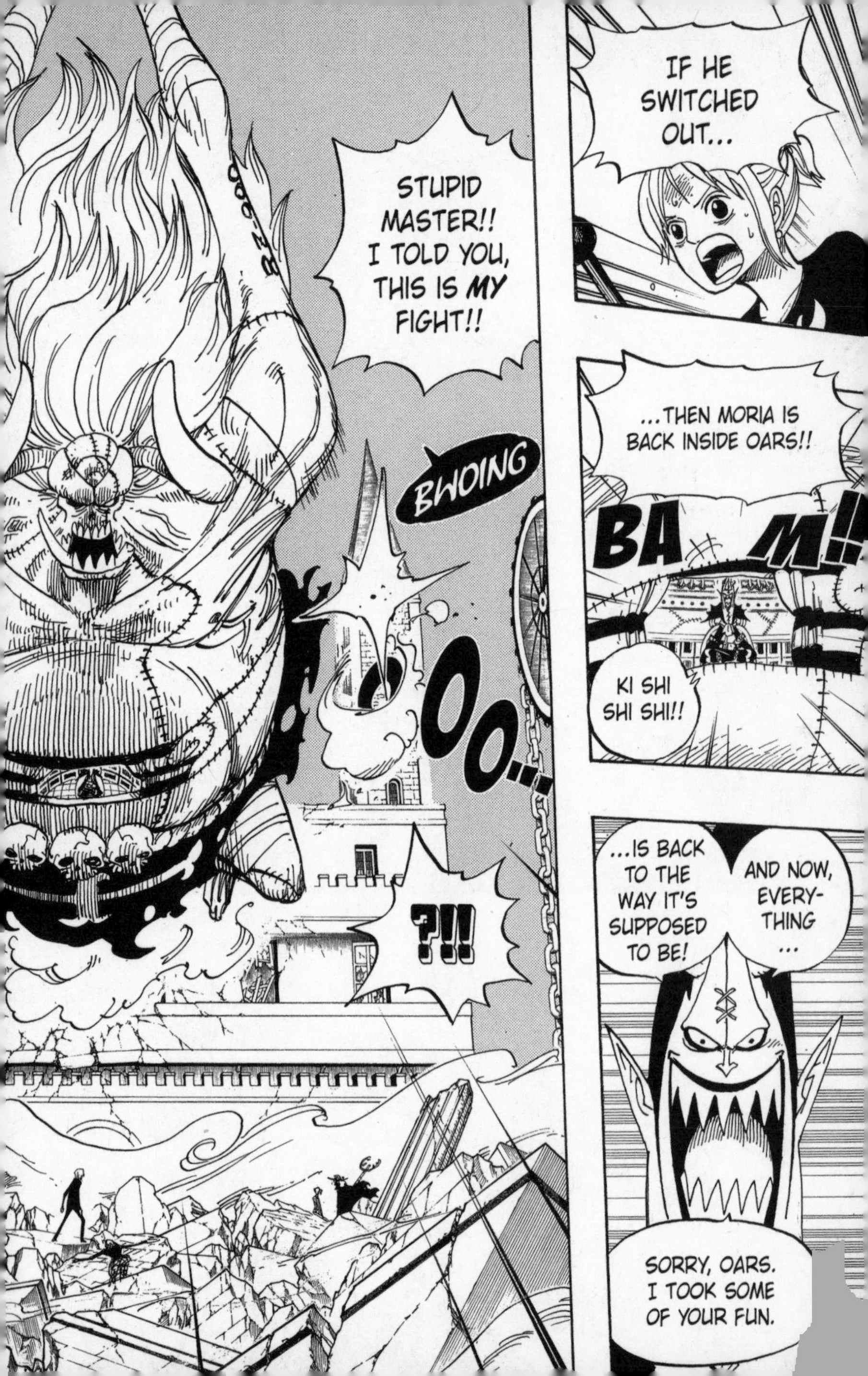
IF HE SWITCHED OUT...
...THEN MORIA IS BACK INSIDE OARS!!
BA M!!
KI SHI SHI SHI!!
AND NOW, EVERY-THING...
...IS BACK TO THE WAY IT'S SUPPOSED TO BE!
SORRY, OARS. I TOOK SOME OF YOUR FUN.
STUPID MASTER!! I TOLD YOU, THIS IS MY FIGHT!!
BWOING
OO...
?!!

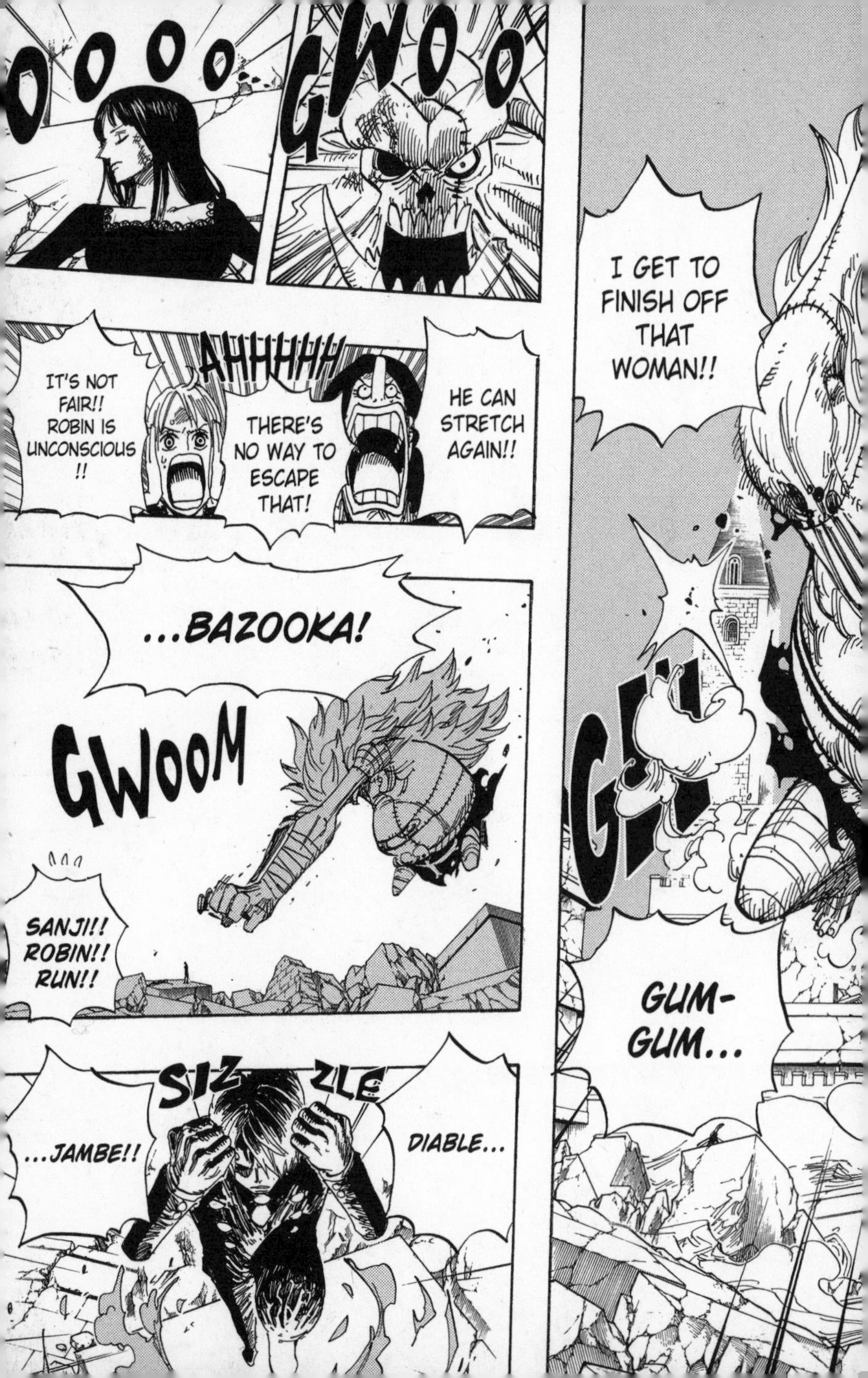
I GET TO FINISH OFF THAT WOMAN!!
GUM-GUM...
GWOOO
OOOO
HE CAN STRETCH AGAIN!!
AHHHHH
THERE'S NO WAY TO ESCAPE THAT!
IT'S NOT FAIR!! ROBIN IS UNCONSCIOUS!!
...BAZOOKA!
GWOOM
SANJI!! ROBIN!! RUN!!
SIZZLE
DIABLE...
...JAMBE!!

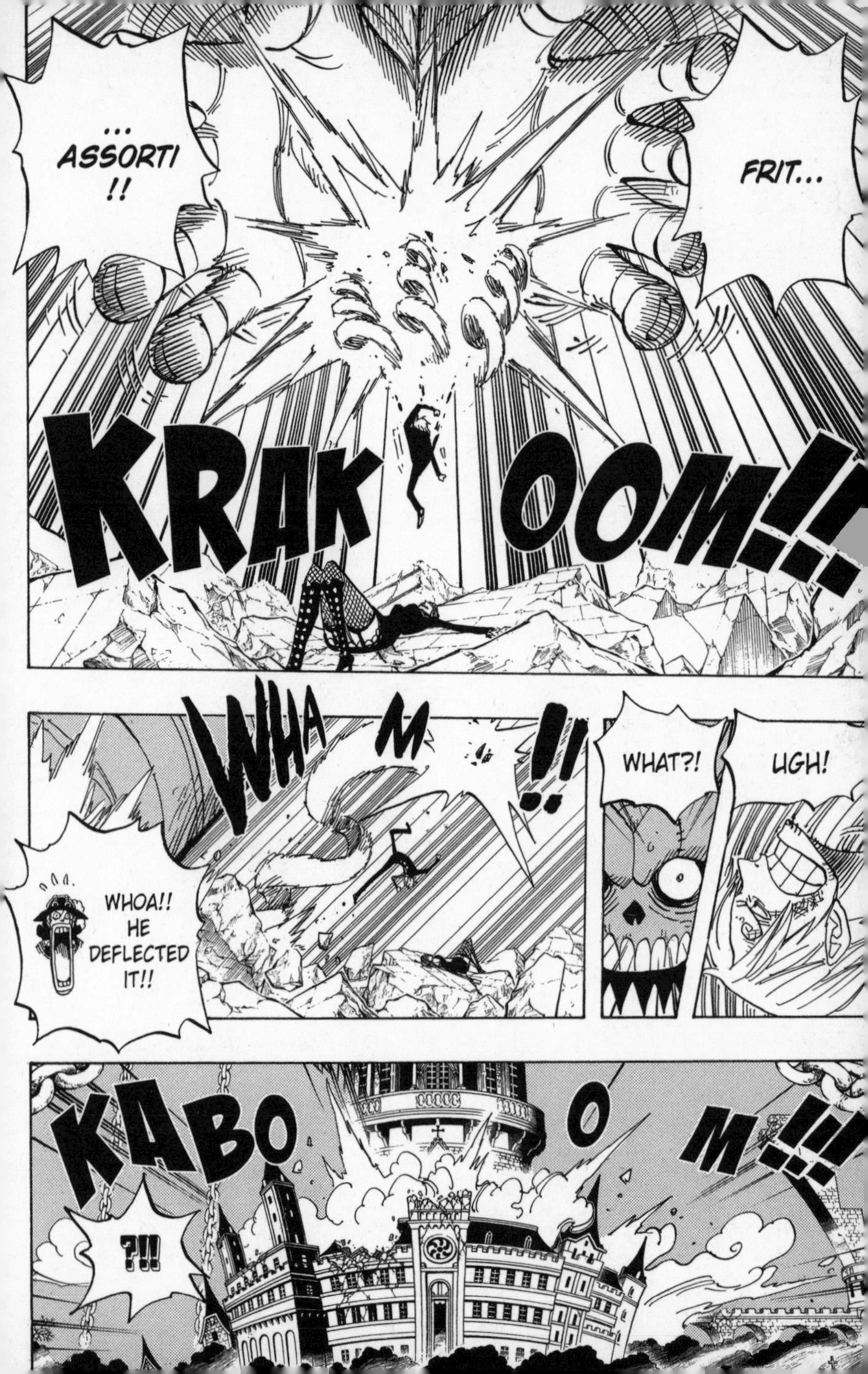
FRIT...
... ASSORTI !!
KRAK OOM!!!
UGH!
WHAT?!
WHA M !!
WHOA!! HE DEFLECTED IT!!
KABO O M!!!
?!!

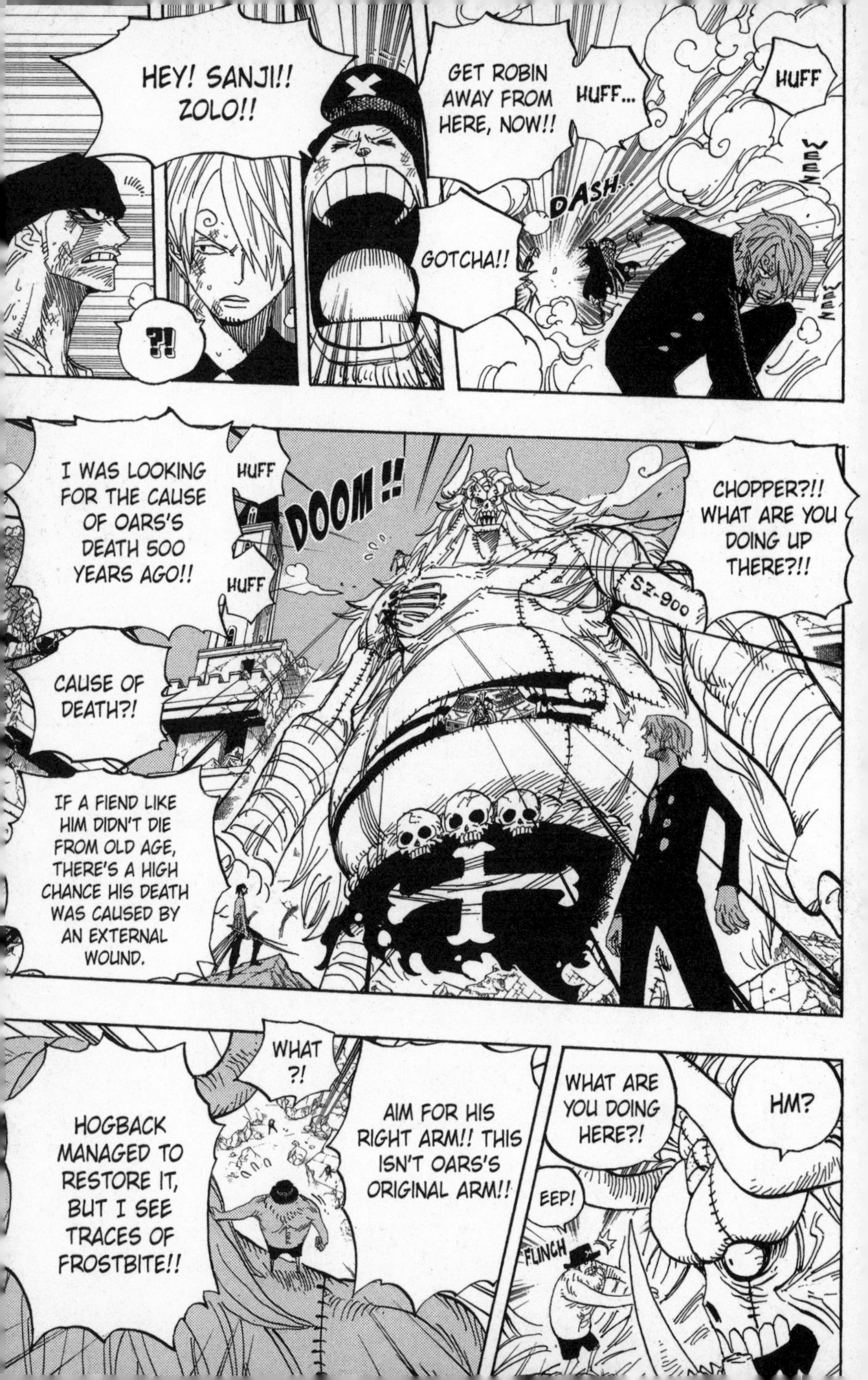
HUFF
WEEZ
HUFF...
DASH
GOTCHA!!
WEEZ
GET ROBIN AWAY FROM HERE, NOW!!
HEY! SANJI!! ZOLO!!
?!
CHOPPER?!! WHAT ARE YOU DOING UP THERE?!!
SZ-900
DOOM!!
HUFF
I WAS LOOKING FOR THE CAUSE OF OARS'S DEATH 500 YEARS AGO!!
HUFF
CAUSE OF DEATH?!
IF A FIEND LIKE HIM DIDN'T DIE FROM OLD AGE, THERE'S A HIGH CHANCE HIS DEATH WAS CAUSED BY AN EXTERNAL WOUND.
HM?
WHAT ARE YOU DOING HERE?!
EEP!
FLINCH
WHAT ?!
AIM FOR HIS RIGHT ARM!! THIS ISN'T OARS'S ORIGINAL ARM!!
HOGBACK MANAGED TO RESTORE IT, BUT I SEE TRACES OF FROSTBITE!!

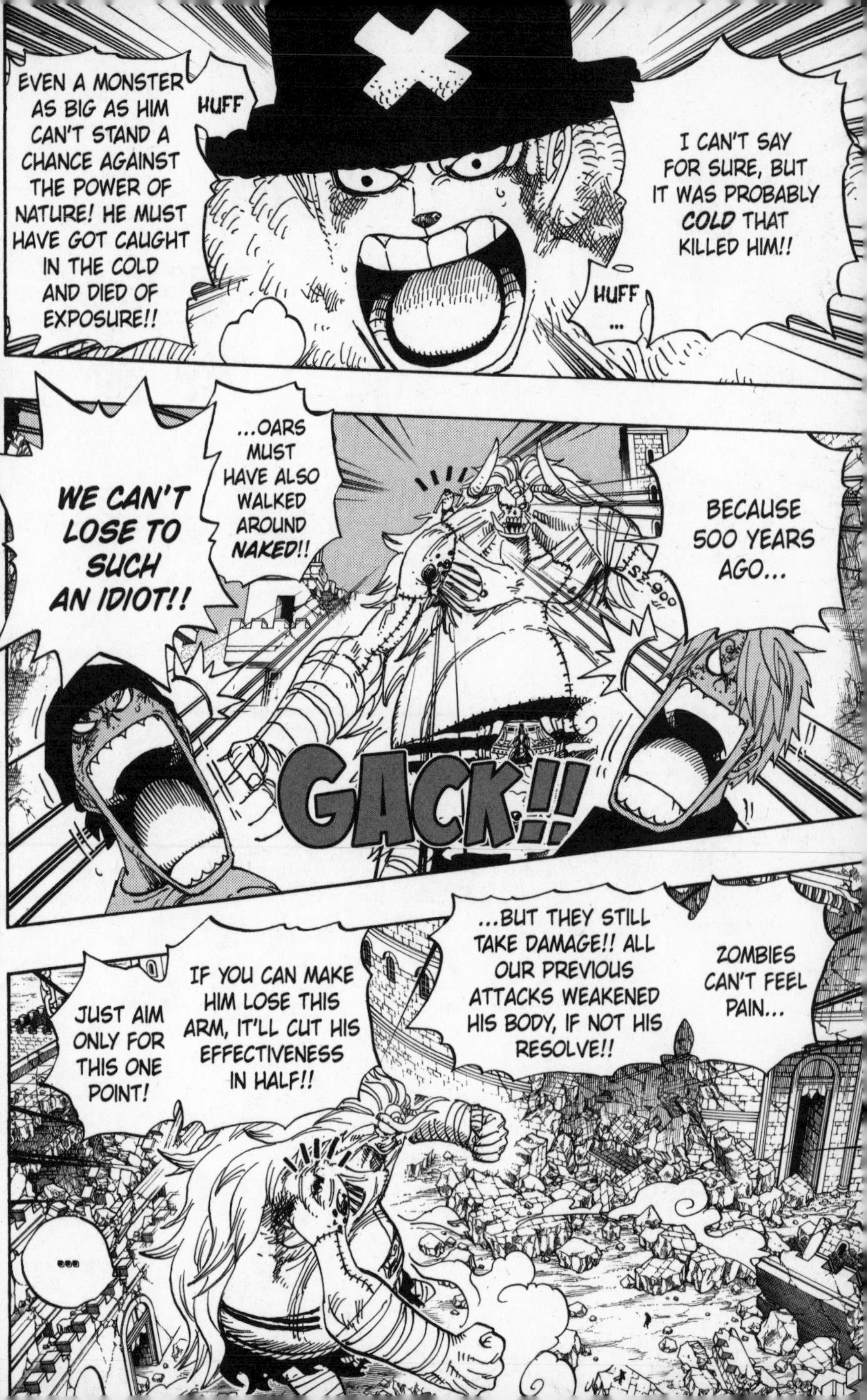
I CAN'T SAY FOR SURE, BUT IT WAS PROBABLY COLD THAT KILLED HIM!!
HUFF ...
HUFF
EVEN A MONSTER AS BIG AS HIM CAN'T STAND A CHANCE AGAINST THE POWER OF NATURE! HE MUST HAVE GOT CAUGHT IN THE COLD AND DIED OF EXPOSURE!!
BECAUSE 500 YEARS AGO...
...OARS MUST HAVE ALSO WALKED AROUND NAKED!!
WE CAN'T LOSE TO SUCH AN IDIOT!!
GACK!!
ZOMBIES CAN'T FEEL PAIN...
...BUT THEY STILL TAKE DAMAGE!! ALL OUR PREVIOUS ATTACKS WEAKENED HIS BODY, IF NOT HIS RESOLVE!!
IF YOU CAN MAKE HIM LOSE THIS ARM, IT'LL CUT HIS EFFECTIVENESS IN HALF!!
JUST AIM ONLY FOR THIS ONE POINT!
...

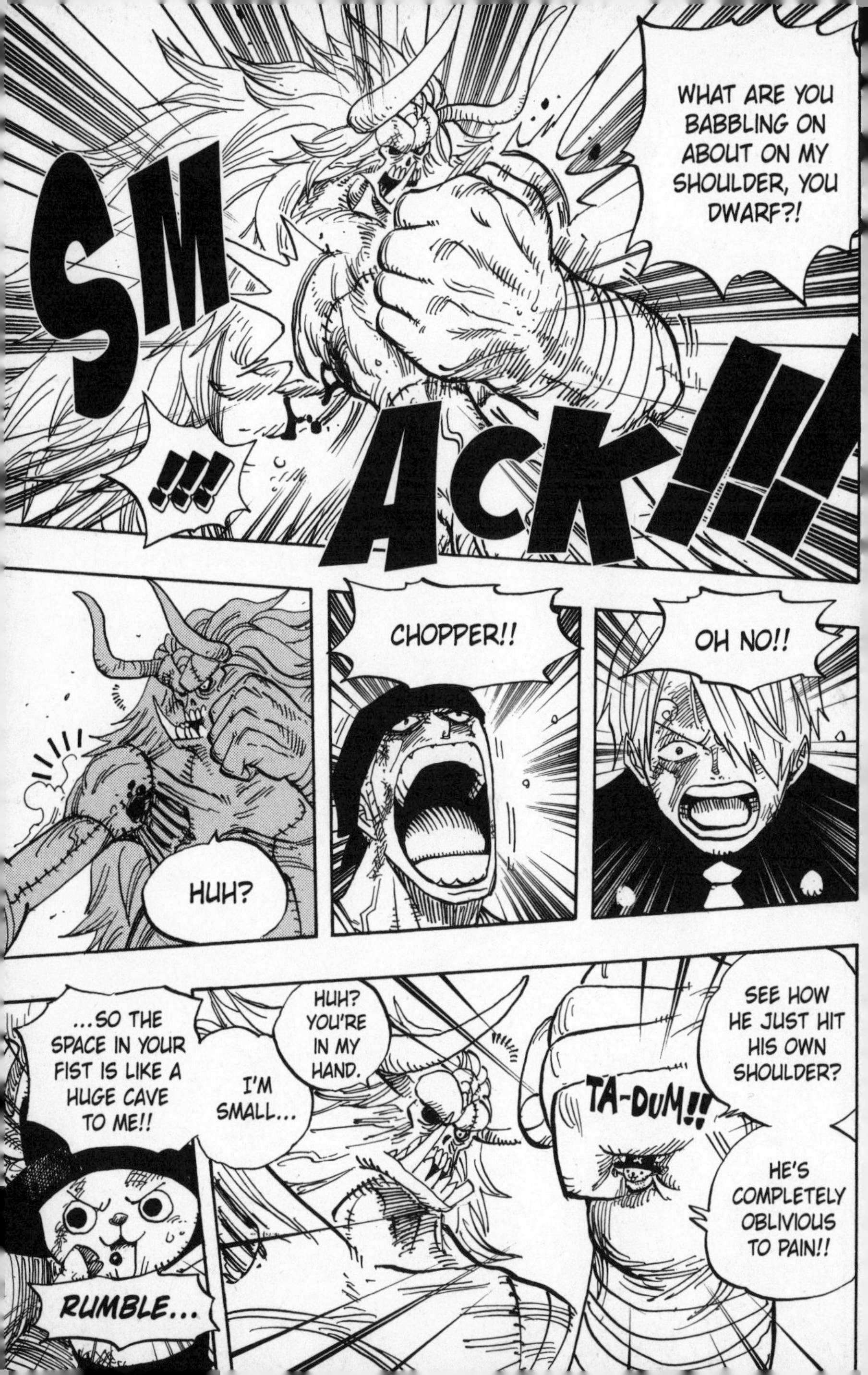
WHAT ARE YOU BABBLING ON ABOUT ON MY SHOULDER, YOU DWARF?!
SMACK!!!
...!!!
OH NO!!
CHOPPER!!
HUH?
SEE HOW HE JUST HIT HIS OWN SHOULDER?
TA-DUM!!
HE'S COMPLETELY OBLIVIOUS TO PAIN!!
HUH? YOU'RE IN MY HAND.
I'M SMALL...
...SO THE SPACE IN YOUR FIST IS LIKE A HUGE CAVE TO ME!!
RUMBLE...

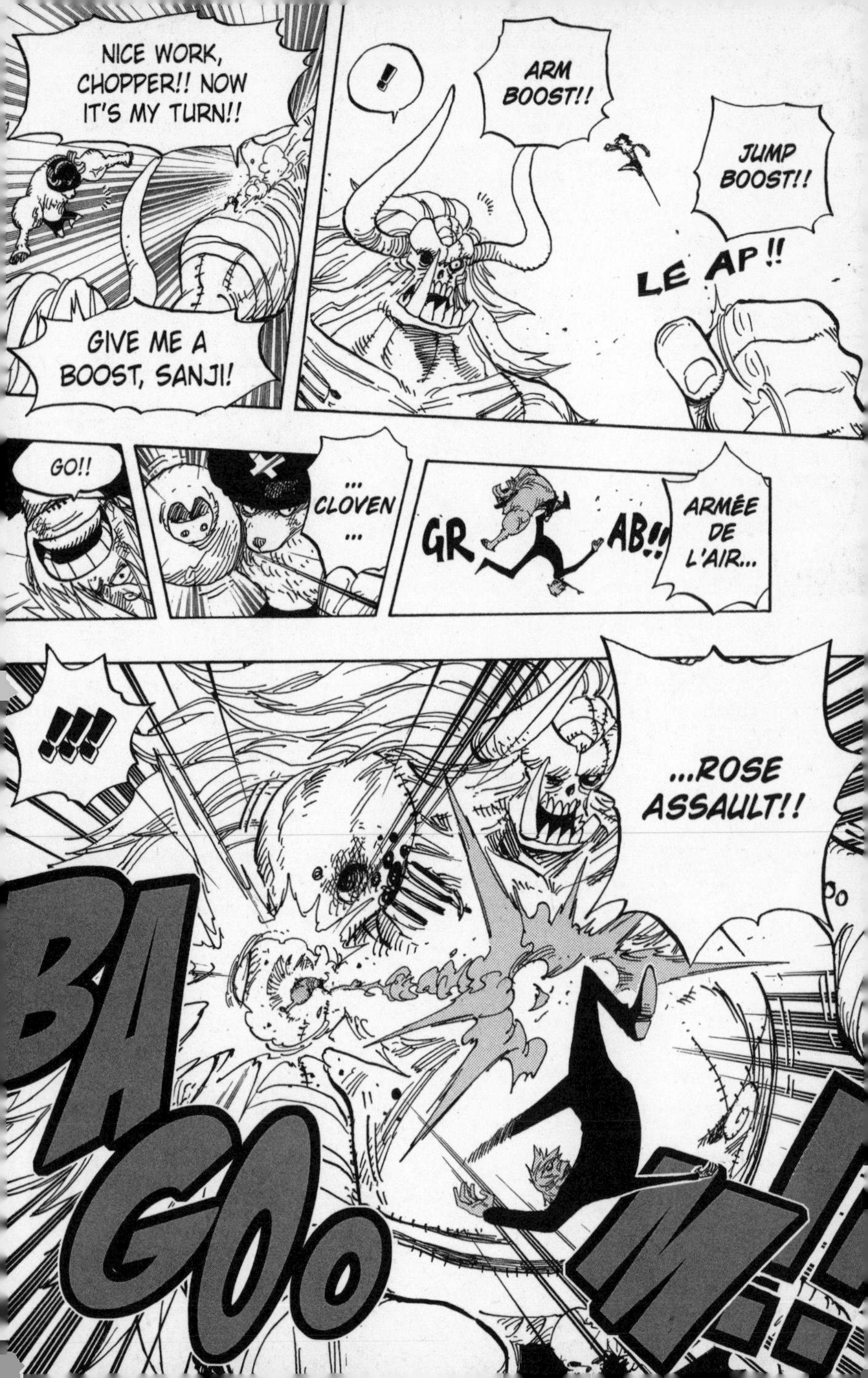
!
ARM BOOST!!
JUMP BOOST!!
LE AP!!
NICE WORK, CHOPPER!! NOW IT'S MY TURN!!
GIVE ME A BOOST, SANJI!
ARMÉE DE L'AIR...
GR AB!!
...CLOVEN...
GO!!
...ROSE ASSAULT!!
!!!
BA GOO M!!

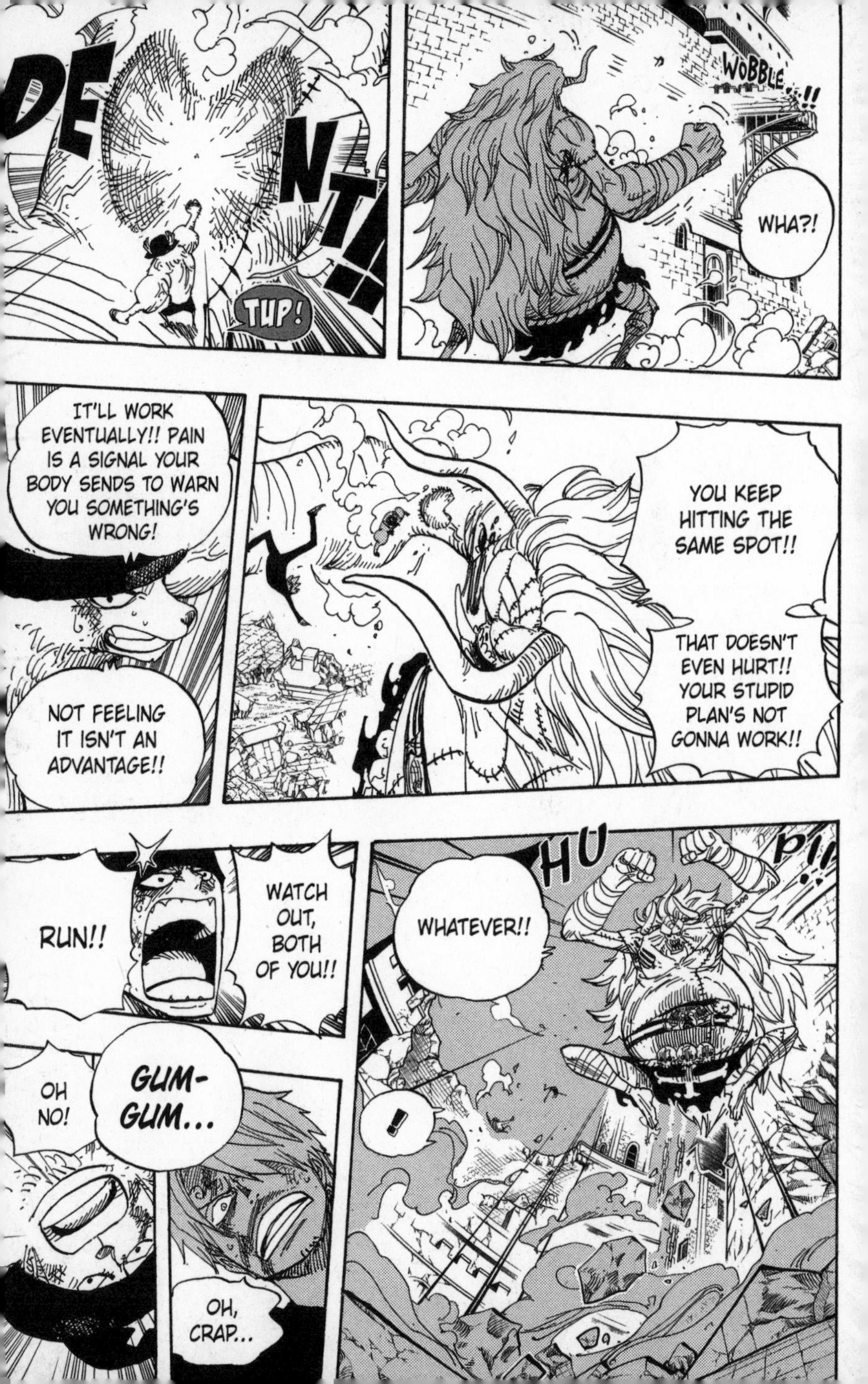
WOBBLE...!!
WHA?!
DENT!!!
TUP!
YOU KEEP HITTING THE SAME SPOT!!
THAT DOESN'T EVEN HURT!! YOUR STUPID PLAN'S NOT GONNA WORK!!
IT'LL WORK EVENTUALLY!! PAIN IS A SIGNAL YOUR BODY SENDS TO WARN YOU SOMETHING'S WRONG!
NOT FEELING IT ISN'T AN ADVANTAGE!!
PI!!
HU
WHATEVER!!
!
WATCH OUT, BOTH OF YOU!!
RUN!!
GUM-GUM...
OH NO!
OH, CRAP...

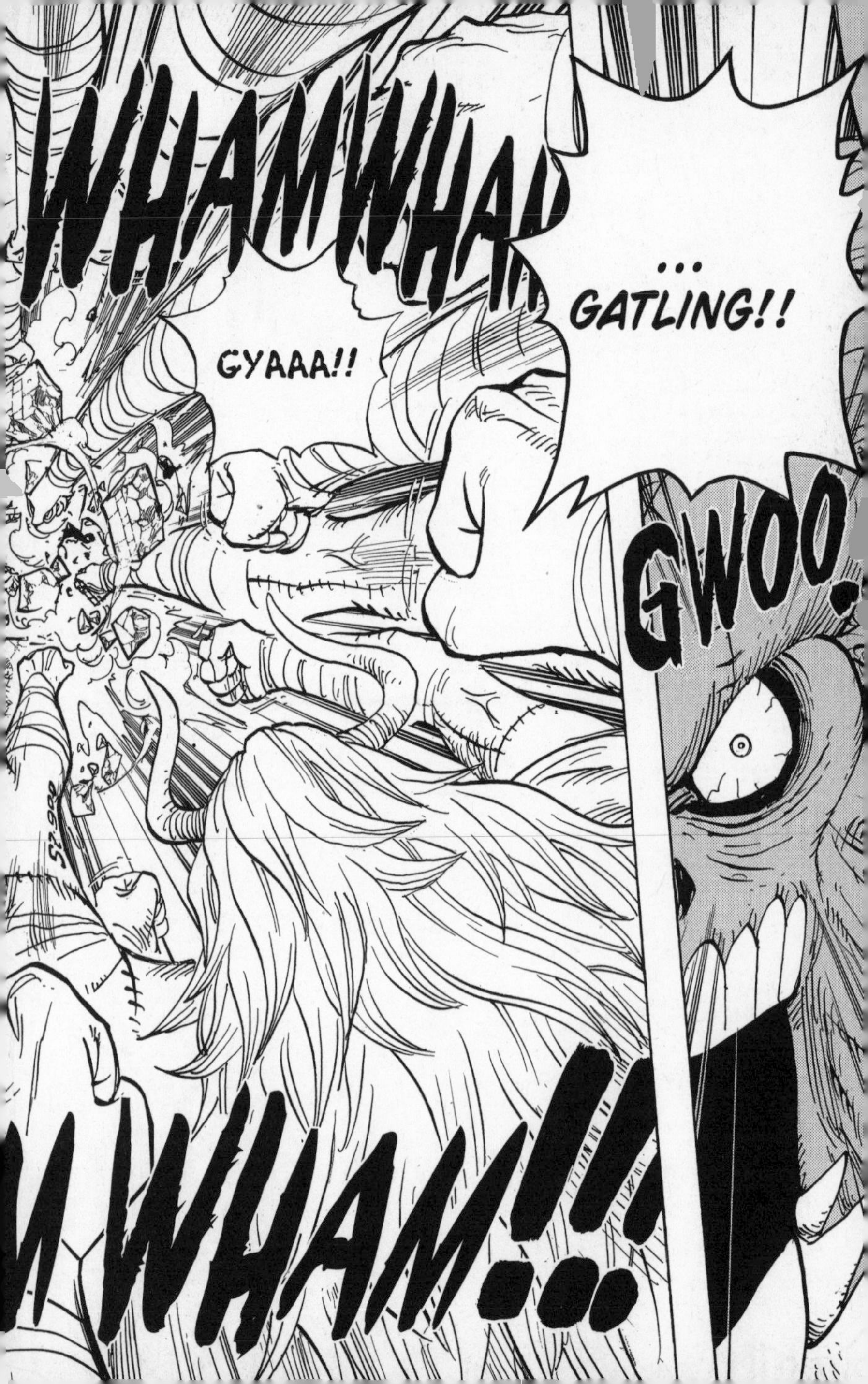
...GATLING!!
WHAMWHAM
GYAAA!!
GWOO..
WHAM!!...

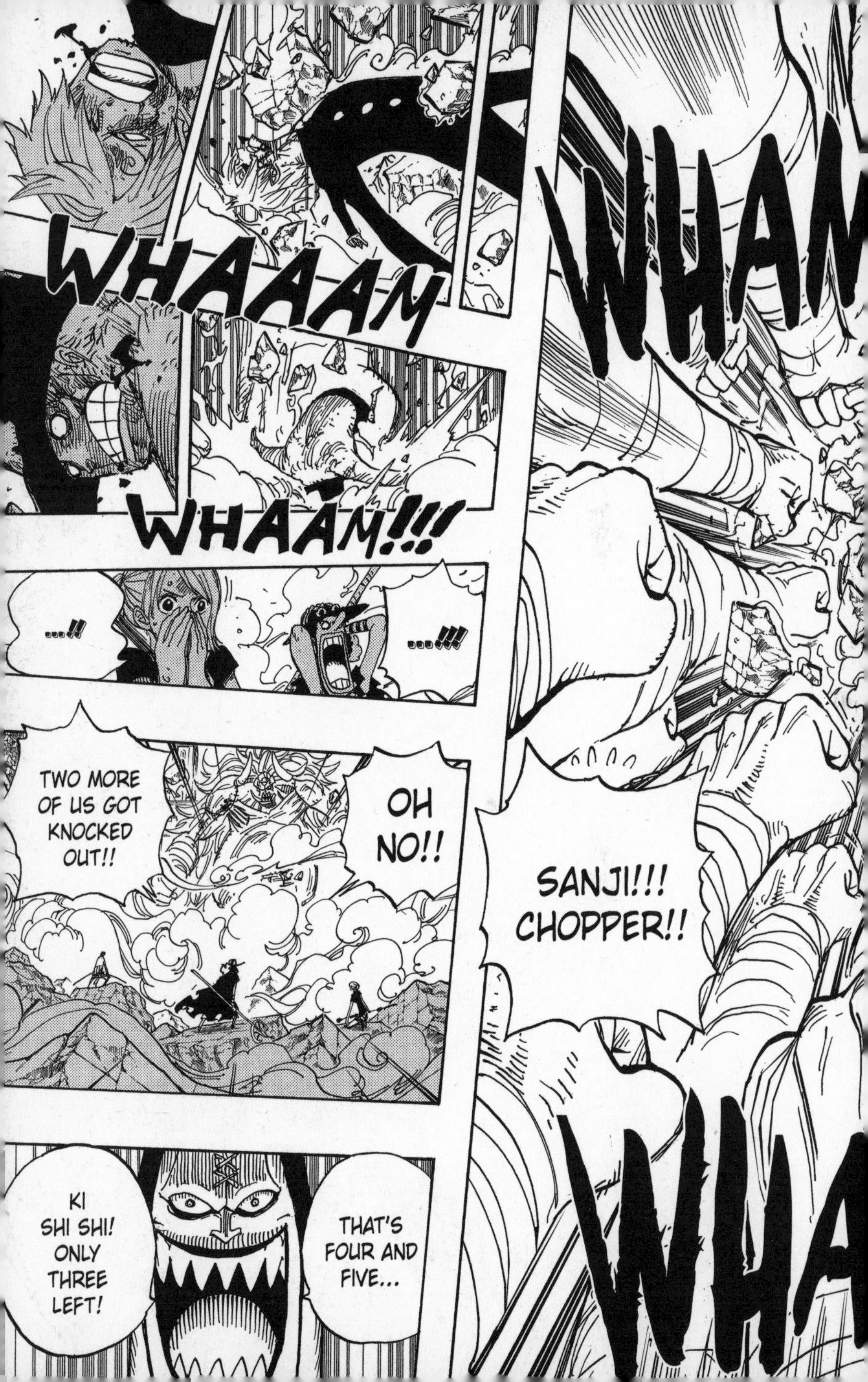
WHAM
SANJI!!! CHOPPER!!
WHA
WHAAAM
WHAAM!!!
...!!!
...!!
OH NO!!
TWO MORE OF US GOT KNOCKED OUT!!
THAT'S FOUR AND FIVE...
KI SHI SHI! ONLY THREE LEFT!

Chapter 478:
LUFFY VS. LUFFY

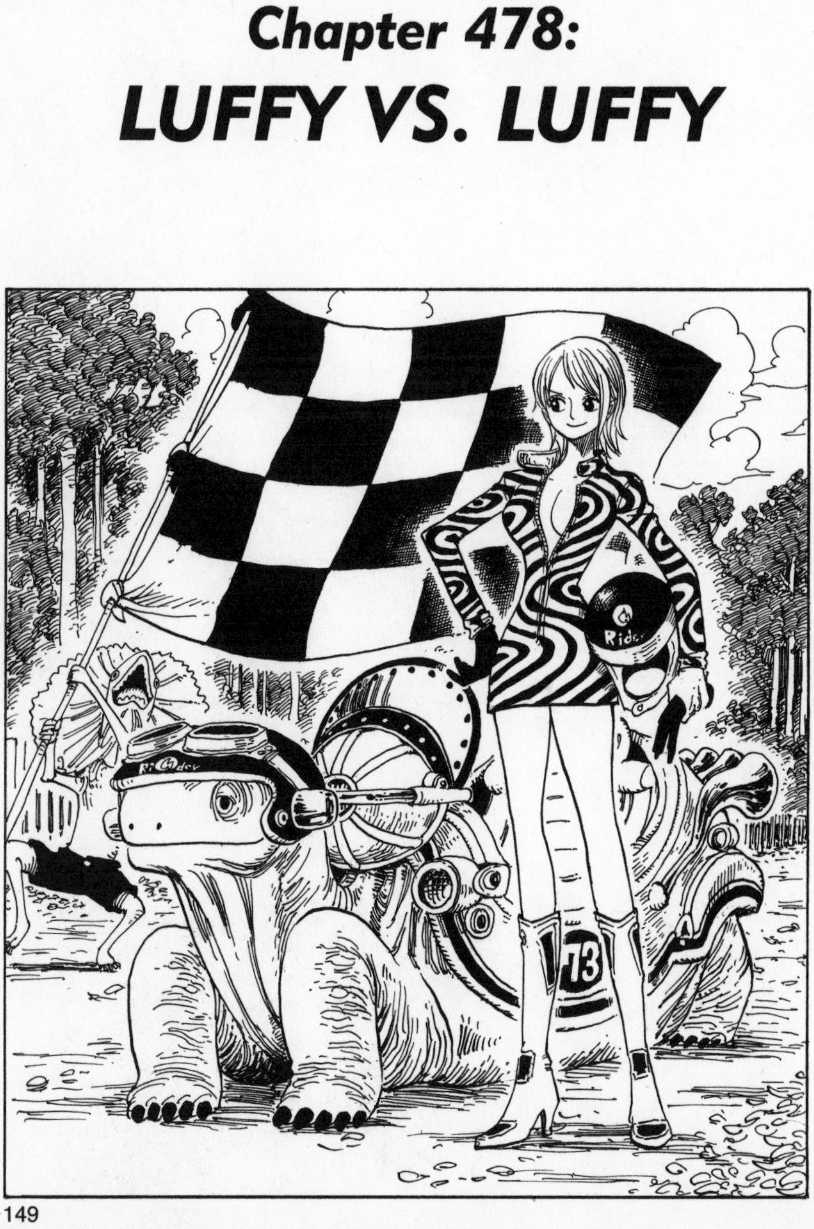
Rider
73

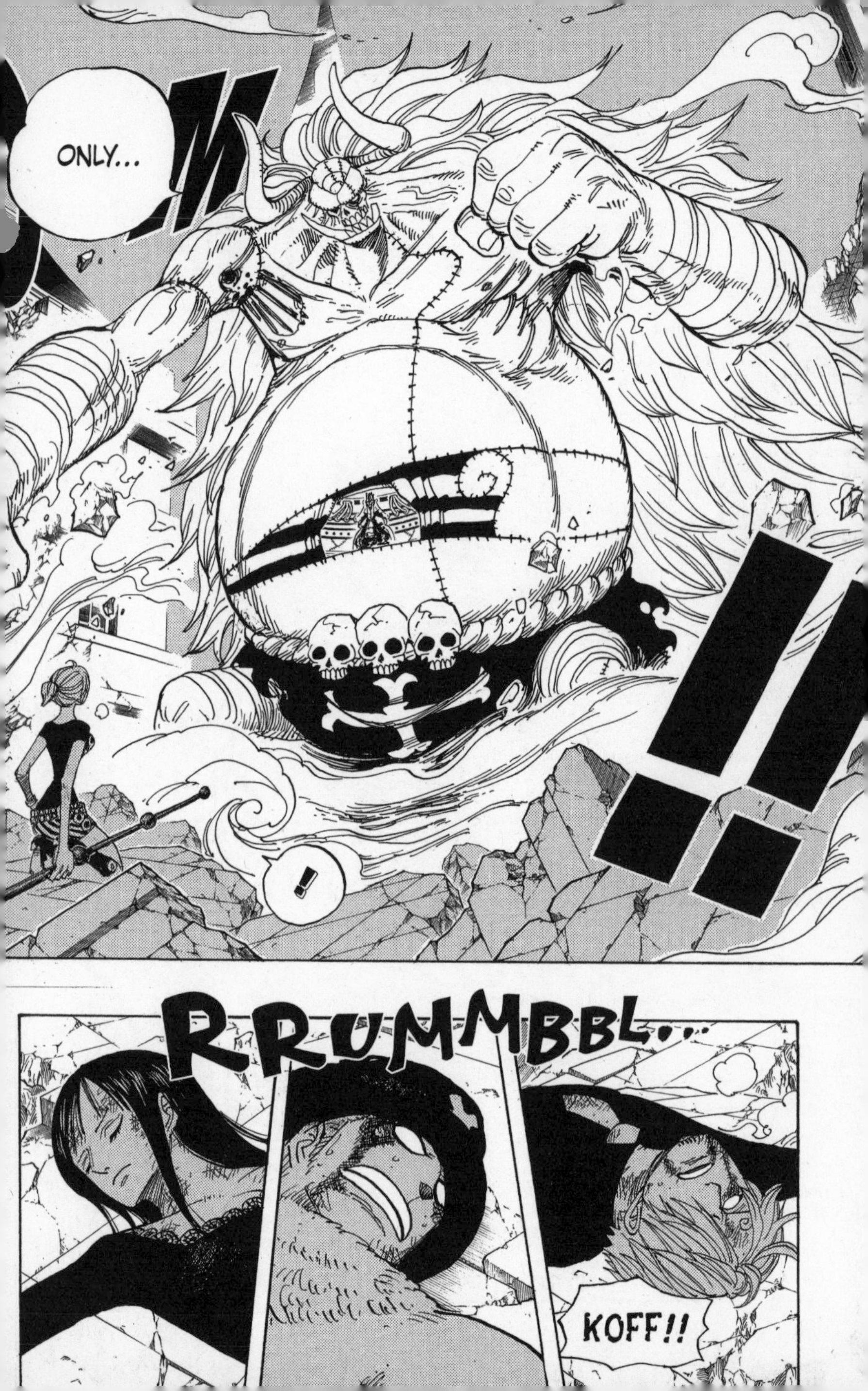
ONLY...
!!
!
RRUMMBBL...
KOFF!!

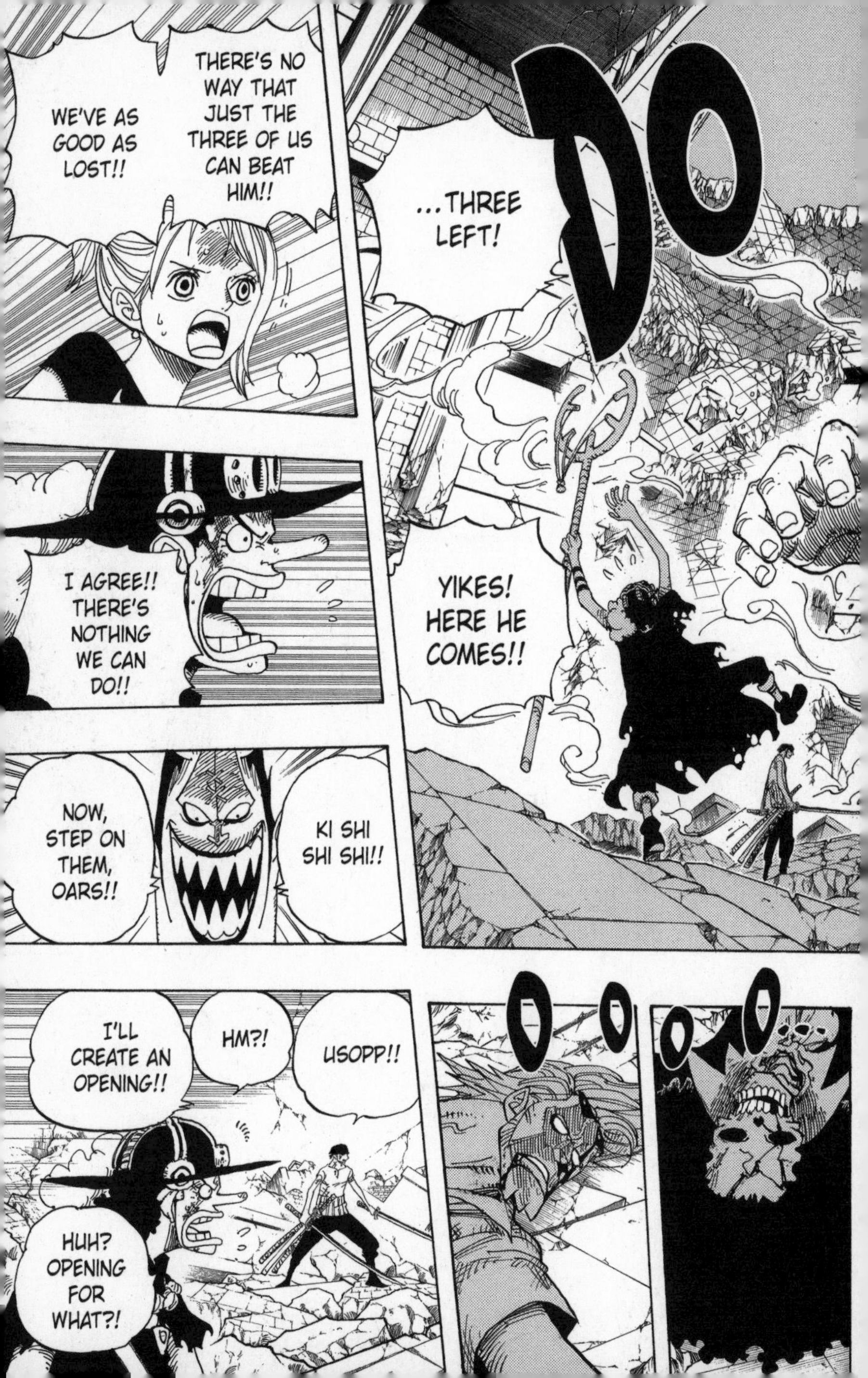
DO
...THREE LEFT!
YIKES! HERE HE COMES!!
THERE'S NO WAY THAT JUST THE THREE OF US CAN BEAT HIM!!
WE'VE AS GOOD AS LOST!!
I AGREE!! THERE'S NOTHING WE CAN DO!!
KI SHI SHI SHI!!
NOW, STEP ON THEM, OARS!!
USOPP!!
HM?!
I'LL CREATE AN OPENING!!
HUH? OPENING FOR WHAT?!

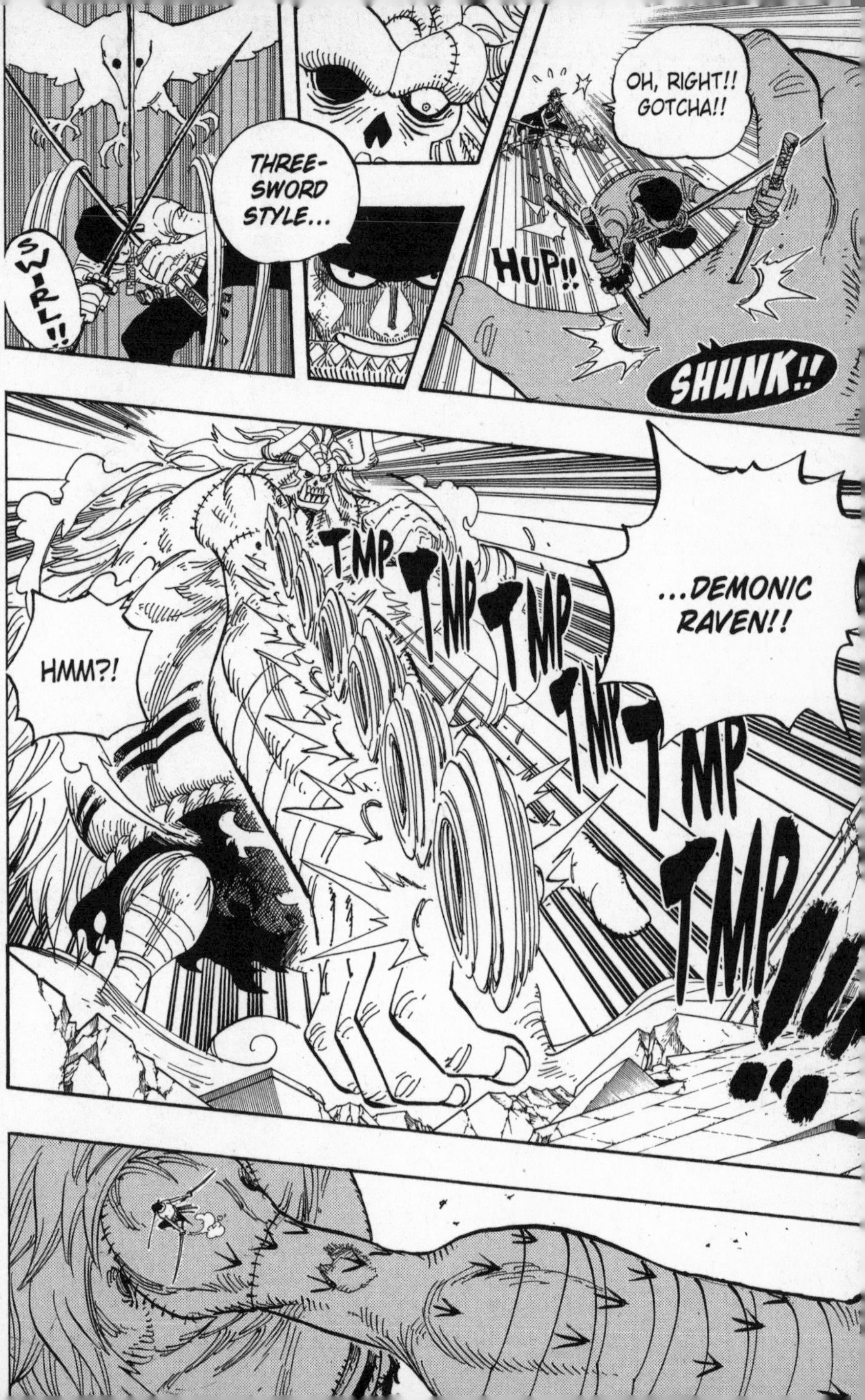
OH, RIGHT!! GOTCHA!!
HUP!!
SHUNK!!
THREE-SWORD STYLE...
SWIRL!!
...DEMONIC RAVEN!!
TMP TMP TMP TMP TMP TMP TMP!!!
HMM?!

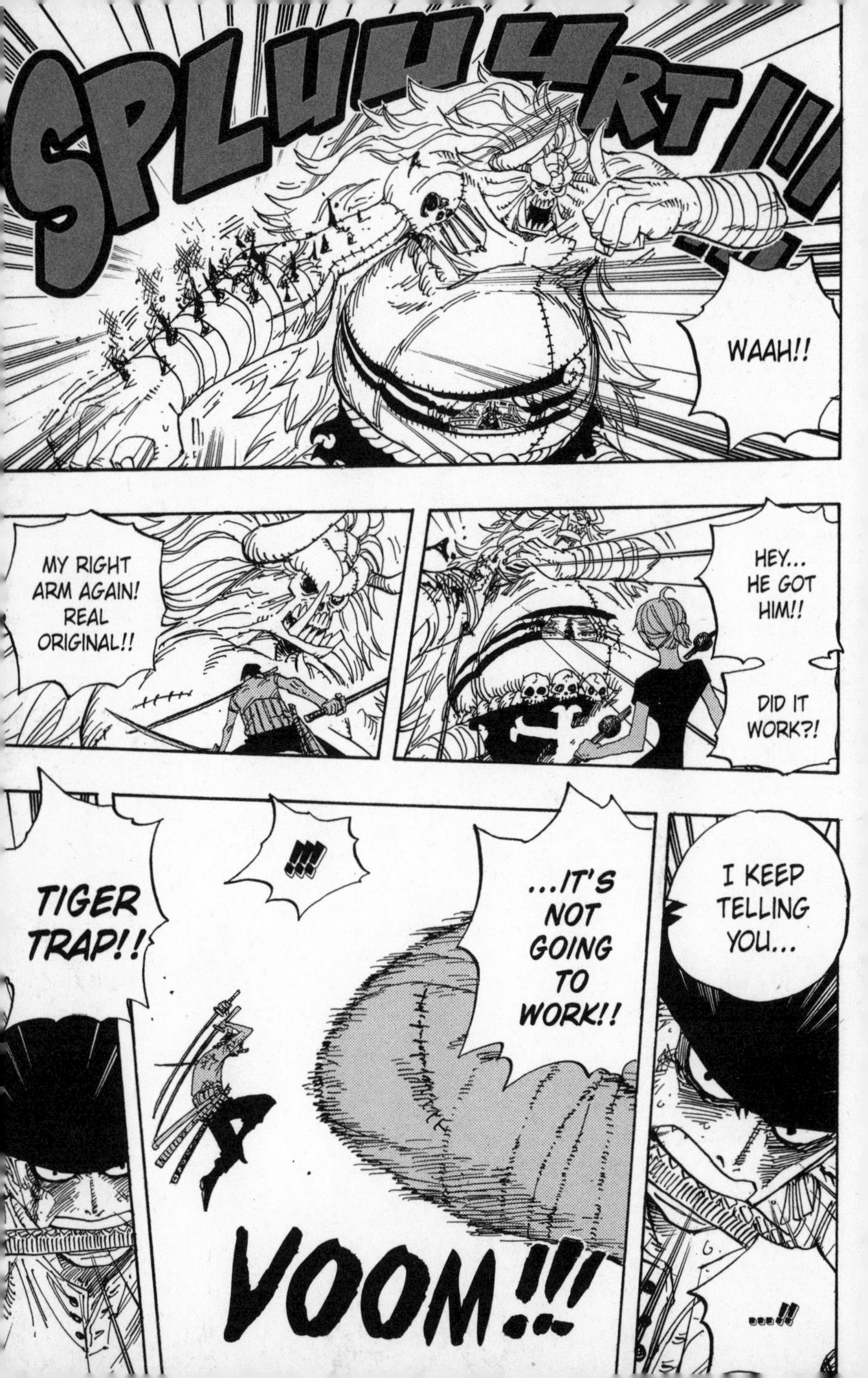
SPLUUURT!!!
WAAH!!
HEY... HE GOT HIM!!
DID IT WORK?!
MY RIGHT ARM AGAIN! REAL ORIGINAL!!
I KEEP TELLING YOU...
...!!
...IT'S NOT GOING TO WORK!!
!!!
TIGER TRAP!!
VOOM!!!

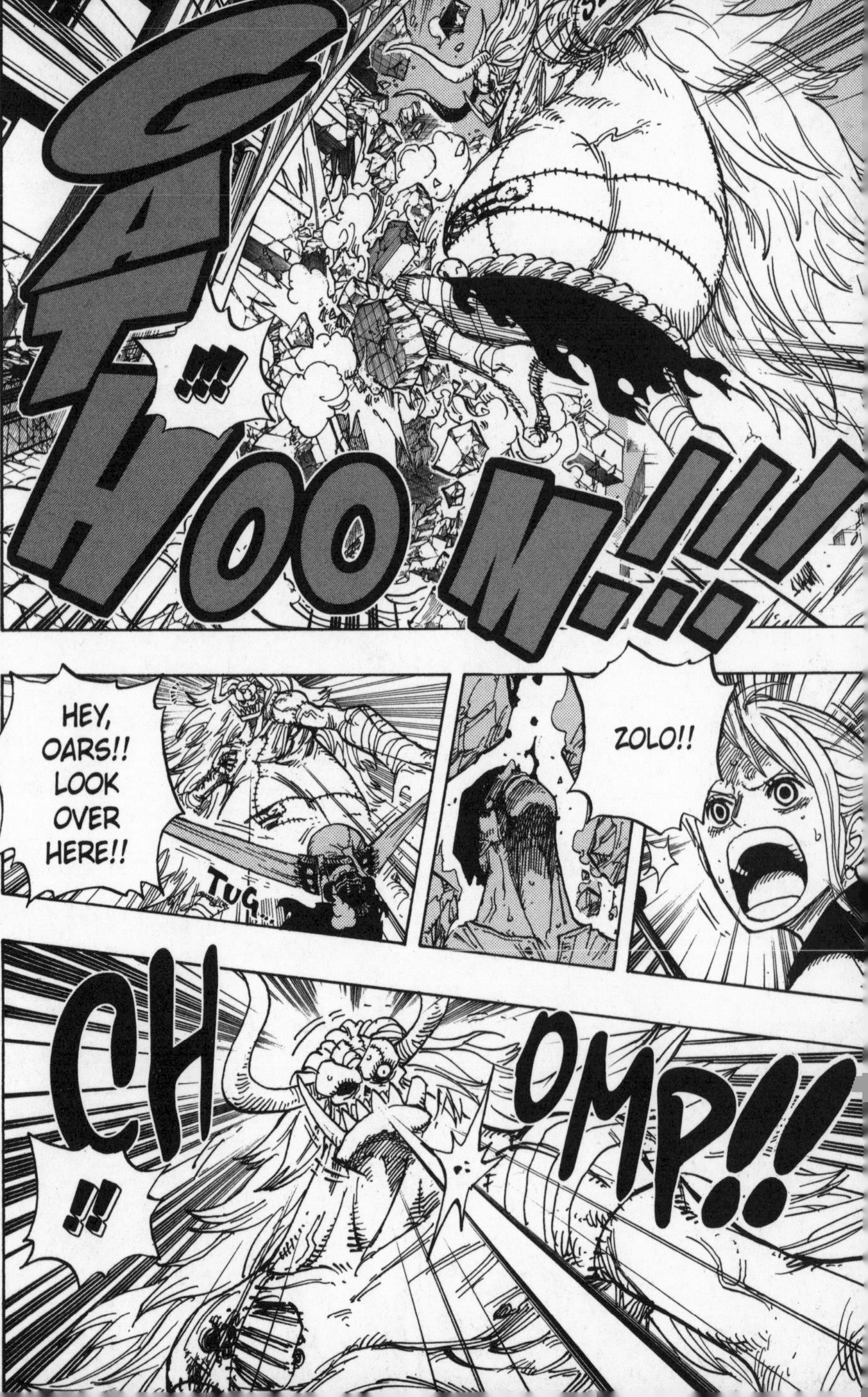
GA!!! HOOM!!!
ZOLO!!
HEY, OARS!! LOOK OVER HERE!!
TUG...
CH!! OMP!!

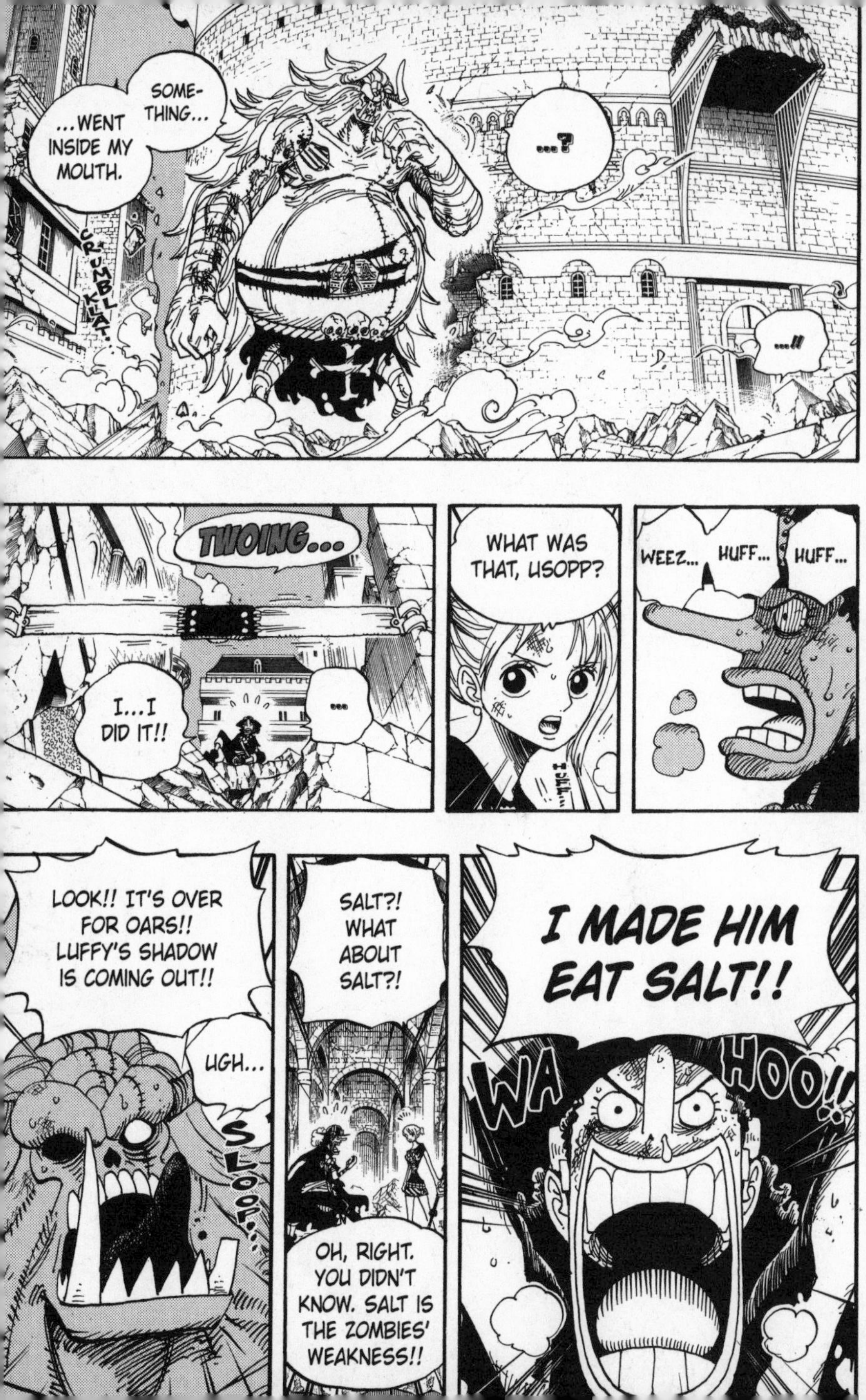

...?
...!!
SOME-THING...
...WENT INSIDE MY MOUTH.
CRUMBL
KLLAT..
WEEZ... HUFF... HUFF...
WHAT WAS THAT, USOPP?
HUFF...
TWOING...
...
I...I DID IT!!
I MADE HIM EAT SALT!!
WA HOO!!
SALT?! WHAT ABOUT SALT?!
OH, RIGHT. YOU DIDN'T KNOW. SALT IS THE ZOMBIES' WEAKNESS!!
LOOK!! IT'S OVER FOR OARS!! LUFFY'S SHADOW IS COMING OUT!!
UGH...
SLOOP...

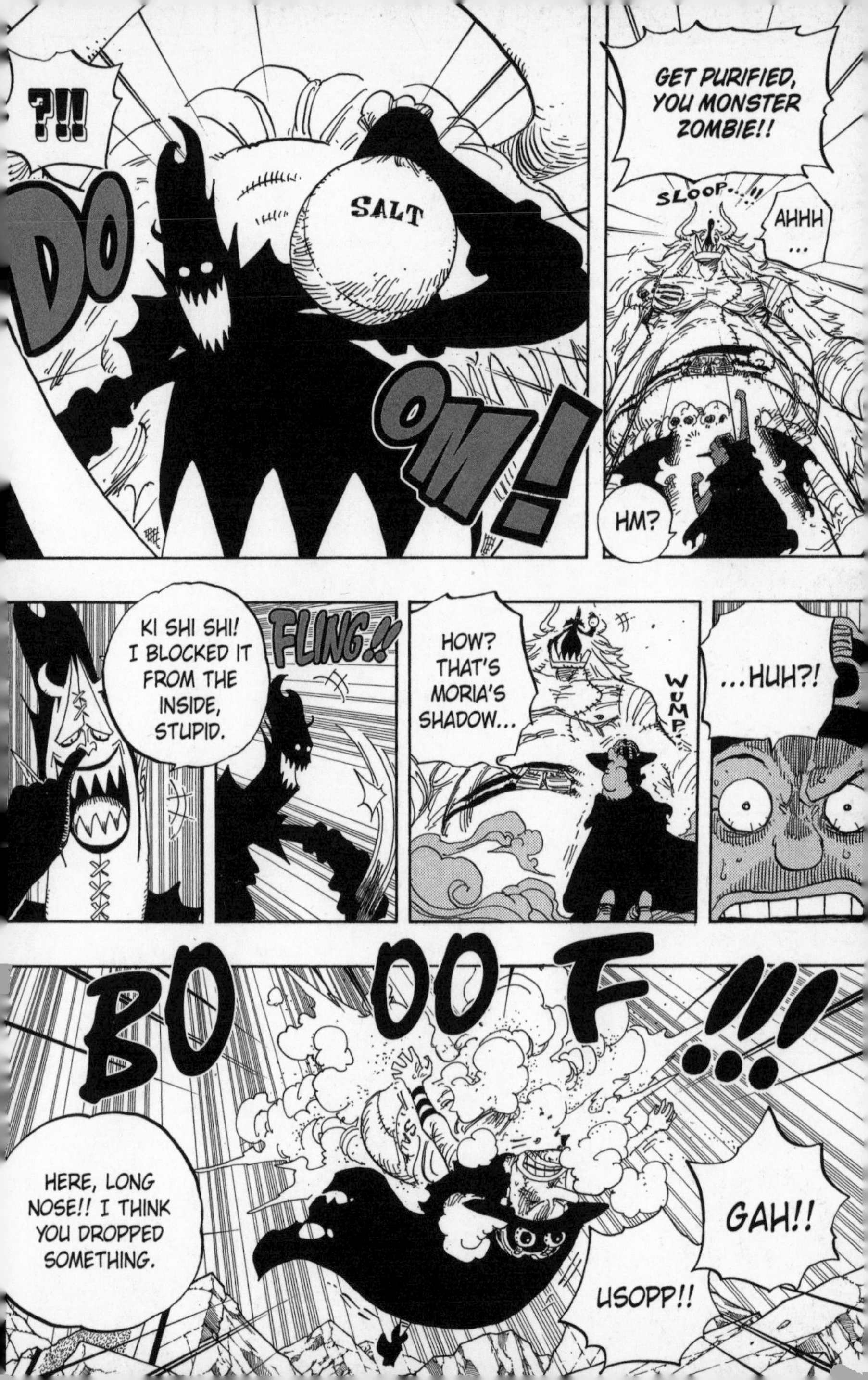
GET PURIFIED, YOU MONSTER ZOMBIE!!
SLOOP...!!
AHHH ...
HM?
?!!
SALT
DOOM!
...HUH?!
HOW? THAT'S MORIA'S SHADOW...
WUMP...
FLING!!
KI SHI SHI! I BLOCKED IT FROM THE INSIDE, STUPID.
BOOOF!!!
GAH!!
USOPP!!
HERE, LONG NOSE!! I THINK YOU DROPPED SOMETHING.

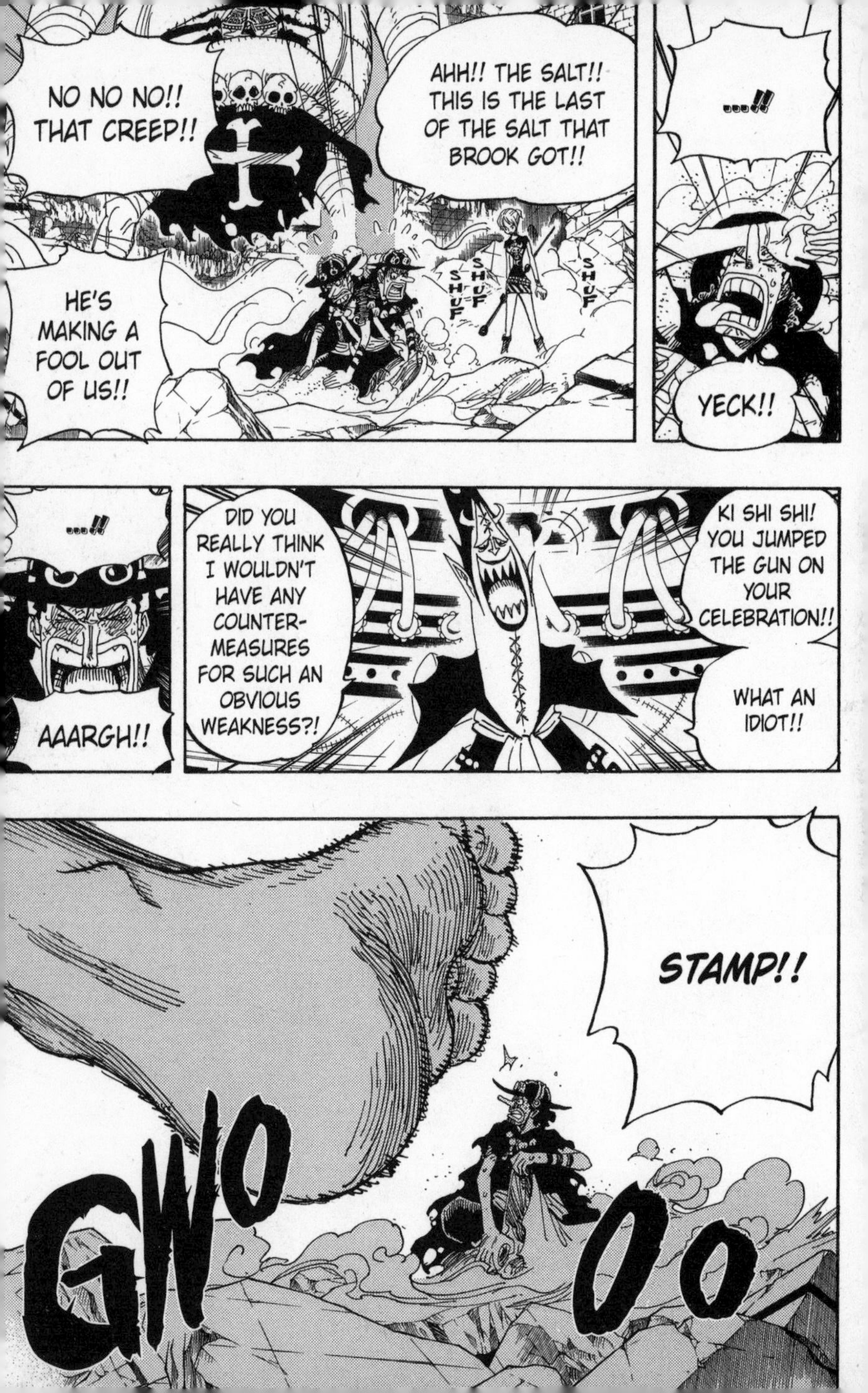
...!!
YECK!!
AHH!! THE SALT!! THIS IS THE LAST OF THE SALT THAT BROOK GOT!!
NO NO NO!! THAT CREEP!!
SHUF SHUF
SHUF
HE'S MAKING A FOOL OUT OF US!!
KI SHI SHI! YOU JUMPED THE GUN ON YOUR CELEBRATION!!
DID YOU REALLY THINK I WOULDN'T HAVE ANY COUNTER-MEASURES FOR SUCH AN OBVIOUS WEAKNESS?!
WHAT AN IDIOT!!
...!!
AAARGH!!
STAMP!!
GWOOO

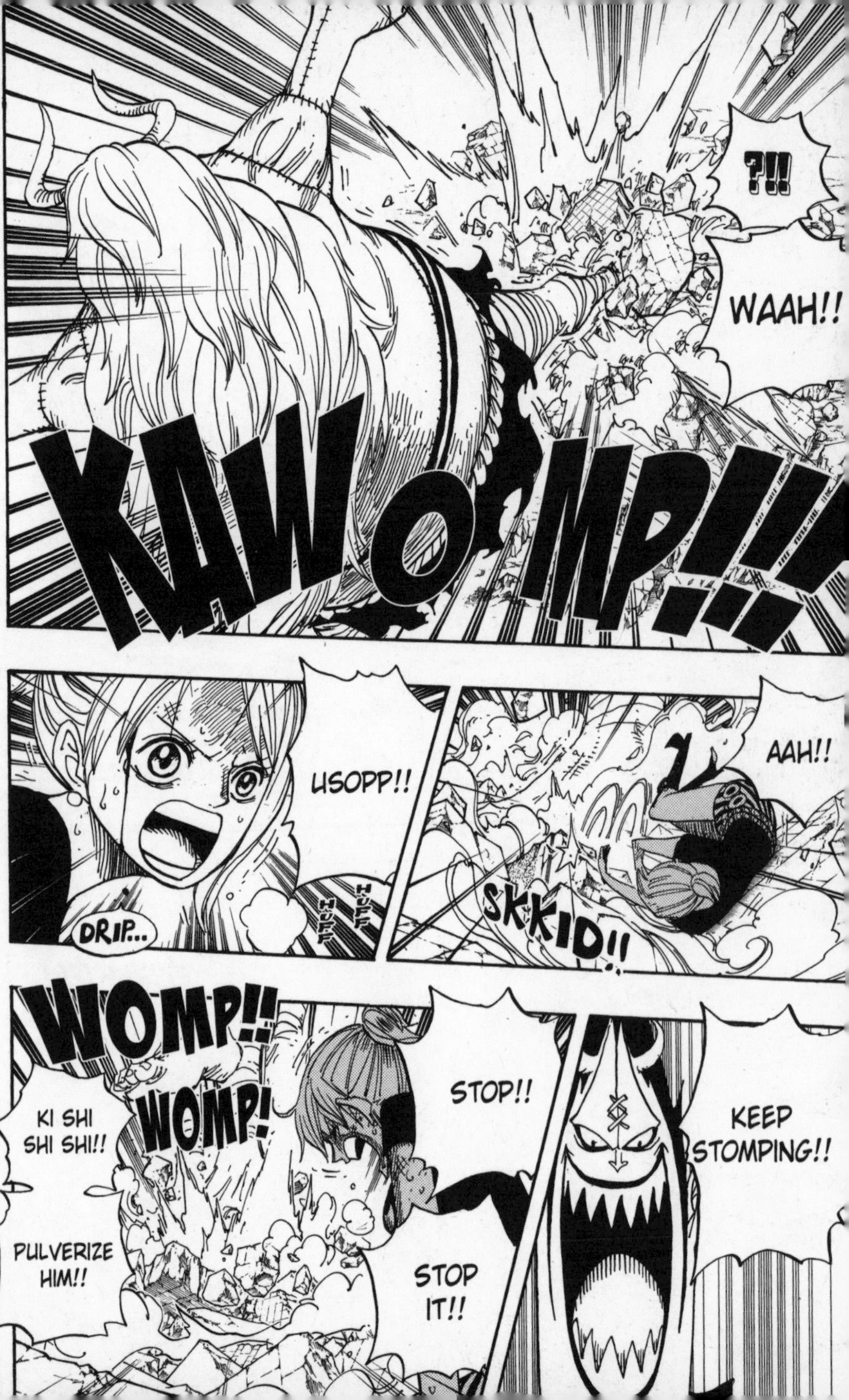
?!!
WAAH!!
KAWOOMP!!!
AAH!!
SKKID!!
USOPP!!
HUFF HUFF
DRIP...
KEEP STOMPING!!
STOP!!
STOP IT!!
WOMP!!
WOMP!
KI SHI SHI SHI!!
PULVERIZE HIM!!

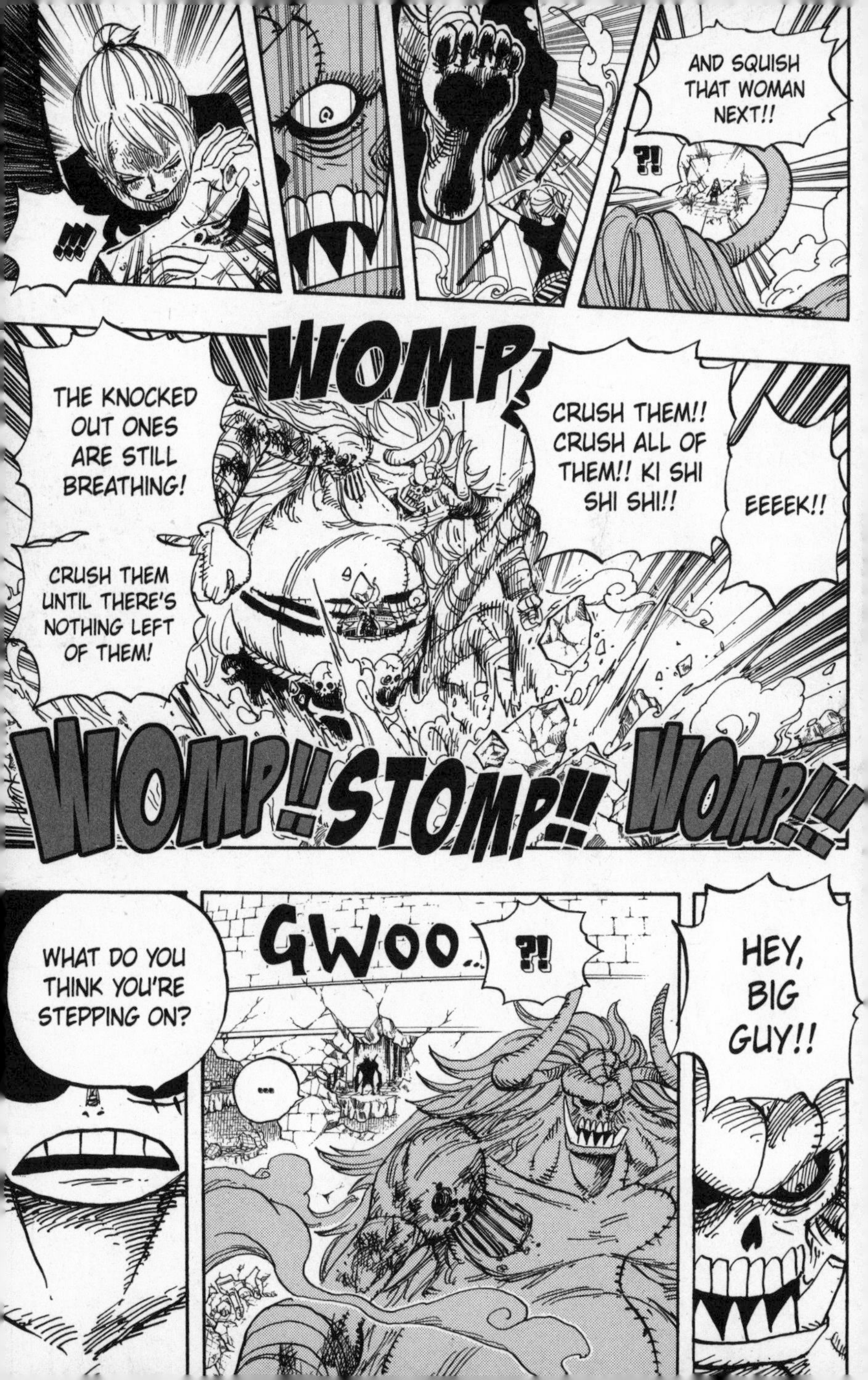
AND SQUISH THAT WOMAN NEXT!!
?!
!!
EEEEK!!
CRUSH THEM!! CRUSH ALL OF THEM!! KI SHI SHI SHI!!
WOMP
THE KNOCKED OUT ONES ARE STILL BREATHING!
CRUSH THEM UNTIL THERE'S NOTHING LEFT OF THEM!
WOMP!!
STOMP!!
WOMP!!
HEY, BIG GUY!!
?!
GWOO...
...
WHAT DO YOU THINK YOU'RE STEPPING ON?

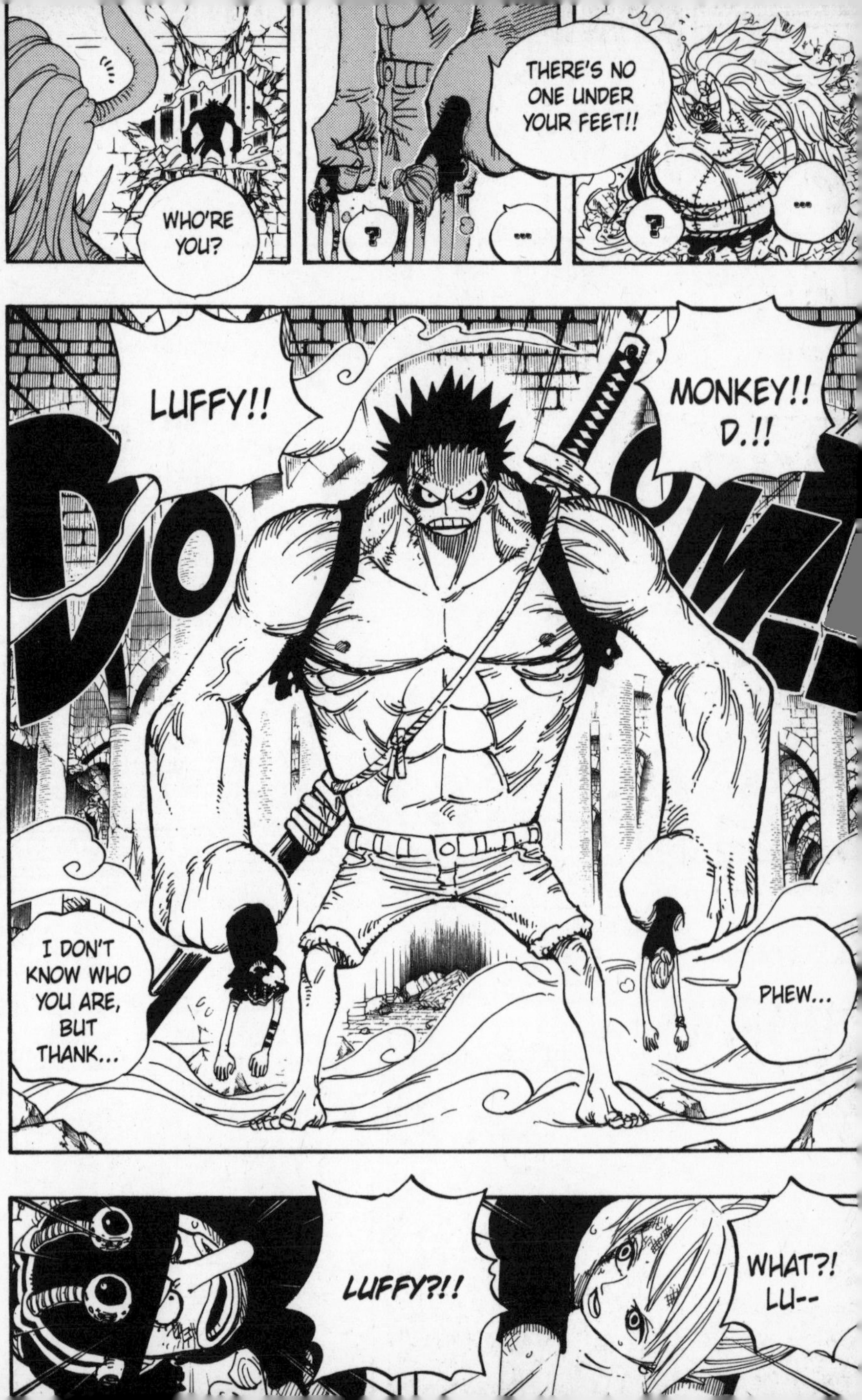
...
?
THERE'S NO ONE UNDER YOUR FEET!!
...
?
WHO'RE YOU?
MONKEY!! D.!!
LUFFY!!
DOOM!!
PHEW...
I DON'T KNOW WHO YOU ARE, BUT THANK...
WHAT?! LU--
LUFFY?!!

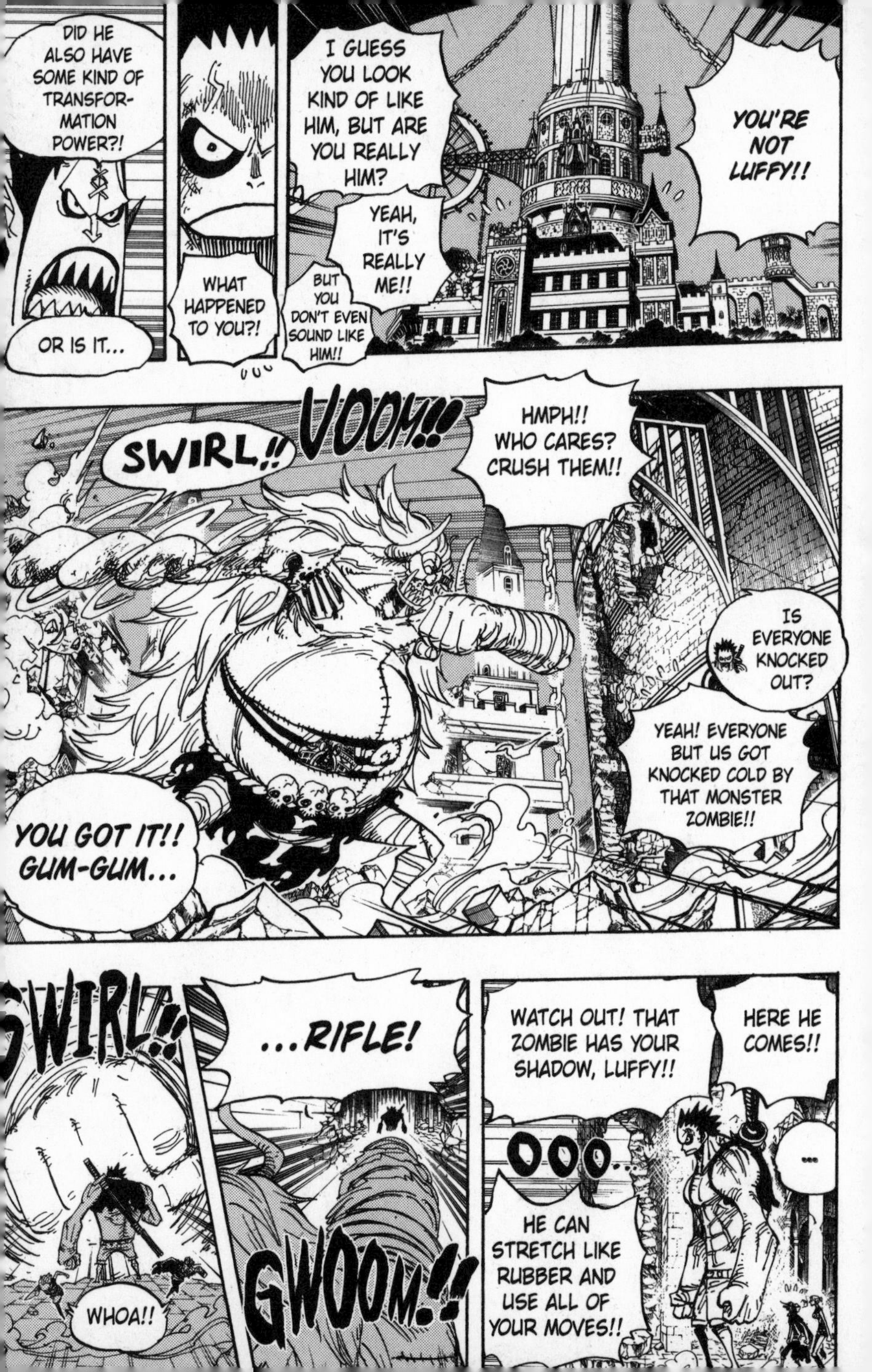
YOU'RE NOT LUFFY!!
I GUESS YOU LOOK KIND OF LIKE HIM, BUT ARE YOU REALLY HIM?
YEAH, IT'S REALLY ME!!
BUT YOU DON'T EVEN SOUND LIKE HIM!!
WHAT HAPPENED TO YOU?!
DID HE ALSO HAVE SOME KIND OF TRANSFORMATION POWER?!
OR IS IT...
HMPH!! WHO CARES? CRUSH THEM!!
VOOM!!
SWIRL.!!
IS EVERYONE KNOCKED OUT?
YEAH! EVERYONE BUT US GOT KNOCKED COLD BY THAT MONSTER ZOMBIE!!
YOU GOT IT!! GUM-GUM...
HERE HE COMES!!
WATCH OUT! THAT ZOMBIE HAS YOUR SHADOW, LUFFY!!
...
OOO...
HE CAN STRETCH LIKE RUBBER AND USE ALL OF YOUR MOVES!!
...RIFLE!
GWOOM!!
SWIRL!!
WHOA!!

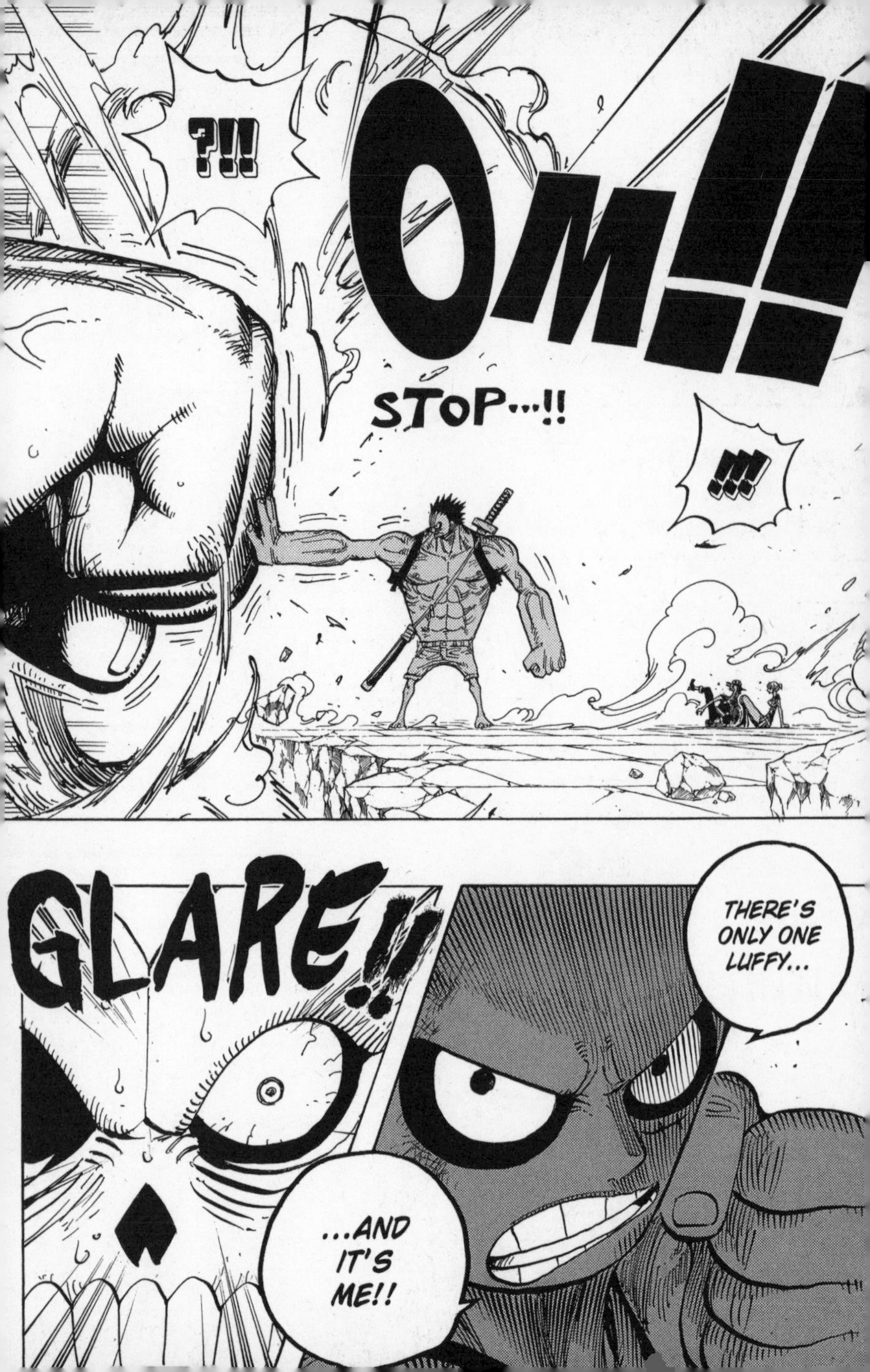
OM!!
?!!
STOP...!!
!!!
THERE'S ONLY ONE LUFFY...
GLARE!!
...AND IT'S ME!!

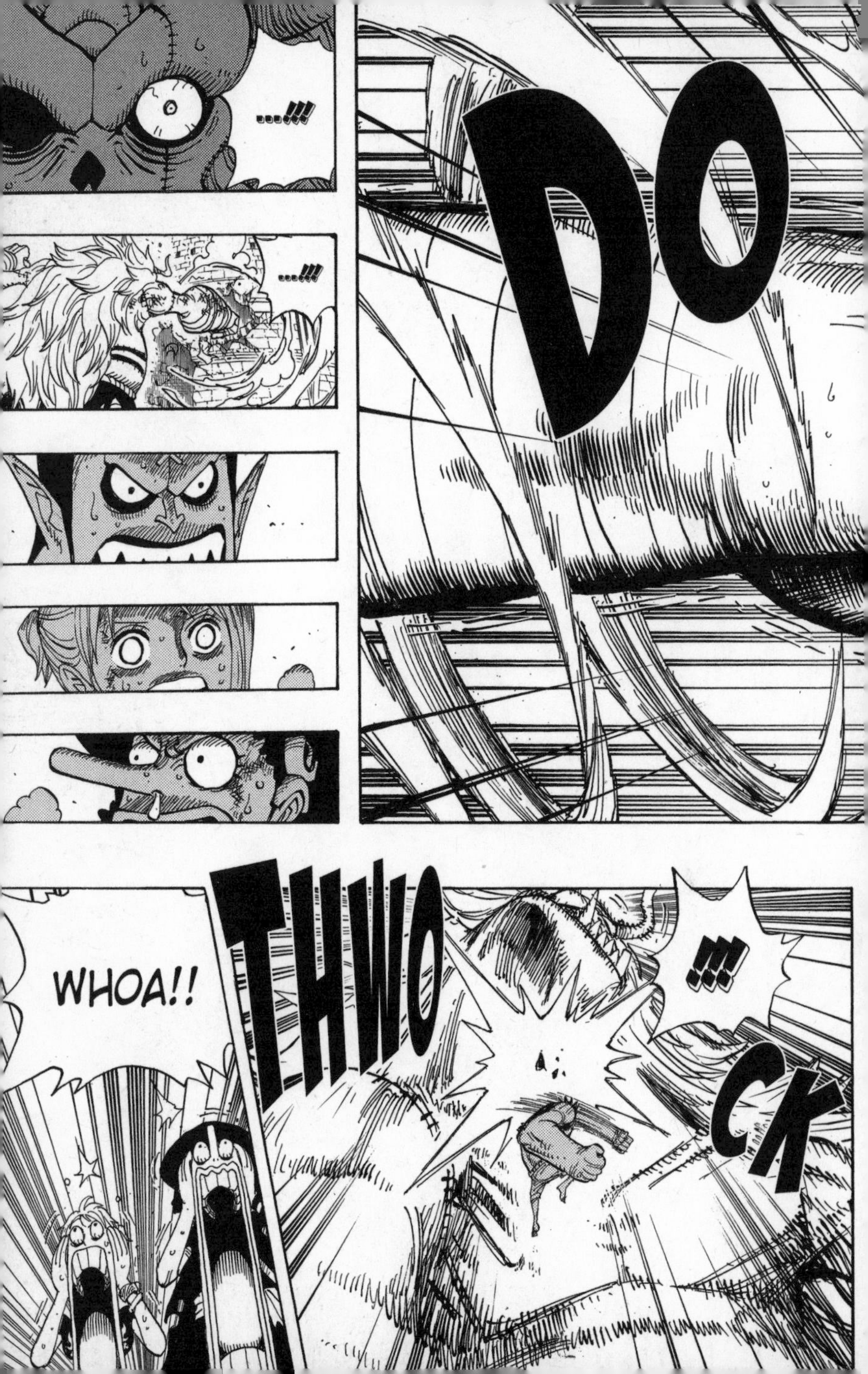
DO
...!!!
...!!!
..!!
!!!
THWOCK
WHOA!!

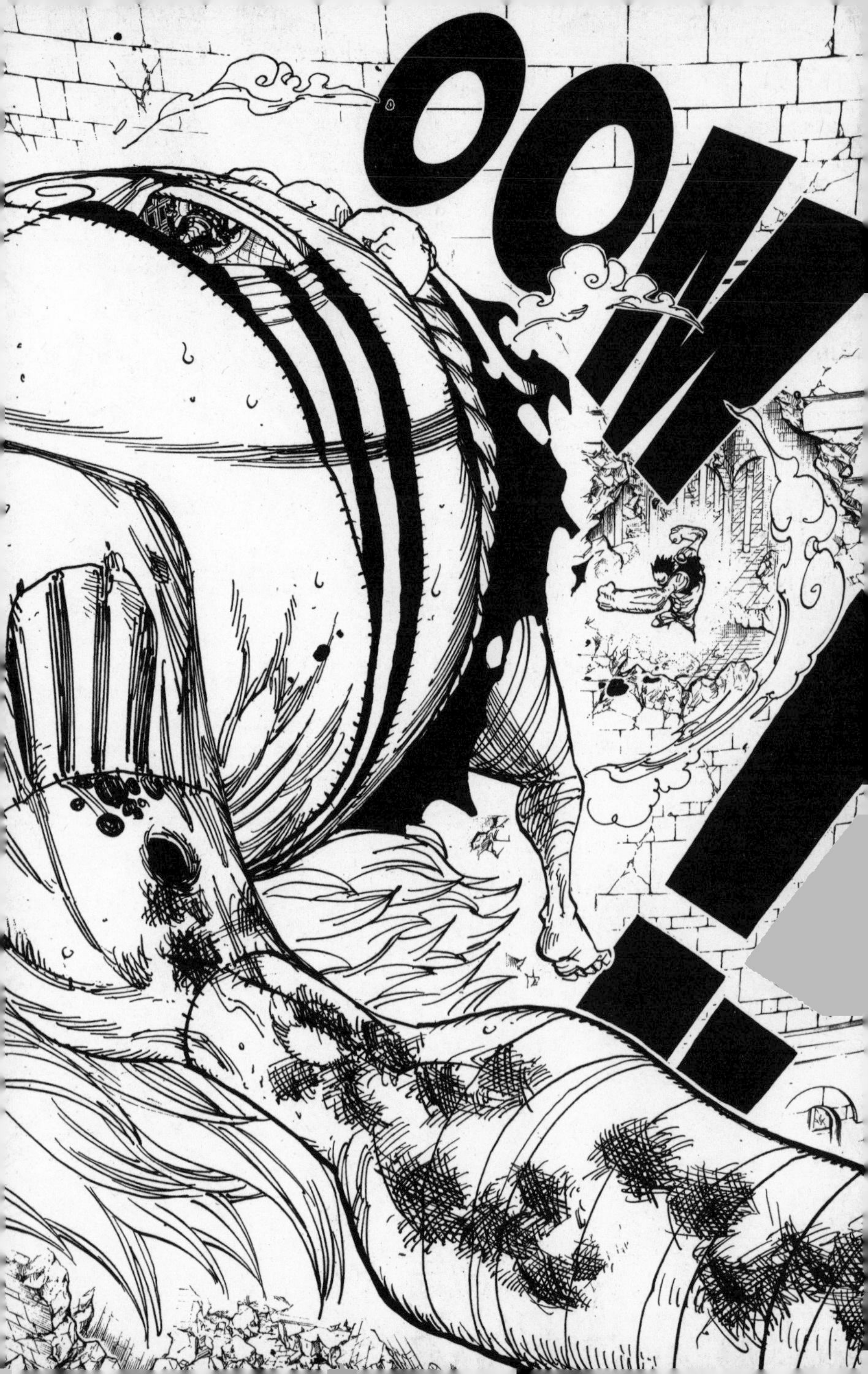
OOM!!

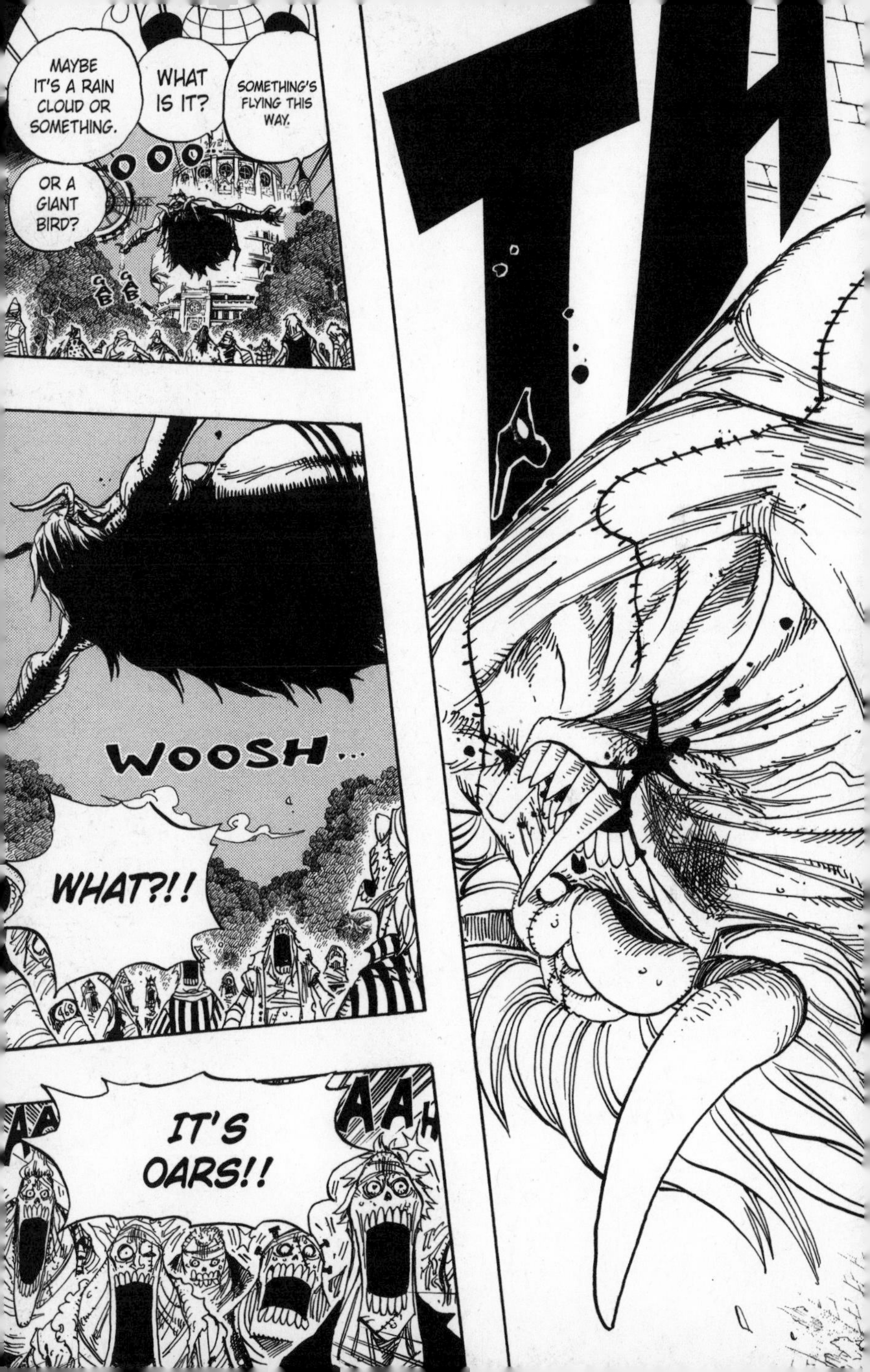
TH
SOMETHING'S FLYING THIS WAY.
WHAT IS IT?
MAYBE IT'S A RAIN CLOUD OR SOMETHING.
OR A GIANT BIRD?
OOO
GAB GAB
WOOSH...
WHAT?!!
AAH
IT'S OARS!!
AA

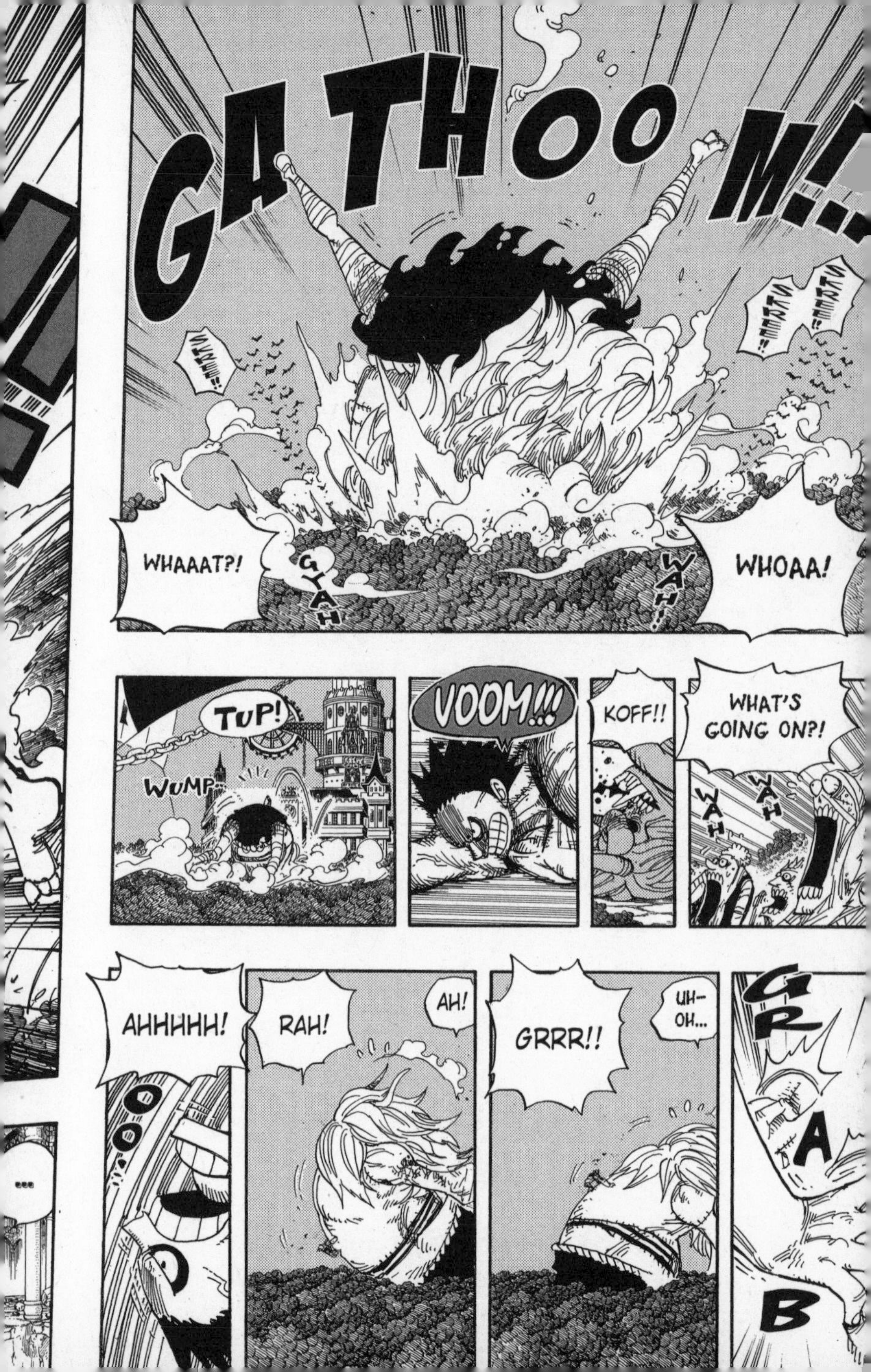
GATHOOM!!..
SKREE!!
SKREE!!
SKREE!!
WHOAA!
WAH!
GYAH
WHAAAT?!
WHAT'S GOING ON?!
WAH
WAH
KOFF!!
VOOM!!!
TUP!
WUMP
GRAB
UH-OH...
GRRR!!
AH!
RAH!
AHHHHH!

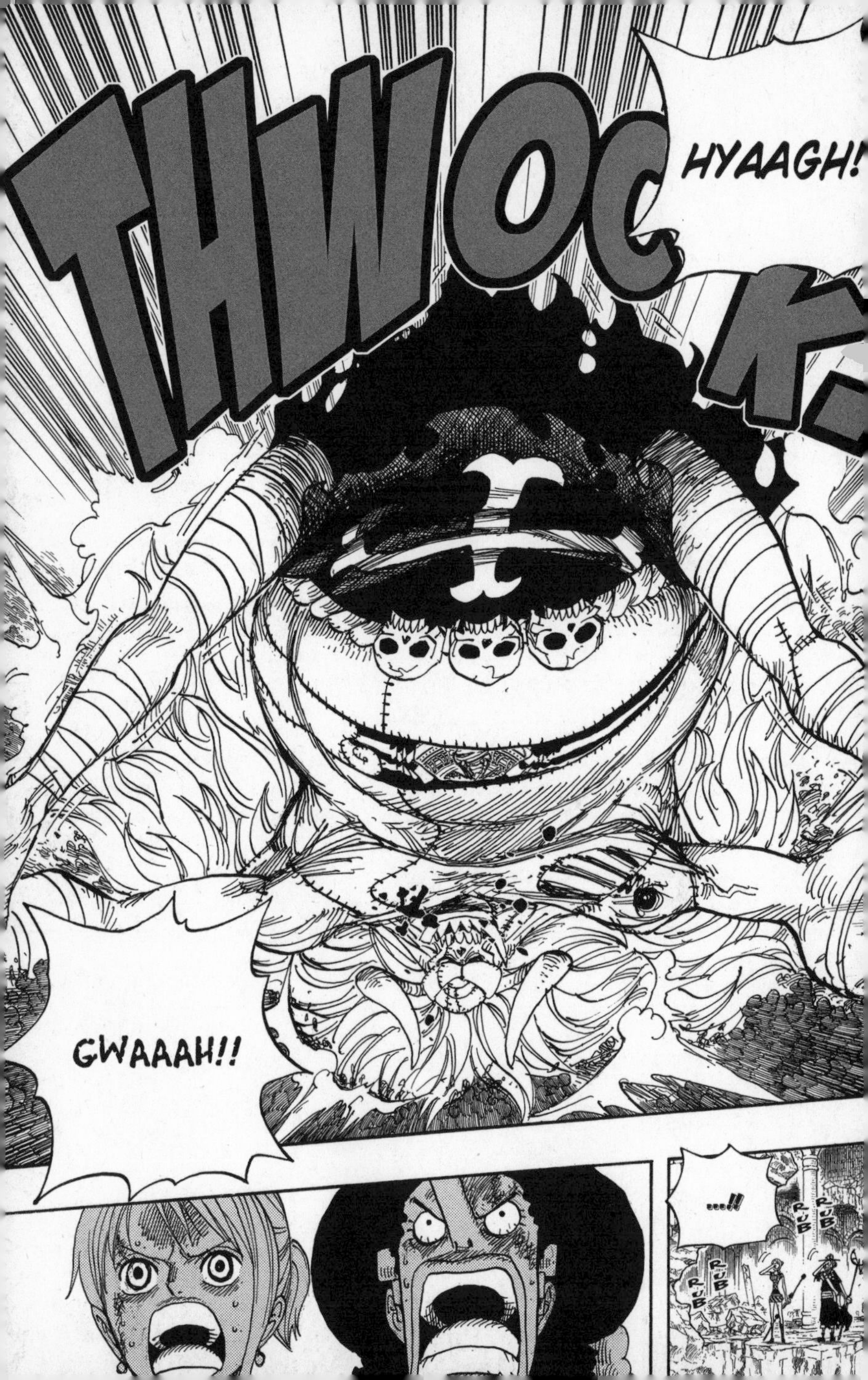
HYAAGH!
THWOCK
GWAAAH!!
...!!
RUB RUB
RUB RUB

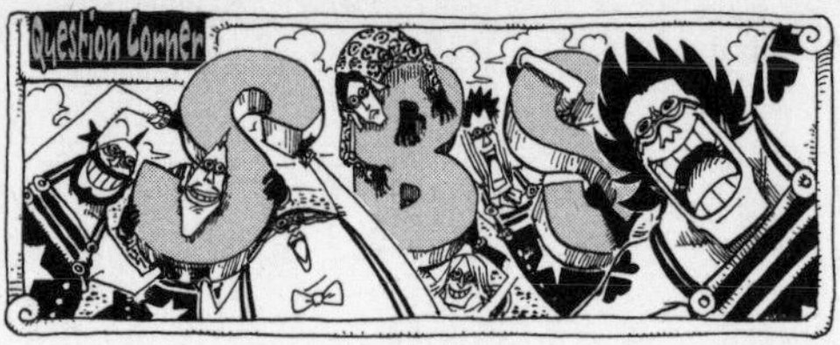
Question Corner
SBS

EXTRA

Q: Hello, Oda Sensei! I have a suggestion that you're gonna love! You know those pictures on top of the Question Corner?! I'm going to assume that it's catching up to the recent chapters, so you might be wondering what to do next! I'm just throwing this out there, but why don't you get fan submissions and put the readers' pictures as the top picture for that volume? --Comic Improvement Committee, Chairman Nisonin Yu

A: I see. Sure? A lot of people do send in fan art, but they don't usually fit the dimensions. That's why I never used them. But if people are willing to draw art for the Question Corner, it'll save me some time. Sure? So I'm going to invite people to send in their drawings for this! Just select any of the old characters that you like. Aside from that, you're free to do whatever you want. But even though I'm agreeing to this, I still get dibs on drawing the Corner picture when I want to.

Question Corner picture dimensions:

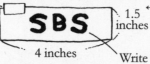

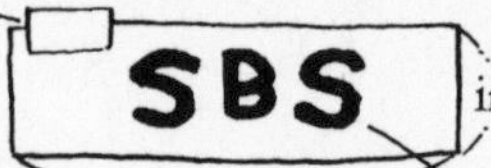
SBS

1.5 inches

4 inches

Write SBS big and clear.

← Send to:
One Piece Editor
P.O. Box 77010
San Francisco, CA 94107

I won't give out any special prizes, but please send in your drawings if you feel nice enough to help me out. This is your chance to be in the book.

*I'm getting a lot of questions for the eight voice actors that I asked for during volume 48. But I'll need a little more time to set things up. So keep sending them in. And they don't have to be so serious, you know? Look for the answers in a future volume.

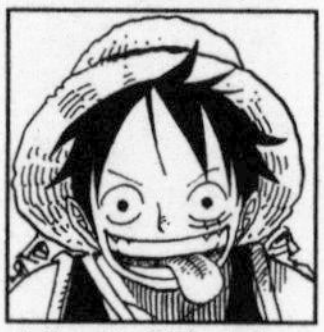
Mayumi Tanaka

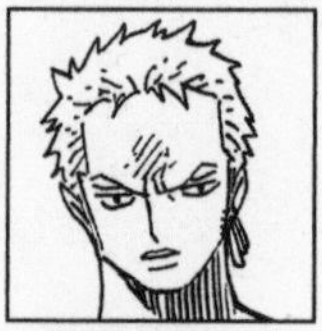
Kazuya Nakai

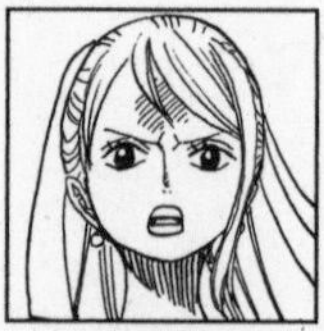
Akemi Okamura

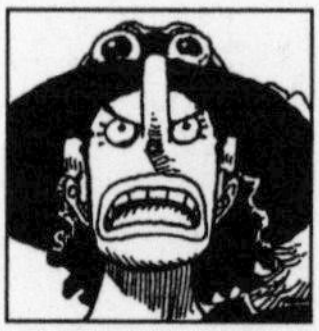
Kappei Yamaguchi

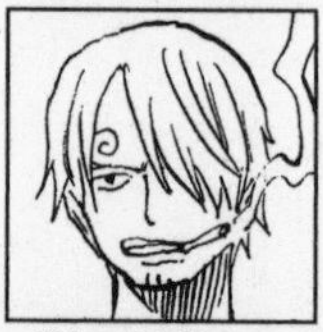
Hiroaki Hirata

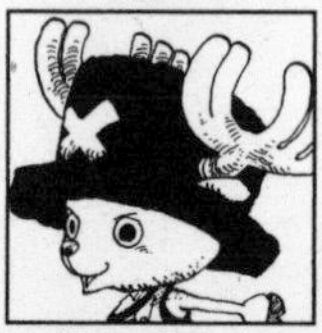
Ikue Otani

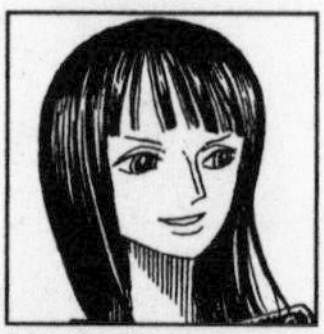
YurikoYamaguchi

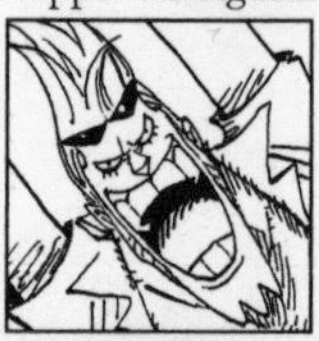
Kazuki Yao

Chapter 479:
WARRIOR OF HOPE

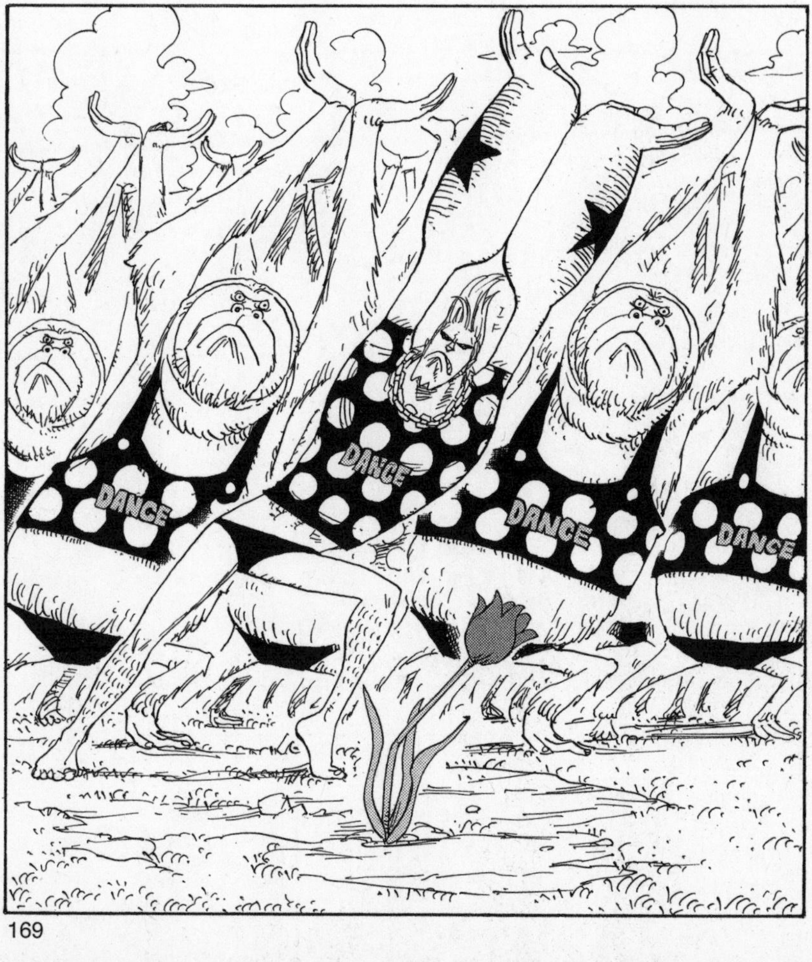
DANCE
DANCE
DANCE
DANCE

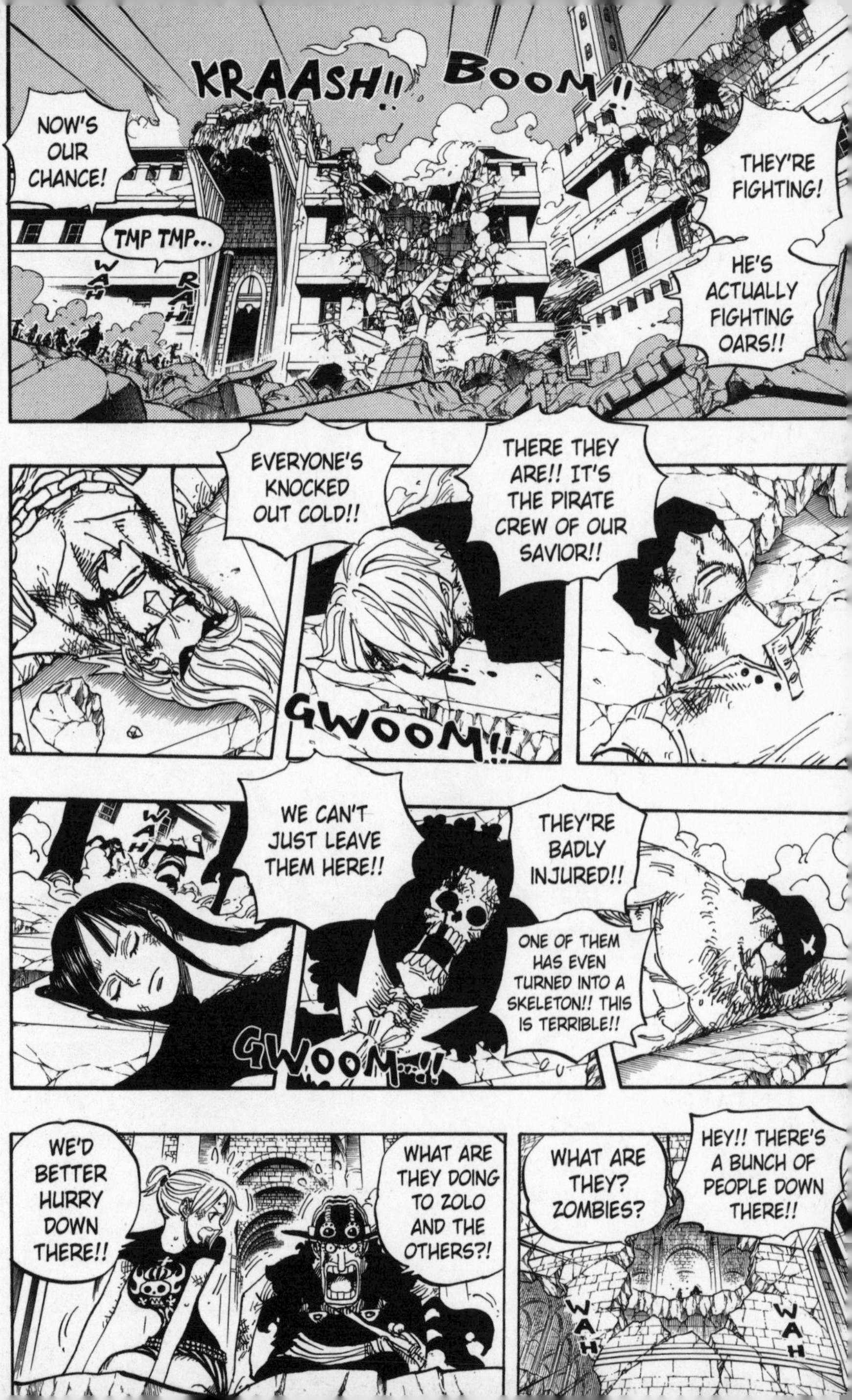
BOOM!!
KRAASH!!
THEY'RE FIGHTING!
HE'S ACTUALLY FIGHTING OARS!!
NOW'S OUR CHANCE!
TMP TMP...
RAH
WAH
THERE THEY ARE!! IT'S THE PIRATE CREW OF OUR SAVIOR!!
EVERYONE'S KNOCKED OUT COLD!!
GWOOM!!
THEY'RE BADLY INJURED!!
ONE OF THEM HAS EVEN TURNED INTO A SKELETON!! THIS IS TERRIBLE!!
WE CAN'T JUST LEAVE THEM HERE!!
GWOOM..!!
WAH
HEY!! THERE'S A BUNCH OF PEOPLE DOWN THERE!!
WHAT ARE THEY? ZOMBIES?
WAH
WAH
WHAT ARE THEY DOING TO ZOLO AND THE OTHERS?!
WE'D BETTER HURRY DOWN THERE!!

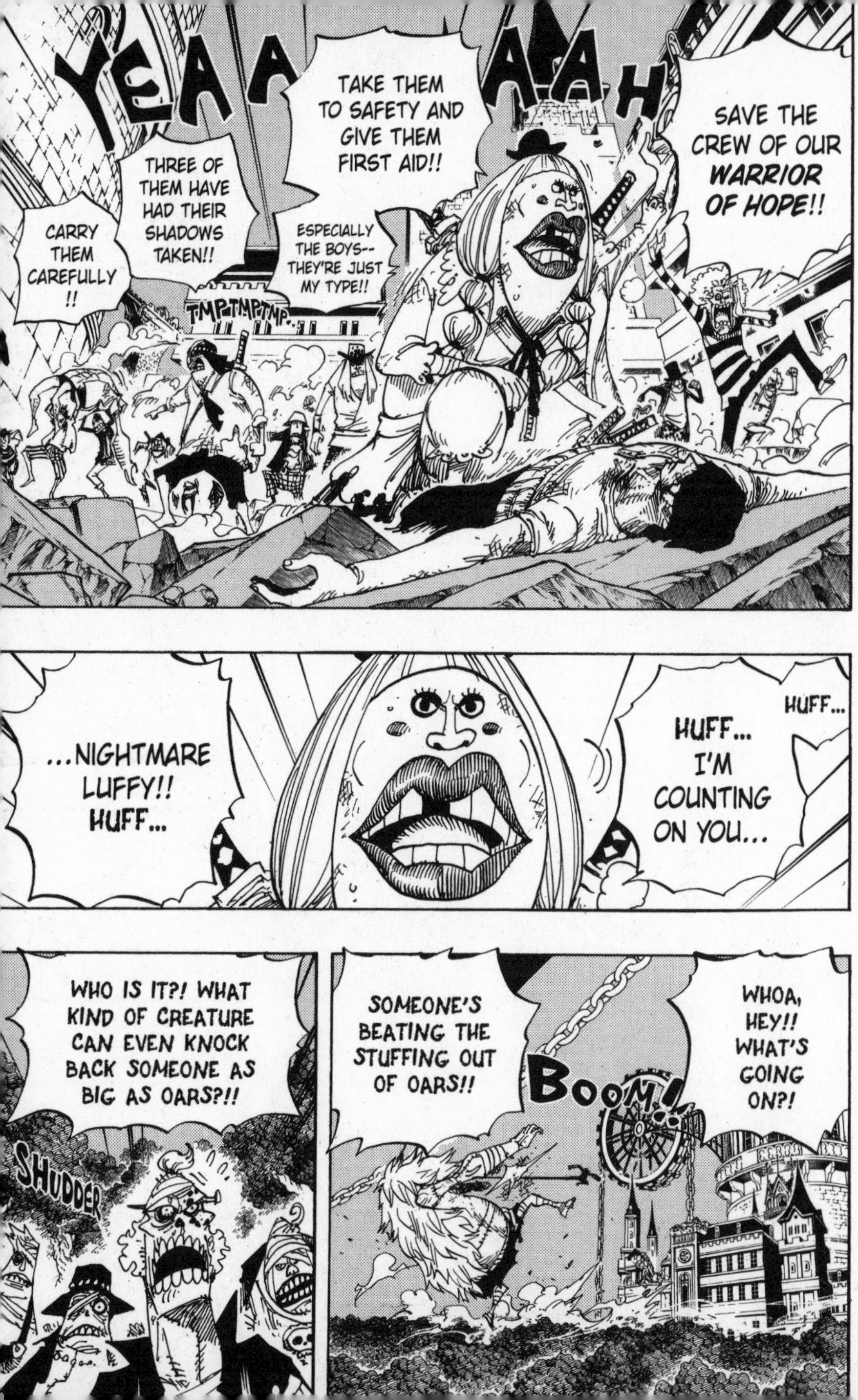
YEAAAAAH
SAVE THE CREW OF OUR WARRIOR OF HOPE!!
TAKE THEM TO SAFETY AND GIVE THEM FIRST AID!!
ESPECIALLY THE BOYS-- THEY'RE JUST MY TYPE!!
THREE OF THEM HAVE HAD THEIR SHADOWS TAKEN!!
CARRY THEM CAREFULLY !!
TMPTMPTMP...
HUFF...
HUFF... I'M COUNTING ON YOU...
...NIGHTMARE LUFFY!! HUFF...
WHOA, HEY!! WHAT'S GOING ON?!
BOOM!!
SOMEONE'S BEATING THE STUFFING OUT OF OARS!!
WHO IS IT?! WHAT KIND OF CREATURE CAN EVEN KNOCK BACK SOMEONE AS BIG AS OARS?!!
SHUDDER

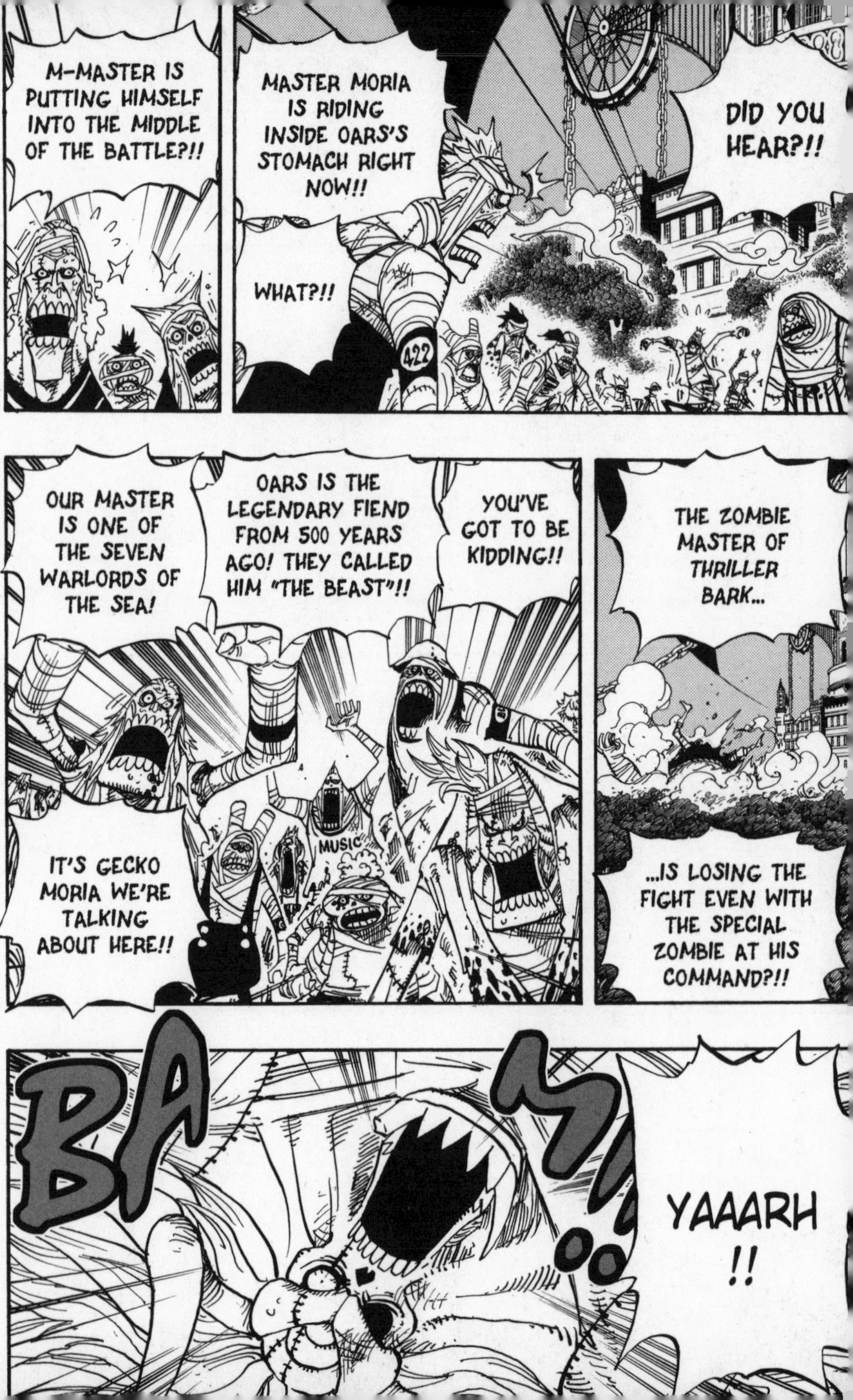
DID YOU HEAR?!!
MASTER MORIA IS RIDING INSIDE OARS'S STOMACH RIGHT NOW!!
WHAT?!!
422
M-MASTER IS PUTTING HIMSELF INTO THE MIDDLE OF THE BATTLE?!!
THE ZOMBIE MASTER OF THRILLER BARK...
...IS LOSING THE FIGHT EVEN WITH THE SPECIAL ZOMBIE AT HIS COMMAND?!!
YOU'VE GOT TO BE KIDDING!!
OARS IS THE LEGENDARY FIEND FROM 500 YEARS AGO! THEY CALLED HIM "THE BEAST"!!
OUR MASTER IS ONE OF THE SEVEN WARLORDS OF THE SEA!
MUSIC
IT'S GECKO MORIA WE'RE TALKING ABOUT HERE!!
YAAARH!!
BAM..

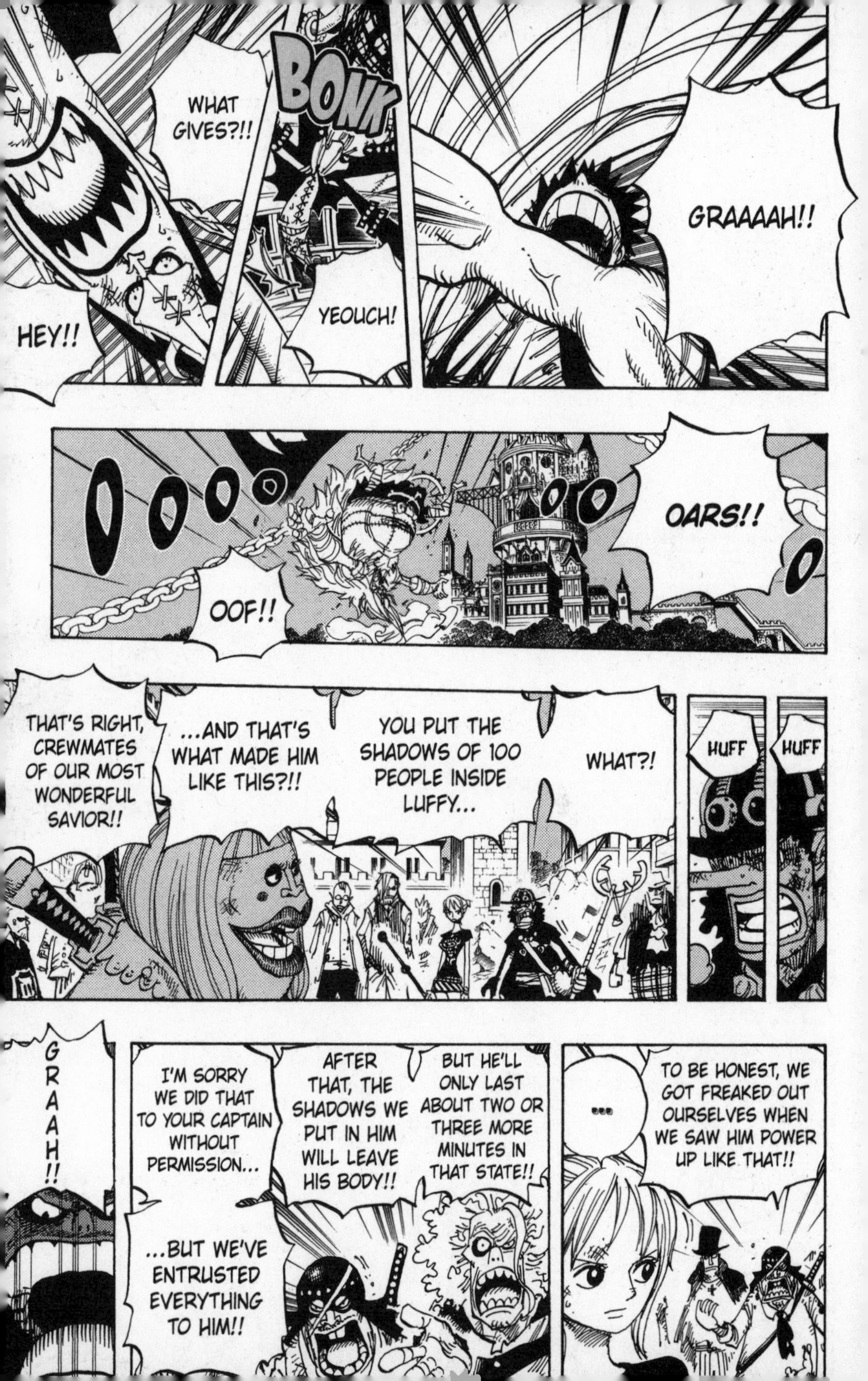
GRAAAAH!!
BONK
YEOUCH!
WHAT GIVES?!!
HEY!!
OARS!!
OOF!!
HUFF
HUFF
WHAT?!
YOU PUT THE SHADOWS OF 100 PEOPLE INSIDE LUFFY...
...AND THAT'S WHAT MADE HIM LIKE THIS?!!
THAT'S RIGHT, CREWMATES OF OUR MOST WONDERFUL SAVIOR!!
TO BE HONEST, WE GOT FREAKED OUT OURSELVES WHEN WE SAW HIM POWER UP LIKE THAT!!
...
BUT HE'LL ONLY LAST ABOUT TWO OR THREE MORE MINUTES IN THAT STATE!!
AFTER THAT, THE SHADOWS WE PUT IN HIM WILL LEAVE HIS BODY!!
I'M SORRY WE DID THAT TO YOUR CAPTAIN WITHOUT PERMISSION...
...BUT WE'VE ENTRUSTED EVERYTHING TO HIM!!
GRAAH!!

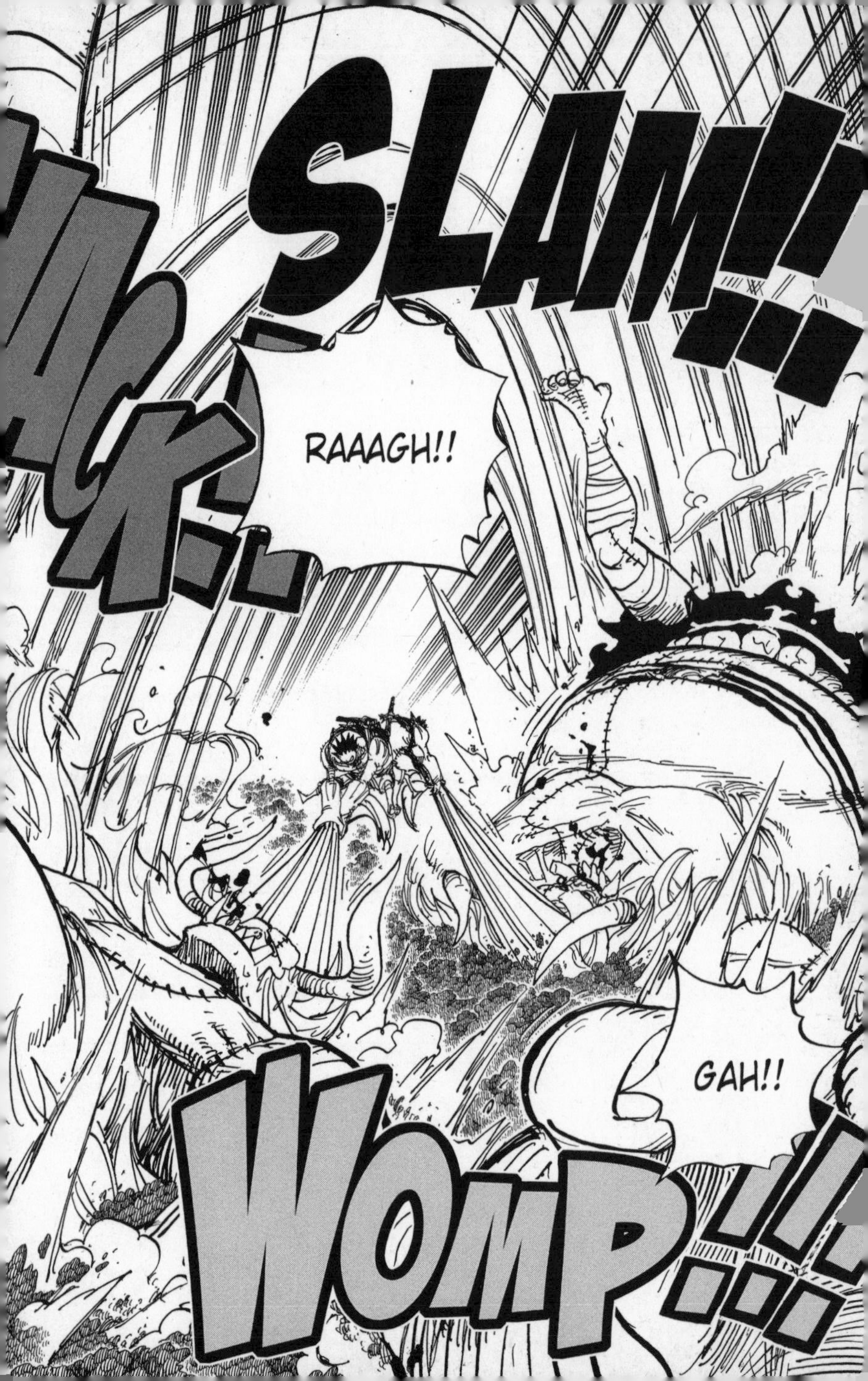
SLAM!!
RAAAGH!!
GAH!!
WOMP!!!

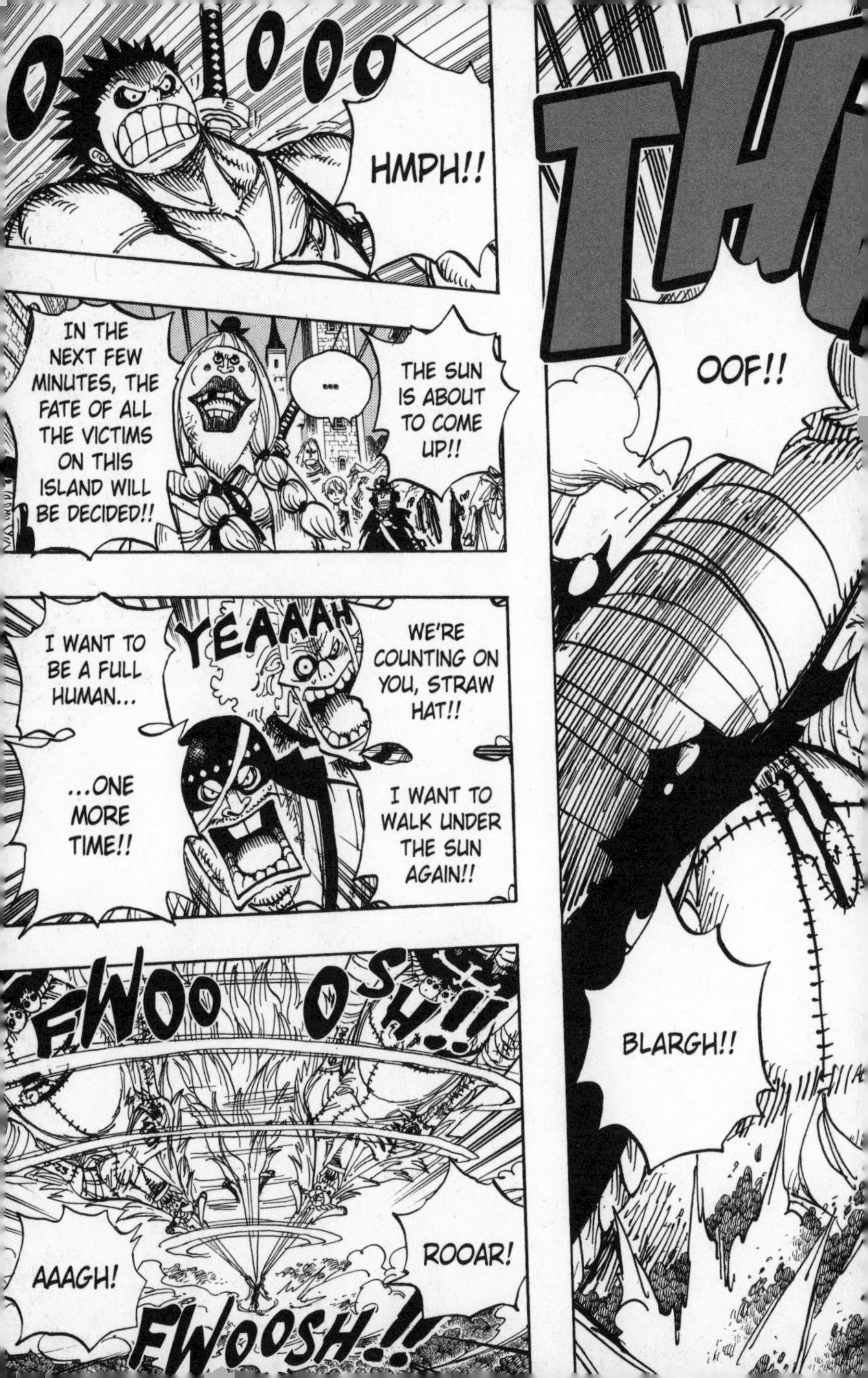

TH
OOF!!
BLARGH!!
OOOOO
HMPH!!
THE SUN IS ABOUT TO COME UP!!
...
IN THE NEXT FEW MINUTES, THE FATE OF ALL THE VICTIMS ON THIS ISLAND WILL BE DECIDED!!
WE'RE COUNTING ON YOU, STRAW HAT!!
YEAAAH
I WANT TO BE A FULL HUMAN...
I WANT TO WALK UNDER THE SUN AGAIN!!
...ONE MORE TIME!!
FWOO OSH!!
ROOAR!
AAAGH!
FWOOSH!!

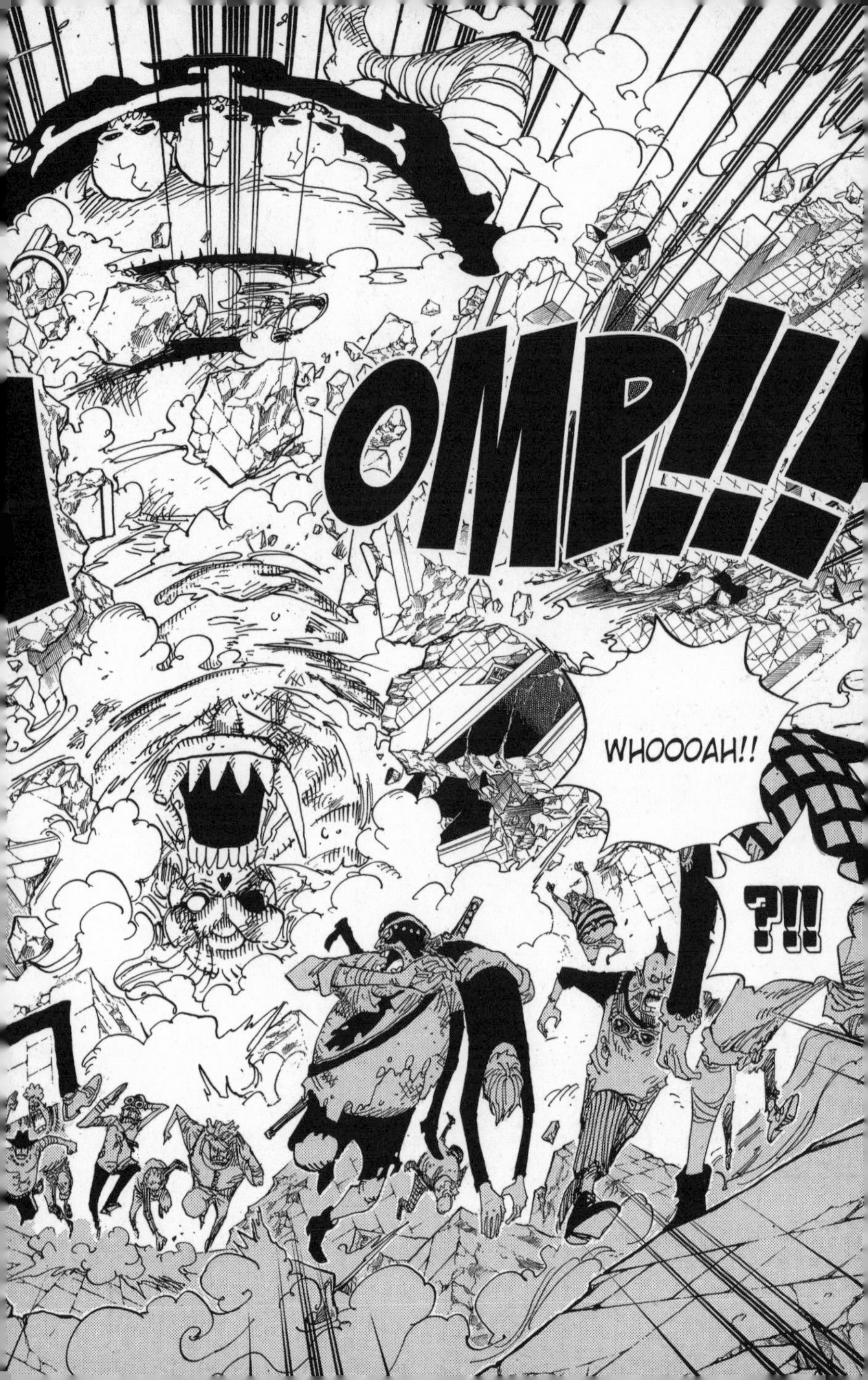
OMP!!!
WHOOOAH!!
?!!

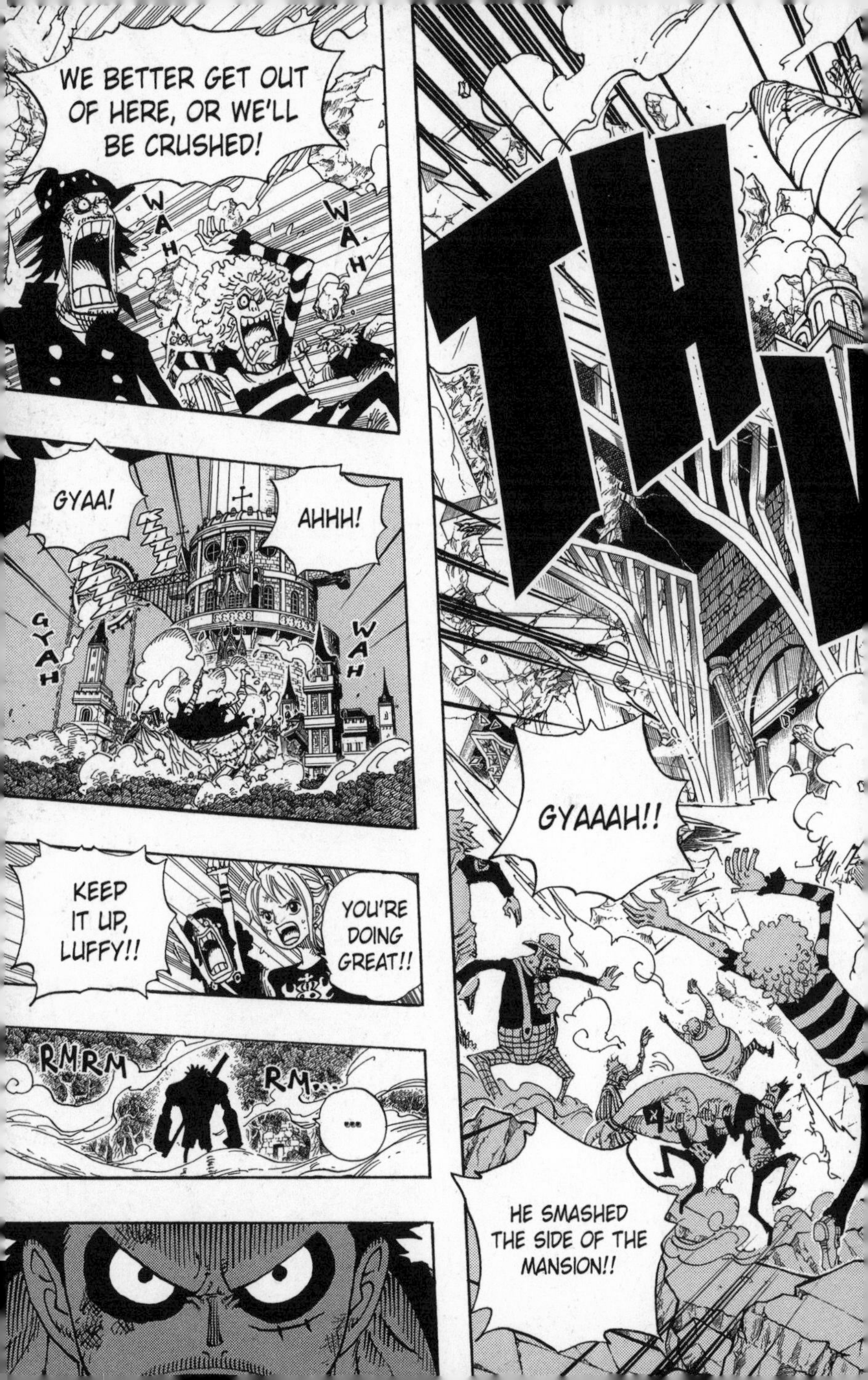
TH
GYAAAH!!
HE SMASHED THE SIDE OF THE MANSION!!
WE BETTER GET OUT OF HERE, OR WE'LL BE CRUSHED!
WAH
WAH
AHHH!
GYAA!
WAH
GYAH
YOU'RE DOING GREAT!!
KEEP IT UP, LUFFY!!
...
RM..
RMRM

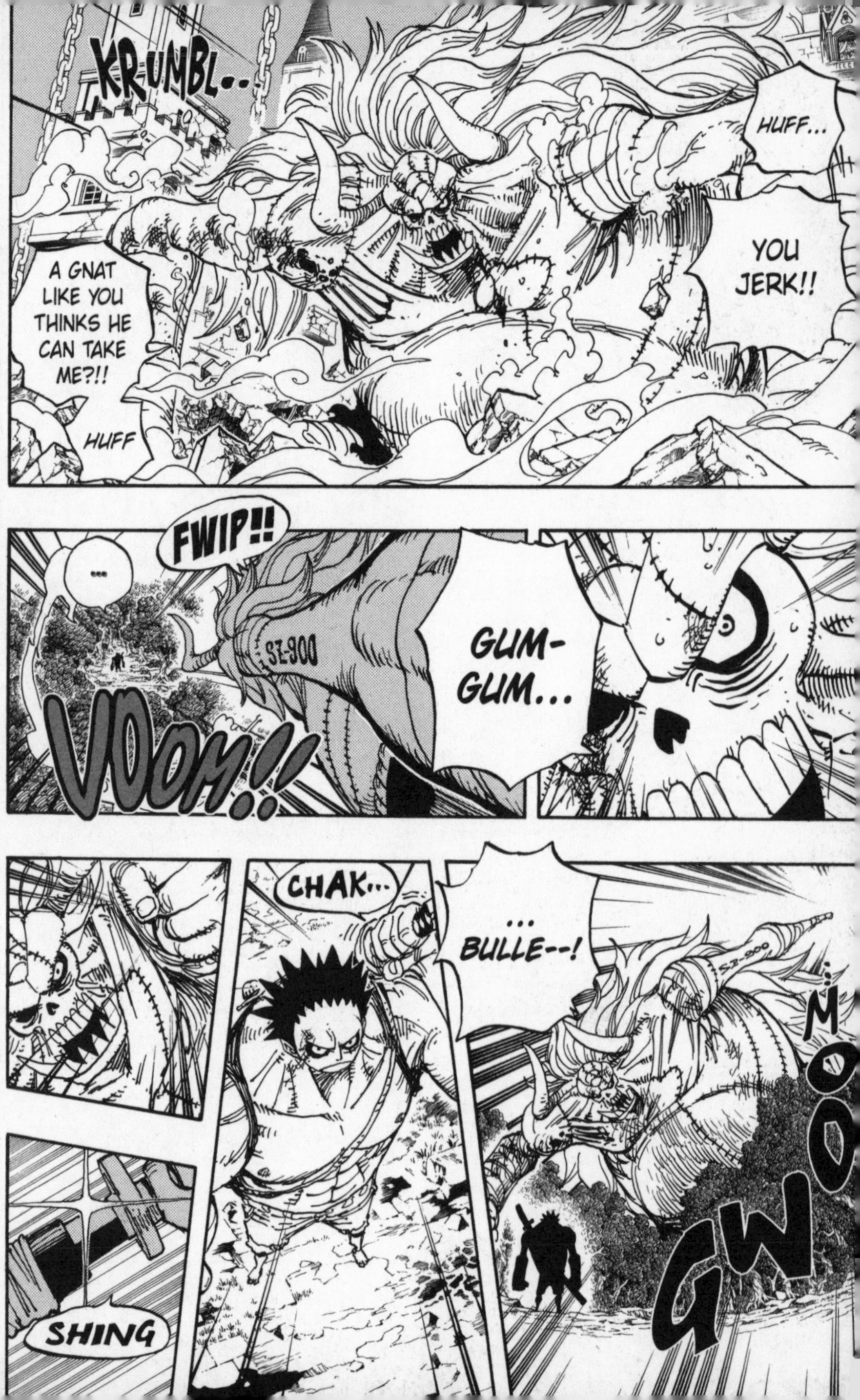
HUFF...
YOU JERK!!
KRUMBL...
A GNAT LIKE YOU THINKS HE CAN TAKE ME?!!
HUFF
GUM-GUM...
FWIP!!
...
VOOM!!
... BULLE--!
M...
GWOOO
CHAK...
SHING

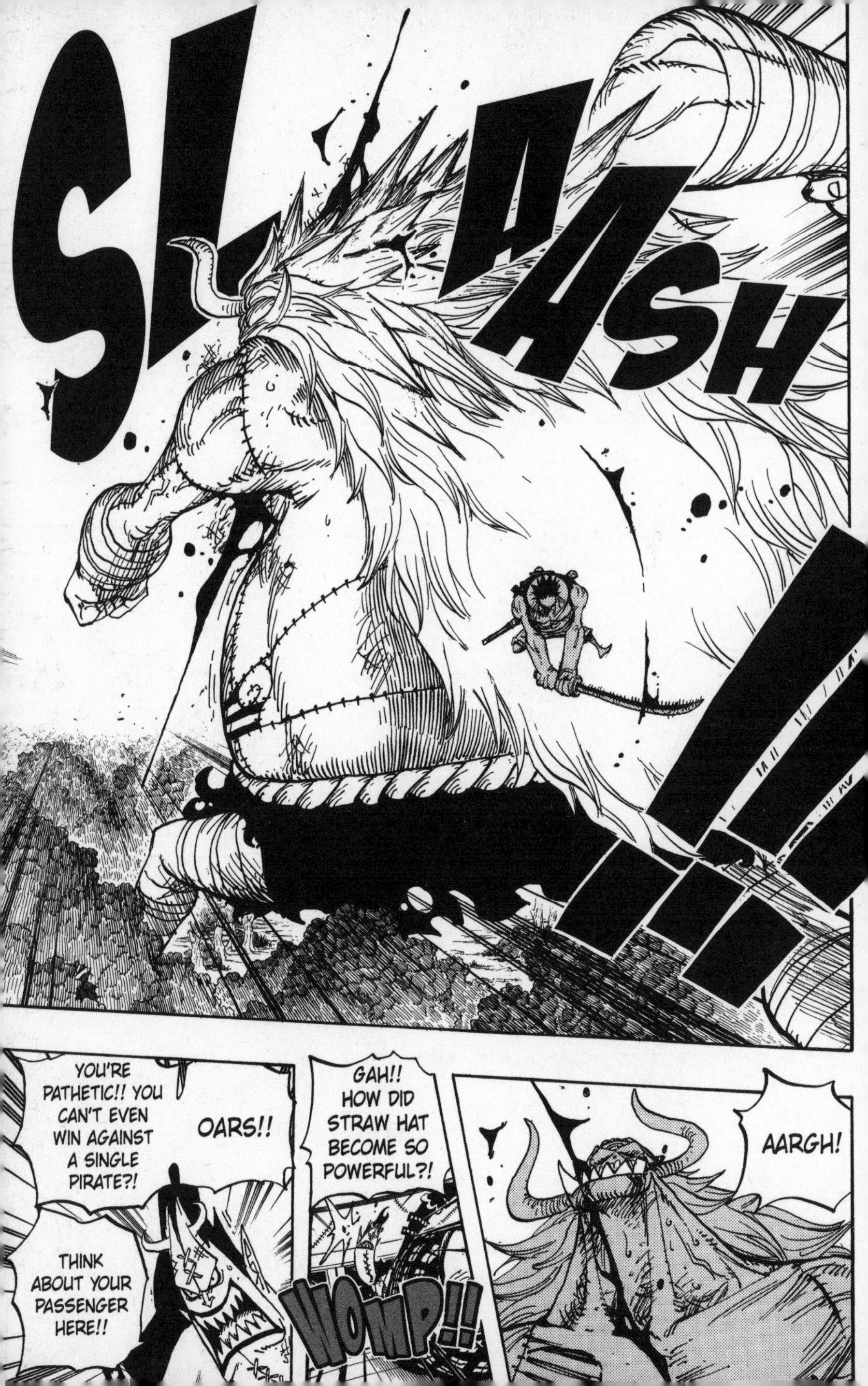
SLAASH!!!
AARGH!
GAH!! HOW DID STRAW HAT BECOME SO POWERFUL?!
WOMP!!
OARS!!
YOU'RE PATHETIC!! YOU CAN'T EVEN WIN AGAINST A SINGLE PIRATE?!
THINK ABOUT YOUR PASSENGER HERE!!

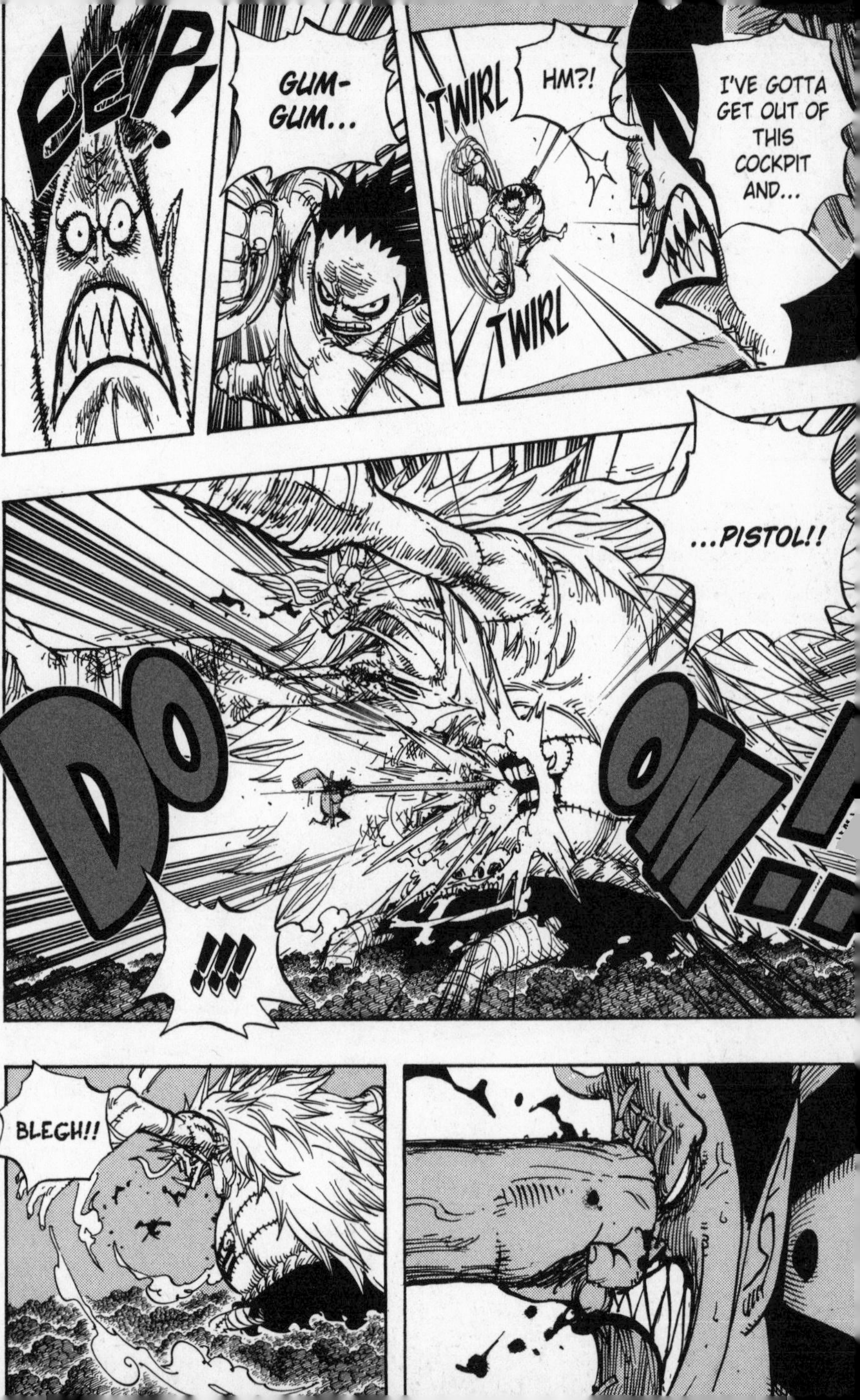
I'VE GOTTA GET OUT OF THIS COCKPIT AND...
HM?!
TWIRL
TWIRL
GUM-GUM...
GEP!
...PISTOL!!
DOOM..!
!!!
BLEGH!!

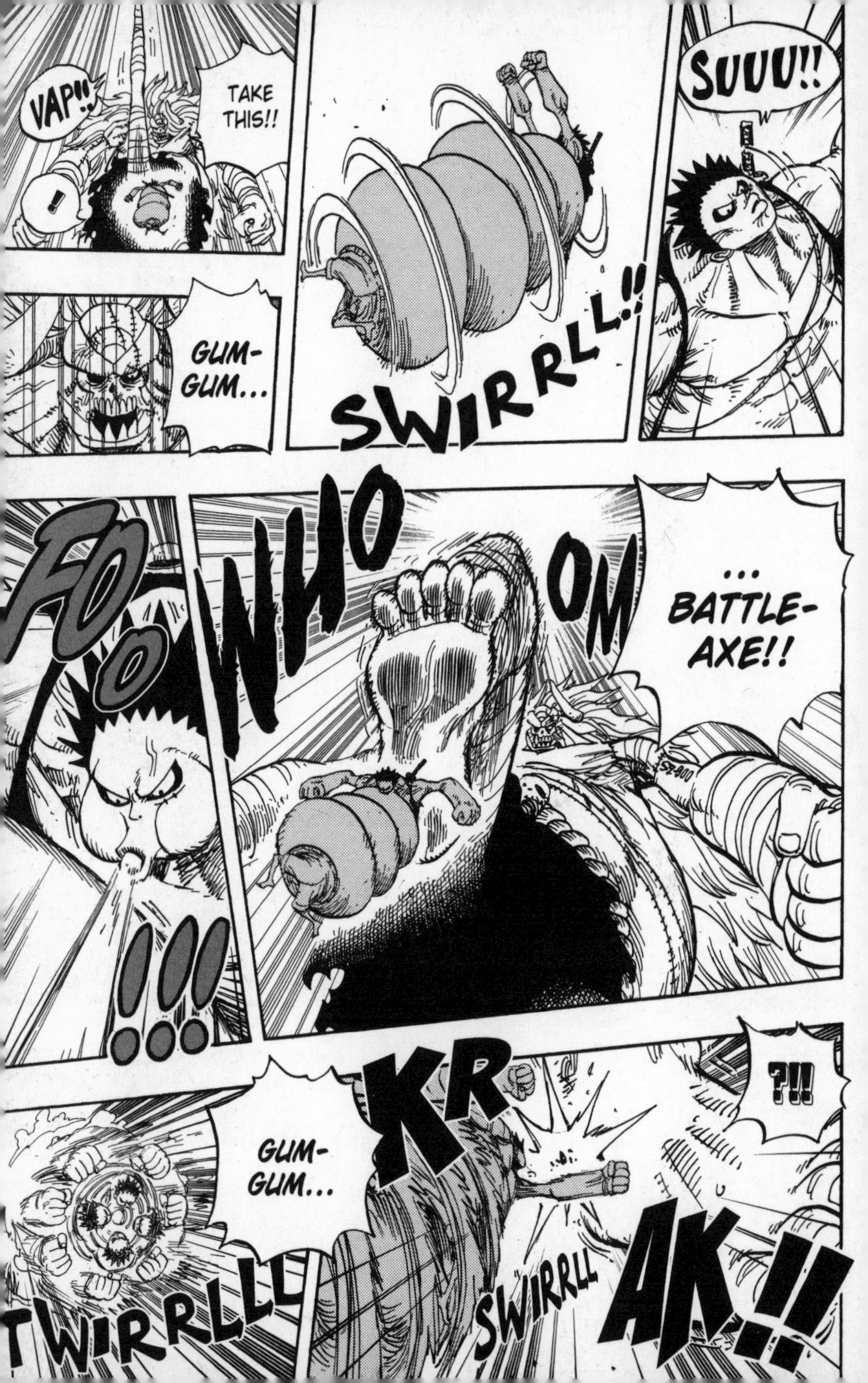
SUUU!!
SWIRRLL!!
VAP!!
TAKE THIS!!
!
GUM-GUM...
... BATTLE-AXE!!
FO O WHO OM
!!!
?!!
KR
AK!!
SWIRRLL
GUM-GUM...
TWIRRLLL

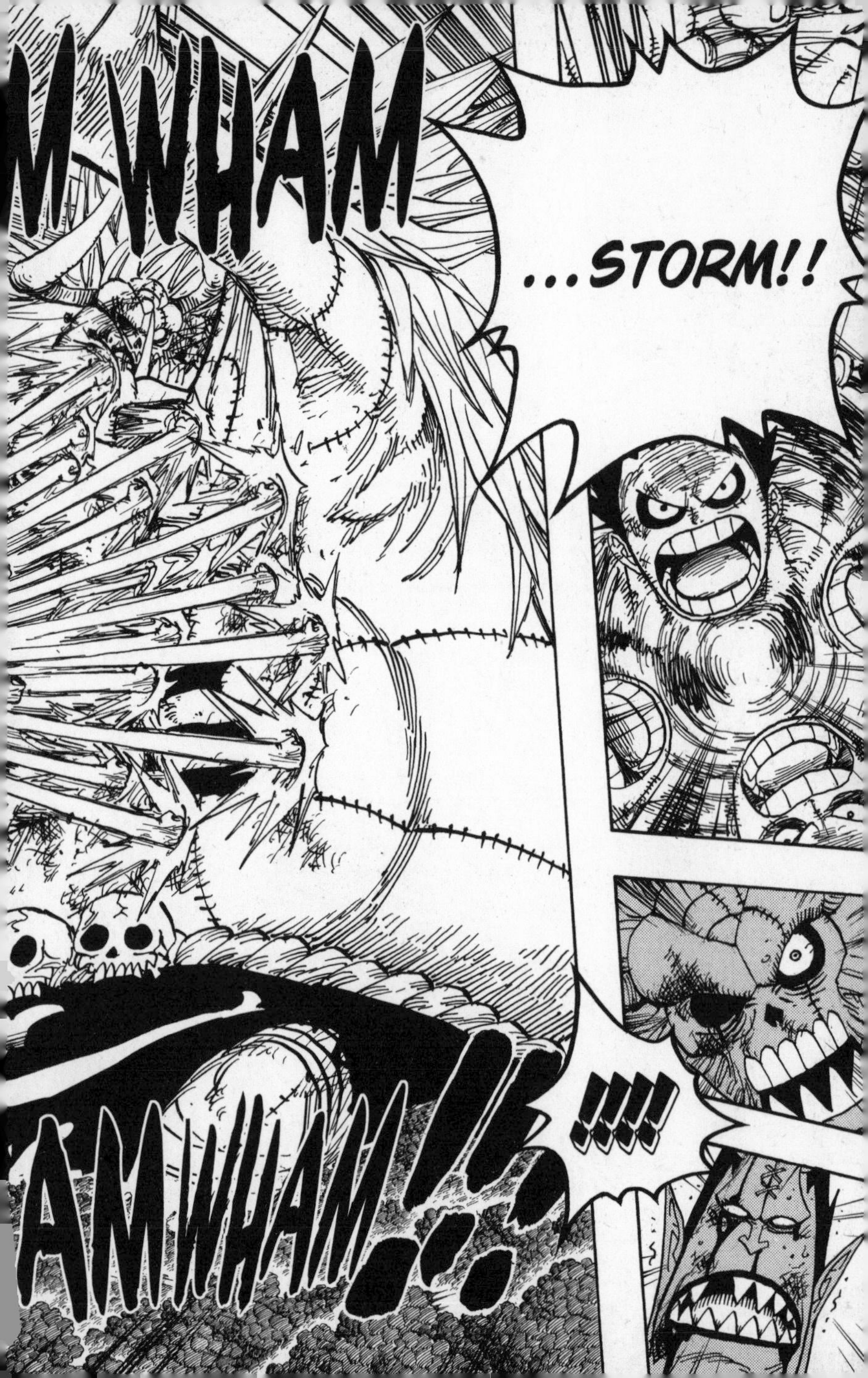
...STORM!!
WHAM
!!!!!
WHAM WHAM!!

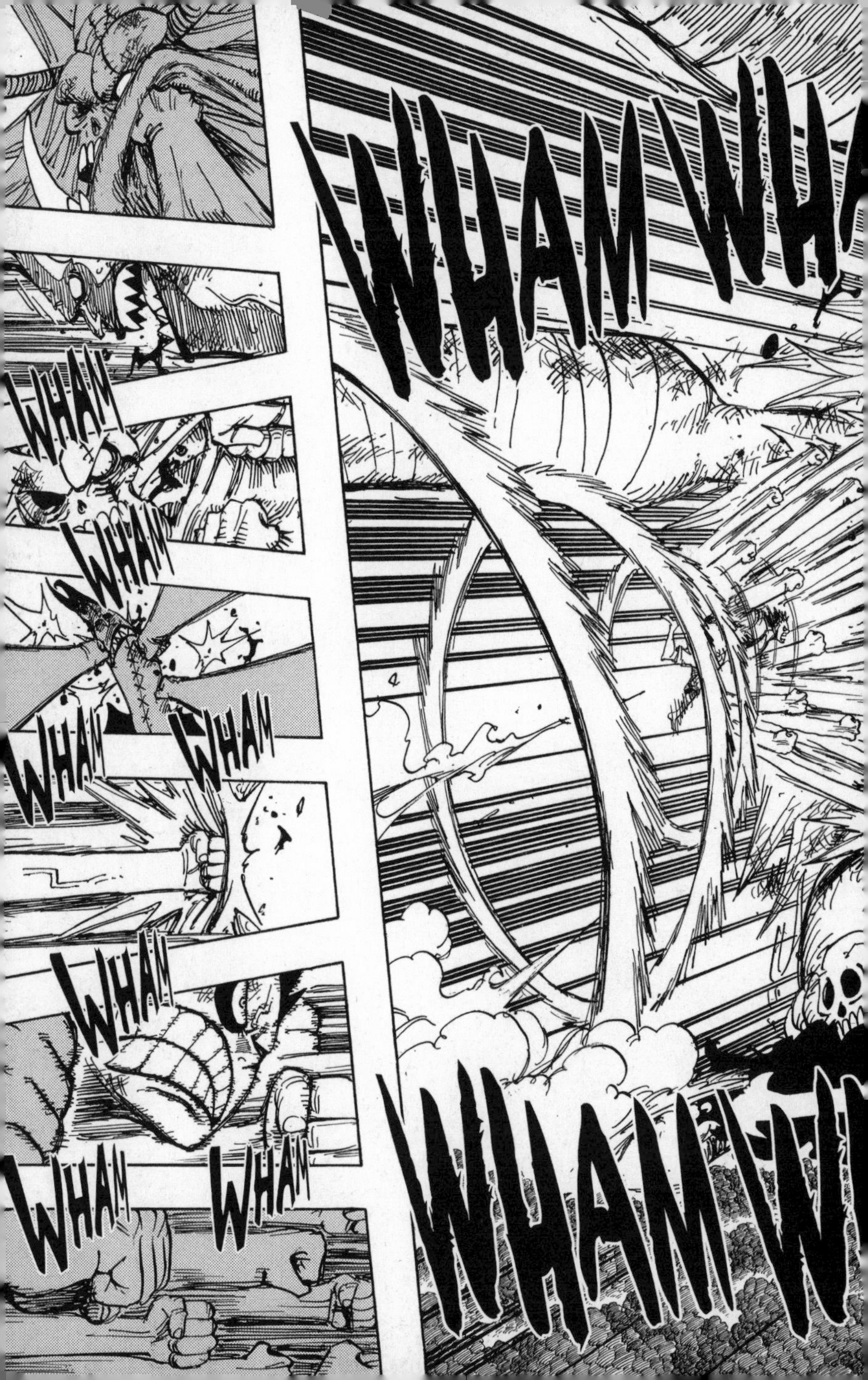

WHAM WHA
WHAM W
WHAM
WHAM
WHAM
WHAM
WHAM
WHAM
WHAM

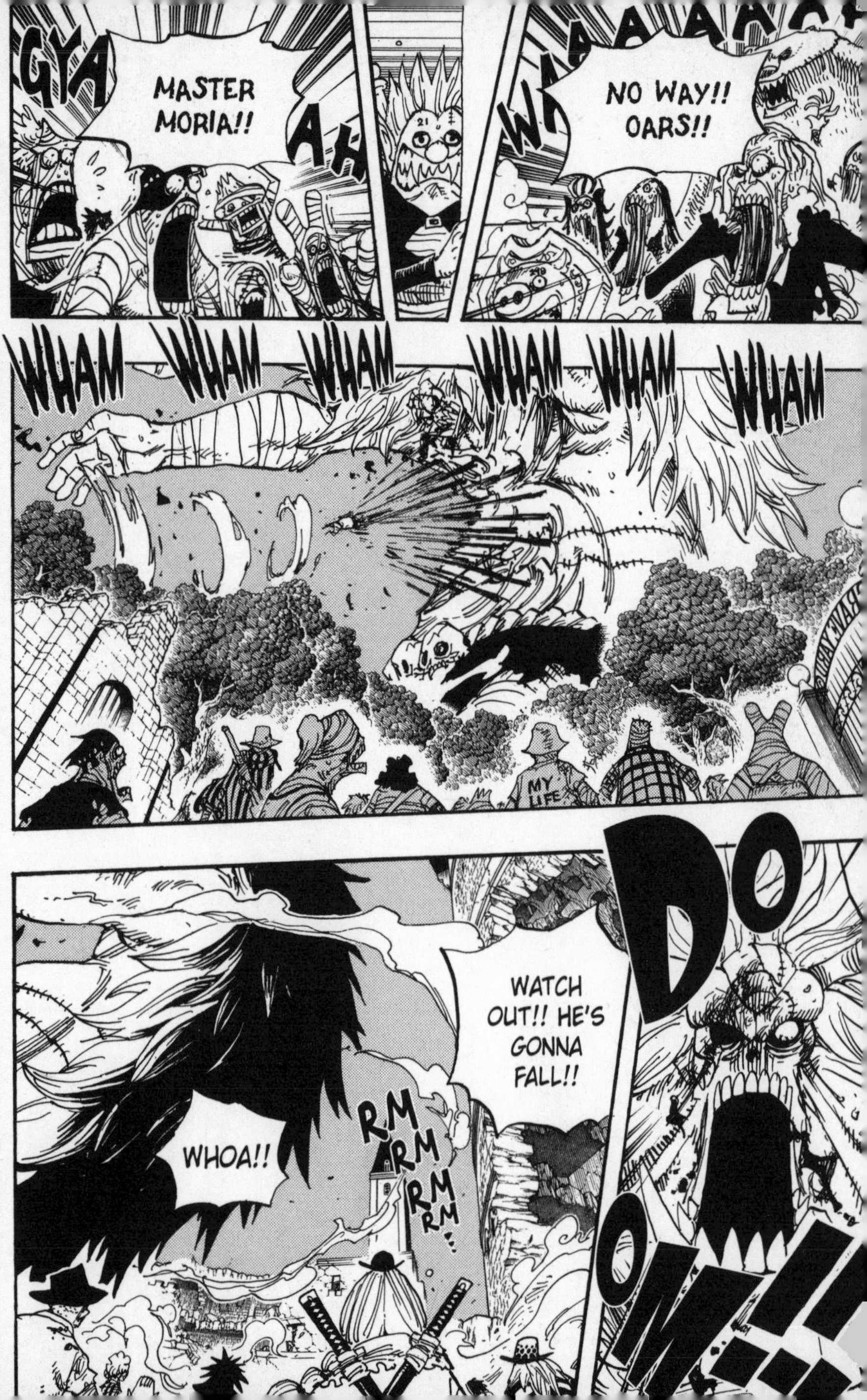
NO WAY!! OARS!!
MASTER MORIA!!
GYA
AH
WHAM WHAM WHAM WHAM WHAM WHAM
MY LIFE
DO
WATCH OUT!! HE'S GONNA FALL!!
RM RM RM RM RM
WHOA!!

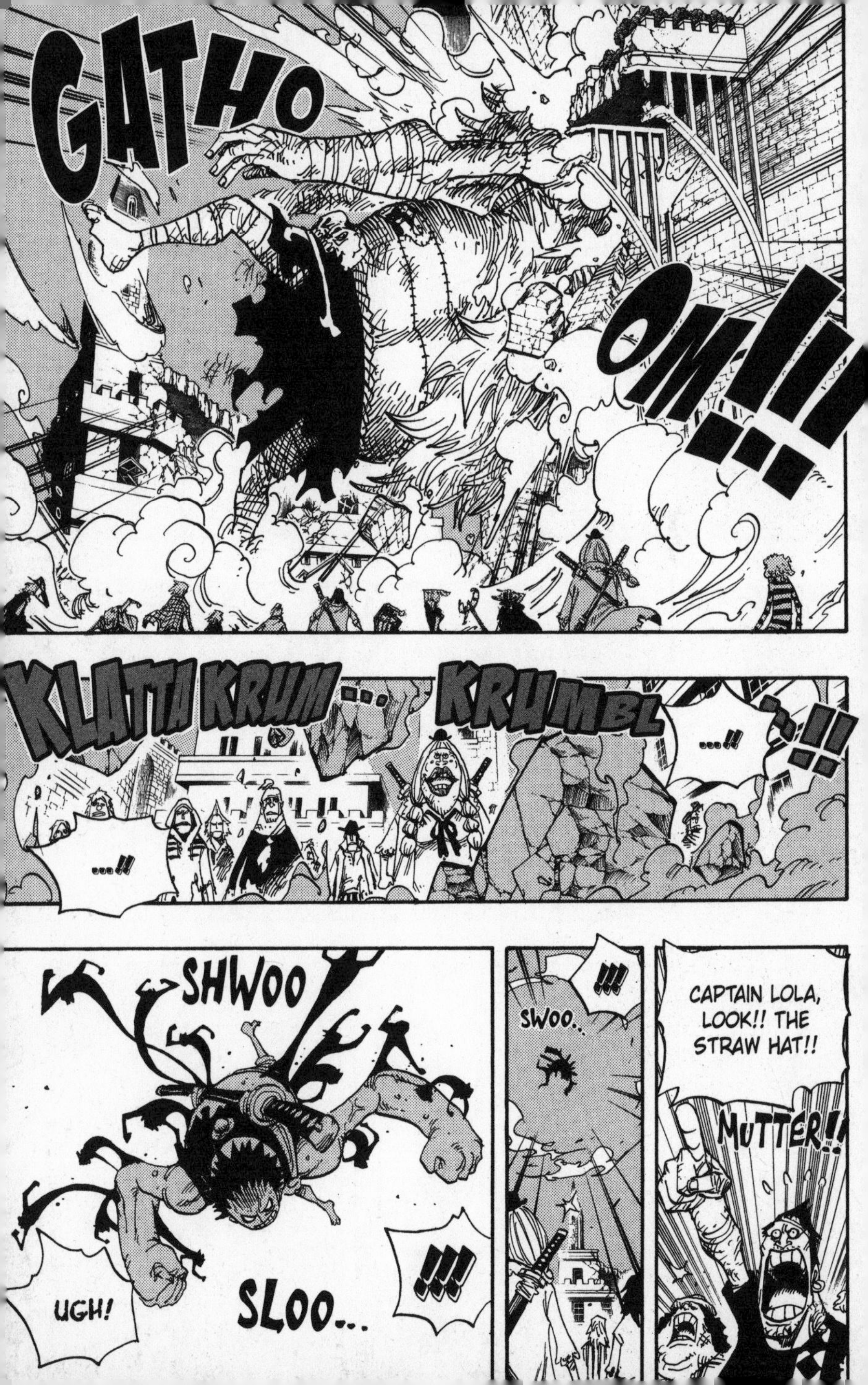

GATHO
OM!!!
KLATTA KRUM...
KRUMBL...!!
...!!
...!!
CAPTAIN LOLA, LOOK!! THE STRAW HAT!!
MUTTER!!
!!!
SWOO..
SHWOO
!!!
UGH!
SLOO...

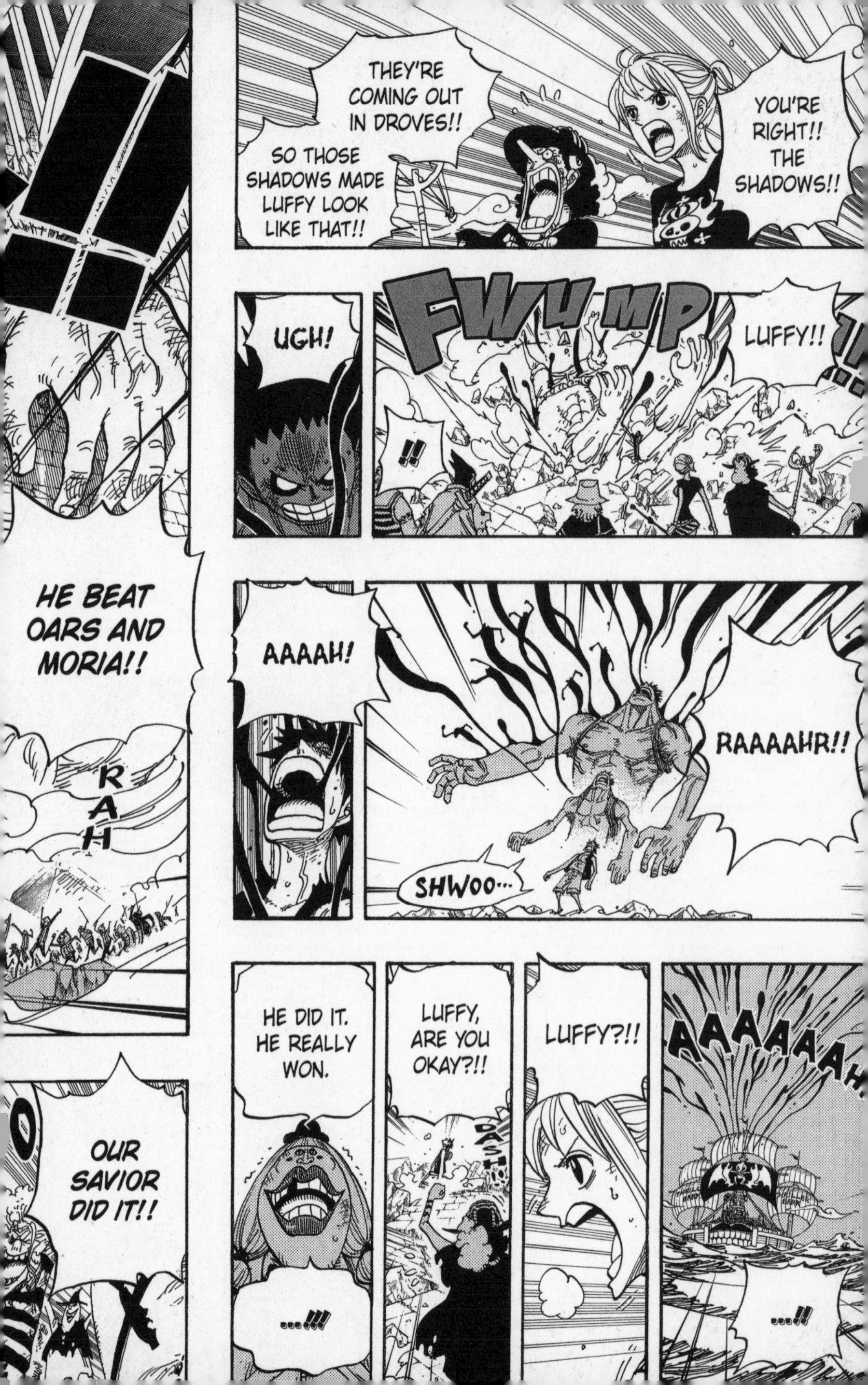

YOU'RE RIGHT!! THE SHADOWS!!
THEY'RE COMING OUT IN DROVES!!
SO THOSE SHADOWS MADE LUFFY LOOK LIKE THAT!!
FWUMP
LUFFY!!
!!
UGH!
RAAAAHR!!
SHWOO...
AAAAH!
AAAAAAAH
...!!
LUFFY?!!
LUFFY, ARE YOU OKAY?!!
DASH
HE DID IT. HE REALLY WON.
...!!!
HE BEAT OARS AND MORIA!!
RAH
OUR SAVIOR DID IT!!

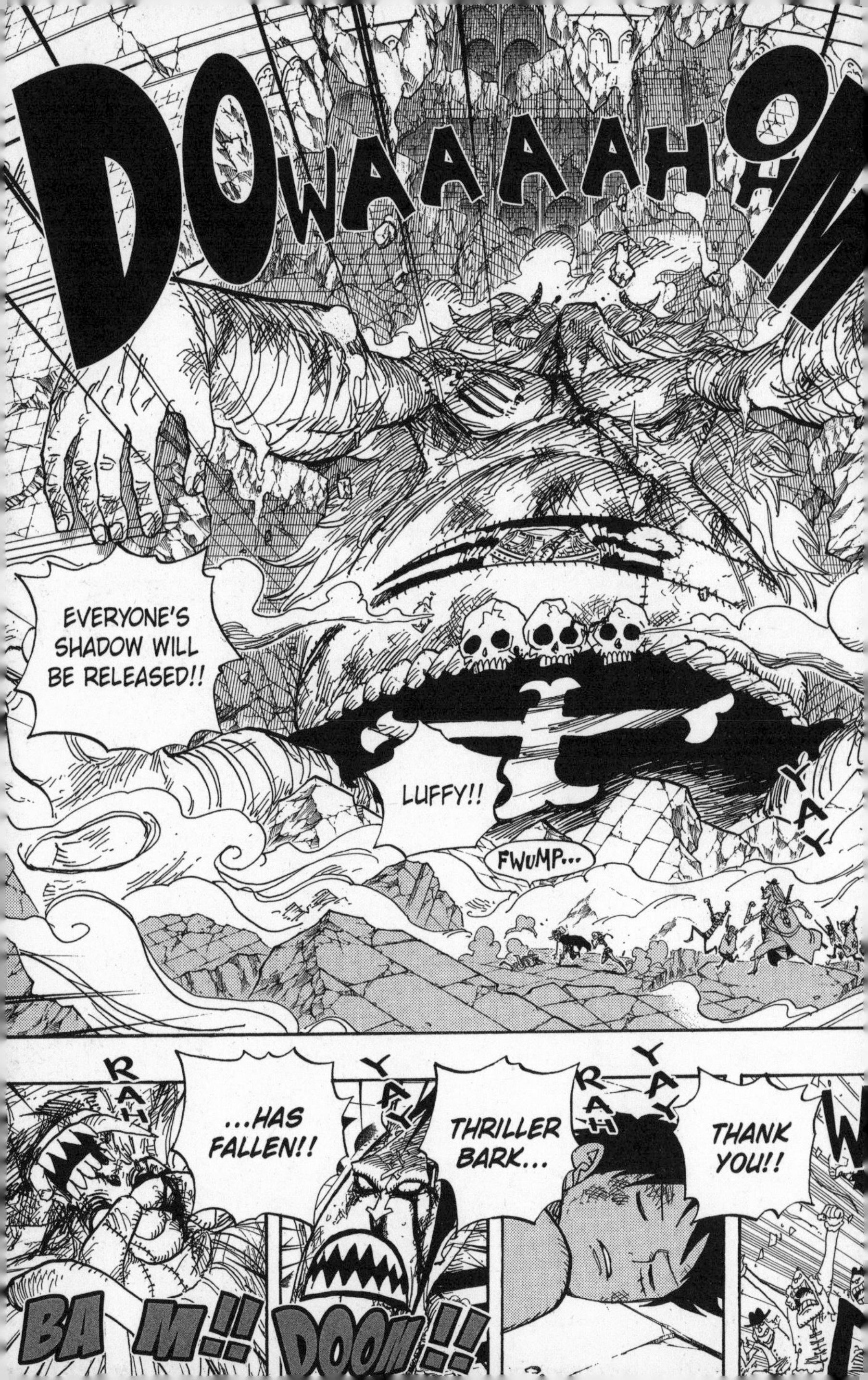
DOWAAAAHOOM
EVERYONE'S SHADOW WILL BE RELEASED!!
YAY
LUFFY!!
FWUMP...
THANK YOU!!
YAY
RAH
THRILLER BARK...
YAY
...HAS FALLEN!!
RAH
BA M!! DOOM!!

ONE PIECE **STORYBOARD PREVIEW!!** #24

FROM VOL. 49, PAGES 182~183 -ED.

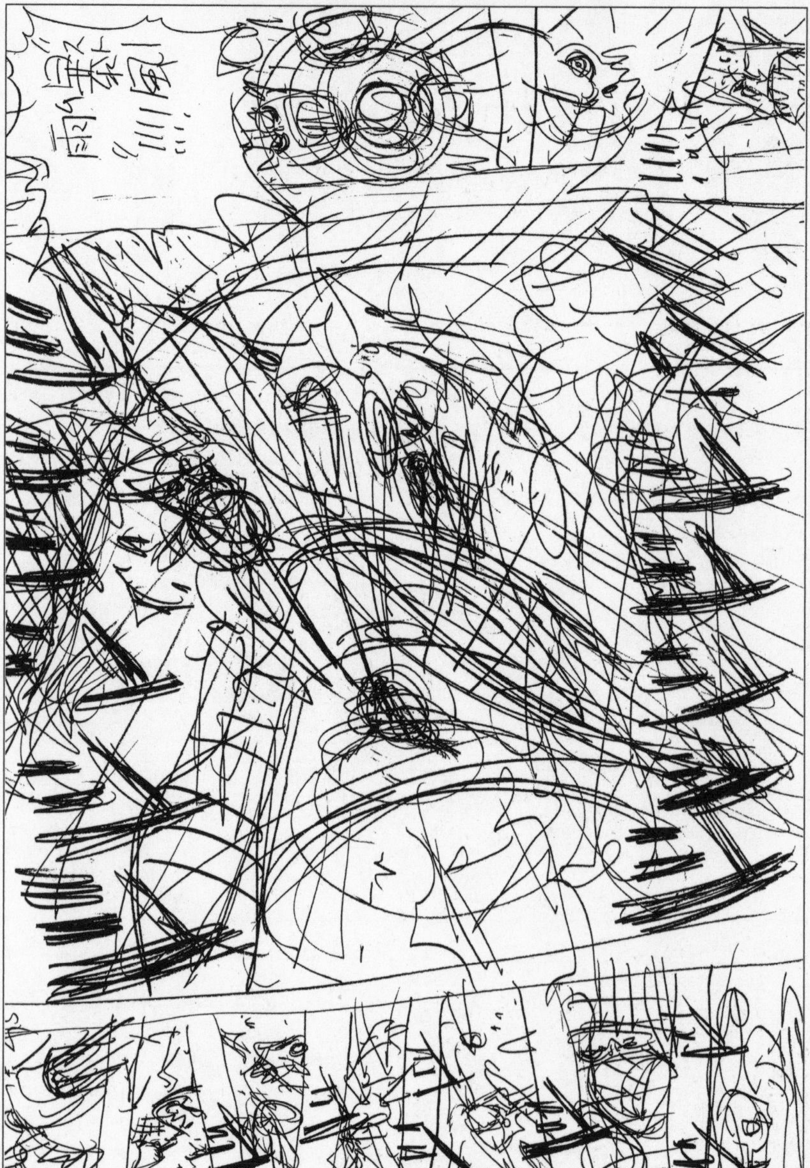

Chapter 480:
INTERCEPTION

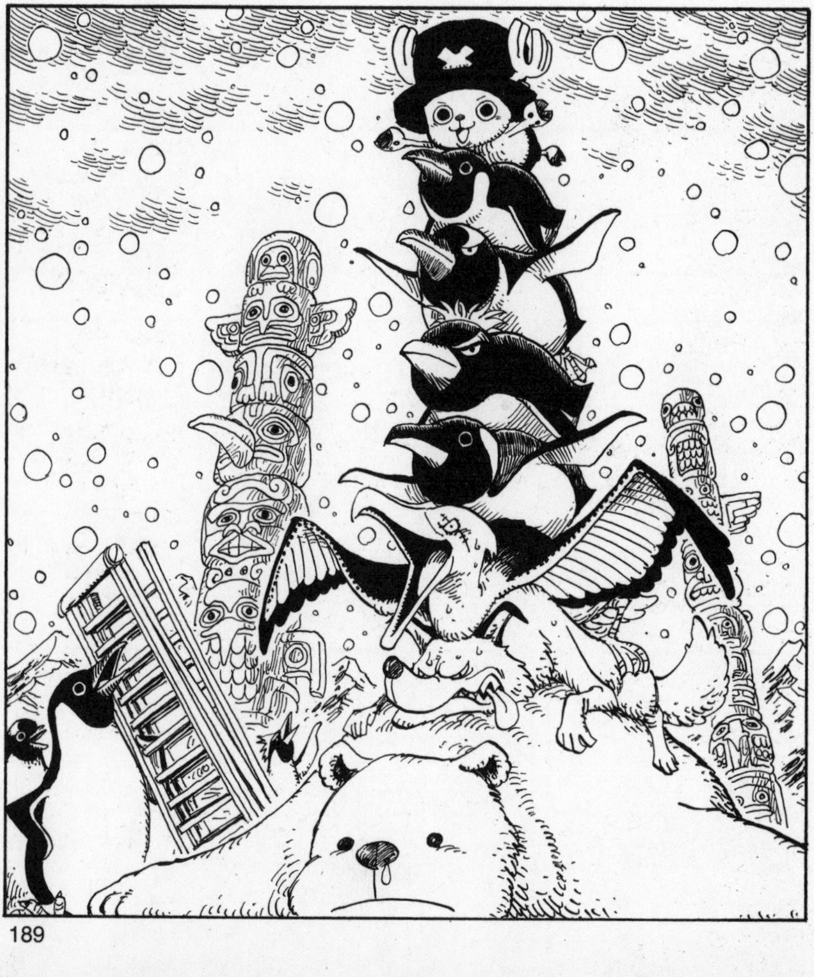

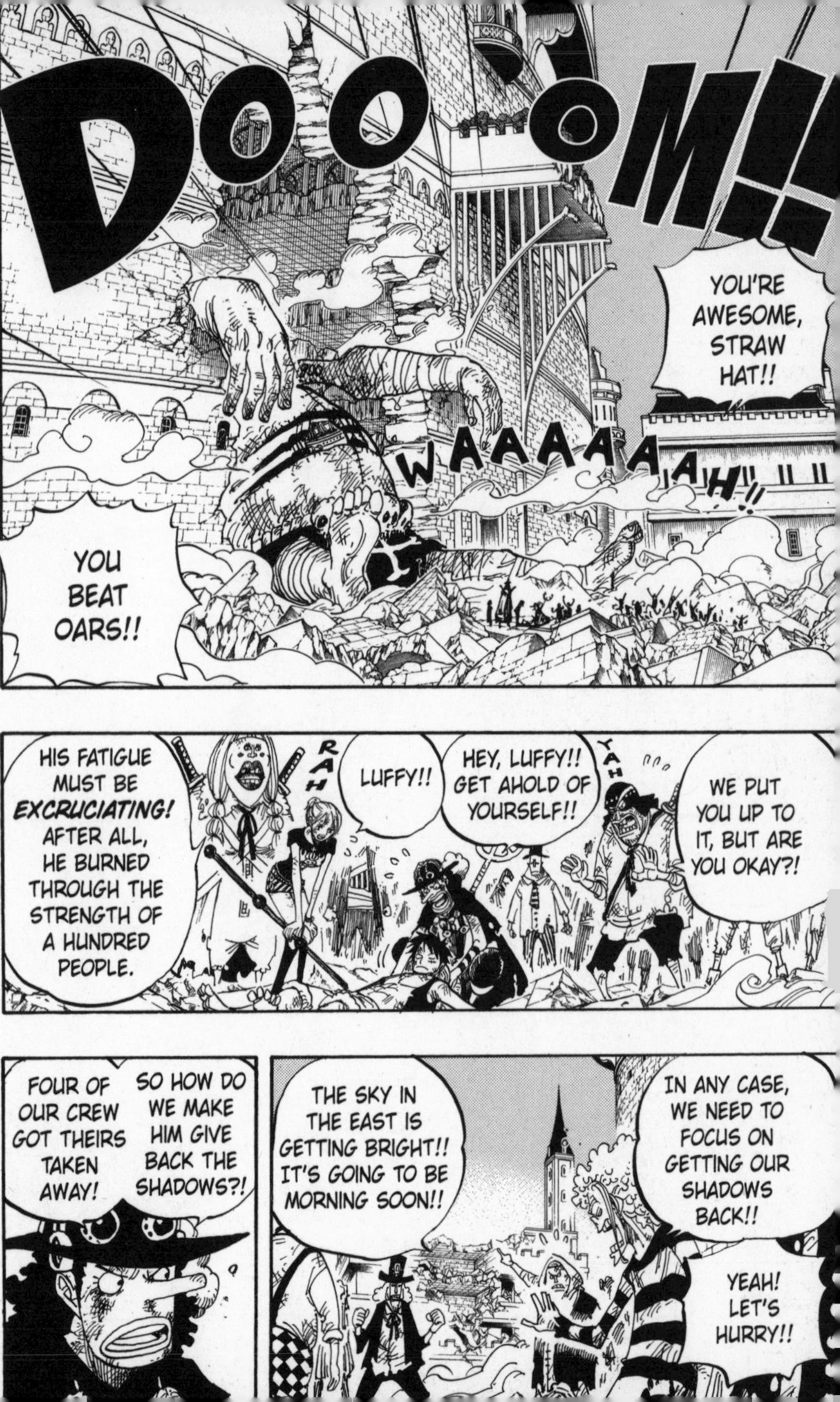
DOOOOM!!
YOU'RE AWESOME, STRAW HAT!!
WAAAAAAH!!
YOU BEAT OARS!!
WE PUT YOU UP TO IT, BUT ARE YOU OKAY?!
YAH
HEY, LUFFY!! GET AHOLD OF YOURSELF!!
LUFFY!!
RAH
HIS FATIGUE MUST BE *EXCRUCIATING!* AFTER ALL, HE BURNED THROUGH THE STRENGTH OF A HUNDRED PEOPLE.
IN ANY CASE, WE NEED TO FOCUS ON GETTING OUR SHADOWS BACK!!
YEAH! LET'S HURRY!!
THE SKY IN THE EAST IS GETTING BRIGHT!! IT'S GOING TO BE MORNING SOON!!
SO HOW DO WE MAKE HIM GIVE BACK THE SHADOWS?!
FOUR OF OUR CREW GOT THEIRS TAKEN AWAY!

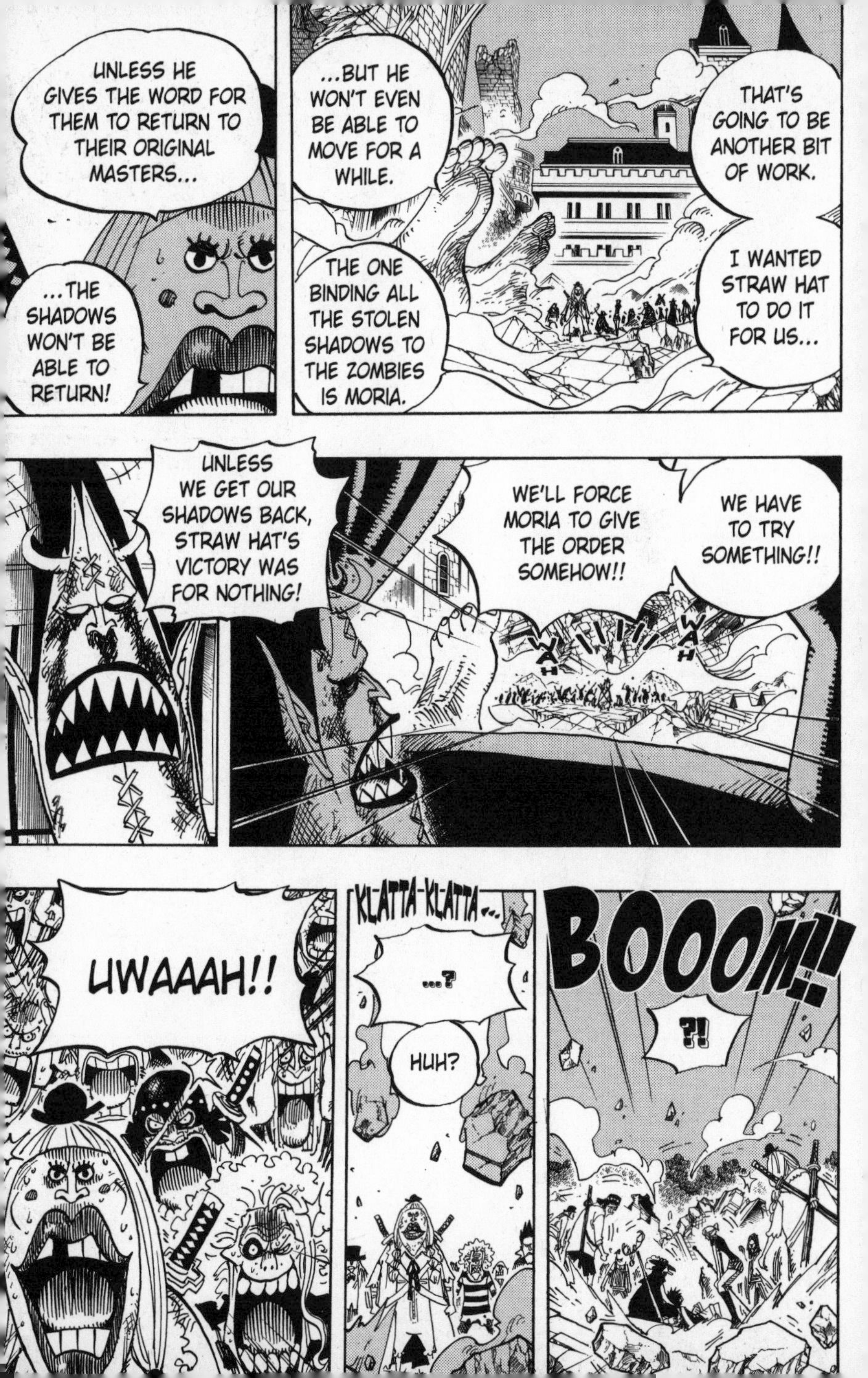
THAT'S GOING TO BE ANOTHER BIT OF WORK.
I WANTED STRAW HAT TO DO IT FOR US...
...BUT HE WON'T EVEN BE ABLE TO MOVE FOR A WHILE.
THE ONE BINDING ALL THE STOLEN SHADOWS TO THE ZOMBIES IS MORIA.
UNLESS HE GIVES THE WORD FOR THEM TO RETURN TO THEIR ORIGINAL MASTERS...
...THE SHADOWS WON'T BE ABLE TO RETURN!
WE HAVE TO TRY SOMETHING!!
WE'LL FORCE MORIA TO GIVE THE ORDER SOMEHOW!!
WAH
WAH
UNLESS WE GET OUR SHADOWS BACK, STRAW HAT'S VICTORY WAS FOR NOTHING!
BOOOM!!
?!
KLATTA-KLATTA...
...?
HUH?
UWAAAH!!

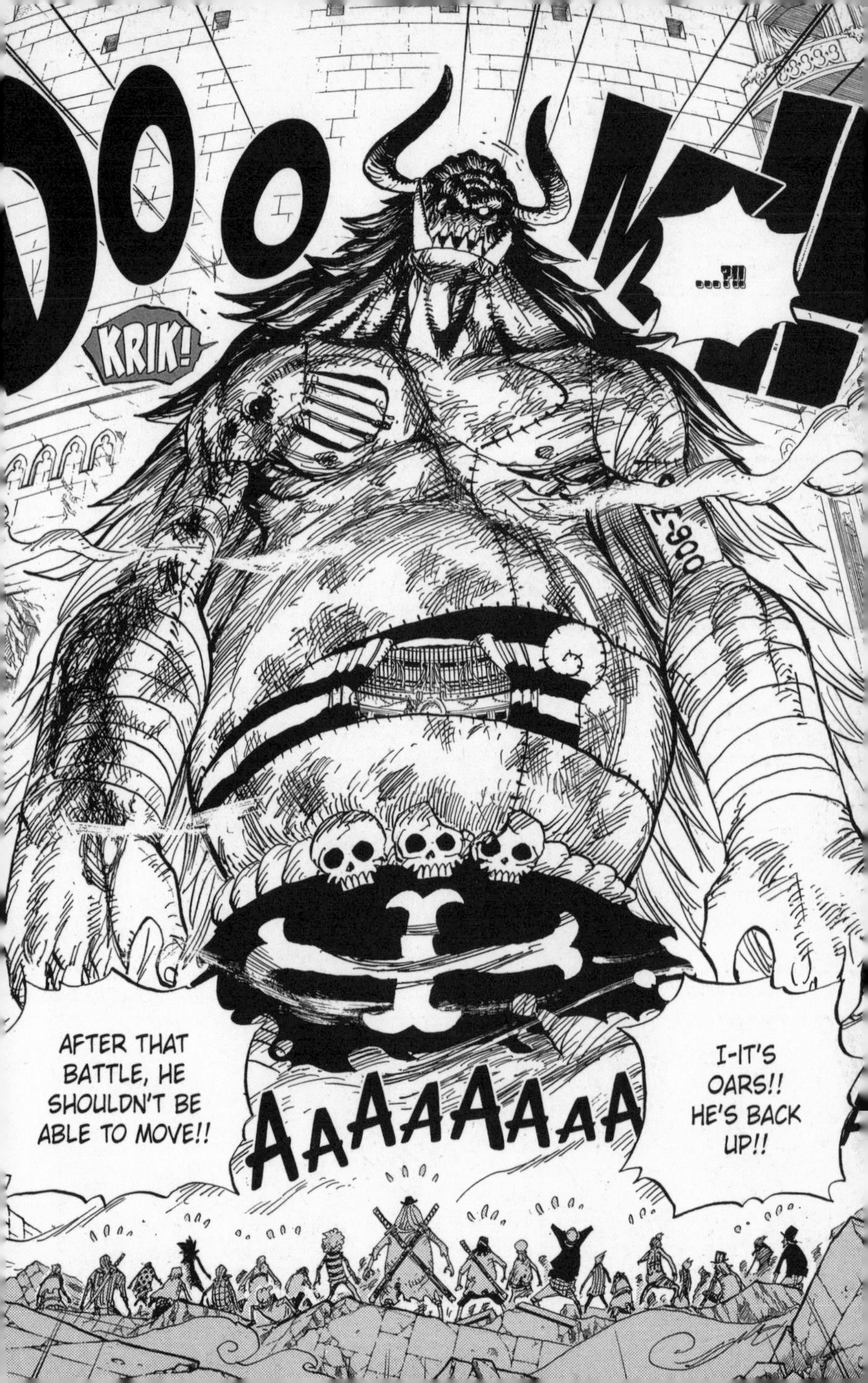
DOOOM
...?!!
KRIK!
I-IT'S OARS!! HE'S BACK UP!!
AAAAAAAA
AFTER THAT BATTLE, HE SHOULDN'T BE ABLE TO MOVE!!

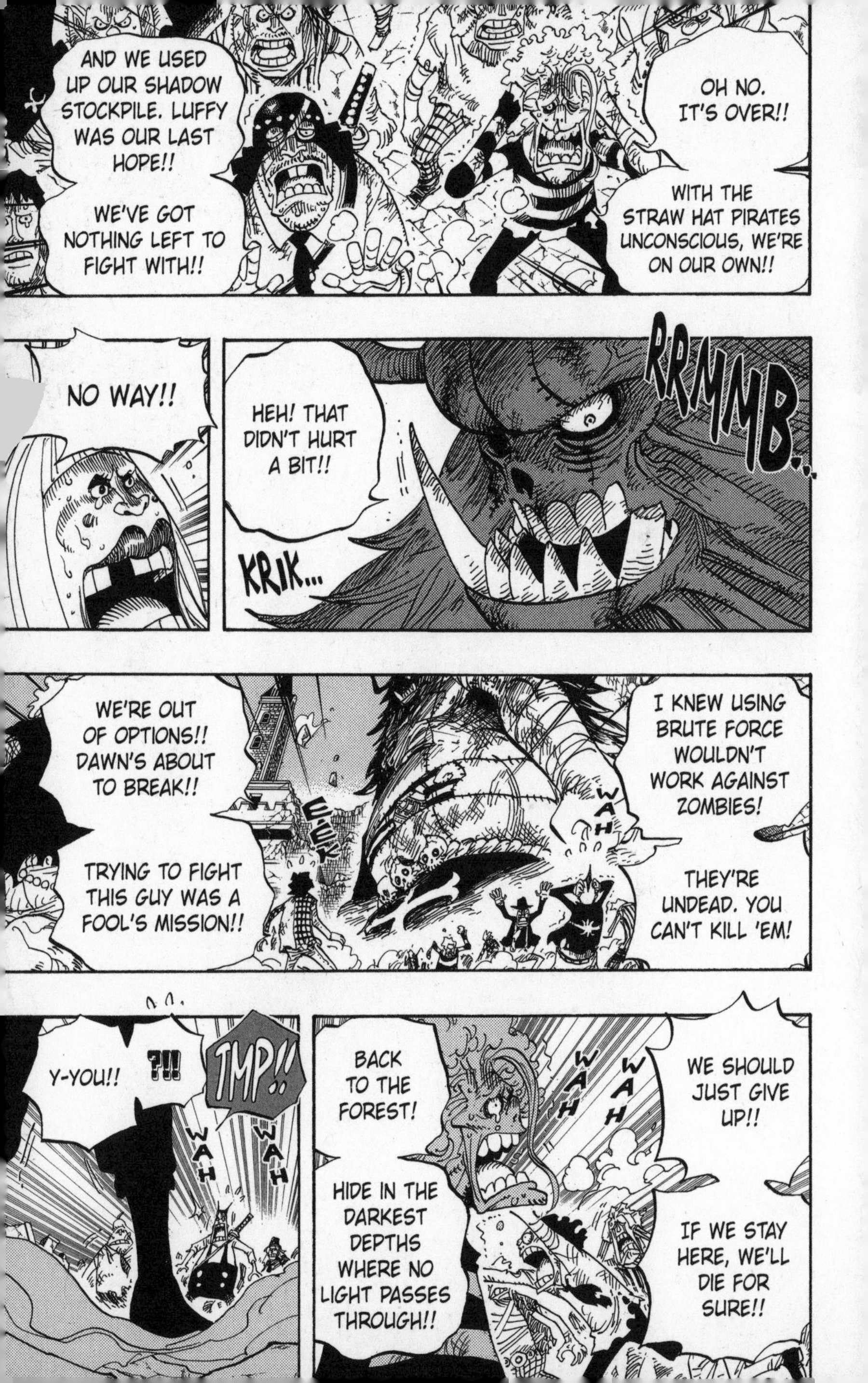
OH NO. IT'S OVER!!
WITH THE STRAW HAT PIRATES UNCONSCIOUS, WE'RE ON OUR OWN!!
AND WE USED UP OUR SHADOW STOCKPILE. LUFFY WAS OUR LAST HOPE!!
WE'VE GOT NOTHING LEFT TO FIGHT WITH!!
RRMMB...
HEH! THAT DIDN'T HURT A BIT!!
KRIK...
NO WAY!!
I KNEW USING BRUTE FORCE WOULDN'T WORK AGAINST ZOMBIES!
WAH
THEY'RE UNDEAD. YOU CAN'T KILL 'EM!
WE'RE OUT OF OPTIONS!! DAWN'S ABOUT TO BREAK!!
TRYING TO FIGHT THIS GUY WAS A FOOL'S MISSION!!
WE SHOULD JUST GIVE UP!!
WAH
WAH
BACK TO THE FOREST!
IF WE STAY HERE, WE'LL DIE FOR SURE!!
HIDE IN THE DARKEST DEPTHS WHERE NO LIGHT PASSES THROUGH!!
TMP!!
?!!
WAH
WAH
Y-YOU!!

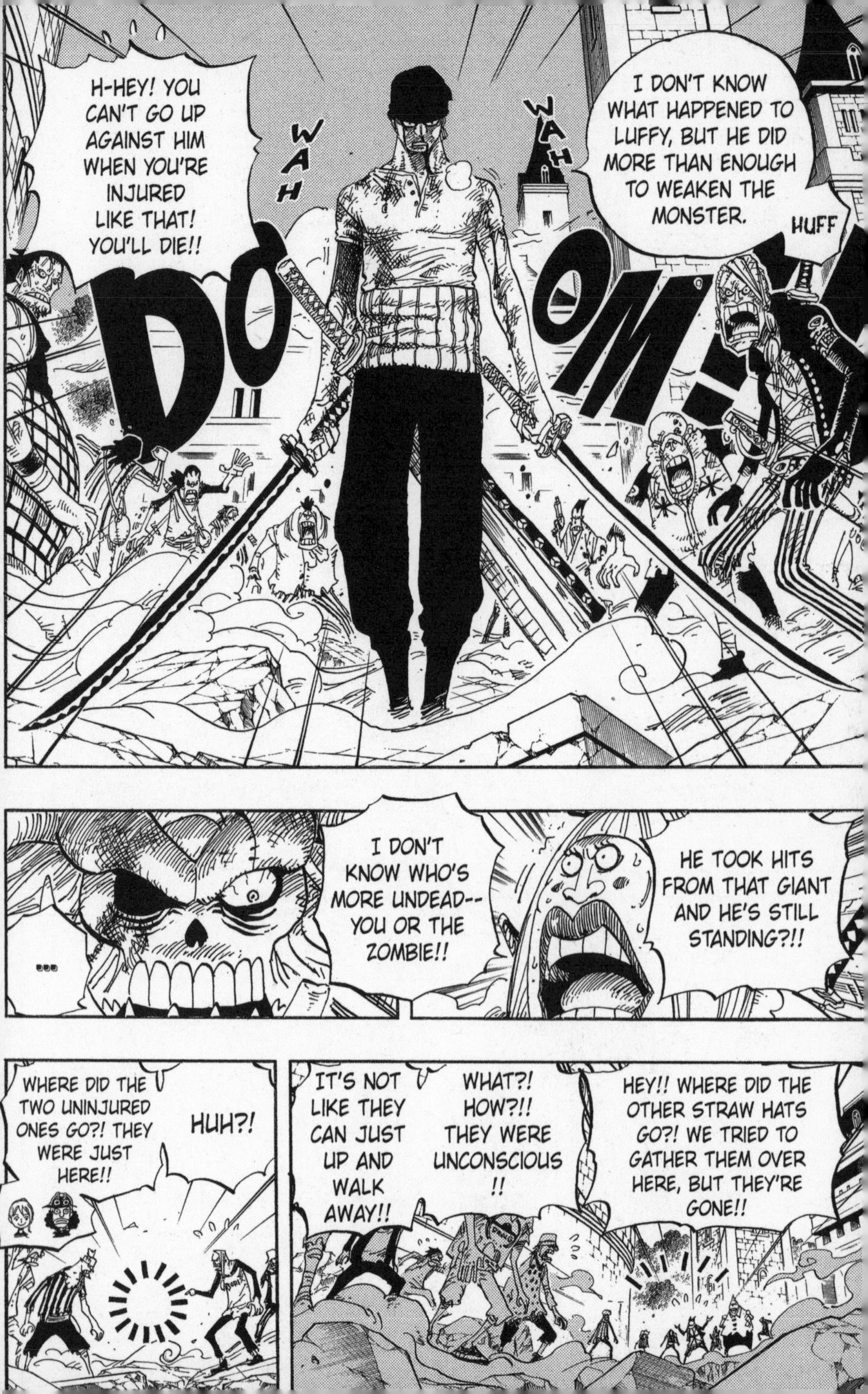
I DON'T KNOW WHAT HAPPENED TO LUFFY, BUT HE DID MORE THAN ENOUGH TO WEAKEN THE MONSTER.
HUFF
WAH
WAH
H-HEY! YOU CAN'T GO UP AGAINST HIM WHEN YOU'RE INJURED LIKE THAT! YOU'LL DIE!!
DO
OM
HE TOOK HITS FROM THAT GIANT AND HE'S STILL STANDING?!!
I DON'T KNOW WHO'S MORE UNDEAD-- YOU OR THE ZOMBIE!!
...
HEY!! WHERE DID THE OTHER STRAW HATS GO?! WE TRIED TO GATHER THEM OVER HERE, BUT THEY'RE GONE!!
WHAT?! HOW?!! THEY WERE UNCONSCIOUS!!
IT'S NOT LIKE THEY CAN JUST UP AND WALK AWAY!!
WHERE DID THE TWO UNINJURED ONES GO?! THEY WERE JUST HERE!!
HUH?!

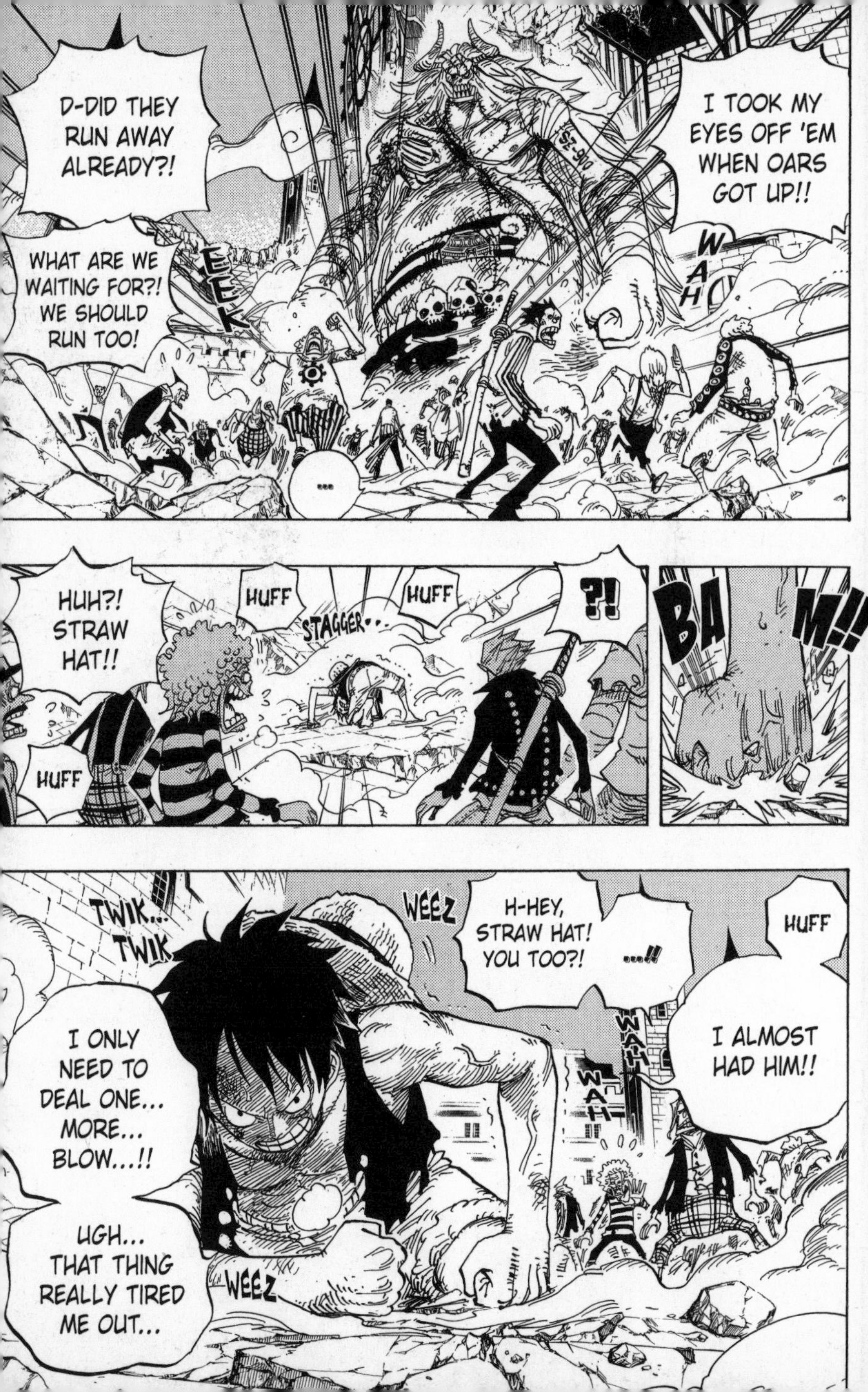
I TOOK MY EYES OFF 'EM WHEN OARS GOT UP!!
WAH
D-DID THEY RUN AWAY ALREADY?!
EEEK
WHAT ARE WE WAITING FOR?! WE SHOULD RUN TOO!
...
BAM!!
?!
HUFF
STAGGER...
HUFF
HUH?! STRAW HAT!!
HUFF
HUFF
...!!
H-HEY, STRAW HAT! YOU TOO?!
WEEZ
TWIK... TWIK
I ALMOST HAD HIM!!
WAH
WAH
I ONLY NEED TO DEAL ONE... MORE... BLOW...!!
UGH... THAT THING REALLY TIRED ME OUT...
WEEZ

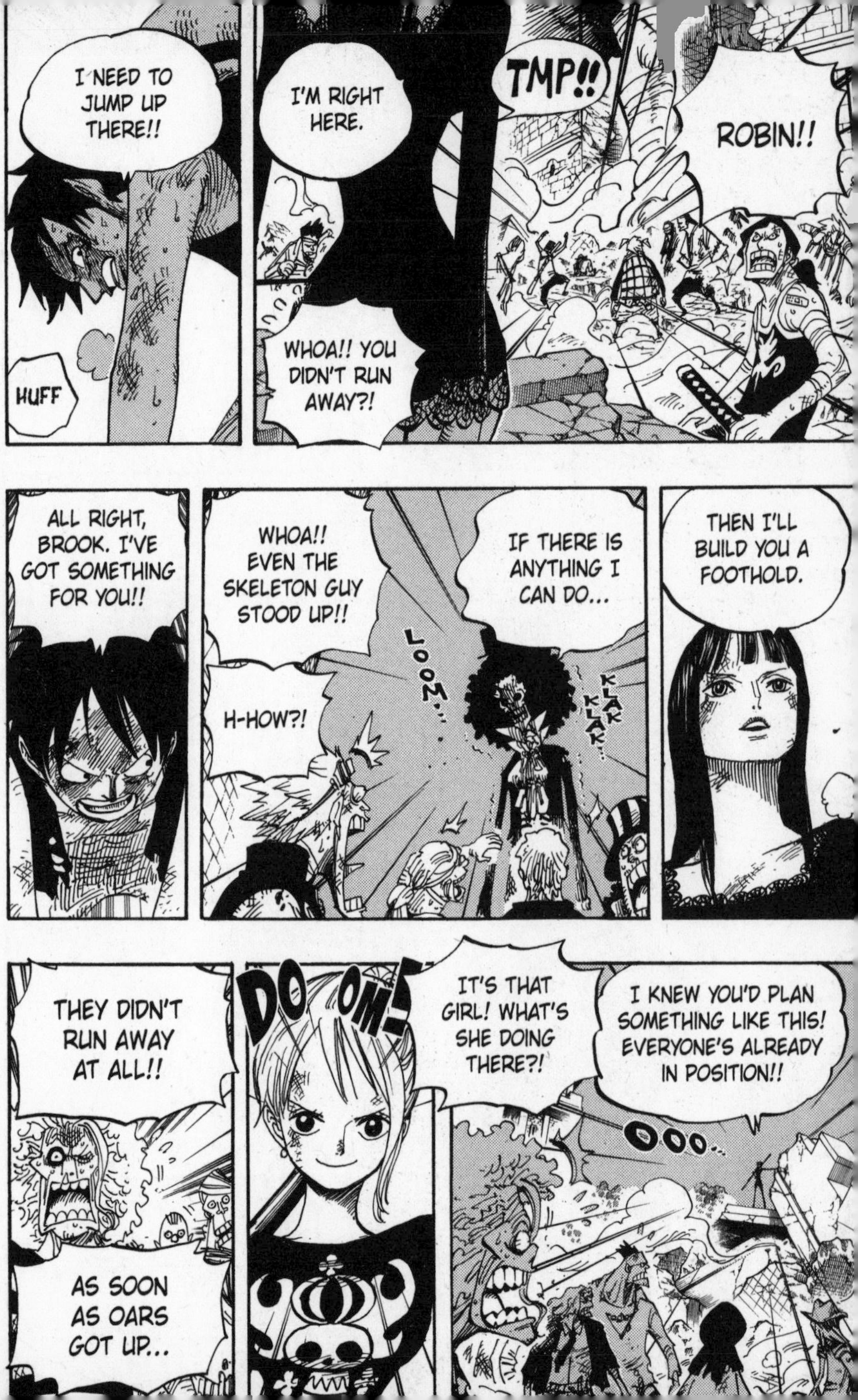
ROBIN!!
TMP!!
I'M RIGHT HERE.
WHOA!! YOU DIDN'T RUN AWAY?!
I NEED TO JUMP UP THERE!!
HUFF
THEN I'LL BUILD YOU A FOOTHOLD.
IF THERE IS ANYTHING I CAN DO...
KLAK KLAK...
LOOM...
WHOA!! EVEN THE SKELETON GUY STOOD UP!!
H-HOW?!
ALL RIGHT, BROOK. I'VE GOT SOMETHING FOR YOU!!
I KNEW YOU'D PLAN SOMETHING LIKE THIS! EVERYONE'S ALREADY IN POSITION!!
IT'S THAT GIRL! WHAT'S SHE DOING THERE?!
OOO...
DOOM!
THEY DIDN'T RUN AWAY AT ALL!!
AS SOON AS OARS GOT UP...

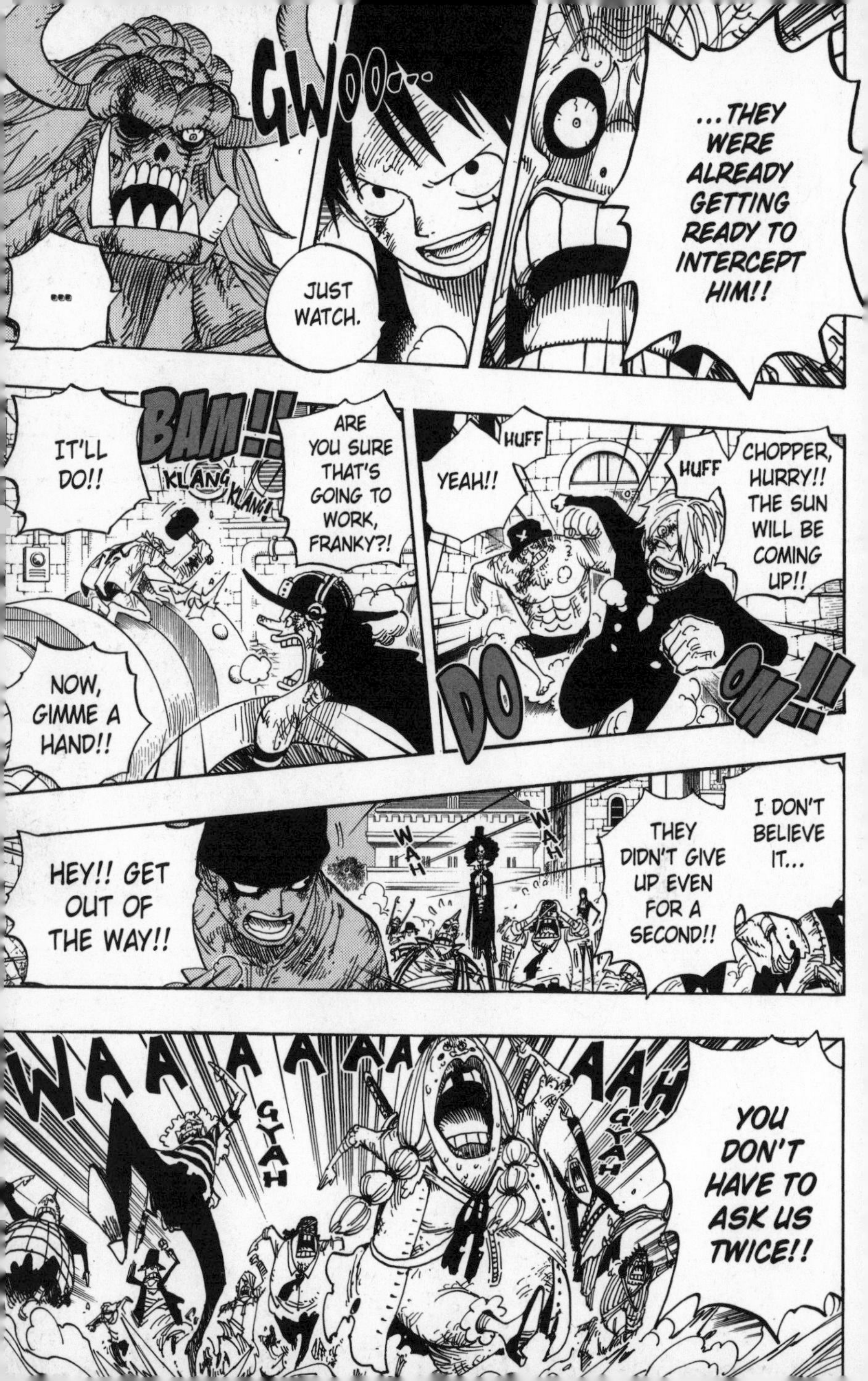
...THEY WERE ALREADY GETTING READY TO INTERCEPT HIM!!
GWOO...
JUST WATCH.
...
CHOPPER, HURRY!! THE SUN WILL BE COMING UP!!
HUFF
HUFF
YEAH!!
DOOM!!
ARE YOU SURE THAT'S GOING TO WORK, FRANKY?!
BAM!!
KLANG
KLANG!
IT'LL DO!!
NOW, GIMME A HAND!!
I DON'T BELIEVE IT...
THEY DIDN'T GIVE UP EVEN FOR A SECOND!!
WAH
WAH
HEY!! GET OUT OF THE WAY!!
YOU DON'T HAVE TO ASK US TWICE!!
GYAH
GYAH
WAAAAAAAAH

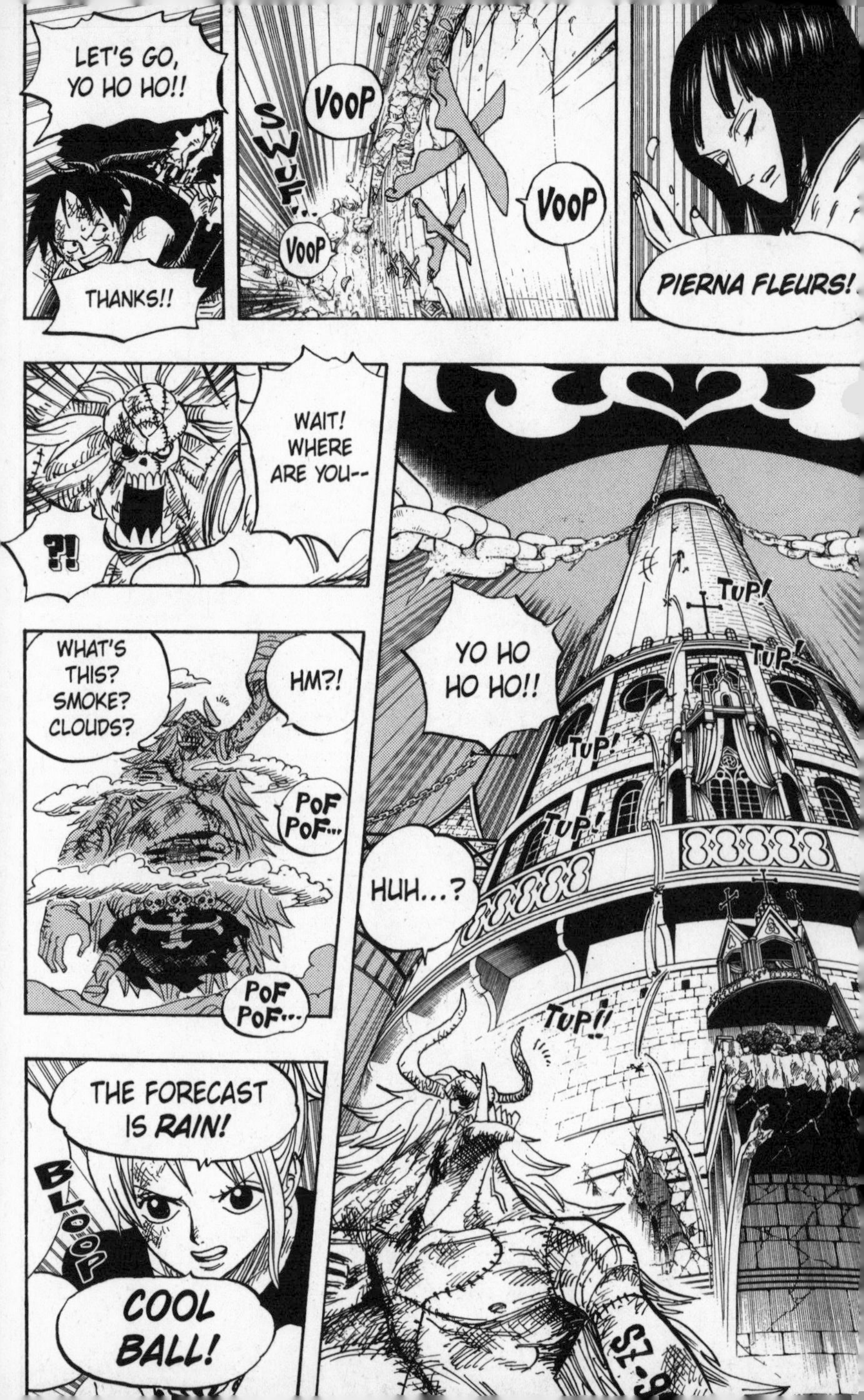
PIERNA FLEURS!
VOOP
SWUF...
VOOP
VOOP
LET'S GO, YO HO HO!!
THANKS!!
YO HO HO HO!!
TUP!
TUP!
TUP!
TUP!
HUH...?
TUP!!
WAIT! WHERE ARE YOU--
?!
HM?!
WHAT'S THIS? SMOKE? CLOUDS?
POF POF...
POF POF...
THE FORECAST IS RAIN!
BLOOP
COOL BALL!

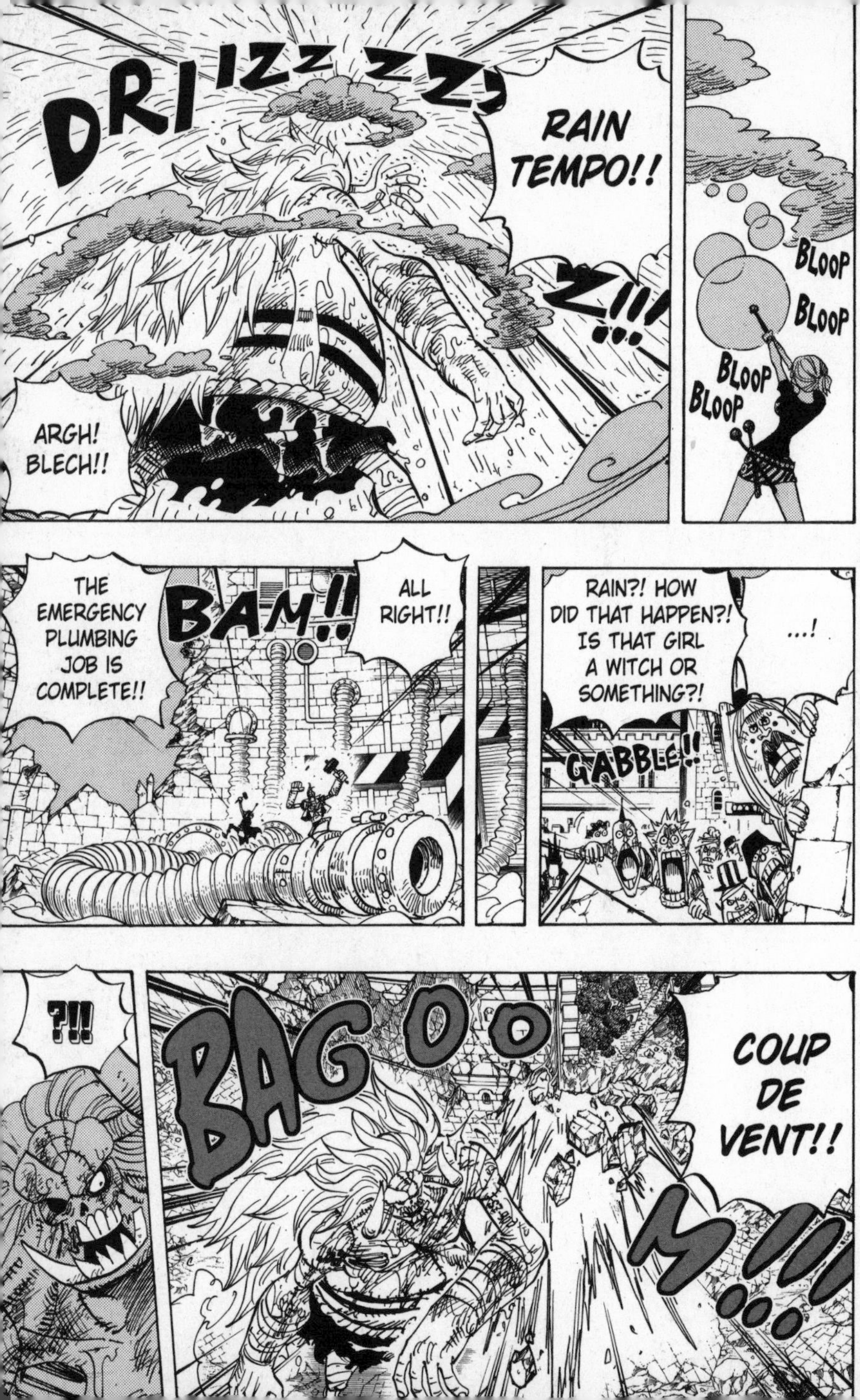
BLOOP
BLOOP
BLOOP
BLOOP
RAIN TEMPO!!
DRIZZZZZ
Z!!!
ARGH! BLECH!!
...!
RAIN?! HOW DID THAT HAPPEN?! IS THAT GIRL A WITCH OR SOMETHING?!
GABBLE!!
ALL RIGHT!!
BAM!!
THE EMERGENCY PLUMBING JOB IS COMPLETE!!
COUP DE VENT!!
BAGOOOM!!!
?!!

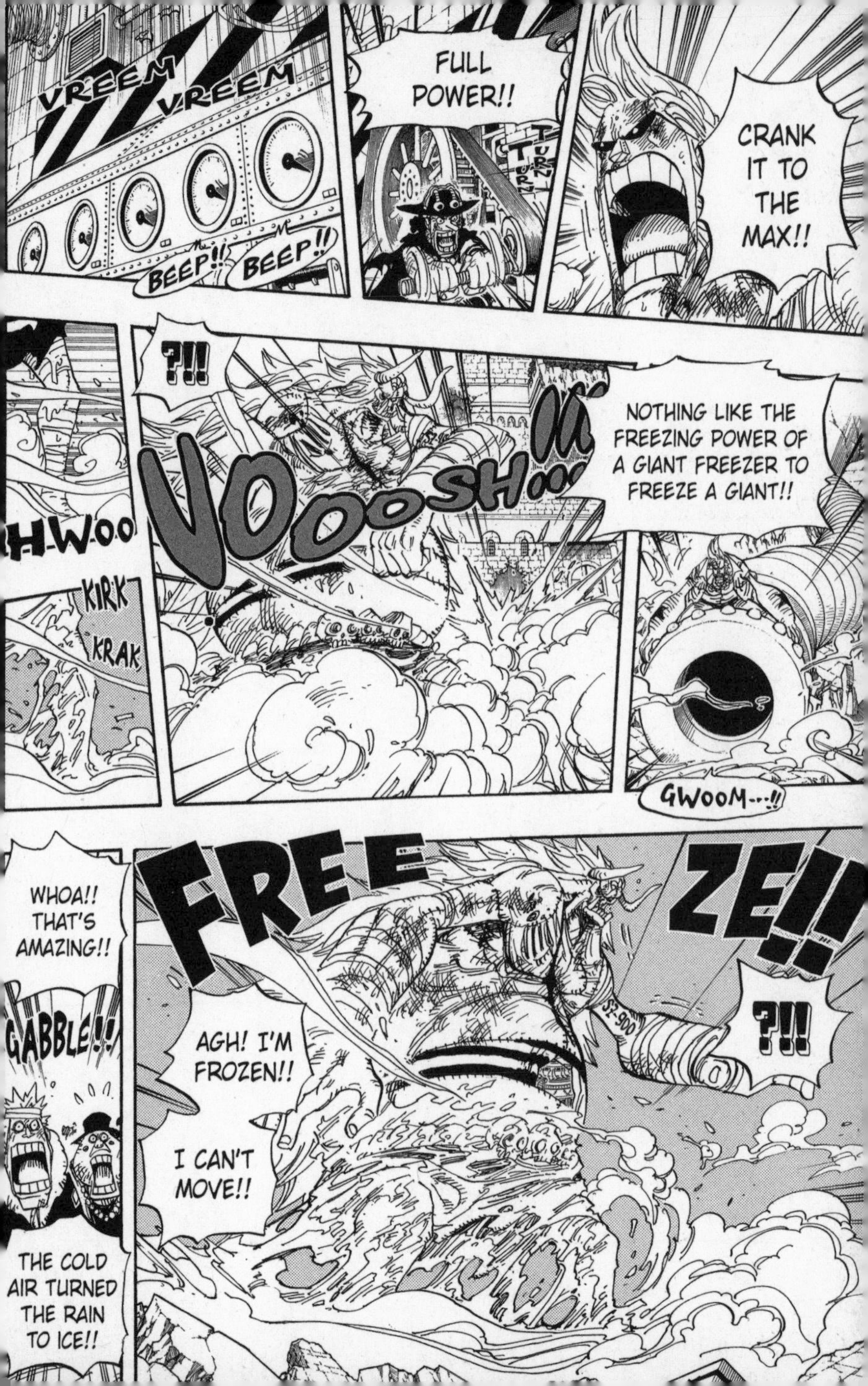
CRANK IT TO THE MAX!!
FULL POWER!!
TURN TURN
VREEM VREEM
BEEP!! BEEP!!
NOTHING LIKE THE FREEZING POWER OF A GIANT FREEZER TO FREEZE A GIANT!!
GWOOM...!!
?!!
VOOOSH...!!
H-W-O-O
KIRK KRAK
FREE ZE!!
?!!
AGH! I'M FROZEN!!
I CAN'T MOVE!!
WHOA!! THAT'S AMAZING!!
GABBLE!!
THE COLD AIR TURNED THE RAIN TO ICE!!

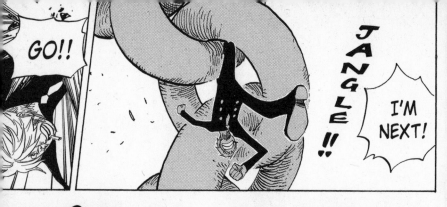

GO!!

JANGLE!!

I'M NEXT!

GASHANK!!!

ARGH! A CHAIN!!

?!!

KLANK!!

THROW ME!!

GREAT JOB, SANJI!

KLAKA!

WAAGH!

HE DID IT!!

THANKS!

TMP!

IT'S THE CHAIN THAT CONTROLS THE RUDDER!!

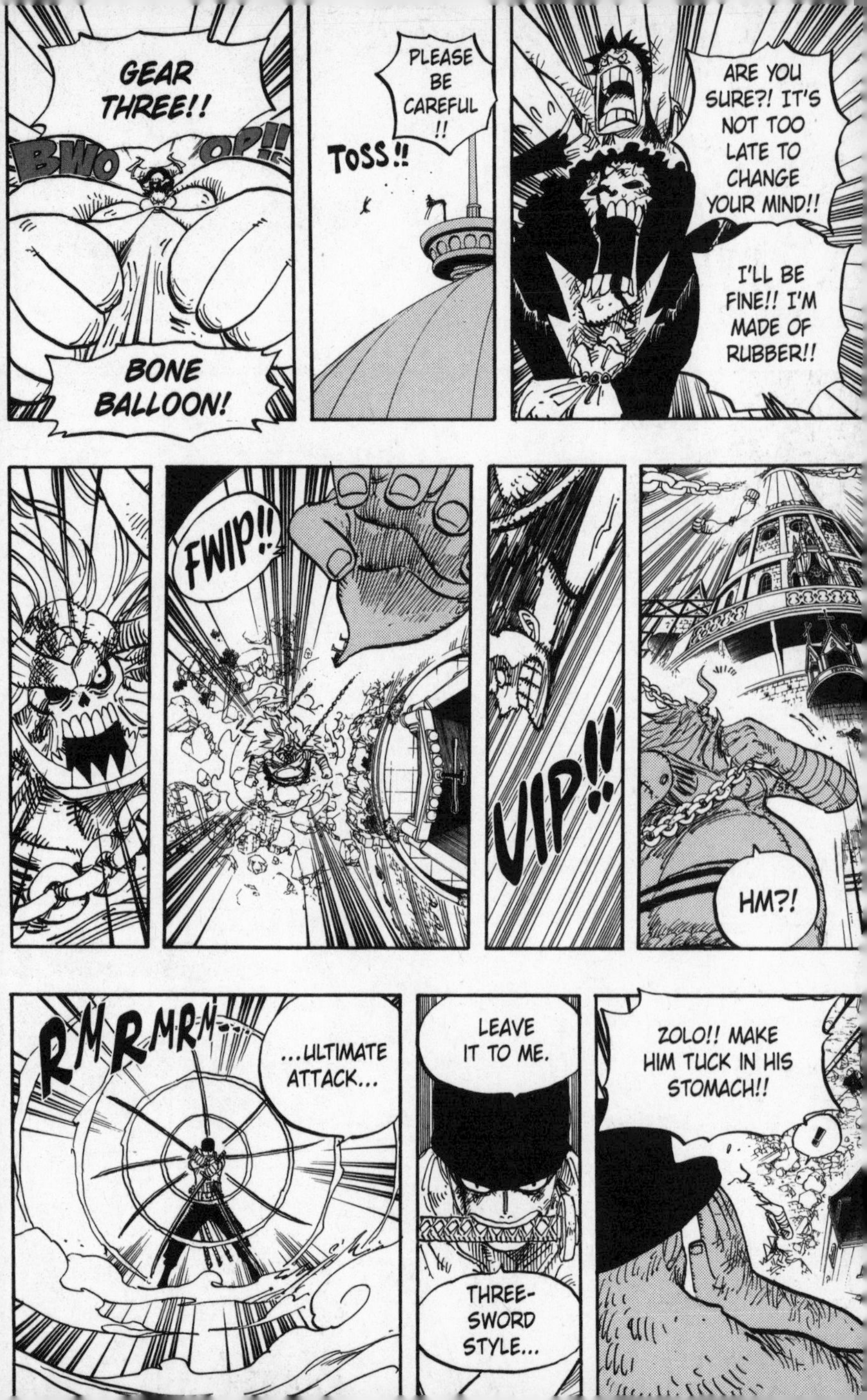
ARE YOU SURE?! IT'S NOT TOO LATE TO CHANGE YOUR MIND!!
I'LL BE FINE!! I'M MADE OF RUBBER!!
PLEASE BE CAREFUL!!
TOSS!!
GEAR THREE!!
BWOOP!!
BONE BALLOON!
HM?!
VIP!!
FWIP!!
ZOLO!! MAKE HIM TUCK IN HIS STOMACH!!
!
LEAVE IT TO ME.
THREE-SWORD STYLE...
...ULTIMATE ATTACK...
RMRMRM...

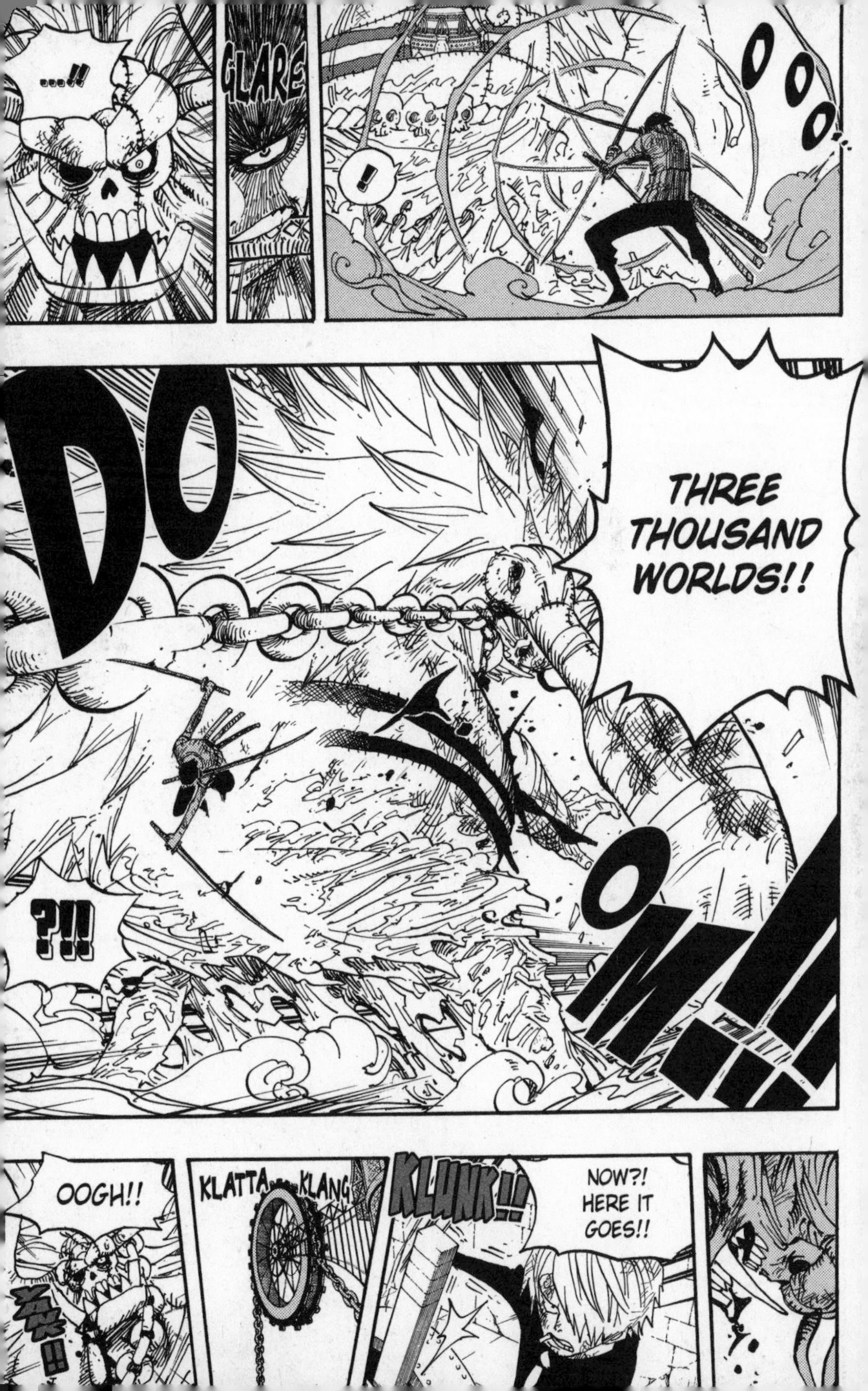
OOO...
!
GLARE
...!!
THREE THOUSAND WORLDS!!
DO
OM!!
?!!
KLUNK!!
NOW?! HERE IT GOES!!
KLATTA... KLANG
OOGH!!
YANK!!

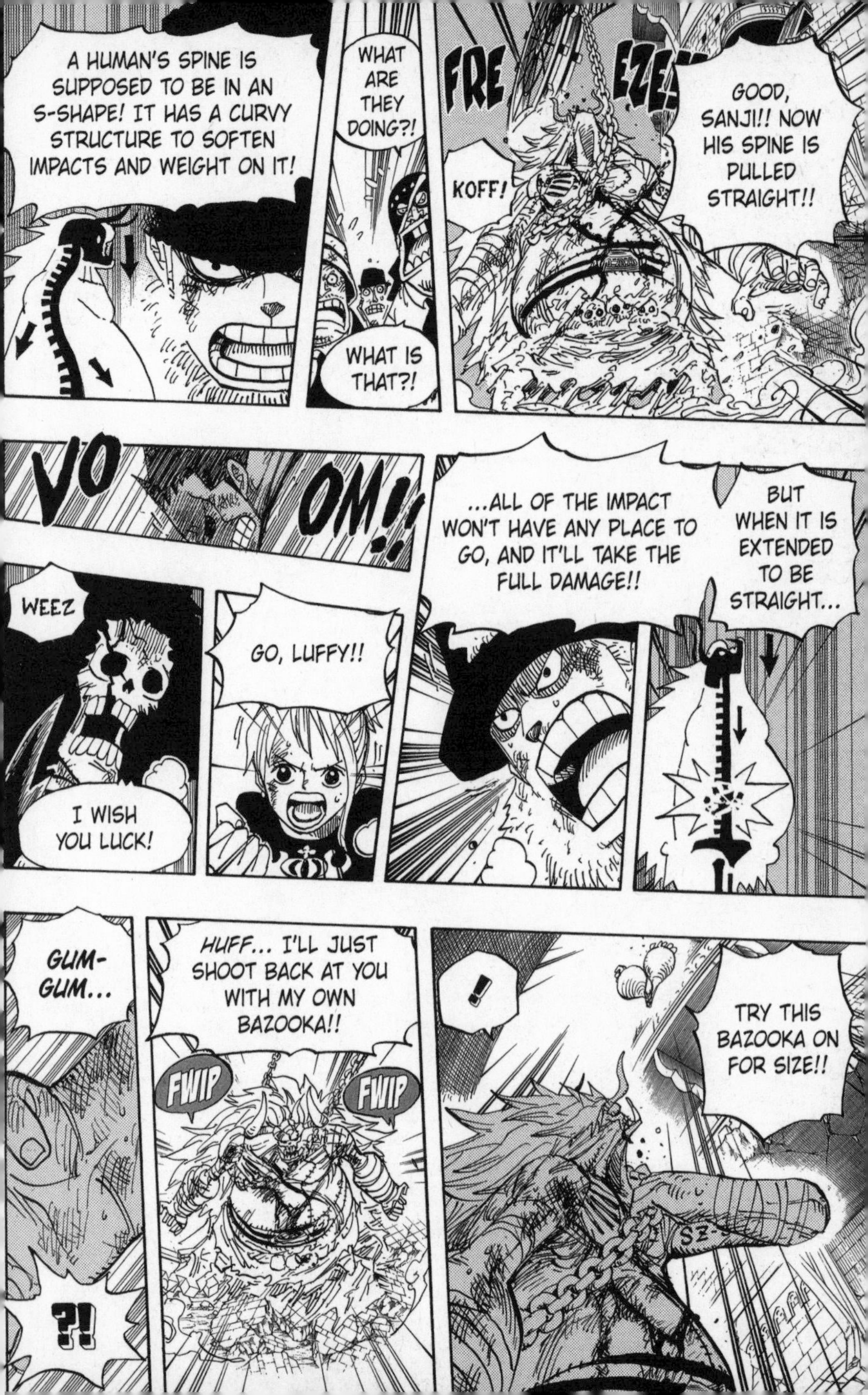
FREEZE!!
GOOD, SANJI!! NOW HIS SPINE IS PULLED STRAIGHT!!
KOFF!
WHAT ARE THEY DOING?!
WHAT IS THAT?!
A HUMAN'S SPINE IS SUPPOSED TO BE IN AN S-SHAPE! IT HAS A CURVY STRUCTURE TO SOFTEN IMPACTS AND WEIGHT ON IT!
BUT WHEN IT IS EXTENDED TO BE STRAIGHT...
...ALL OF THE IMPACT WON'T HAVE ANY PLACE TO GO, AND IT'LL TAKE THE FULL DAMAGE!!
VOOM!!
GO, LUFFY!!
WEEZ
I WISH YOU LUCK!
!
TRY THIS BAZOOKA ON FOR SIZE!!
SZ-
HUFF... I'LL JUST SHOOT BACK AT YOU WITH MY OWN BAZOOKA!!
FWIP
FWIP
GUM-GUM...
?!

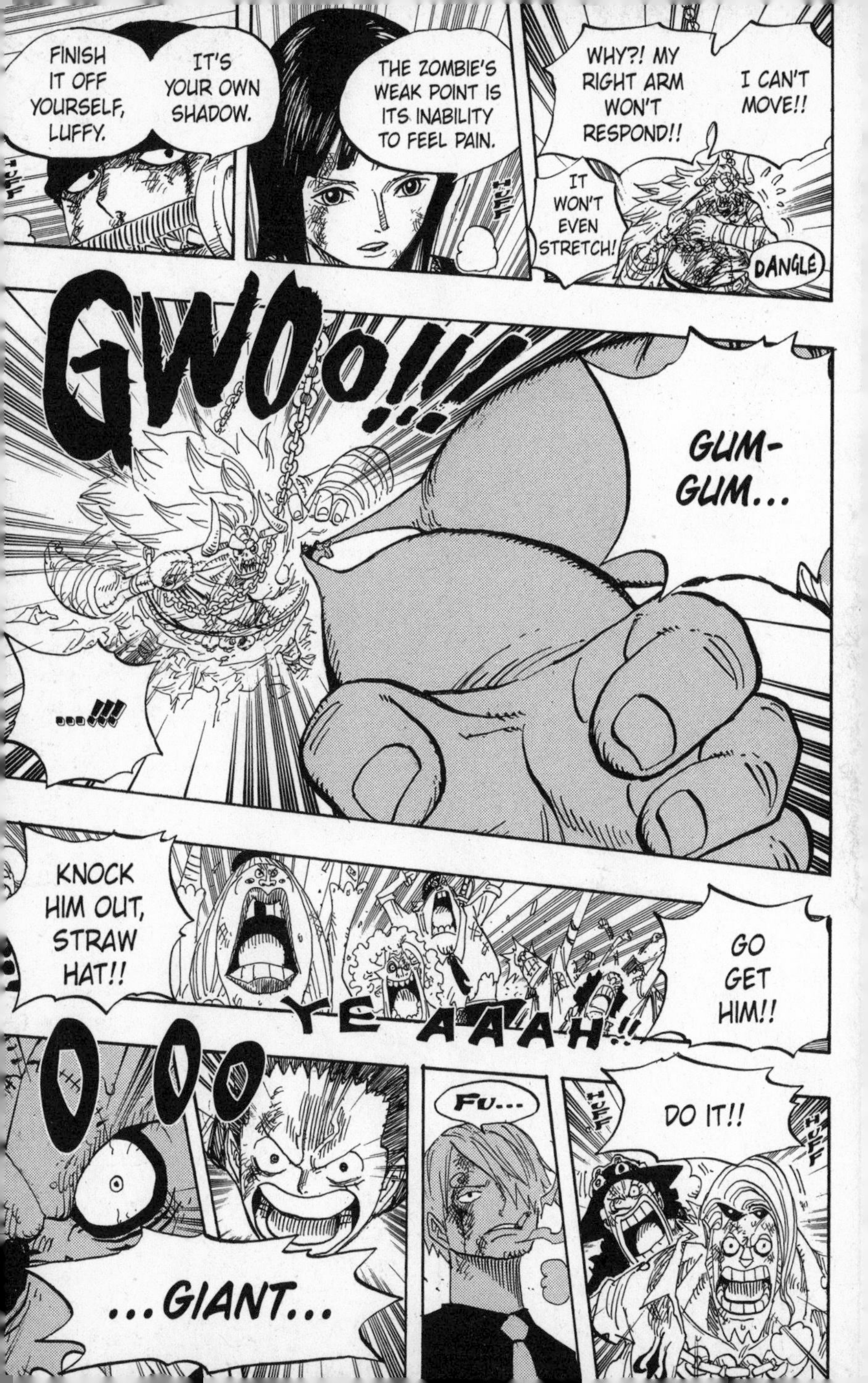
I CAN'T MOVE!!
WHY?! MY RIGHT ARM WON'T RESPOND!!
IT WON'T EVEN STRETCH!
DANGLE
THE ZOMBIE'S WEAK POINT IS ITS INABILITY TO FEEL PAIN.
HUFF
IT'S YOUR OWN SHADOW.
FINISH IT OFF YOURSELF, LUFFY.
HUFF
GUM-GUM...
GWOO!!!
...!!!
GO GET HIM!!
YEAAAH!!
KNOCK HIM OUT, STRAW HAT!!
HUFF
DO IT!!
HUFF
FU...
OOO
...GIANT...

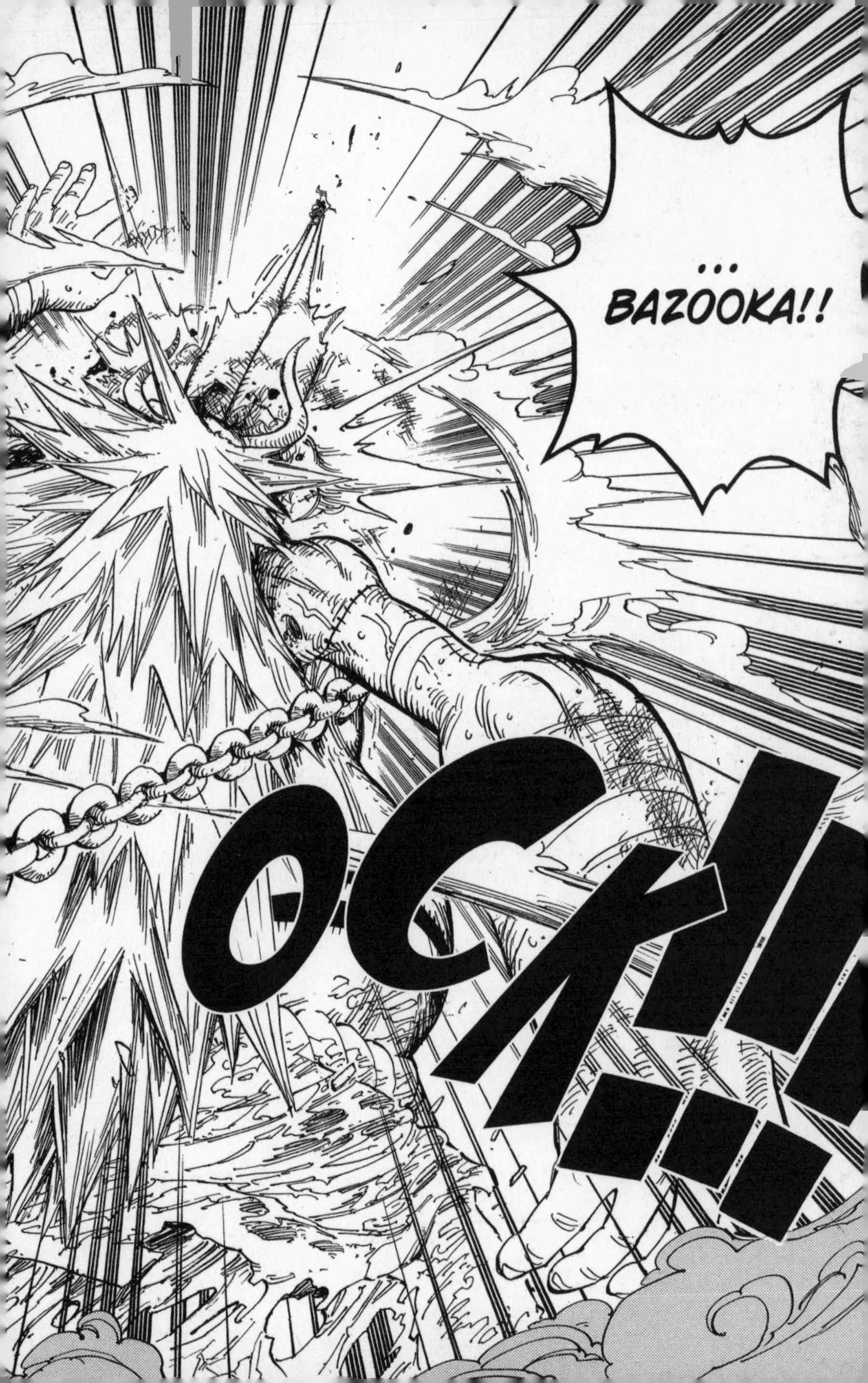
...
BAZOOKA!!

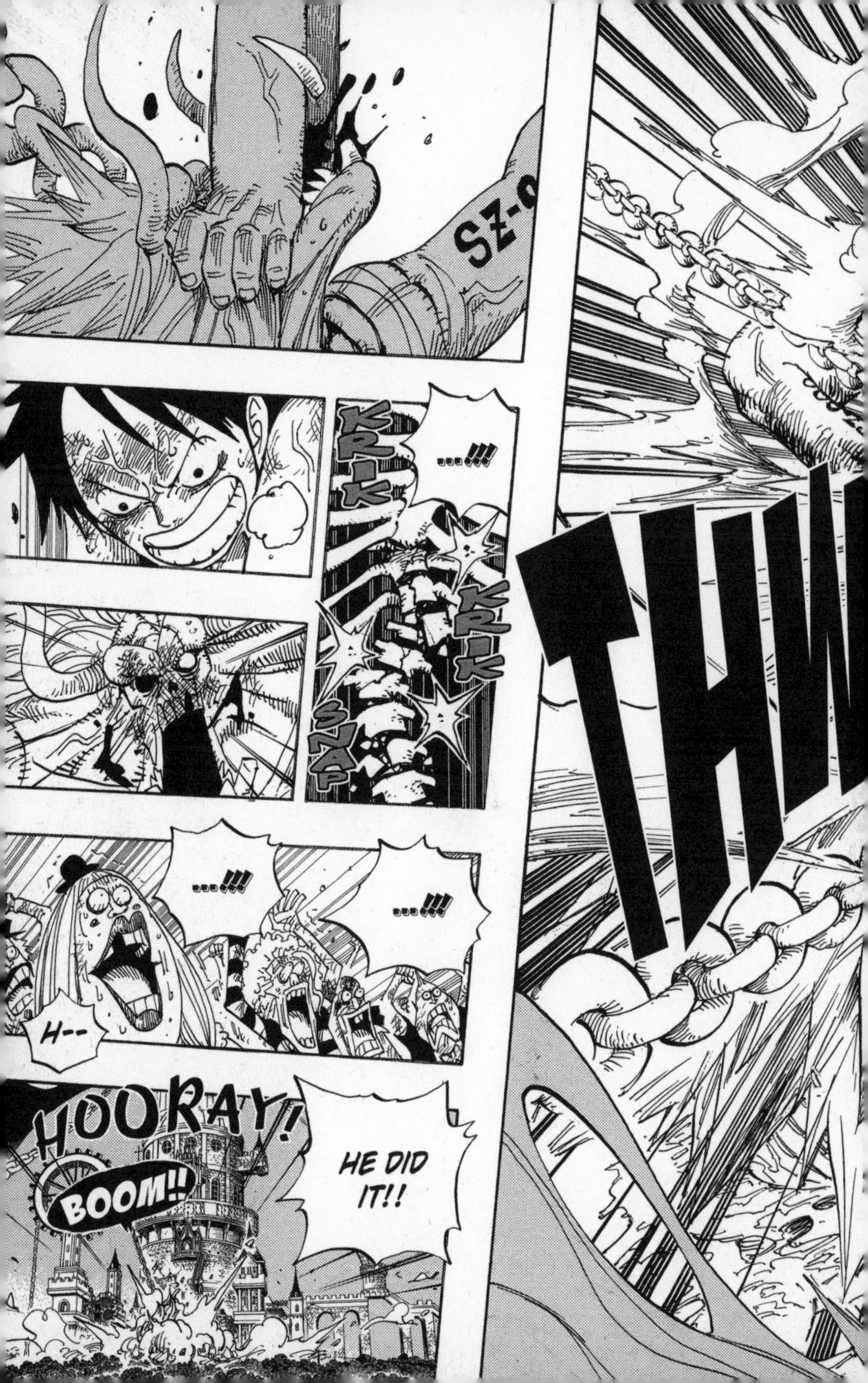
THW
SZ-0
KRIK
...!!!
KRIK
SNAP
...!!!
...!!!
H--
HE DID IT!!
HOORAY!
BOOM!!

Chapter 481:
SHADOWS ASGARD

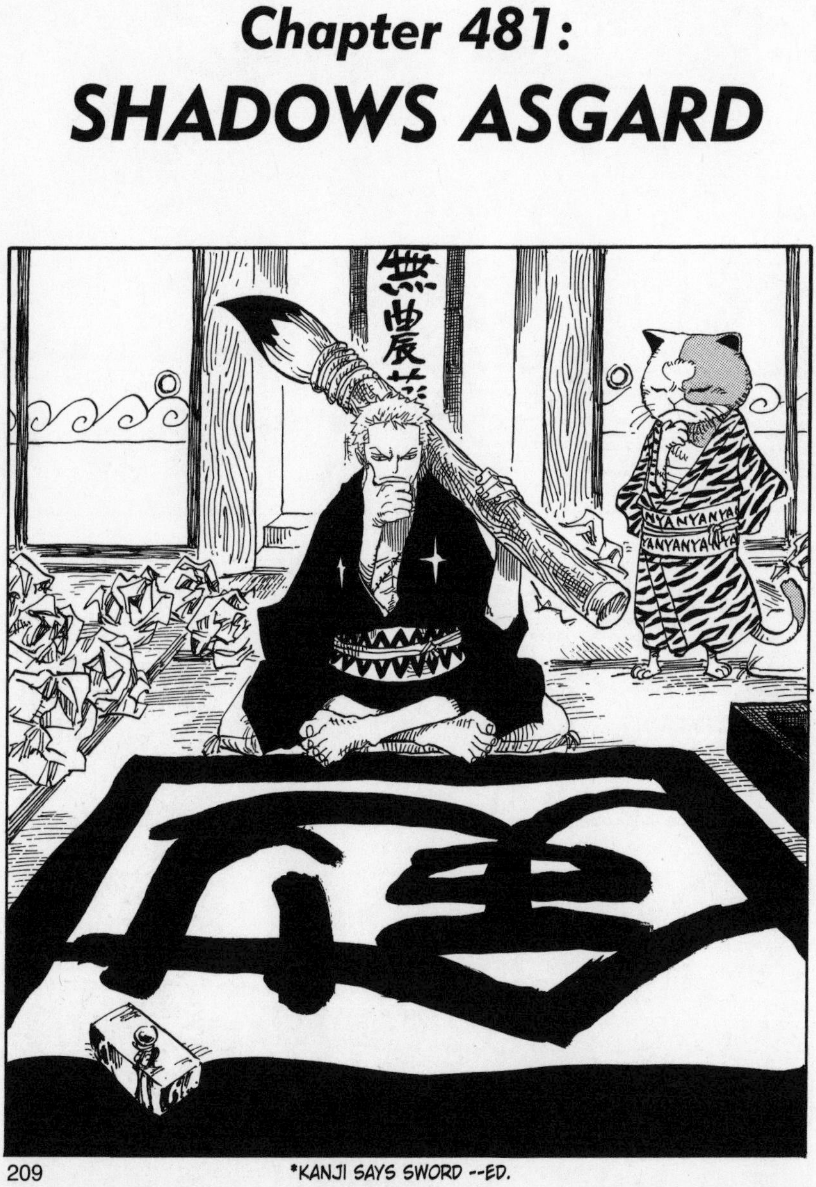
NYANYANYA
YANYANYANYA

*KANJI SAYS SWORD --ED.

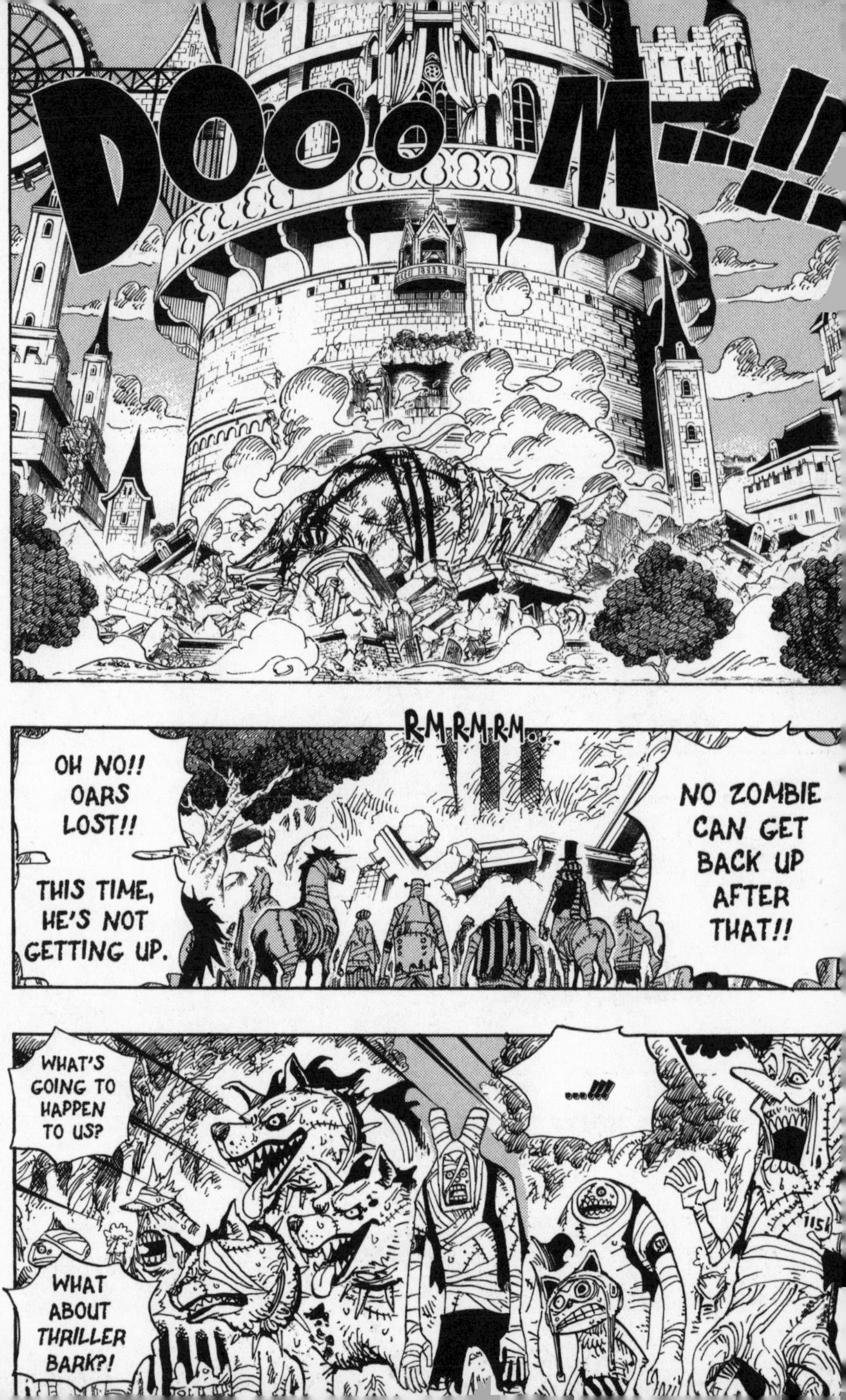
DOOOM...!!
R-M-R-M-R-M...
NO ZOMBIE CAN GET BACK UP AFTER THAT!!
OH NO!! OARS LOST!!
THIS TIME, HE'S NOT GETTING UP.
...!!!
WHAT'S GOING TO HAPPEN TO US?
WHAT ABOUT THRILLER BARK?!

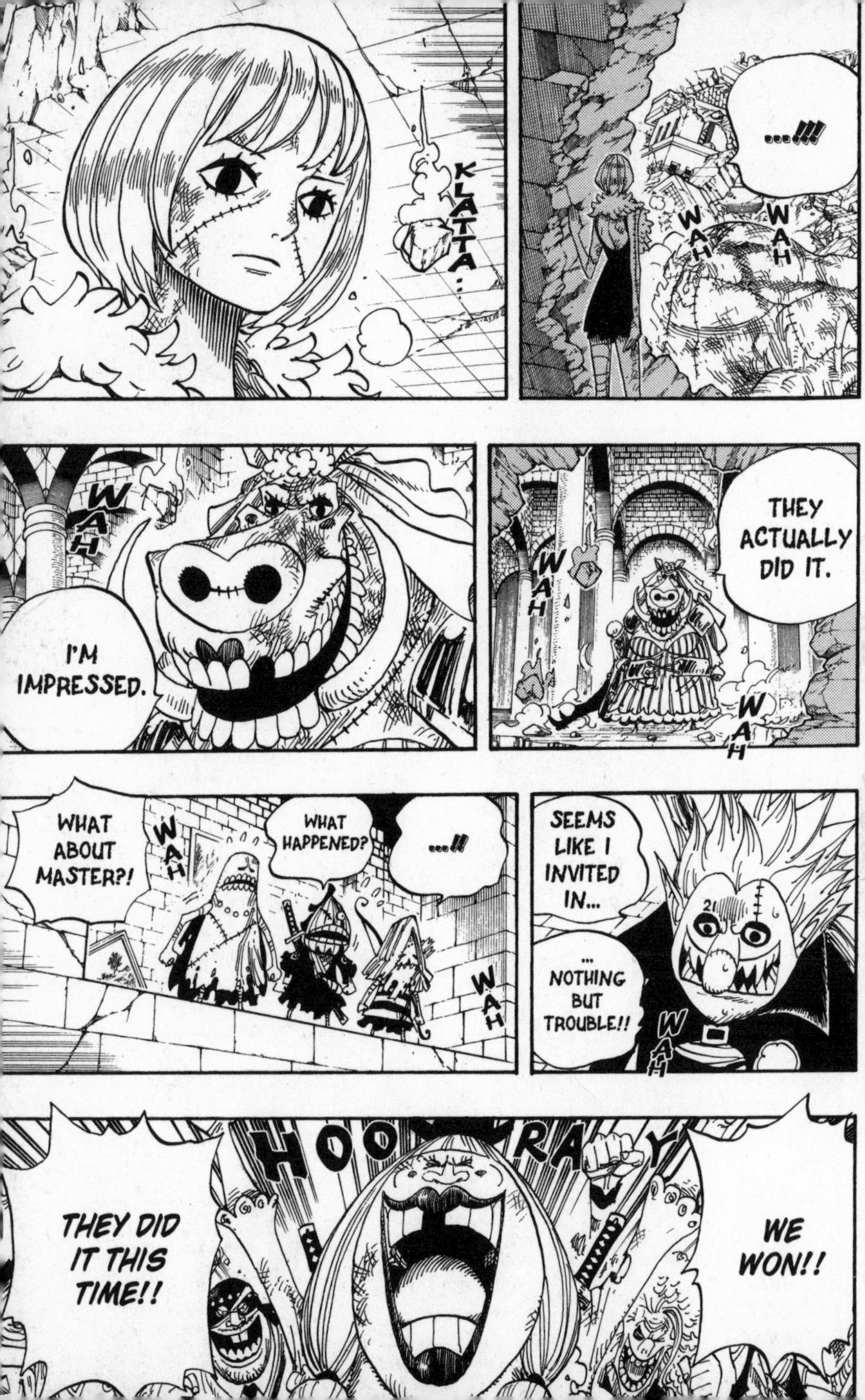
...!!!
WAH
WAH
KLATTA...
THEY ACTUALLY DID IT.
WAH
WAH
WAH
I'M IMPRESSED.
SEEMS LIKE I INVITED IN...
... NOTHING BUT TROUBLE!!
WAH
...!!
WHAT HAPPENED?
WHAT ABOUT MASTER?!
WAH
WAH
WE WON!!
THEY DID IT THIS TIME!!

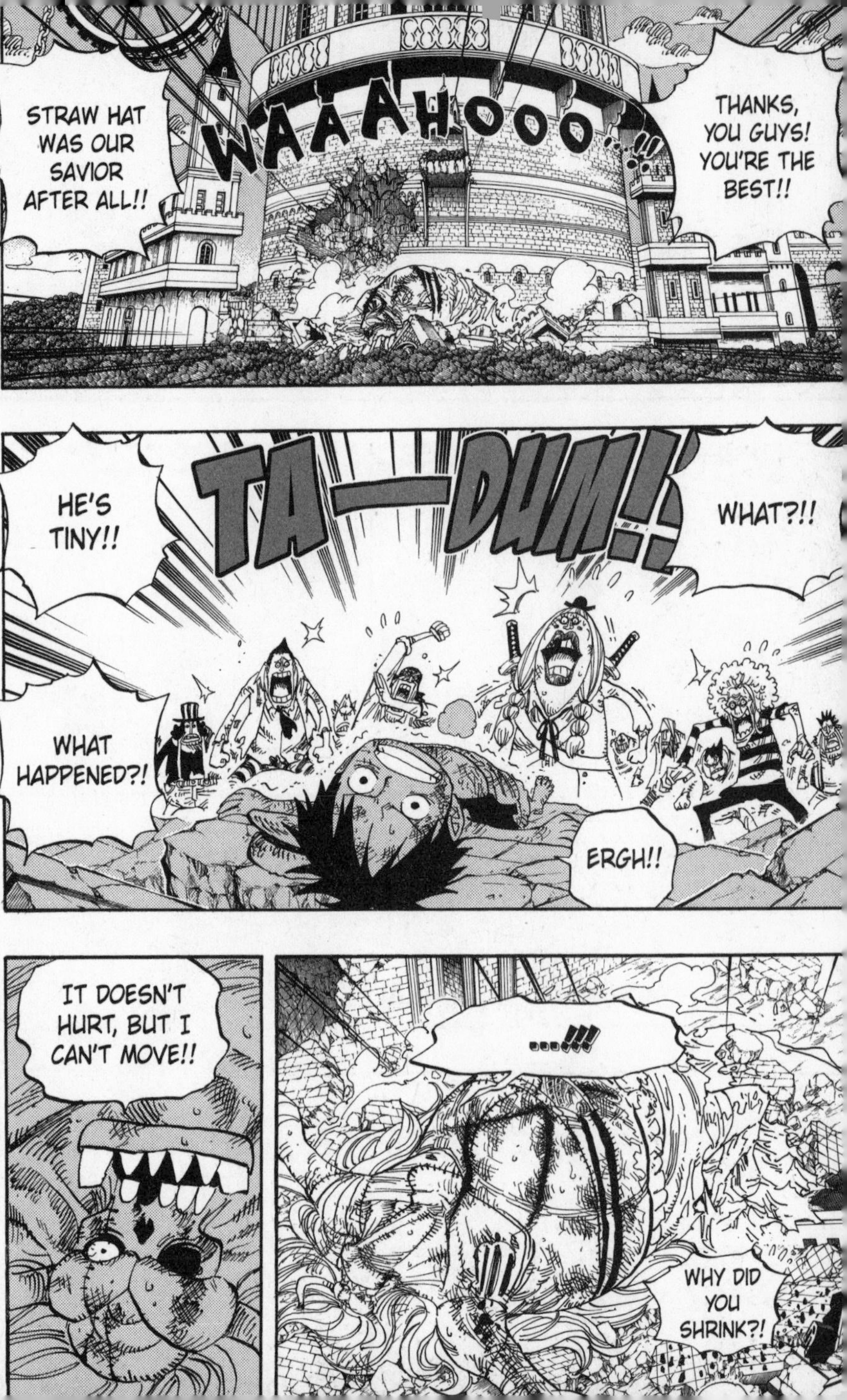
THANKS, YOU GUYS! YOU'RE THE BEST!!
WAAAHOOO...!!
STRAW HAT WAS OUR SAVIOR AFTER ALL!!
WHAT?!!
TA—DUM!!
HE'S TINY!!
ERGH!!
WHAT HAPPENED?!
...!!!
WHY DID YOU SHRINK?!
IT DOESN'T HURT, BUT I CAN'T MOVE!!

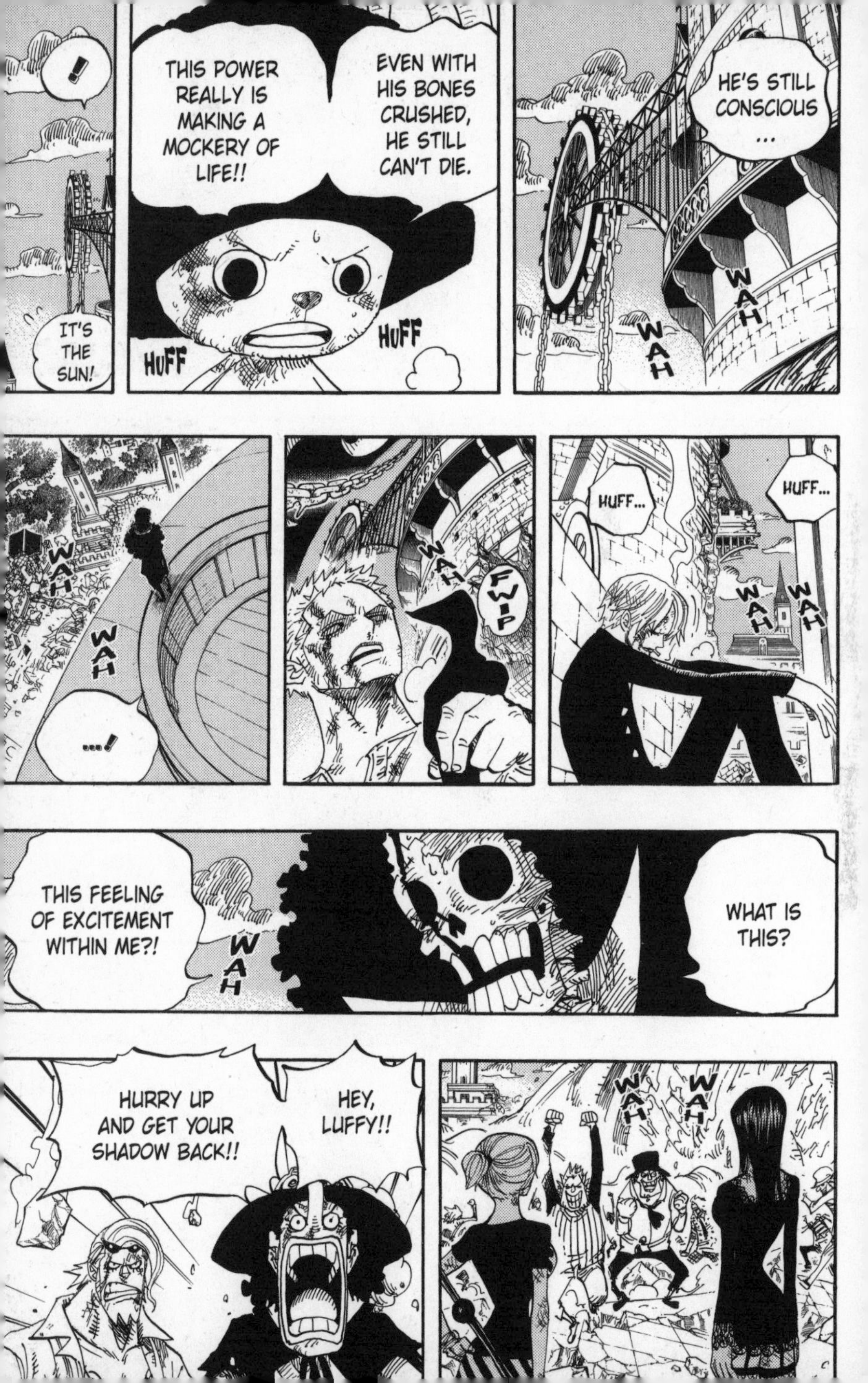
HE'S STILL CONSCIOUS ...
WAH
WAH
EVEN WITH HIS BONES CRUSHED, HE STILL CAN'T DIE.
THIS POWER REALLY IS MAKING A MOCKERY OF LIFE!!
HUFF
HUFF
!
IT'S THE SUN!
HUFF...
HUFF...
WAH
WAH
WAH
FWIP
WAH
WAH
...!
WHAT IS THIS?
WAH
THIS FEELING OF EXCITEMENT WITHIN ME?!
WAH
WAH
HEY, LUFFY!!
HURRY UP AND GET YOUR SHADOW BACK!!

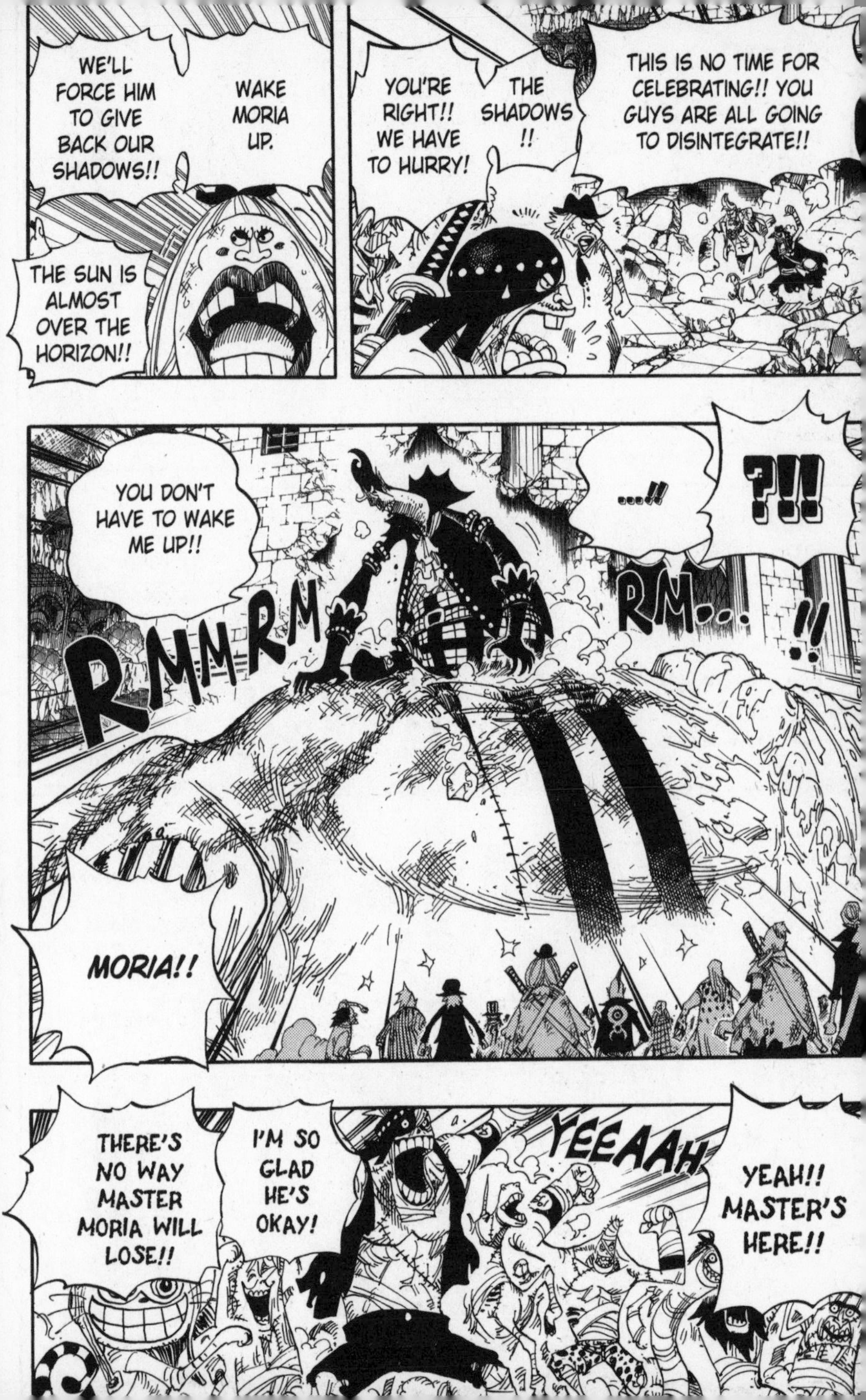
THIS IS NO TIME FOR CELEBRATING!! YOU GUYS ARE ALL GOING TO DISINTEGRATE!!
THE SHADOWS !!
YOU'RE RIGHT!! WE HAVE TO HURRY!
WAKE MORIA UP.
WE'LL FORCE HIM TO GIVE BACK OUR SHADOWS!!
THE SUN IS ALMOST OVER THE HORIZON!!
?!!
...!!
RM...!!
YOU DON'T HAVE TO WAKE ME UP!!
RMMRM
MORIA!!
YEAH!! MASTER'S HERE!!
YEEAAH
I'M SO GLAD HE'S OKAY!
THERE'S NO WAY MASTER MORIA WILL LOSE!!

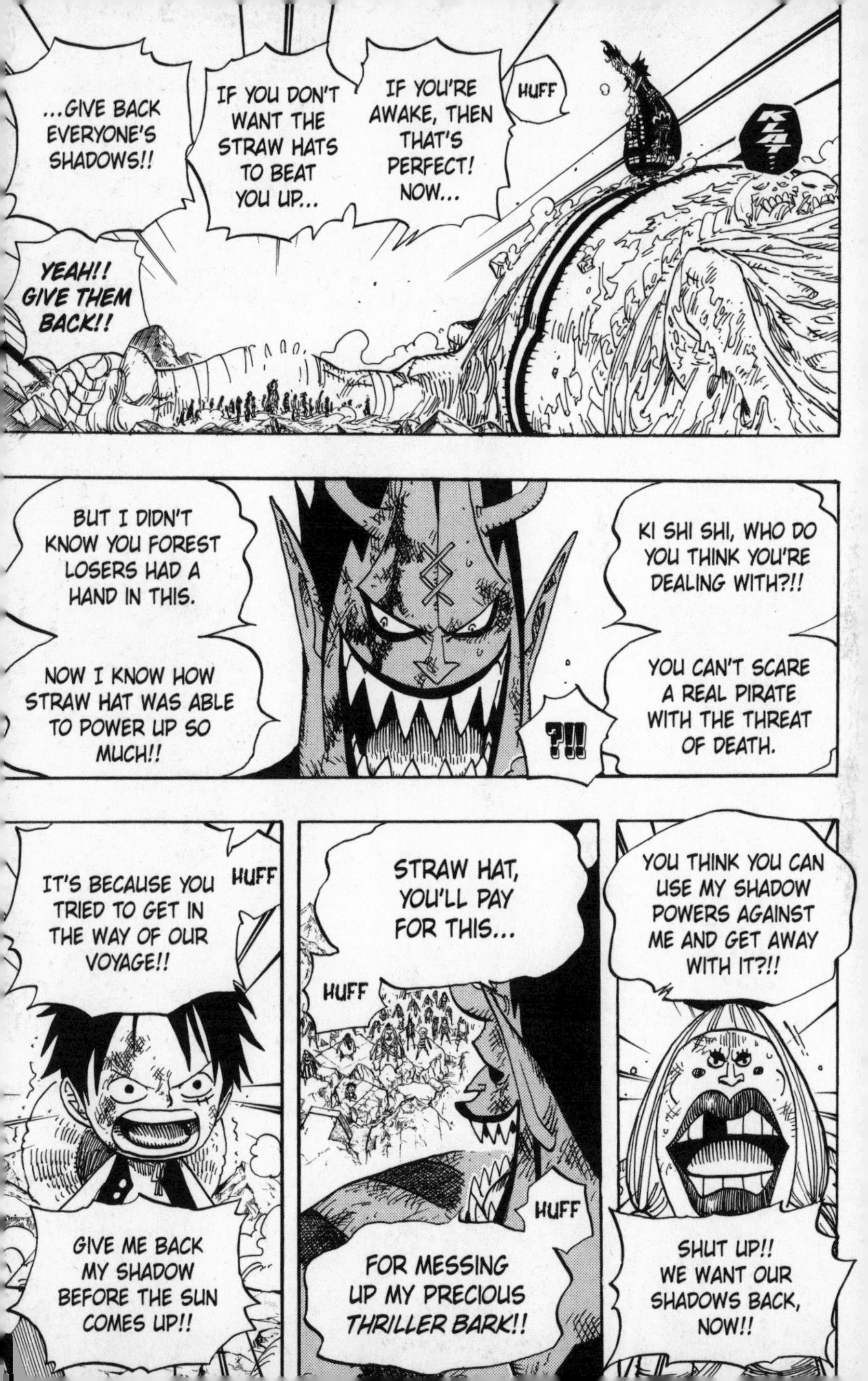
HUFF
KLAT
IF YOU'RE AWAKE, THEN THAT'S PERFECT! NOW...
IF YOU DON'T WANT THE STRAW HATS TO BEAT YOU UP...
...GIVE BACK EVERYONE'S SHADOWS!!
YEAH!! GIVE THEM BACK!!
KI SHI SHI, WHO DO YOU THINK YOU'RE DEALING WITH?!!
YOU CAN'T SCARE A REAL PIRATE WITH THE THREAT OF DEATH.
?!!
BUT I DIDN'T KNOW YOU FOREST LOSERS HAD A HAND IN THIS.
NOW I KNOW HOW STRAW HAT WAS ABLE TO POWER UP SO MUCH!!
YOU THINK YOU CAN USE MY SHADOW POWERS AGAINST ME AND GET AWAY WITH IT?!!
SHUT UP!! WE WANT OUR SHADOWS BACK, NOW!!
STRAW HAT, YOU'LL PAY FOR THIS...
HUFF
HUFF
FOR MESSING UP MY PRECIOUS THRILLER BARK!!
HUFF
IT'S BECAUSE YOU TRIED TO GET IN THE WAY OF OUR VOYAGE!!
GIVE ME BACK MY SHADOW BEFORE THE SUN COMES UP!!

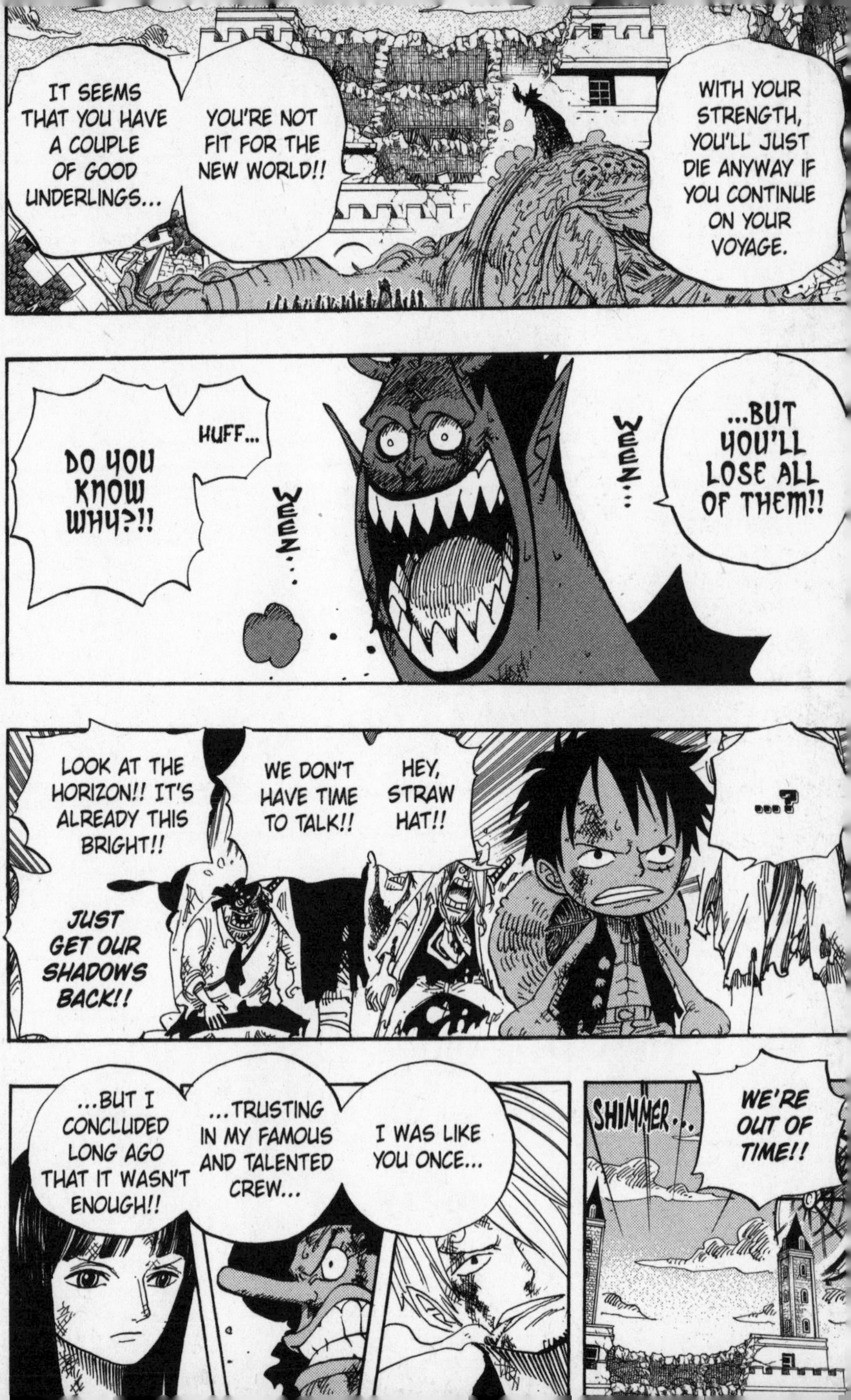
WITH YOUR STRENGTH, YOU'LL JUST DIE ANYWAY IF YOU CONTINUE ON YOUR VOYAGE.
YOU'RE NOT FIT FOR THE NEW WORLD!!
IT SEEMS THAT YOU HAVE A COUPLE OF GOOD UNDERLINGS...
...BUT YOU'LL LOSE ALL OF THEM!!
WEEZ...
WEEZ...
HUFF...
DO YOU KNOW WHY?!!
...?
HEY, STRAW HAT!!
WE DON'T HAVE TIME TO TALK!!
LOOK AT THE HORIZON!! IT'S ALREADY THIS BRIGHT!!
JUST GET OUR SHADOWS BACK!!
WE'RE OUT OF TIME!!
SHIMMER...
I WAS LIKE YOU ONCE...
...TRUSTING IN MY FAMOUS AND TALENTED CREW...
...BUT I CONCLUDED LONG AGO THAT IT WASN'T ENOUGH!!

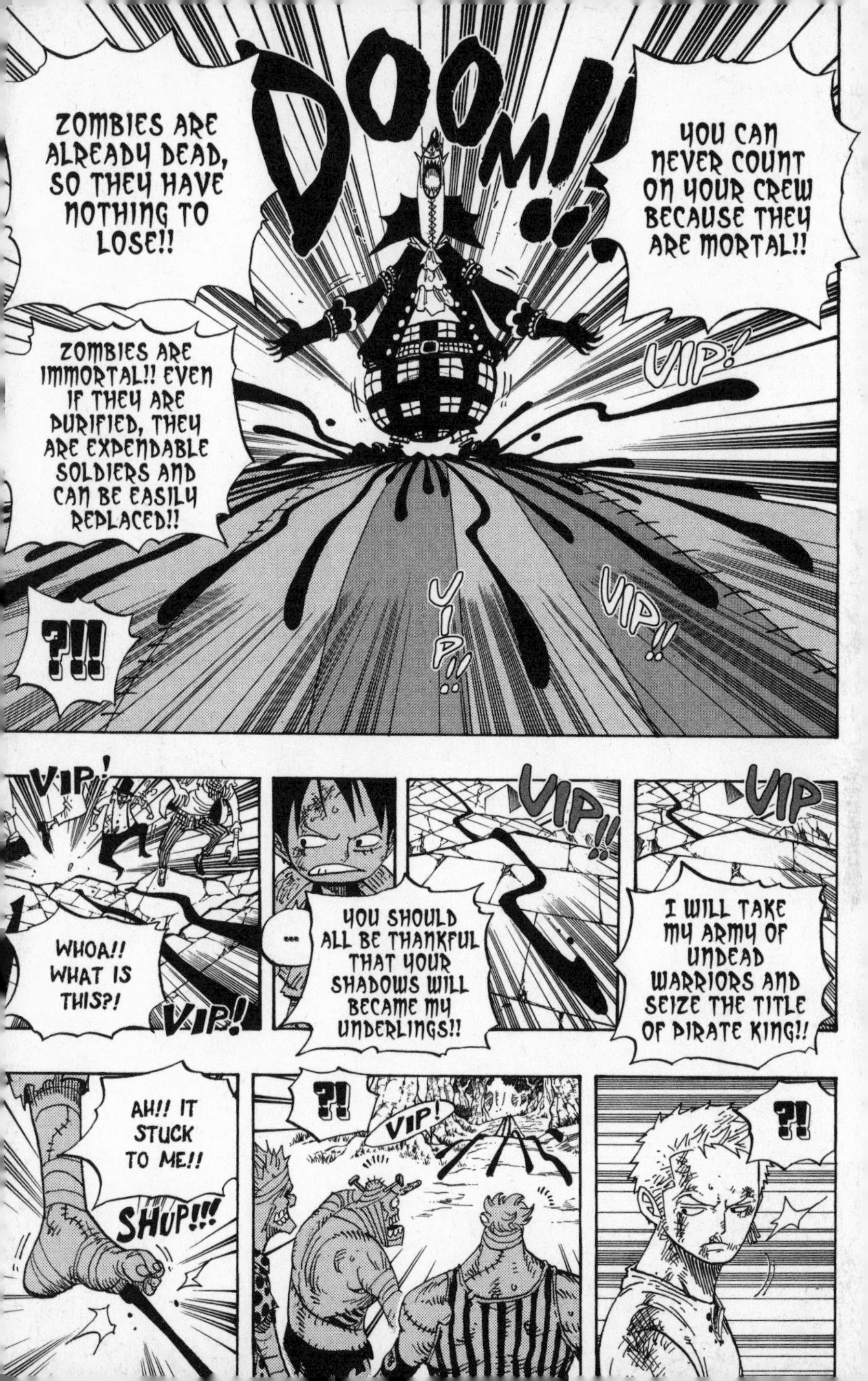
YOU CAN NEVER COUNT ON YOUR CREW BECAUSE THEY ARE MORTAL!!
DOOM!!
ZOMBIES ARE ALREADY DEAD, SO THEY HAVE NOTHING TO LOSE!!
VIP!
ZOMBIES ARE IMMORTAL!! EVEN IF THEY ARE PURIFIED, THEY ARE EXPENDABLE SOLDIERS AND CAN BE EASILY REPLACED!!
VIP!!
VIP!!
?!!
VIP
I WILL TAKE MY ARMY OF UNDEAD WARRIORS AND SEIZE THE TITLE OF PIRATE KING!!
VIP!!
YOU SHOULD ALL BE THANKFUL THAT YOUR SHADOWS WILL BECAME MY UNDERLINGS!!
...
VIP!
WHOA!! WHAT IS THIS?!
VIP!
?!
?!
VIP!
AH!! IT STUCK TO ME!!
SHUP!!!

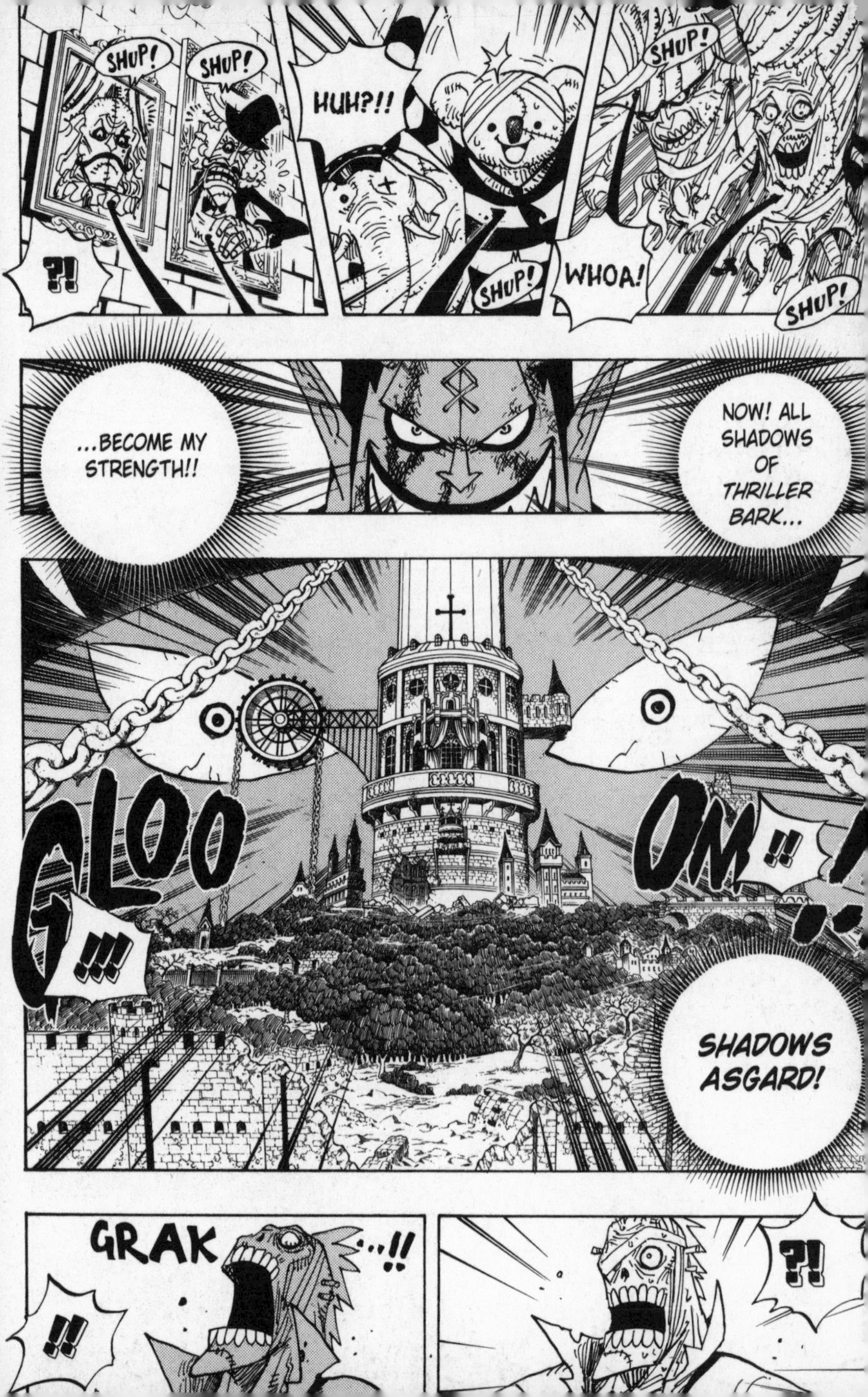
SHUP!
SHUP!
WHOA!
HUH?!!
SHUP!
SHUP!
SHUP!
?!
NOW! ALL SHADOWS OF THRILLER BARK...
...BECOME MY STRENGTH!!
GLOOOM!!
SHADOWS ASGARD!
?!
GRAK...!!
!!

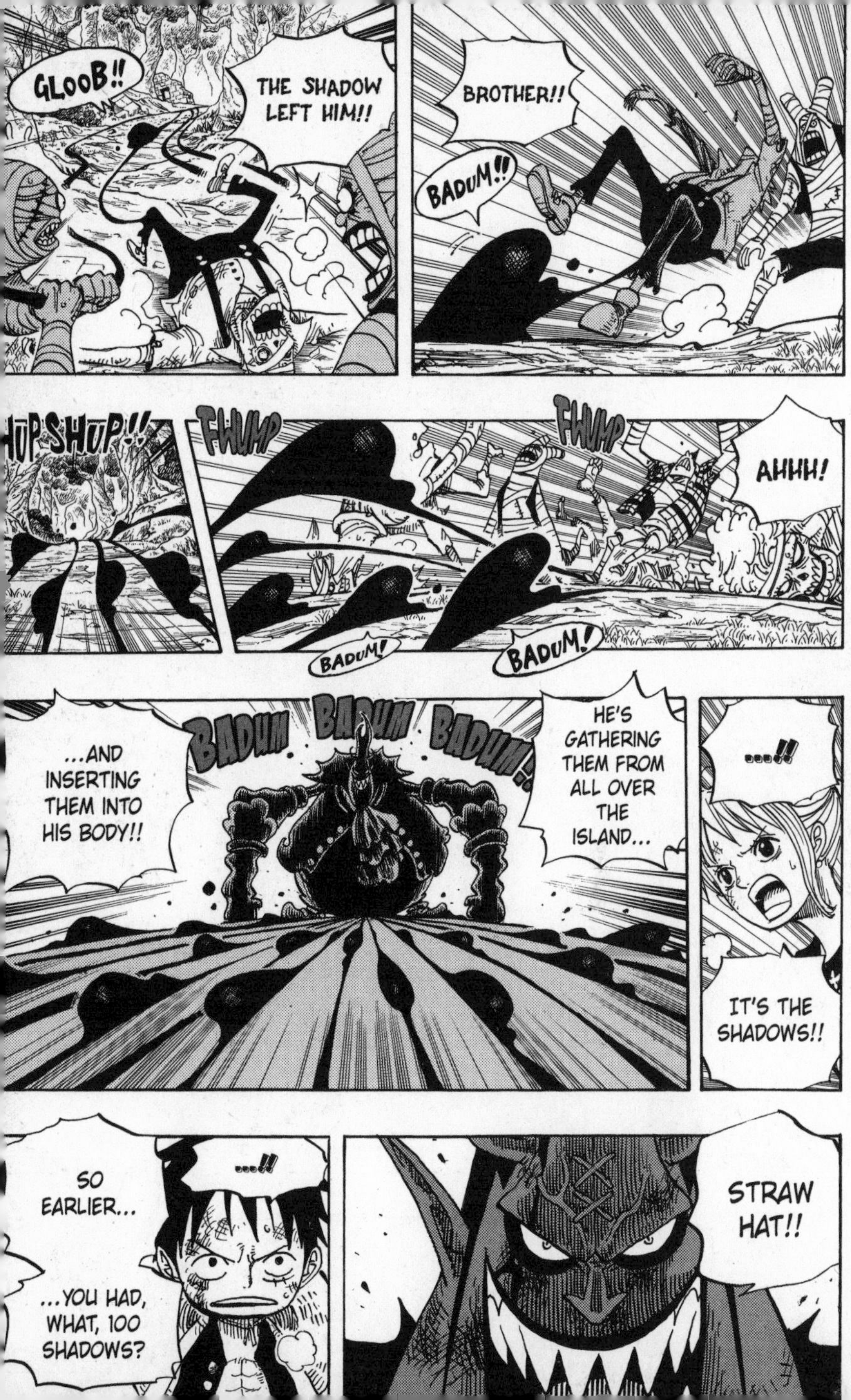
BROTHER!!
BADUM!!
THE SHADOW LEFT HIM!!
GLOOB!!
AHHH!
FWUMP
FWUMP
BADUM!
BADUM!
HUP SHUP!!
...!!
IT'S THE SHADOWS!!
HE'S GATHERING THEM FROM ALL OVER THE ISLAND...
BADUM BADUM BADUM!!
...AND INSERTING THEM INTO HIS BODY!!
STRAW HAT!!
...!!
SO EARLIER...
...YOU HAD, WHAT, 100 SHADOWS?

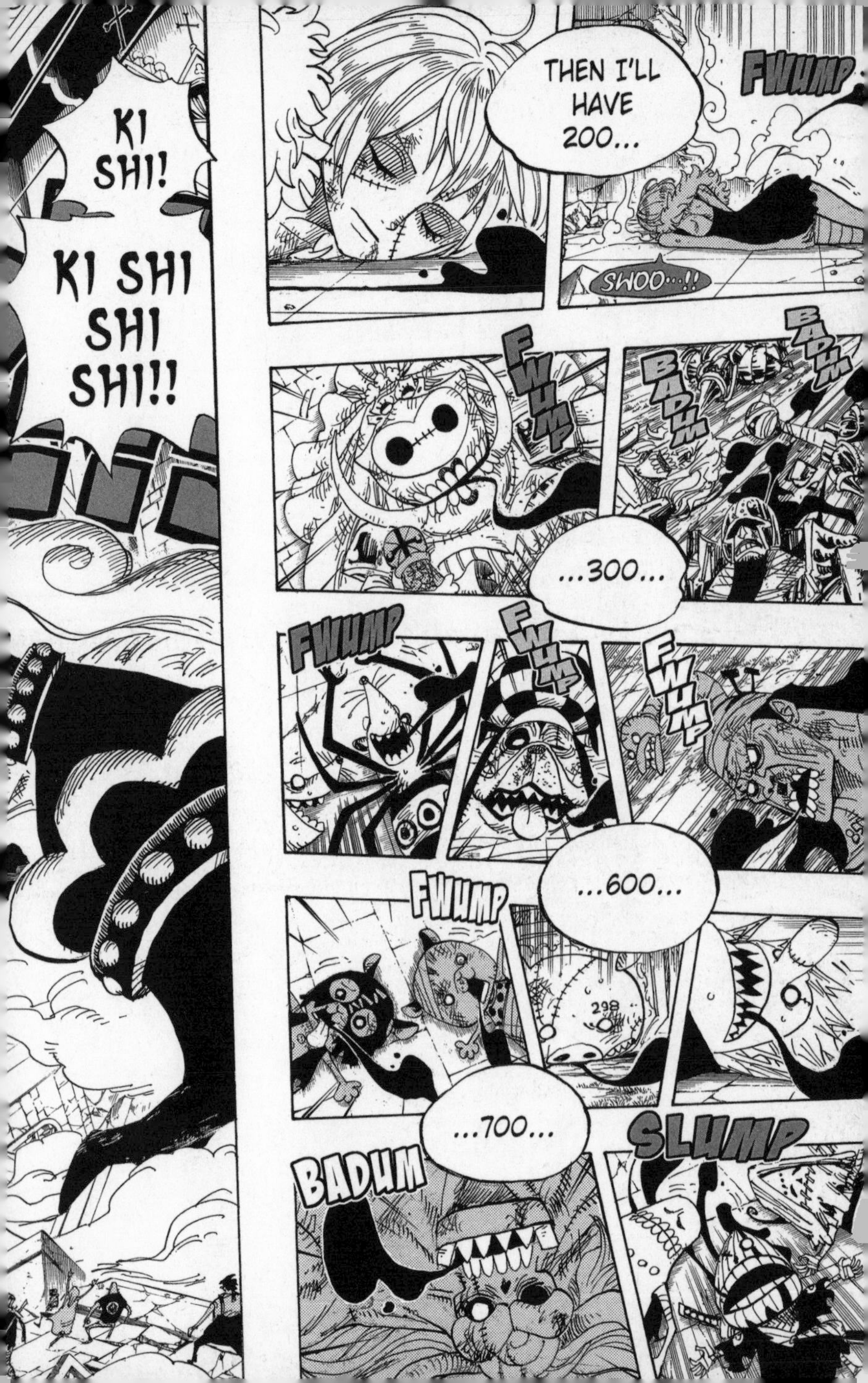
FWUMP
SWOO...!!
THEN I'LL HAVE 200...
BADUM
BADUM
FWUMP
...300...
FWUMP
FWUMP
FWUMP
...600...
FWUMP
SLUMP
...700...
BADUM
KI SHI!
KI SHI SHI SHI!!

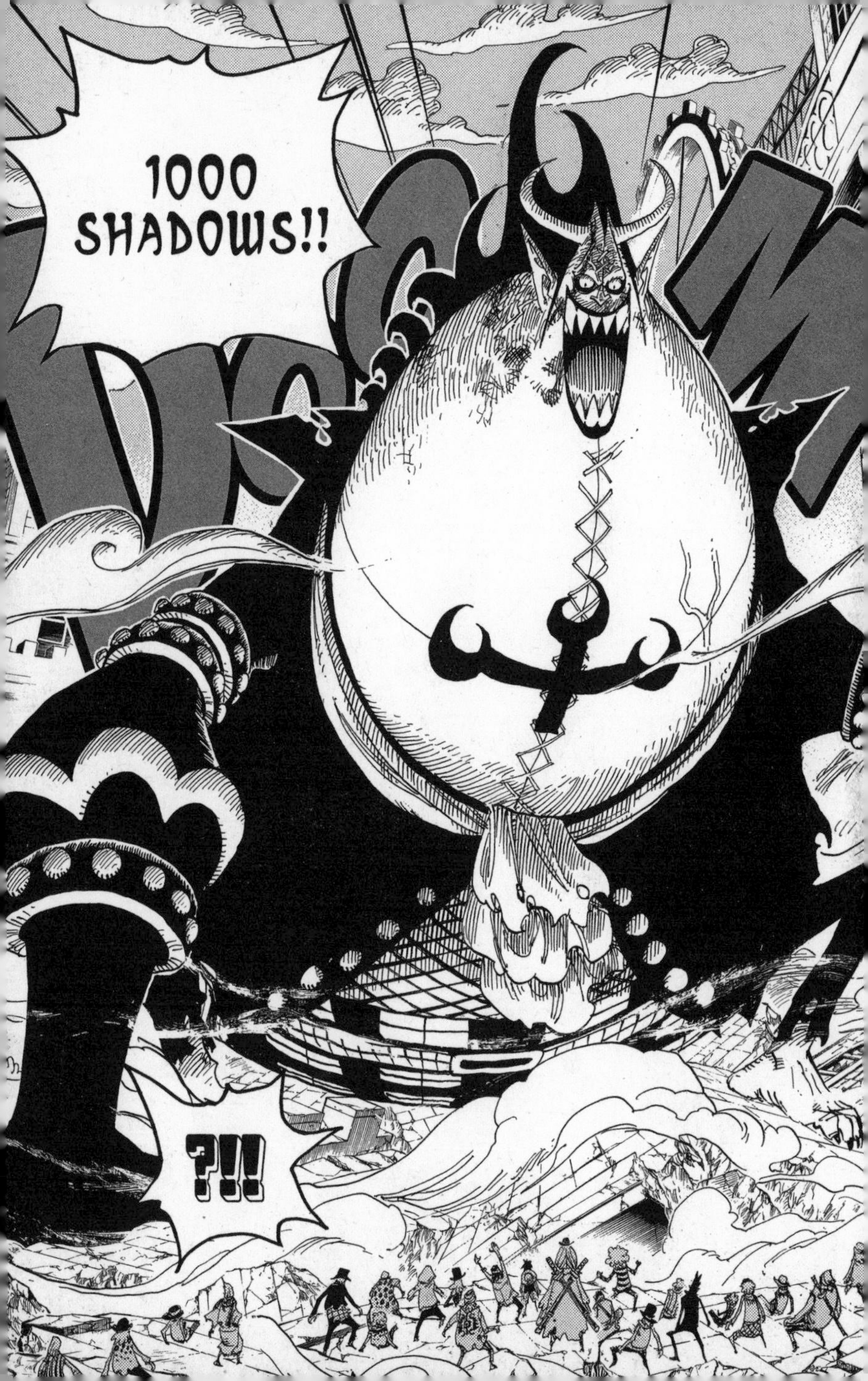
1000 SHADOWS!!
?!!

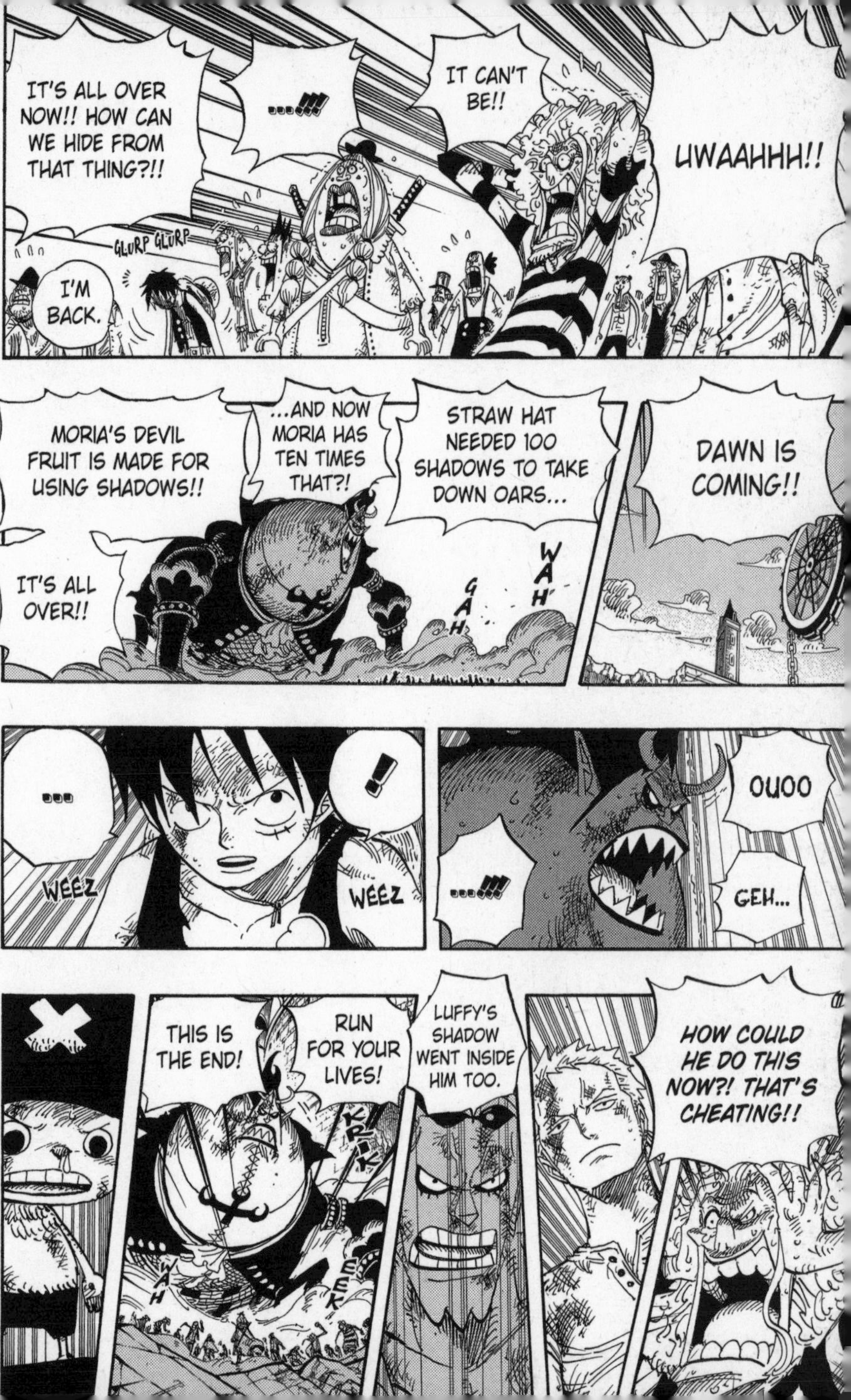
UWAAHHH!!
IT CAN'T BE!!
...!!!
IT'S ALL OVER NOW!! HOW CAN WE HIDE FROM THAT THING?!!
GLURP GLURP
I'M BACK.
DAWN IS COMING!!
STRAW HAT NEEDED 100 SHADOWS TO TAKE DOWN OARS...
...AND NOW MORIA HAS TEN TIMES THAT?!
MORIA'S DEVIL FRUIT IS MADE FOR USING SHADOWS!!
WAH
GAH
IT'S ALL OVER!!
OUOO
GEH...
...!!!
!
WEEZ
...
WEEZ
HOW COULD HE DO THIS NOW?! THAT'S CHEATING!!
LUFFY'S SHADOW WENT INSIDE HIM TOO.
RUN FOR YOUR LIVES!
KRIK
THIS IS THE END!
WAH
EEK

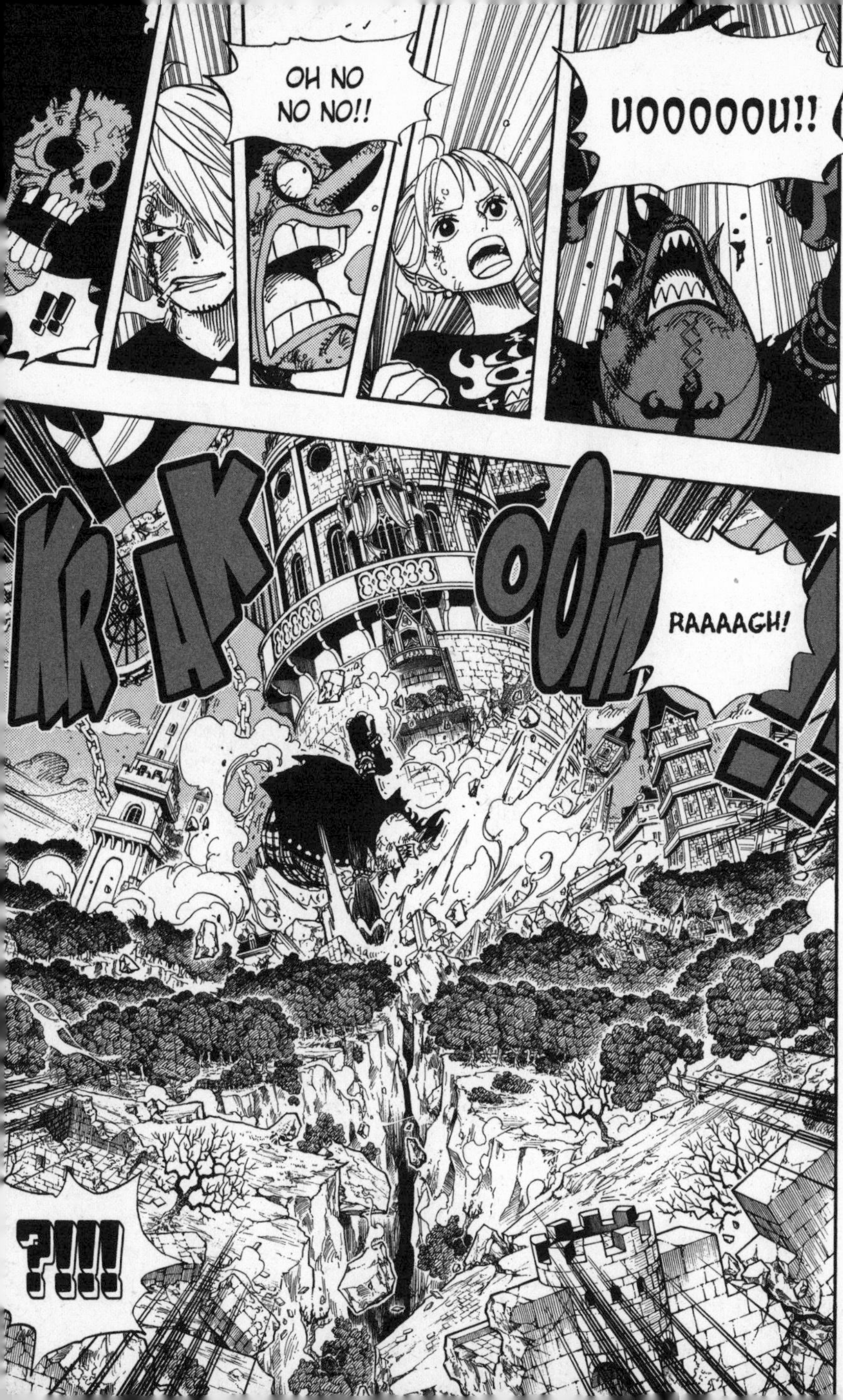
UOOOOOU!!
OH NO NO NO!!
!!
RAAAAGH!
KRAKOOOM
?!!!

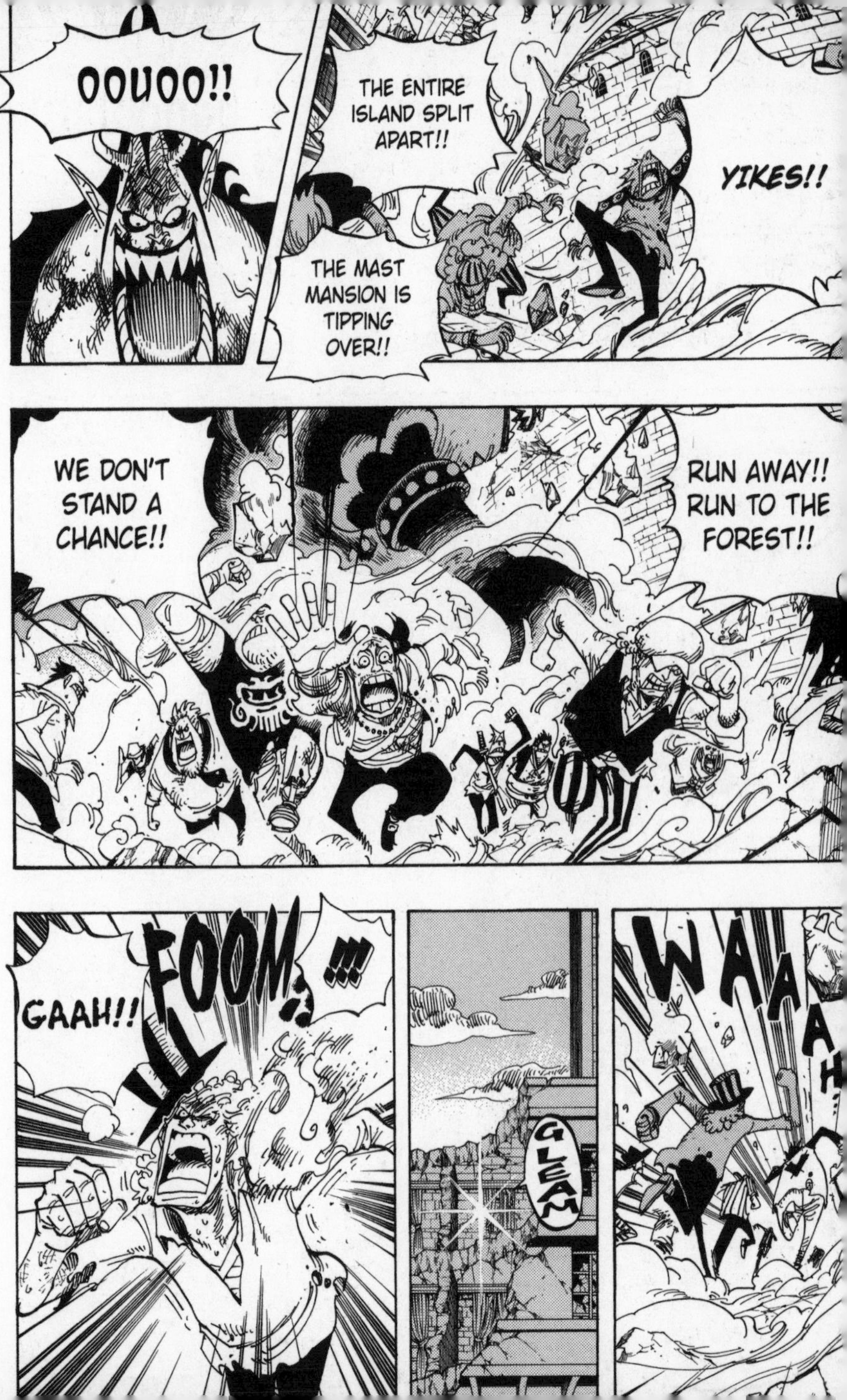
THE ENTIRE ISLAND SPLIT APART!!
YIKES!!
THE MAST MANSION IS TIPPING OVER!!
OOUOO!!
RUN AWAY!! RUN TO THE FOREST!!
WE DON'T STAND A CHANCE!!
WAAAH
GLEAM
FOOM
GAAH!!

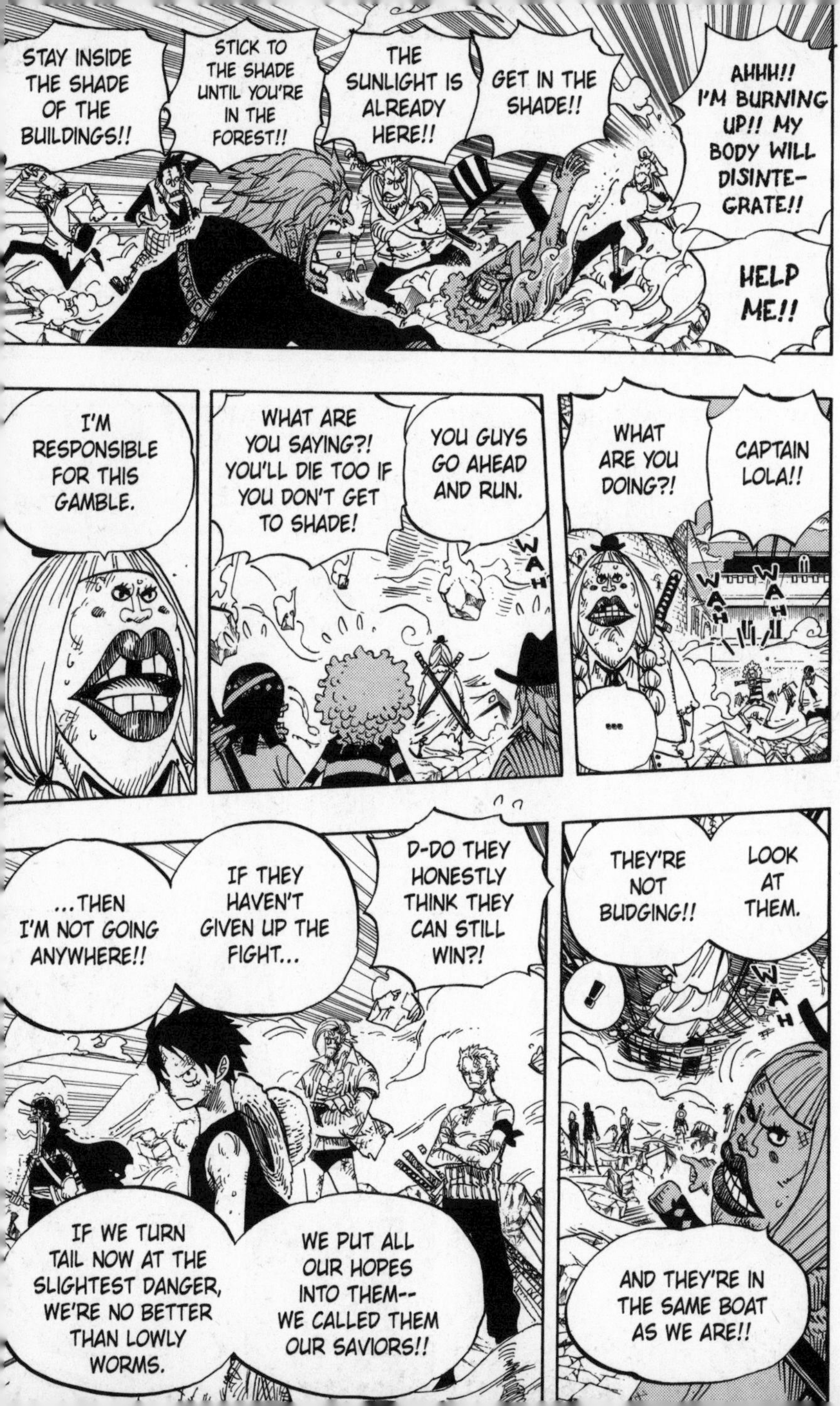
AHHH!! I'M BURNING UP!! MY BODY WILL DISINTE-GRATE!!
HELP ME!!
GET IN THE SHADE!!
THE SUNLIGHT IS ALREADY HERE!!
STICK TO THE SHADE UNTIL YOU'RE IN THE FOREST!!
STAY INSIDE THE SHADE OF THE BUILDINGS!!
CAPTAIN LOLA!!
WHAT ARE YOU DOING?!
WAH
WAH
...
YOU GUYS GO AHEAD AND RUN.
WHAT ARE YOU SAYING?! YOU'LL DIE TOO IF YOU DON'T GET TO SHADE!
WAH
I'M RESPONSIBLE FOR THIS GAMBLE.
LOOK AT THEM.
THEY'RE NOT BUDGING!!
!
WAH
AND THEY'RE IN THE SAME BOAT AS WE ARE!!
D-DO THEY HONESTLY THINK THEY CAN STILL WIN?!
IF THEY HAVEN'T GIVEN UP THE FIGHT...
...THEN I'M NOT GOING ANYWHERE!!
WE PUT ALL OUR HOPES INTO THEM-- WE CALLED THEM OUR SAVIORS!!
IF WE TURN TAIL NOW AT THE SLIGHTEST DANGER, WE'RE NO BETTER THAN LOWLY WORMS.

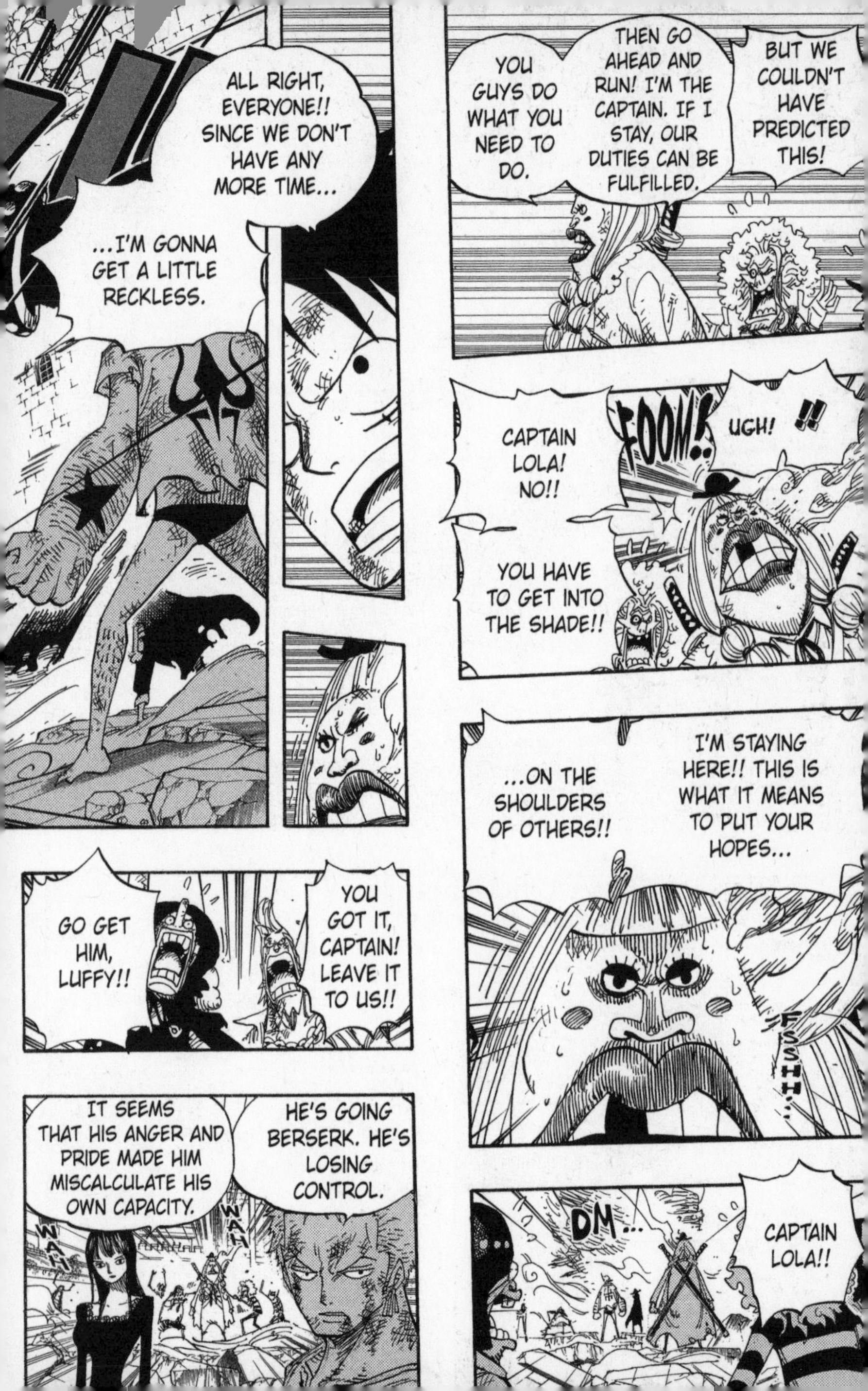
BUT WE COULDN'T HAVE PREDICTED THIS!
THEN GO AHEAD AND RUN! I'M THE CAPTAIN. IF I STAY, OUR DUTIES CAN BE FULFILLED.
YOU GUYS DO WHAT YOU NEED TO DO.
UGH!!
FOOM!
CAPTAIN LOLA! NO!!
YOU HAVE TO GET INTO THE SHADE!!
I'M STAYING HERE!! THIS IS WHAT IT MEANS TO PUT YOUR HOPES...
...ON THE SHOULDERS OF OTHERS!!
FSSHH...
CAPTAIN LOLA!!
DM...
ALL RIGHT, EVERYONE!! SINCE WE DON'T HAVE ANY MORE TIME...
...I'M GONNA GET A LITTLE RECKLESS.
YOU GOT IT, CAPTAIN! LEAVE IT TO US!!
GO GET HIM, LUFFY!!
HE'S GOING BERSERK. HE'S LOSING CONTROL.
IT SEEMS THAT HIS ANGER AND PRIDE MADE HIM MISCALCULATE HIS OWN CAPACITY.
WAH
WAH

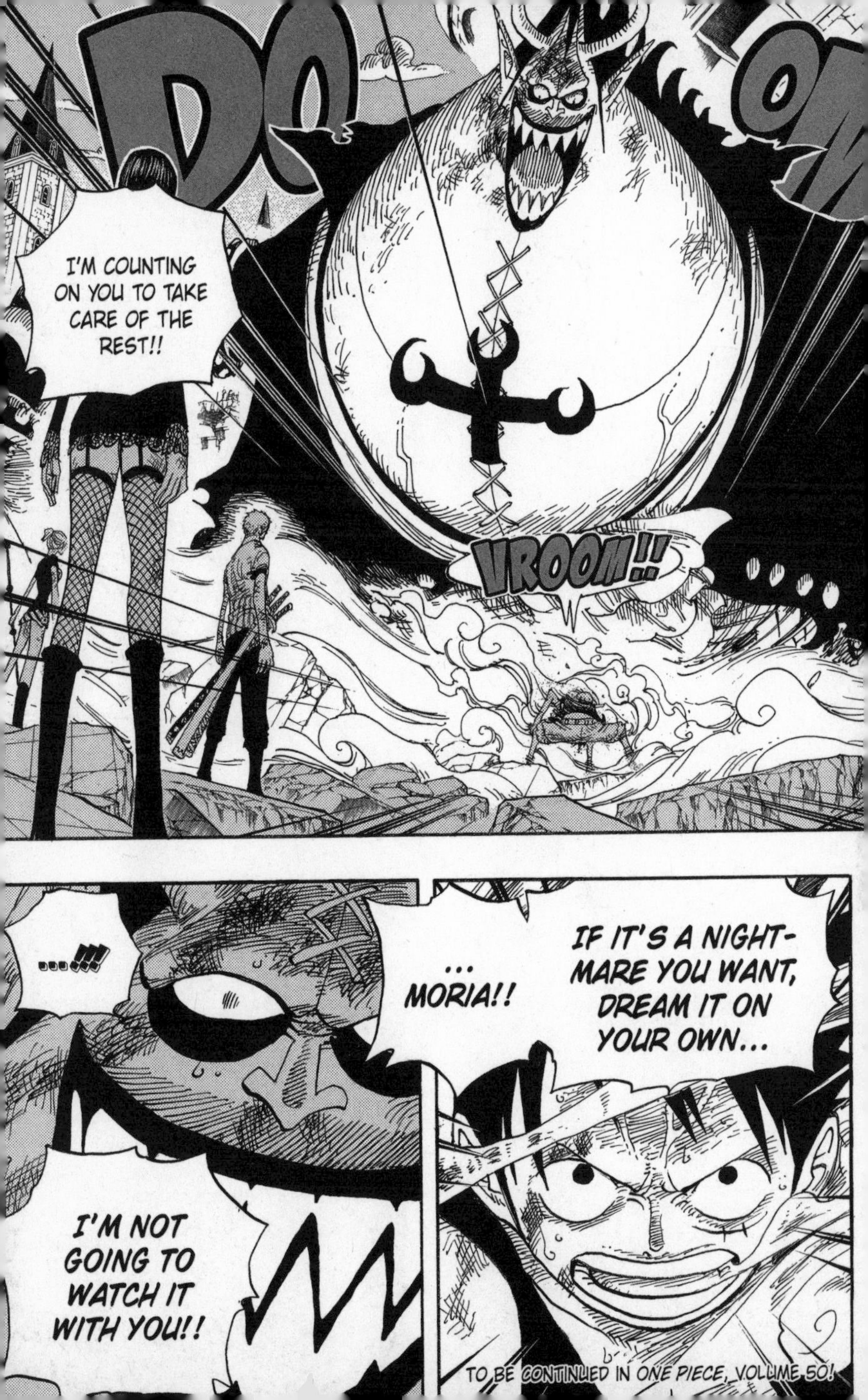
I'M COUNTING ON YOU TO TAKE CARE OF THE REST!!
VROOM!!
IF IT'S A NIGHT-MARE YOU WANT, DREAM IT ON YOUR OWN...
... MORIA!!
...!!!
I'M NOT GOING TO WATCH IT WITH YOU!!
TO BE CONTINUED IN ONE PIECE, VOLUME 50!

COMING NEXT VOLUME:

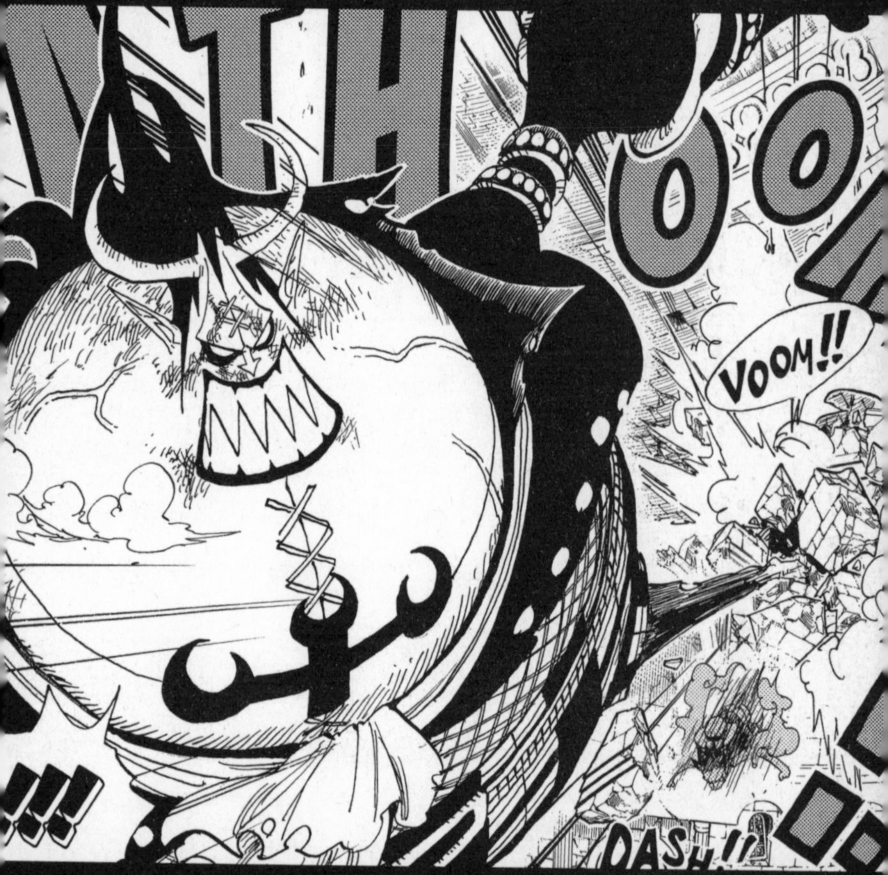
VOOM!!
DASH!!

The Straw Hats are in a desperate battle against time and Gecko Moria to get their shadows back before dawn. Gecko Moria unleashes his devastating power of a thousand shadows, but Luffy counters with his "Gear" powers. To save his crew, will Luffy have to make the ultimate sacrifice?

ON SALE NOW!

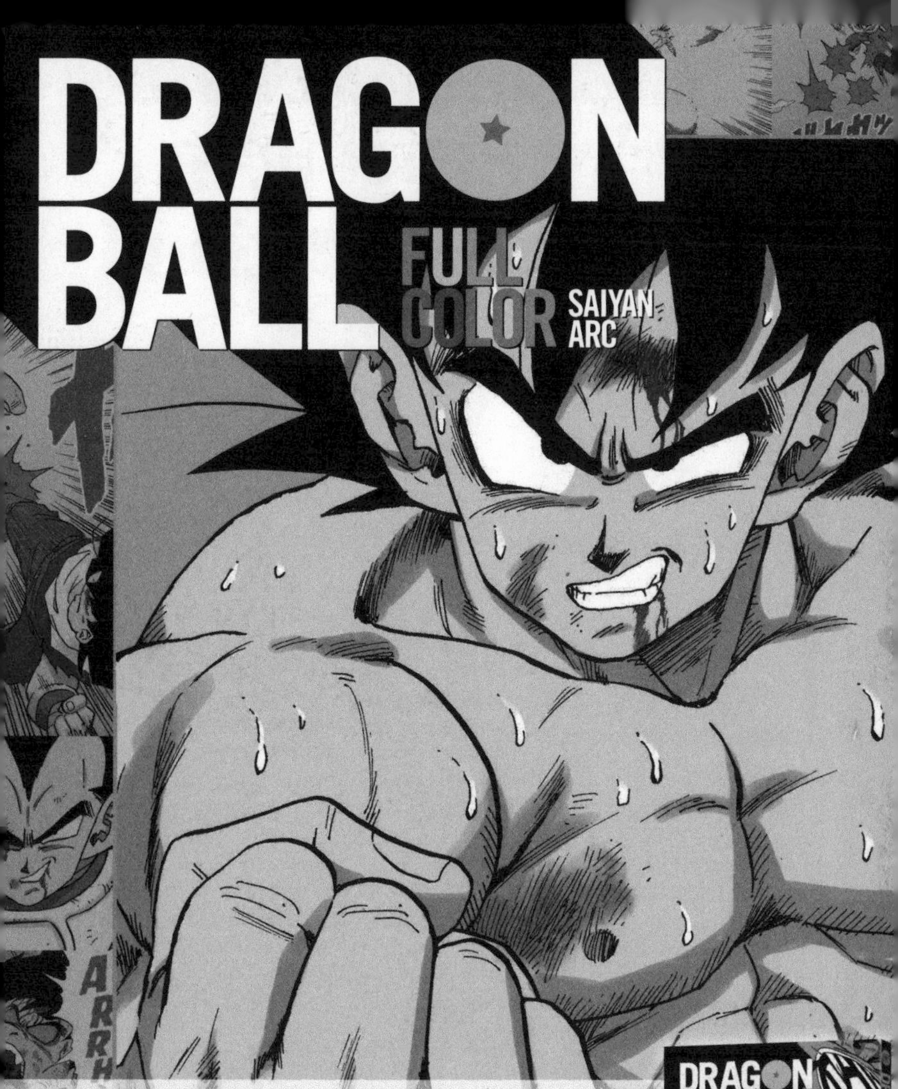
DRAGON BALL
FULL COLOR
SAIYAN ARC
ARRH

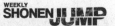

You're Reading in the Wrong Direction!!

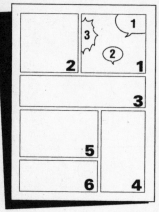

Whoops! Guess what? You're starting at the wrong end of the comic!

...It's true! In keeping with the original Japanese format, **One Piece** is meant to be read from right to left, starting in the upper-right corner.

Unlike English, which is read from left to right, Japanese is read from right to left, meaning that action, sound effects and word-balloon order are completely reversed...something which can make readers unfamiliar with Japanese feel pretty backwards themselves. For this reason, manga or Japanese comics published in the U.S. in English have sometimes been published "flopped"— that is, printed in exact reverse order, as though seen from the other side of a mirror.

By flopping pages, U.S. publishers can avoid confusing readers, but the compromise is not without its downside. For one thing, a character in a flopped manga series who once wore in the original Japanese version a T-shirt emblazoned with "M A Y" (as in "the merry month of") now wears one which reads "Y A M"! Additionally, many manga creators in Japan are themselves unhappy with the process, as some feel the mirror-imaging of their art skews their original intentions.

We are proud to bring you Eiichiro Oda's **One Piece** in the original unflopped format. For now, though, turn to the other side of the book and let the journey begin...!

—Editor